From Carnegie to Fort Book

The History of the Huntsville-Madison County Public Library

By

Paul A. Hays

To Jack Bissinger,
My good friend and good neighbor.

Paul A. Hays
12 april 2005

ISBN 0-7414-2488-6

Published by:

PUBLISHING.COM

1094 New DeHaven Street, Suite 100
West Conshohocken, PA 19428-2713
Info@buybooksontheweb.com
www.buybooksontheweb.com
Toll-free (877) BUY BOOK
Local Phone (610) 941-9999
Fax (610) 941-9959

Printed in the United States of America

Printed on Recycled Paper

Published March 2005

Preface

*"To an historian libraries are food, shelter and even muse.
They are of two kinds: the library of published material,
books, pamphlets, periodicals, and the archive
of unpublished papers and documents."*

Barbara Tuchman
Practicing History (1981)
The Quotable Book Lover

The United States Army was my life for 27 years after graduation from college. I also worked as a defense contractor after the Army until my total retirement. I became active in the Academy for Lifetime Learning at The University of Alabama in Huntsville, primarily as a developer and presenter of original classes. The best way to learn is to become the instructor.

In recent years there was an increasing interest in capturing the stories of the veterans of World War II. I was a veteran of the Cold War, and so I wrote *Never The Same Job Twice, Wandering Through a Military Life in Historical Context*, which was about my 40-plus years' association with the United States Army. That effort whetted my appetite for historical writing. A writer said that one has to read 30 books in order to write one. Reading, writing and teaching became my retirement life, because that combination led to maximum fulfillment.

I continued to read to learn about being a better non-fiction writer. But three-fourths of the fun is in the researching phase, because that allows the writer to wander over the landscape to find new information that can be developed into a book. In 2003 I wrote the ten-year history of the Academy for Lifetime Learning and *Harem of Books*, which was about my personal library.

This history of the Huntsville-Madison County Public Library was chosen as my next effort for several reasons. First, it offered the opportunity to research primary sources, which makes the historian happiest. Second, the subject dovetailed with my interest in the great libraries of the world and teaching courses about books and libraries. Third, since no one had written extensively about Huntsville's library, it seemed to be a noble community project along with the other Huntsville, Alabama and Southeast Regional histories. Fourth, it allowed me to pursue a goal with passion, which is a key element of a successful retirement life. Fifth, it was a reason to visit different parts of the city and county to keep current with local progress. Sixth, it was an opportunity to undertake a creative project, because that is also another factor in a successful retirement.

I wish to acknowledge the cooperation and assistance of the following people who provided information and valuable insights to this history: Shawana Ariel, Al Bellingrath, Myrtle Binford, Julia Blackwell, Sarah Bradford, Mrs. Robert Cook, Anne Corley, Carolyn Courtney, Kathryn Dilworth, Storm Dovers, Jack Fitzpatrick, Marie Garrett, Betty George, Patsy Gray, Nellie Hackworth, E. Cutter Hughes, Larrel Hughes, Thomas Hutchens, Geoffrey Jolly, Mary Lacey, Helen Lee, David Lilley, Earl Mathews, Mayme Claire Maples, Susan Markham, Kate McLemore, Diane Metrick, Gail Phillips, Ranee´ Pruitt, Judy Purinton, Jane Roberts, Sue Royer, Donna Schremser, Priscilla Scott, Melissa Shepherd, Alice Sisk, Lucy Thrasher, Teresa Thrower, Martin Towery, Floyd Turner, and Joyce Welch.

A special thanks goes to Bob Ludwig, publisher of *The Huntsville Times*, for allowing the use of voluminous material from that newspaper.

The photograph of the Huntsville Carnegie Library is the courtesy of the Huntsville Public Library archives. The other photographs are the author's.

Any errors in this book are mine.

This book is dedicated to my wife, Margaret, who also loves books, for tolerating the many hours I spent going, coming and visiting the libraries cited in this effort. She also contributed with her editing and photo manipulation skills.

Paul A. Hays

Contents

List of Illustrations

Introduction

*"A public library is a deep freeze that thaws with the
touch of a hand on the front door.*

John Winterich, author
The 1977 AB Bookman's Yearbook

The evolution of the Huntsville public library over the 186 years covered by this history requires a definition of "public." The library was always considered public, as differentiated from private, meaning one owner. The library started on a subscription basis, as presumably every white male could join if they paid the requisite fee. Later there was a circulating library, which charged per item and was a commercial enterprise. The Carnegie Library in 1916 was public and free for whites only. It was also public because it was owned and operated by the local government. During the 1950's the library became free and public for all residents, based on having an address in Madison County.

The library history is a story of change, first, in the served area over time, and second, the response of the library to its surroundings. Changes were almost nonexistent in the first half of the history. The second half produced significant changes, as the library was a lagging agency to its environment for a long time until professional management and skills turned it into an aggressive outreach organization utilizing the latest technological tools and building a stronger financial base.

The growth of libraries will follow the evolution of schools and literacy, and industrialization in the country. Librarian professionalism increased as both a cause and effect of the proliferation and internal growth of libraries.

The Huntsville newspapers reported on library activities throughout the period. *The Huntsville Times* has been especially supportive over the past 40 years with its coverage and particularly its editorials supporting reading and adequate funding for this important educational, cultural and recreational agency.

The library history consists of many distinct activities and stories, which are related as they occurred for the most part. This approach allows the reader to better appreciate the roles of the personalities, as many of the events were concurrent and not always related to other events.

The source and amount of construction money for the three main library buildings was a reflection of the economic well being of the Huntsville and Madison County area.

The growth of the library system, both externally and internally, will demonstrate the professionalism of the library employees over the years as innovative workers and good stewards of the public trust and money.

Each director of the library brought his/her own management style to the job, based on different experiences, and most importantly, different professional aspirations. Career aspirations are the driving factor in the individual's motivation, which is manifested in several ways; capability and willingness to innovate; expansion of the personal and organization's mission; and the demonstrated willingness to work extra hours to make things happen. Each director of the Huntsville-Madison County Public Library was in a different social, economic, and demographic environment than earlier directors. Each had a different base upon on which to build and each was standing on the shoulders of the earlier directors. There is no basis for trying to compare directorships over the years.

The Library Board minutes are identified by the date and a hyphen, for example, "August 4, 1936 – " to depict the chronology of different issues which faced the boards. These items will not be footnoted. The library boards were the principal decision authority and the interface between outside governing bodies with money and the library director. The boards' minutes provided many details and much of the official history of the library. Newspaper articles also provided many details, as well as editorial support, in the later years.

The following mission statement was on the walls of the library buildings in 2004.

"THIS IS THE PUBLIC'S LIBRARY

Our mission is to enrich the educational, recreational, and cultural life
of our community. Our knowledgeable and courteous staff will serve as
the gateway to library materials, information, and programs."

I ask my readers to keep that statement in mind as they travel through the history of the Huntsville-Madison County Public Library and see how earlier and current library personnel achieved that mission of service to the community.

Chapter 1

The First Century

*"The library is a part of society as a whole and does not in any
sense exist in a vacuum, nor does it pursue its own course
isolated from the happenings around it."*

William F. Ogburn, 1937
Persistent Issues in American Librarianship[1]

William Ogburn's statement above is certainly true. The evolution of libraries from the earliest times through the 186-year history of the Huntsville-Madison County Public Library reflects on that statement. The library is a part of civilization and society, but is a lagging component of societies.

Professor Ogburn also said in the same speech that high school attendance was increasing and there was growth in adult education. He even hinted at the "possible growth of our leisure time." He was correct on all three accounts and would probably be shocked at the growth of leisure time as we knew it in 2004. He did not address the tremendous increase in longevity since 1937, which was also a major factor in the growth of our libraries.[2]

Education is the imparting and acquisition of knowledge. Libraries are the main repositories of accumulated history. The cultural status of a community can in part be assessed by the extent and quality of its library's holdings.[3]

"Libraries arrived on the North American continent with the first European settlers. Religious books, primarily for the use of the clergy, formed the center of most 17th-century collections. The richest colonial merchants and planters often developed their own libraries, but the number of people regularly reading books, other than the Bible, was quite small.

Books became available to a broader public as the 18th century progressed. Improvements in printing methods lowered their cost, making them affordable to more people. Increased interest in commerce, science, and art spurred a demand for more information—a demand that was often best satisfied through reading. Colonists began to form social libraries in which individuals contributed money to purchase books. Public libraries sprang up in urban centers; outstanding examples include those still existing in Philadelphia, Pennsylvania, Charleston, South Carolina, and New York, New York. However, such societies generally only lent their books to those who donated money. But, libraries are urban phenomenon, and so were unlikely to be in expanding frontiers and agricultural areas.

Libraries continued to develop after the Revolutionary War. Women, for example, created their own collections, with books often circulating great distances among farms and plantations. Libraries such as the women's libraries are characterized as social libraries because they were for people of the upper social status and interests. Between 1815 and 1850, library societies increasingly concentrated on specialized subjects, usually of a professional nature. Mercantile libraries held books of interest to clerks and businessmen, while collections of mechanics' and seamen's libraries in their particular trades. These libraries were supported by business owners and provided educational and social opportunities for young men."[4]

The social libraries tended to become legal entities, because the books were owned by the group, not individuals. This was the initial situation in Huntsville, as you will see below.

The oldest newspaper in Alabama, the Huntsville *Republican,* was established in 1816. It later became the Huntsville *Southern Advocate.* In 1823 the Huntsville *Democrat* was founded to fight the aristocratic Georgia Machine.[5] Alabama was actually part of the Mississippi Territory before statehood. James Madison was the fourth president of the United States, but Madison County had already taken his name on December 13, 1808 before he was inaugurated. Madison County was "Made a county in 1808 by order of Governor of Mississippi Territory. Area ceded 1805, 1806 by Cherokees, Chickasaws. This was the first land in Alabama ceded by these great civilized tribes." according to the marker in the northeast corner of Huntsville's courthouse square.

The background above about the development of libraries sets the stage for the Huntsville library story. A notice in the *Alabama Republican*, a Huntsville newspaper, on June 20, 1818 stated, "A number of citizens request that all those who are disposed to encourage the establishment of a public circulating library in Huntsville would meet in Mr. Boardman's room in Monday 5. o'clock p.m. for the purpose of organizing an association to carry out that highly beneficial object into effect."[6] President James Monroe was in his second year.

John Boardman came to Huntsville in early 1818 as editor of the *Alabama Republican*, a weekly newspaper published on Saturday. Republican at that time referred to republic, not to Republican and Democrat, which were not named as such until the mid-19th century. Boardman's printing shop is in the Huntsville Constitution Village fronting on Madison Street (circa 2004).

Dr. Thomas Fearn wrote Clement Clay in July 1818 suggesting the need for a library, "how pleasing it would be to see the hours lost at the card table, with the dice box, or even those more innocently thrown away in idle chitchat, exchanged for profitable employment, and would it not be well to break in the avaricious calculations of the speculator occasionally?"[7] Dr. Thomas Fearn studied medicine at the University of Pennsylvania under Dr. Benjamin Rush, 1745-1813, American physician and political leader, as well as the author of medical treatises. Dr. Rush signed the Declaration of Independence in 1776 as a delegate from Philadelphia.

Two 8 &1/2 x 10 &1/2-inch notebooks written by Dr. Fearn, as a student under Dr. Rush in 1809, are in the Huntsville Library's archives. The notebooks were brown and on the spines were "Medical Notes' in gold on a black background and "Rush" in gold on a red background. The pages were unlined, but Dr. Fearn had a steady writing hand for over 400 pages as it was as straight as if it were on a line. The reading was legible if one had patience. Dr. Fearn supposedly made the first use of quinine and started Monte Sano (Mountain of Health). The notebooks were in good condition.[8] We now know that Dr. Fearn appreciated the importance of libraries. But, we might wonder how he treated his patients in Huntsville since he was a student of Dr. Benjamin Rush. Dr. Rush was supremely confident of his own opinion and decisions, yet shallow and very unscientific in practice. Rush's chief accomplishment as a physician was in the practice of bleeding the patient. It was said that he considered bleeding to be a cure for nearly every ailment. Even when the practice began to decline, he refused to reconsider the dangers of it. Fearn studied under Rush only four years before Rush died, so those strong views must have been influential on Fearn. Ponder about the citizens of Huntsville.[9] "Never was the liberality of the citizens of Huntsville and its vicinity so cheerfully exercised as on a late application to them to contribute to the establishment of a Public Library. Between $2,000 and $3,000 were subscribed in a few hours for this worthwhile laudable purpose, and agreeable to the terms of the subscription, notice is hereby given to the shareholders, and those who are disposed to have an interest in this active institution to meet at Mr. Simpson's Boarding House on Thursday the 29th inst. at 7 o'clock pm to elect five members to draft a constitution."[10] Notice the refined wording of the two newspaper notices. The positive leadership demonstrated by the citizens of Huntsville toward the establishment of the library was established early, and continued through 2004.

"At a meeting of the subscribers to the Public Library in Huntsville, agreeable to notice, the following gentlemen were chosen a committee to Draft a Constitution for its government and instructed to report the same to the shareholders on Friday evening the 20th November next at Mr. Minor's office at the courthouse. (Doct. David Moore, Maj. John M. Taylor, Henry Minor, Samuel Hazard, John Boardman, Committee Esquires) Those who are disposed to encourage this institution can subscribe to the articles and become shareholders upon the original terms previous to or at the above meeting time and apply to either of the committees."[11]

"The subscribers to the Public Library in Huntsville are desired to attend at Mr. Minor's office in the courthouse on Friday evening the 20th inst. to adopt a constitution and By-Laws. John Boardman, Secy"[12]

A "CERTIFICATE OF STOCK IN THE HUNTSVILLE LIBRARY COMPANY, Share No. 59. This is to certify that William Atwood having this day paid to the Treasury the sum of $20 agreeable to the provision of the Constitution is entitled to one share in the Huntsville Library Company. Dated the 10th day of December, 1818. Robert Fearn Treas. Thomas G. Percy Pres. "[13] The library was only open to men.[14] "Public" means the opposite of private, but does not mean all citizens, only those men who pay.

It is assumed that the first books purchased were collected and located in Mr. Minor's office in the courthouse. The law office of John Nelson Spotswood Jones is credited with the location of the first library in October 1819, as Jones opened his law office in September 1819. A replica of the office faces Madison Street next to the Boardman printing building in the Constitution Village.[15] No evidence of the library was found between December 1818 and October 1819.

"The stockholders of the Huntsville Library Co. are herby notified that the annual [first?] Meeting will be held on Thursday next, at early candlelight, at the room occupied by Mr. Minor in the Court House, for the purpose of electing nine Directors and a Treasurer for the ensuing 12 months. The report of the Directors will also be read. Delinquent Stockholders are requested to make payment before that evening—otherwise their names will be reported. By order of the Directors, Samuel Hazard."[16]

"The stockholders in the Huntsville Library are informed that the Books are opened at the office of J. N. S. Jones, Esq. next door to the Printing Office on the street leading to Ditto's Landing [current Madison & Whitesburg]. The Library will be opened and books delivered every Tuesday and Friday from half past 11 o'clock A. M. to half past 12. John Boardman, Librarian.[17] "Delivered" does not mean that the books were actually delivered to individual readers homes, it means that the books were available to be checked out at these times and were delivered by the custodian across the counter to the recipient.[18]

Books contained in Huntsville's first library included:
- "*Annals of Scotland*, by David Dalrymple Lord Hailes, Vol. 3, Edinburgh, 1797.
- *Apocalypse or Book of Revelations*, by Emanuel Swedenburg, Vols. 4 and 5, London, 1814.
- *Guy Mannering or the Astrologer*, vol. 2, New York, 1818.
- *Quarterly Review*, August and November, vol. 2, 1809, April and July, Vol. 17, 1817.
- *Works of John Locke in Ten Volumes*, vols. 7, 8, 9, London, 1812.

- *Arcana Celestia; or Heavenly Mysteries,* by a Society of Gentleman, vol. 5, 1808; vol. 7, 1812; vol. 8, 1812.
- *Ecclesiastical History, Ancient and Modern* by John Lawrence Moshelm, Charleston, 1811.
- *History of Rome,* by Titus Livina, Vols. 1 and 6.
- *History of Rome* by George Baker, vols. 2, 4, 5, London, 1814."[19]

The first book cited above had an incomplete title, because books of that era usually had very descriptive titles, so here is the full title: *Annals of Scotland, from the accession of Malcolm III. in the year M.LVII. to the accession of the House of Stuart in the year M.CCC.LXXI. To which are added, tracts relative to the history and antiquities of Scotland.* Don't you feel more enlightened knowing the full title? The library's holding was a second edition, which was published in three volumes and the library held only the third volume. The work was originally published in 1776 and 1779 in two volumes. A third edition was published in 1819 in three volumes. Those three volumes were available on the Internet in 2004 for $450 from a bookseller in Johannesburg, South Africa. The volumes from the bookseller were in fine condition, with half leather marbled covers and gilt decorated bands.[20]

The last two items on the list above were actually the same book. Titus Livius (Livy), 59 B.C.-A.D. 17, was a Roman historian, and George Baker was the translator for the 1814 publication. The library, therefore, had volumes 1, 2, 4, 5 and 6.

The library had only three volumes of John Locke, and all volumes can be bought on the Internet in 2004 for $900-$1000.[21]

It is difficult to imagine more than a handful of Huntsvillians in 1819 reading the original books cited above, as they were rather weighty tomes. The books were probably more useful for show on the shelf than reading. On second thought, it's hard to imagine more than a handful of Huntsvillians in 2004 reading those books. Many of the books in private and social libraries in the colonial days of the northeastern United States were religious in nature. Two of Huntsville's were.

The Alabama constitutional convention convened in Huntsville on July 5, 1918. President James Monroe signed the bill for Alabama admission to the Union as the 22nd state on December 14, 1819. The state's nickname is "Heart of Dixie" and the motto is "We dare defend our rights." Huntsville was the state's capital for less than a year, and then the capital was moved to Cahaba, just south of Selma.

The constitution of 1819 provided that "schools and the means of education shall forever be encouraged in this state." That sounded good, but the legislature failed to provide the means, and so the Alabama tradition of talking about improved schools, but doing little about it, started early and lasted a long time, some say into 2004.

"A charge of 18 ¾ cents was charged after the first two weeks and the like sum for every succeeding week."[22]

"Huntsville Library. The stockholders and the public are informed, that the Library is moved to the upper room in the court-house which was recently occupied as the Senate chambers and that *Thomas Brandon Esq* is appointed the *Librarian.* The Library will be open for delivery and return of Books *every day of the week,* (Sunday excepted) from the hour of 9 to 12 M.

Non-subscribers may be accommodated with books by making a deposit with the Librarian, and paying for use of each volume, in proportion to its size. By order of the Board. *SAMUEL HAZARD, Sec'y* January 15"[23] Thomas Brandon and his brother, William, were masons and are credited with turning a Huntsville of wood houses into a town of stone and brick structures.[24]

The *Universal Gazetteer*, published in 1821, described Huntsville, "It is regularly laid out, and contains a court-house, market, printing office, bank and about 100 houses. The town is supplied with good water. It is in fertile country, and is rapidly increasing."[25]

Imagine the town of Huntsville based on the descriptions in the two small paragraphs above. The census of all of Madison County in 1820 was:

- 3,144 white males over 21 years of age
- 3,218 white males under 21 years of age
- 1,606 white females over 21 years of age
- 3,134 white females under 21 years of age
- 9,255 slaves
- 54 free persons of color
- 45% of the total population were slaves
- There were 95% more white males than white females over age 21.[26] "

"Huntsville Library Company. STOCKHOLDERS are informed that the annual meeting will be held in the Library Room in the Court House, on Wednesday the 19th inst. at 6 o'clock, P. M. Directors to be elected. N.B. The annual contribution must be paid on or before the annual meeting. SAM'L HAZARD, Sec'ry"[27]

"Huntsville Library – We are much pleased to see an entirely new arrangement in the Library. This institution contains a great number of very valuable works, which are now neatly arranged under their appropriate heads, and are kept in a neat and systematic order."[28] This is the first identified editorial praise from the local newspaper. There will be many more of them in the 1960's and later.

"Huntsville Library Company. A SPECIAL MEETING of the Stockholders will be held at the Library Room, on the 8th of March, at 6 0'clock, to consider some alteration and amendments of the constitution which will then be proposed. By order of the Directors. SAMUEL HAZARD, Sec'y"[29] In April 1823 the Alabama State Senate and House of Representatives approved "AN ACT TO INCORPORATE THE HUNTSVILLE LIBRARY COMPANY. ...Thomas Fearn, Samuel Hazard, John Boardman, James G. Bivney (sic-Birney), George Fearn, Miles S. Watkins, Henry Minor, Thomas Brandon and others associated with them, for the purpose of establishing a library in the town of Huntsville, are hereby incorporated as a body politick and corporate, in deed and in law, by the name and style of the 'Huntsville Library Company.'" There was a further description of the powers and legal responsibilities of the corporation which ended thusly: "...and to make such rules and regulations not repugnant to the constitution and laws of this state, or of the United States, as they may deem expedient: Provided, that they shall not possess, and enjoy real estate to a greater amount that five thousand dollars."[30] The lack of home rule by local communities was instituted early in Alabama's history and still is a dominant factor codified by the 1901 Alabama Constitution, as amended over 700 times as of 2004.

"Huntsville Library. THE STOCKHOLDERS in the Huntsville Library are hereby informed, that in pursuance of a resolution of the Board of Directors, Books will hereafter be delivered from the Library on *Mondays, Wednesdays and Saturdays,* ONLY, from 11 to 1 o'clock each day. THE LIBRARIAN."[31] The constitution of the Huntsville Library Company was revised in June 1824.

"At a meeting of the Stockholders of the Huntsville Library Company, on the 12 instant, - the annual contribution of members was reduced to $3, payable in two installments of $1.50 each, on the first Mondays in January and July.

The following preamble and resolutions were also adopted: --

WHEREAS, all the Stockholders of the Huntsville Library Company are in arrears for annual contributions, agreeably to the existing Constitution and By-Laws of the said Company, and for some of which the said company have ordered their stock to be publicly sold, which was done – And for the purpose of reinstating all delinquents to the full use of the library, and to the privileges of membership – *Be it Resolved,* That all stockholders be reinstated in all their rights and privileges, by paying, in lieu of all fines, forfeitures and contributions which have heretofore accrued, the sum of two dollars, to the Treasurer of the said Company, on or before the first day of July next, at the same time subscribing their acceptance of the Charter which has been granted to the said Company by the late act of the legislature, and the Constitution and By-Laws recently adopted.

Be it further resolved, That new certificates of stock shall be issued to all those stockholders whose shares have been publicly sold, on their paying to the Treasurer the sum of two dollars, agreeably to the foregoing resolution and subscribing to the Charter & Constitution.

All shares having originally cost 20 dollars, and the price of shares having reduced to 10 dollars each – *It is resolved,* That the old certificates of stock may be surrendered by the holder, and in lieu thereof two shares shall be issued for each original share.

Resolved, That stockholders be deprived the use of the Library until all arrears are paid agreeably to the foregoing resolutions.

Pursuant to the foregoing resolutions, the Charter, Constitution and By-Laws have been transcribed and deposited with the Librarian for the signatures of stockholders.

Persons who have lost their certificates of stock, or to whom certificates have never been issued, are directed to make application to the Directors.

New certificates of stock will be issued as soon as practical after the surrender of the old ones.

N. B. All persons having books belonging to the Library are requested to return them without delay. GEORGE FEARN, Sec'y"[32]

Less than a year after the problem about the stock price dropping and the company in financial trouble, an advertisement appeared in the *Alabama Republican,* April 29, 1825, "2 or 3 shares in the Huntsville Library may be obtained for about one half their original cost, on application at this office."[33] "HUNTSVILLE LIBRARY All persons having BOOKS belonging to the library, which have been retained longer than the lawful period, are requested to return them. A. WOODWARD, Librarian April 16, 1826."[34] The problem of returning books in a timely manner was an age-old continuing problem.

"Notice to the Stockholders in the Huntsville Library Company. All persons indebted to the Company are required to make payment on or before the 13th March next; and in default thereof, notice is hereby given, that the stock of all who shall then be indebted to the amount of 85; for fines or contributions, will be sold at public auction, at the Town Hall. Contributions due since the 24th August, 1833, have been remitted by order of the Company. Geo. Fearn, Treasurer."[35]

The disappearance of the Huntsville Library Company in the 1830s, and other similar companies, was characterized by Reverend John B. Wight, a library activist in the Boston area, as he addressed the Massachusetts General Court in 1854:

"While they have contributed much to a more general diffusion of knowledge and mental culture among their associated proprietors, experience has fully shown that their permanence is not to be depended on. With the exception of a few in the large towns which have been well maintained, their fate has been very much as follows. For a few years after the formation of the library everything goes well. Its books are read with avidity. New books are occasionally added. Those who have shares find it pleasant and improving to participate in its advantages. But before many years its prosperity begins to decline. Some of the proprietors have deceased. Others have removed from town. Others have been unfortunate in business. The annual assessments cease to be paid. New publications are no longer purchased. The library falls into disuse. For a long time there are no books in circulation and then perhaps when the attention of some influential person happens to be drawn to the subject the old library is reorganized or a new one is formed, to pass through a similar course of growth, decline and neglect."[36]

"The second library was known as The Hermathenian Library. No dates of this library have been found but we do know by the bookplates that they used many of the same books that were in the Huntsville Library."[37] It is presumed that Hermathenian is a combination of Hermes, the Greek god of commerce, eloquence, invention, and travel, and Athena, the Greek goddess of wisdom.

The third library was The Cliosophic Society of the Greene Academy for young men. This school was in operation from 1821 until it was burned by northern soldiers during the War Between the States. The Greene Academy was on the site of the existing East Clinton Elementary School at Clinton Avenue and Calhoun Street.[38] The Cliosophic Society was a debating society founded on June 7, 1770. It was one of several literary societies in American colleges. They constructed and taught their own curricula, selected and bought their own books, and operated their own libraries, which were sometimes larger than that of the host institution. Their libraries afforded undergraduates easy access to the world outside; their debates trained generations to consider the great public issues of the day, from slavery to American expansion, from women's rights to the dismemberment of the union.[39]

The Greene Academy mentioned above was one of more than 250 academies (private high schools) chartered by the Alabama legislature between 1820 and 1860. There was no regulation, as the people in each area and town could apply for a charter, give the academy a name and direct in any way the leaders decided.[40]

The *William's Huntsville City Directory, 1859-60,* owned by Benjamin P. Young, was still in the library archives in 2004. The *Huntsville City Council Code of Ordinances, 1861,* printed by William Acken, Esq., was also in the 2004 archives. Huntsville individuals and businesses were listed in the directory, as well as all the post offices in the United States. [without zip codes] The Hermathenian Library, organized in 1854, meets at Greene Academy every Saturday night, was in the directory.[41]

Clement Claiborne Clay, a son of an Alabama governor, congressman and a U.S. Senator, was elected a United States Senator from Alabama in 1853. He was an ardent defender of Southern rights and earned the nickname "Copperhead" by his Northern Senate colleagues. He remained an active Confederate politician during the War for Southern Independence. The President of the United States placed a bounty on Clay's head of $25,000 for complicity in the murder of President Abraham Lincoln. Clay surrendered to Union troops on May 12, 1865, three days after the bounty was posted.[42] Clay was imprisoned at Fort Monroe, Virginia with Jefferson Davis, President of the Confederacy. Clay's wife sent her 365-day prayer book to her husband during his internment. He wrote pencil notes about his captivity in the margins of the prayer book. That book was still in fine condition in the library archives in 2004.[43]

Libraries in America evolved slowly as the country expanded westward. Reading books was a leisure activity in a period when leisure time was at a minimum because people spent their time farming and in other labors to make a living. During the middle of the 19th Century,

English library thoughts were picked up in the Eastern United States that public libraries should be tied in with broad educational goals to educate the general public, not just the elite. Education was starting to win battles over theology in that era. Carl Russell Fish described those times,

"Self improvement...under the impulse of national elation...became not merely a solemn duty, with fear of failure always present and with escape from damnation as its most insistent motive; it was a thrilling almost gay, opportunity; a sure key to treasures of heaven and earth. Seldom have people thronged so merrily to school."[44] Educational reform was a necessary precursor to public libraries. Horace Mann was secretary to the Massachusetts Board of Education in the 1830s and 1840s. He wrote in his third annual report in 1839: "After the rising generation have acquired habits of intelligent reading in our schools, *what shall they read?*...for, with no books to read, the power of reading will be useless." He studied the social libraries in the state and determined there were 180,000 volumes in the state's social libraries, but they were available to only one-seventh of the population. He urged more support for school-district libraries. He said, "Had I the power, I would scatter libraries over the whole land, as the sower sows his wheat-field."[45] Ninety-eight years later, a sower of libraries would enter the Huntsville area and change the school and public library situation with a professional approach.

Reverend Wight, of Wayland, Massachusetts, quoted previously, was a state representative and instrumental in getting library legislation passed in Massachusetts in 1851. He continually extolled the many virtues of libraries, for example, he talked about the Wayland library:

"On Saturday afternoon ladies, and young ladies, and girls, frequent it and have a good time of friendly greetings and pleasant intercourse. In the evening men, and young men and boys may be found there, spending an hour or two in a rational and useful manner, under the quiet influence and suggestive association of the place. All carry away with them instructive and interesting books adapted to their peculiar capacities, tastes, and wants, and furnishing them with innocent and improving occupation in their leisure hours....Every Father and Mother who understands the subject, must feel, that in such a library their children will have advantages for acquiring much of the mental culture and general information, which is the principal and most valuable result of an extensive and liberal education."[46]

Several New England towns claim to have the first public library, but it was Boston's tax-supported library that opened in 1854 that is given credit for establishing the public library trend in the United States. It would take Alabama another 50 years to have a public library.

The concept of tying educational goals and libraries for *everybody* did not permeate Alabama. Alabama was a poor agricultural state, growing mostly cotton. The years before the Civil War found northern Alabama farmers switching to grains because the cotton from north Alabama did not bring as good a price as did the cotton from the Mobile area. Decent economic conditions are a precursor to schools, and schools are precursors to libraries. But, just as important is the fact that libraries were urban phenomena, and Alabama was heavily agricultural.

The Mobile area started the first public schools in Alabama in 1852. The Alabama legislature passed the Public School Act of 1854, which provided for centralization of the school system. A state superintendent of education was to be elected by the legislature and hold office for two years. The act appropriated $100,000 from the state treasury each year for public schools and set aside moneys from certain special funds for education. The educational system in Alabama started to make some progress, until the Civil War.[47] There is little evidence of libraries in North Alabama during the mid- to late-19th century. The pre-Civil War conditions got worse during the war, and not much better during the Reconstruction period, generally considered ended in 1877 when Rutherford B. Hayes was elected president.

In 1853 there was a "Call for a Convention of Librarians" to be held in New York City on Thursday, September 15, 1853. Twenty-six librarians from the most prestigious city and university libraries in the northeastern United States signed the Call "...believing that the knowledge of books, and the foundation and management of collections of them for public use, may be promoted by consultation and concert among librarians and others interested in bibliography... for the purpose of conferring together upon the means of advancing the prosperity and usefulness of public libraries, and for the suggestion and discussion of topics of importance to book collectors and readers."[48] The convention came to naught and the Civil War stymied any further progress of this idea. In the 1850s Alabamians were not interested in libraries, but in seceding from the Union.

The new Alabama Constitution of 1868 placed more emphasis on public schools (again) and women's rights. Some historians credit the Carpetbaggers (Northerners who invaded the South during the Reconstruction) with bringing more public schools to Alabama.[49] The Scalawags, white Southerners acting to support Reconstruction, were opposed by the majority of the white population, who were hostile to the Northerners and wanted to restore the pre-Civil War societal structures. The post-Civil War emancipation of the slaves reduced the plantation system to a subsistence level, that is, to produce not for the market but only for the immediate needs of the workers. The waste of human potential during this era was devastating to society and the economic environment. Education and libraries cannot flourish in such an economic society.

The idea of a librarian convention was revived in the aftermath of the Civil War. During October 4-6, 1876, 103 persons, 90 men and 13 women, gathered in the rooms of the Historical Society of Pennsylvania in Philadelphia to found the American Library Association (ALA). The year 1876 was chosen because it was the centennial celebration of the founding of the United States. Six attendees from the 1853 convention were on hand at the 1876 convention to remind the attendees that it was very easy to pass resolutions about annual conferences and cooperative work, but it was a different matter to follow through with action. The ALA did survive from that convention and one hundred years later it had grown and prospered as the oldest, largest, and strongest library association in the world.

In 1876 Alabamians were still not interested in libraries because economic conditions were not good enough. The power structure had approved the Constitution of 1875, which "emphasized white supremacy, economy, honesty and retrenchment in government." The Board of Education was abolished as a "useless appendage."[50] If the government was not interested in pushing education, there was no need for libraries during the 1870's. The number of newspapers in Alabama kept increasing during the last half of the 19th century, so perhaps that encouraged some people to want to learn how to read, but that implies schools. Some of the plantation homes had large libraries, but the number of book readers is questionable.

The First International Conference of Librarians was held in London in October 1877. John Winter Jones, Librarian of the British Museum said, "The idea of holding a Conference of Librarians originated in America—in that country of energy and activity which has set the world so many good examples, and of which a Conference of Librarians is not the least valuable, looking to the practical results which may be anticipated from it." England founded its own library association in October 1877 at the international meeting cited above.[51]

As stated earlier in this chapter, libraries came from Europe as part of the Western civilization and culture. But, it was in an American context of freedom of ideas and expanding country that the associations of like thinking people were allowed to flourish. There were professional organizations in Europe from ancient days, but librarianship was not a profession in the middle of the 19th Century. Only in America could there be an initial coalescing of ideas to found a library association. The early European libraries were founded by monks, churches, kings, and other rich and powerful rulers. European societies had been locked into stratified classes for many centuries of perpetuation of the same system. Change was difficult because the powerful had no incentive to change old power structures. Public libraries are trailing cultural activities that depend on a critical mass of urban populations before libraries are founded. Only in an expanding American not driven by old stratification could the idea of equality be the driving force for educating the general population, which in turn made possible our public library system. The industrial age in the United States was magnified by the Civil War and it continued to expand throughout the late 1800s. In 1870 the total population of librarians in the United States was reported at 213. In 1976, on the one hundredth anniversary of the American Library Association, the membership in the ALA was more than 33,000.

Alabama, along with most of the southeastern states, has long been a laggard in providing for public education. The plantation owners of the 19th Century had a strong abiding economic interest in having slave labor and keeping the general white population from raising themselves upward. This trend continued in Alabama into the 20th Century because the steel mills, owned by northern white industrialists, were largely populated by slaves and poor whites. Although Alabama had steel mills, the age of iron, steam and industry generally bypassed Alabama. All of this constrained the growth of public libraries, which equally affected Huntsville until the 1940's.

Richard Rogers Bowker (1848-1933) was the publisher of the *Publishers Weekly* and the editor of the *Library Journal*, which were instrumental in maintaining the momentum of the newly founded American Library Association. He was one of the giants of the early ALA. His company continued uninterrupted to 2004 as R.R. Bowker, which is the official United States agency for the issuance of International Standard Book Numbers (ISBN). ISBN's identify the publishing company and provide a unique number for each book. Commercial books require an ISBN to be accepted within the book publishing and selling community. ISBN's are readily available to self-publishers, such as this author. Several years ago I self-published a book and I paid a fee of $195 to R.R. Bowker, for which I received a block of ten ISBN's that I control and can assign the number for any new book published by my publishing name.

Melvil Dewey (1851-1931) was another of the early ALA leaders. Dewey was the organizer of the 1876 convention. He was the first secretary of the ALA at the tender age of 25. He was the originator of the Dewey Decimal System, the book classification still in use today in some libraries. Dewey, anonymously, while a student at Amherst College, wrote a 42-page booklet titled *Classification and Subject Index for Cataloguing and Arranging Books and Pamphlets of a Library.* Others have since adopted the Library of Congress system, which starts with a letter. In 1876, the first *Library Journal* was named the *American Library Journal*, but at the International Library Conference in 1877 it was agreed to drop "American" so the journal would apply to both the English and American associations. Melvil Dewey was the energetic editor that made the journal a valuable element on both sides of the Atlantic.[52]

"The first library after the War Between the States was the library of the Huntsville Literary Debating Society, which was organized March 1, 1870. The library has some of the books which had belonged to the old Huntsville Library and the Hermathenian Library. One book still contains the three book plates.

The Young Men's Christian Association (YMCA) had established a library in its building on Estes Street. Mrs. Anthony, widow of Dr. LeRoy Anthony, gave his large and valuable library to this organization. A Reverend J. T. Thompson also donated many valuable books"[53]

The Huntsville Circulating Library was established about June 1891 and had the motto, "Vita sine literis mors est" (Latin: Life without literature (or books) is death). The library was located in a corner in Murray and Smith's Book Store. Mrs. V. A. Betts was the librarian. The library moved to the YMCA in August 1891. Earlier in this chapter the social library was discussed. The circulating library was generally based on people paying to read the books, but there was no corporation as with the social library. The circulating library was a commercial enterprise to make money, so it had to match the popular taste in books. That meant it did not stock the history of Rome, but had fiction and romance novels, etc.

Upon the library's departure from the Murray and Smith store, Mrs. Betts wrote the following letter to the owners.

"We cannot leave the genial firm that always smiled us a kindly welcome without offering them our grateful acknowledgement for their unexceptional deportment during our stay of three months in their home. To their assistance and encouragement we really owe our beginning.

We would also offer thanks to Mr. Kolb, the eye of the establishment, for more than one act of kindness, and to Mr. Daniel, the accomplished engraver, our remembrance of such delicate courtesies as only a refined man knows how to show a woman.

Nor would we pass out of these pleasant doors without the recognition of the services of their excellent porter, Marion Moore, whose thoughtfulness spared us many a weary step.

Adieu to a pleasant past.

Very respectfully,
(Signed) V. A. Betts'
Librarian"[54]

The establishment of the circulating library in 1891 was coincidently with the changing fortunes of Huntsville during the 1890s. Electricity had been introduced into Huntsville in 1882. The Northern capitalists introduced their capital into Huntsville in the form of multiple cotton mills and other small industries. The first free mail delivery was in 1892 and the first long distance telephone call in 1896. A non-agricultural infrastructure was slowly coming to a town that had gone nowhere since before the Civil War. The population of Huntsville "boomed" from 4,977 in 1870 to 8,068 in 1900, a 62 percent increase in 30 years, albeit not impressive by modern standards. But remember, Huntsville was "nowhere."

There was another significant event in 1896 that impacted Huntsville and the entire South. The United States Supreme Court decision, Plessy versus Ferguson, set the precedent that "separate" facilities for blacks and whites were constitutional as long as they were "equal." The "separate but equal" doctrine extended to almost every aspect of public life. It would remain that way until the "Brown versus the Board of Education of Topeka, Kansas" Supreme Court decision of 1954.

"We can really feel the atmosphere so that corner library in Murray and Smith's. Imagine it. Surrounded by Haviland china, cutglass, rare Delph, Venetian glass, cases of silver, and shelves of books for sale. Mr Murray was a large, broad-faced, large-mouthed man who was interested in fine things. Having been superintendent of schools in Huntsville, he was interested in keeping culture alive. His taste for beautiful things was seen in the articles he selected for his store. The library was lucky to have such a place.

"The candidates for the position of librarian in 1895 were Mrs. M.V. Douglass, Miss Etta Matthews, Miss Meneese Pattison, and Miss Virginia Clay. Miss Mathews was appointed. Mr. Conrad O'Shaughnessy was elected secretary and treasurer. The librarian was in the library from three o'clock to five o'clock twice a week to check loans, collect dues, and to order new books and repair old ones. As the books were on open shelves, they were selected by the borrower.

Every now and then the members gave benefits for its maintenance. There was also a charge of One Dollar a year for membership and fines for books which are overdue. The first lot of books were procured by private subscriptions collected by Miss Matthews, Mrs. L.S. Noble, one Mrs. Connor, and Mr. Conrad O'Shaughnessy. An addition of the books from the Young Men's Christian Association was a good increase in the number of books for public [not really public since it was for members only] use. Other books were added by receipts from public entertainment.

Such an evening's amusement was arranged by Mrs. L.S. Noble and Mrs. S. Morgan at the Huntsville Hotel on April 23, 1895. Dancing was always a popular amusement. Mrs. Noble employed a good band and obtained permission to use the hotel dining room. She succeeded in drawing a large crowd who danced until dawn was breaking – a scandalous thing to do, very much against the health and morals of the community. But it was done nevertheless."[55]

In 1895 the Library was moved from the Y.M.C.A. to the Gordon Building on Franklin Street. It was now open to the public on Tuesday and Thursday afternoons, but by 1897 the circulation has increased to such an extent that it was necessary to operate every afternoon to take care of the public. The hours were also changed from 2:30 to 4:30 P.M. At the election of the Huntsville Library Association in 1897, Miss Emma Wells was chosen president. "She was an active person, pleasing in manner and earnest in public service. Mrs. Felix Baldridge, the beautiful wife of Dr. Felix Baldridge, was elected vice-president. She was a college woman, and inveterate reader, aggressive, and determined to make the library a certainty. She was one of its chief workers. Miss Etta Matthews retained her post and Mrs. Henry Dillard was elected in Mr. O'Shaughnessy's place. The directors were also a strong group: Misses Katie Mastin, Belle Farris, Lula Miller, Lizzie Vogel, Dr. P.L. Brouillette, and Mr. Jere Murphy. They began a series of entertainments.

Twice that year they selected living pictures as a means of drawing a crowd to supply money when Mr. Charles Dana Gibson was a recognized artist – recognized, that is, by the public. His ink drawings were sold by the foot. His heads were prized possessions. He turned them out by the hundreds it seemed just to show that he could. His work was chosen for tableaux at the Huntsville Hotel. There were two presentations at Twenty Five Cents at entrance. Tea, chocolate, and pictures were also sold. Patrons were asked to donate books, too. Mrs. Felix Baldridge and Mrs. Walter I. Wellman served the chocolate. Both were beautiful women; one a brunette, the other a blonde. Mrs. D.I. White, also a handsome woman, served tea. They were assisted by Misses May Steele, Felica Hubbard, Grace Russel, Olive Nucholls, Mamie Fletcher, Byrd Ludlow, Kate Mastin, Betty Mathews, and Mabel Hinchcliffe.

Dr. J.E. Darwin and Mr. W.I. Wellman auctioned reprints of Edwin A. Abbey, A.B. Frost, Charles Dana Gibson, Wells H. Lowe, Howard Pike, W.T. Smedley, and Alice Barbour Stevens. The net receipts of this entertainment were Forty Dollars.

Miss Etta Matthews made a capable and agreeable librarian. She was a handsome blond with lovely blue eyes and golden hair. Her quiet manner and deep musical voice won many friends without effort. She was an asset to the work. By the close of the century the library had many regular members and a nice book collection."[56]

"Public Library Association, Annual Meeting of Stockholders. The regular Annual meeting of the members of said Association will be held at the city hall at 7:30 p.m. on Thursday, January 7th, 1897, for the election of new officers for the year 1897, and the transaction of other business as may come before them. All members in good standing are entitled to vote, and are urged to be present at said meeting, or send their proxies. Paul Speake, Pres't"[57]

"In about 1899 or 1900 the library was carried to a room over the Fire Hall, which was then located in the old City Hall-Market House building where the Twickenham Hotel now stands. Miss Emma Wells and Mrs. Arthur Owen Wilson acted as librarians without remunerations.

From there it was moved to an upstairs room in the Hundley Building on the East Side of the Square. Mrs. Wilson continued as librarian. Rabbi Jacobs and Miss Nora Davis were very interested in a library for Huntsville and did much to help it in its early struggles. [We will see more about Nora Davis later.] The library remained at that site until it was moved to the Carnegie Building which it now occupies."[58]

In his 1984 book, *Public Libraries in America*, William Fletcher wrote, "librarianship affords a fine field for women's work, and a decided majority of all American librarians are women." He said that precisely half of the largest 100 libraries listed in his book were headed by women. Fletcher did not mention that women did not head the largest and most significant libraries. The number of men and women librarians heading the Huntsville-Madison County Public Library should be remembered as this history marches through time.

Membership in the American Library Association passed over 1,000 in 1902. The association was growing stronger along with the country. The issue of whether librarianship was a profession, not just a job, was debated frequently in the group and continued to be debated for several decades. Professionalism implies ethics, a code of conduct, a scientific approach to the management of the activities and an educational process to learn the necessary job skills. During this era the Library of Congress first began the distribution of printed catalog cards and began to assume leadership for future cataloguing rules. During this same period Andrew Carnegie started to distribute money for public and school libraries. The activities above set the stage for Alabama librarians to finally get moving and organize themselves.

The Alabama Library Association was formed on Monday, November 21, 1904 at a meeting in Montgomery in the Carnegie Library building. No one from Huntsville attended, although two persons from Athens did. The first president was Thomas M. Owen, LL. D., Director, Department of Archives and History, Montgomery.

"Dr. Owen again addressed the meeting, calling attention to recent press reports in reference to the closing of the Huntsville library. Such a step, he thought, would be extremely unfortunate, and the moral influence of the Association should be set against it. He therefore offered the following resolution, which, after being read, was seconded by several, and unanimously adapted, viz: 'This body having heard with profound regret that the Huntsville Library Association expects to close the library it has maintained in that city for the past eleven years; now therefore be it '*Resolved, by the Alabama Library Association,* That a most earnest appeal is hereby made to the said Huntsville Library Association to reconsider its determination to discontinue its library, and hope is expressed that some means may be devised whereby future support may be obtained'" (Proc, 1st, AL-21)

The last section of the *Proceedings of the First Meeting of the Alabama Library Association* contained a list of all the public and school libraries in the State, to the best of its knowledge. Huntsville was listed as having a Garrisonia Library founded in 1870. The date, but not the name, corresponds to the earlier cited Huntsville library in 1870.[59]

"First serious consideration of library legislation by the state legislature results in the Library Act of 1907, which establishes the principle of state support for library services by authorizing and financing the Library Extension Division of the Department of Archives and History. This division was to operate a system of traveling libraries for the entire state. These mobile libraries would consist of 25-35 books sent to rural counties and schools for a period of up to four months; shipping and transportation costs were to be paid by recipients. Establishment of school and public libraries was to be encouraged and assisted, and a summer course in library instruction instituted."[60]

Theodore Roosevelt was the twenty-sixth president of the United States in 1907 and the Panama Canal was under construction. The first 90-some years of the Huntsville library went through fits and starts with limited success, but that was also true for the entire state. Potential progress was stifled by the Civil War, but more importantly, the power-hungry, selfish, state leadership failed miserably to improve the lot of its citizens in every respect throughout the 19th century.

Chapter 2

Carnegie Was Here

*"What is more important in a library than anything
else — is the fact that it exists."*

Archibald MacLeish
"The Premise of Meaning"
American Scholar (June 5, 1972)
The Quotable Book Lover

On February 29, 1916, a leap year Tuesday, The Huntsville Carnegie [Public] Library was formally opened to the public. This was the genesis of the modern era Huntsville-Madison County Public Library. Public is in brackets because of the varied definitions of public. Was it an auspicious coincidence or purposefully chosen that the Carnegie Library opened on a leap-year day? Perhaps we will never know, but it was a well-timed event for Huntsville. In the previous chapter, social and circulating libraries were defined. One of the characteristics of a public library is that it is supported by a government entity, while social and circulating libraries had no relationship to government. Woodrow Wilson was the twentieth-eighth president of the United States.

The Carnegie Library was so named because the library building was constructed by money donated by Andrew Carnegie. Carnegie, 1835-1919, was born in Scotland, but moved with his family to the United States in 1846 and settled in Allegheny, Pennsylvania, a suburb of Pittsburgh. He worked for the Pennsylvania Railroad from 1853 until 1865. He invested in railroad sleeping cars and introduced the first successful sleeping car on an American railroad. He invested in oil development in 1862, three years after oil was discovered in Titusville, Pennsylvania. He eventually founded the Carnegie Steel Company and sold that business in 1901 for $250 million. He was one of the richest men in America.

Carnegie then retired and devoted the rest of his life to philanthropy. Before he sold his company he was already considering what to do with his money. In 1889 he wrote a famous essay entitled "The Gospel of Wealth," in which he stated that wealthy men should live without extravagance, provide moderately for their dependents, and distribute the rest of their riches to benefit the welfare and happiness of the common man—with the consideration to help only those who would help themselves. His second essay "The Best Fields for Philanthropy," listed seven fields to which the wealthy should donate: universities, libraries, medical centers, public parks, meeting and concert halls, public baths, and churches. He later expanded this list to include gifts that promoted scientific research, the general spread of knowledge, and the promotion of world peace.

Carnegie's formal education was from 8 to 11 years of age. Children did not go to school very much in the mid-1800s. In his birthplace of Dunfermline, about 12 miles northwest of Edinburgh across the Firth of Forth, he participated in discussions about books borrowed from the Tradesmen's Subscription Library that his father, a weaver, helped create. Subscription means paying for the opportunity to read books, neither free nor public.

While working as a messenger for the railroad in the early 1850s, Carnegie was introduced to Colonel James Anderson of Allegheny, who every Saturday opened his personal library to any young worker who wished to borrow a book. Carnegie later said the colonel opened the windows through which the light of knowledge streamed. In 1853, when the colonel's representatives tried to restrict the library's use, Carnegie wrote a letter to the editor of the *Pittsburgh Dispatch* defending the right of all working boys to enjoy the pleasures of the library. More important, he resolved that, should he ever be wealthy, he would make similar opportunities available to other poor workers. He was obviously a believer in the power of knowledge and kept his word.

When Carnegie died in 1919 he had given away $350,695,653, mostly through the Carnegie Foundation started in 1911. He endowed over $62 million of that for the building of 2,811 Free Libraries in communities across the United States and other English speaking countries, including 1,946 in the United States.[1] Huntsville received a grant of $12,500 from the Carnegie Foundation on 8 May 1914 for the establishment of a public library. Huntsville did not have a public library before that.[2]

The Constitution and By-Laws of the Carnegie Library Governing Board of Huntsville, Alabama were derived from an ordinance adapted by the City Commissioners of Huntsville on 17 December 1915.

- "The Board was to be known as the Carnegie Library Board.
- The Board was authorized to solicit donations for equipment and maintenance.
- The city reserves the right to elect the librarian.
- There was to be strict accounting of receipts and expenditures of money.
- The Board consisted of ten members.
- There were three standing committees: Library; House and Grounds; and Book.
- "The use of the Library is hereby limited to residents of Madison County, of the white race." (Copy of original document, undated)

Fourteen Carnegie Libraries were established in Alabama, which placed 28th among the 46 states in the number of libraries, and was 3rd among 11 southeastern states. Alabama rated 32nd in the total amount of dollars received with $195,800. Alabama ranked 42nd in the number of dollars received per 100 population with $7.40 per 100 people.[3] An Alabama State Library Association was organized in 1904 and a State Library Commission organized in 1907.

The list of communities in Alabama receiving a Carnegie Grant is below. The towns are listed in the chronological order when they each received the grant, which was generally correlated to the timing of the paperwork submission by the town. In each case the name of the town will be followed by a yes or no, which answers the question, "Was a public library established before the Carnegie Grant?" That will be followed by the amount of money and the date.

- Montgomery/No/$50,000/February 13, 1901
- Eufaula/No/$10,000/February 2, 1903
- Decatur/No/$12,500/February 12, 1903
- Selma/No/$11,800/April 13, 1903
- Gadsden/No/$10,000/November 18, 9003
- Ensley/No/$10,000/March 25, 1905
- Bessemer/No/$10,000/February 13, 1906
- Talladega/No/$12,500/February 13, 1906
- Avondale/No/$10,000/December 13, 1907

- Troy/No/$10,000/April 6, 1908
- West End/No/$10,000/February 1, 1909
- Union Springs/No/$7,000/January 6, 1911
- Huntsville/No/$12,500/May 8, 1914
- Anniston/No/$20,000/May 15, 1916[4]

Decatur was eleven years ahead of Huntsville, or stated another way, Huntsville was eleven years behind its neighbor. In 1910 the population of Huntsville was 7,611 people, while Decatur's was 4,228. Decatur was on the most direct line between Nashville and Birmingham, as there was a railroad bridge over the Tennessee River before the Civil War.

Now that the principal statistics are out of the way, let us go back and explore the inner workings of the Carnegie library philanthropy operation.

Andrew Carnegie supplied the money, but the man who did all the work and made almost all decisions was James Bertram. Bertram was a fellow Scot like Carnegie and was born in the village of Corstorphine, now part of Edinburgh, in 1872. He was educated in the equivalent of a business high school. After several jobs and some sickness, he applied for the position of private secretary to Carnegie. After a three-month trial period, he was Carnegie's confidential secretary for seventeen years, from 1897 to 1914, and secretary to the Carnegie Corporation of New York from 1911 to 1934.

Bertram was the consummate administrative secretary. When word of Carnegie's decision to give away most of his fortune, requests flooded in from all over the world, to include churches and libraries. Bertram organized the chaos into order and ran the operation from Carnegie's home, which was in two consecutive locations in New York City. He was the buffer between the hordes of applicants and Carnegie, and also served as a watchdog on the treasury.

Bertram published procedures and a questionnaire to be returned by the town applicants. Bertram was businesslike and brevity was the norm. This led to a certain abruptness, rudeness, and lack of tact and patience. For example, a newspaper editor wrote a letter asking for information on how to obtain a grant. Bertram replied,

"Dear Sir:

It is an extraordinary fact that after Mr. Carnegie has given some thirty or forty libraries in Indiana, and the detailed applications and also Mr. Carnegie's response have been printed in its daily press, a Newspaper Editor writes and professes ignorance as to how to proceed or as to what is required."

Bravo, Mr. Bertram, that was well stated. And to another letter that asked for a copy of an important misplaced letter, Bertram asked, "Do you mean to say that you have lost the letter promising you $10,000? This is extraordinary!" To repeat a common phrase, Bertram suffered no fools.[5]

When towns sent a request letter to Bertram, he sent back the following questionnaire (several similar versions):

1. Name of Town_____
2. Population_____
3. Has it a Library at present?_____
4. Number of books (excluding government reports)?_____
5. Circulation for the last year?_____
6. How is Library housed?_____
7. Number of rooms, their measurements and uses?_____
8. Finances according to the last annual report:

```
Receipts                      Expenditures
From Taxes_____               Rent_____
Other Income_____             Other Costs_____
Total_____
```

   9. a) Rate at which municipality will pledge annual support (with a tax levy) if building is obtained_____

       b) What is the highest rate of tax levy allowed by law?_____

       c) How much income would this rate have yielded for the last five years?_____

  10. Is the requisite site available?_____

  11. Amount, if any, already collected toward building_____

"To facilitate Mr. Carnegie's consideration of your appeal, will you oblige by filling in the above, and return with a statement of any particulars likely to assist in making decision? It is necessary to give explicit answers to each question, as in absence of such, there is no basis for action, and the matter will be delayed pending further communication."

The following form was utilized to show that the community accepted the library grant as well as the specified responsibilities.

"A Resolution to Accept the Donation of Andrew Carnegie

Whereas, Andrew Carnegie has agreed to furnish_____Dollars to the _____(name of community) to erect a Free Public Library Building, on condition that the said community shall pledge itself by a Resolution of Council, to support a Free Public Library, at a cost of not less than_____Dollars a year, and provide a suitable site for the said building.

Now therefore be it resolved by Council of _____(name of community) that said community accept said donation, and it does hereby pledge itself to the requirements of Andrew Carnegie. Resolved that it will furnish a suitable site for said building when erected, at a cost of not less than_____Dollars. Resolved that an annual levy shall hereafter be made upon the taxable property of said community sufficient in amount to comply with the above requirements." The signatures of the clerk and mayor and witnessing statement of clerk followed.[6]

Some explanation of the rationale behind some of the requirements is necessary. Carnegie wanted to ensure that maintenance funds were approximately ten percent of the building's cost, and not by donations but came from the city's tax structure on a continuing basis. Carnegie would not pay for the books to fill the library. Two operative words in the document were: "Free Public." It was intended that there be no fees for entrance nor for each book borrowed. The Carnegie group was well aware of the conditions of segregation in the South. It imposed no political statement about those conditions and overlooked the fact that the libraries would be free to whites, and that Negroes would be excluded.

The Carnegie documentation provided six sample-building plans with specific layouts and guidance. But this approach only started in 1908 after James Bertram began to examine building plans. Before 1908 there was no guidance to grant recipients. For example, in 1902 Bertram was shown a drawing of a library in Denver and wrote, "I am sorry to have money wasted in this way – This is no practical plan. Too many pillars."[7] Library planners were told to guard against wasted space at the building entrance, as large elaborate entrance ways were costly and space-consuming. Bertram gave little guidance about the exterior, except to keep it plain and dignified, and warned against "Greek temples."[8] The picture of the Huntsville Carnegie Library certainly shows good taste in architecture and compliance with Bertram's guidance. Of course, the larger the town, the more emphasis on constructing a "Greek Temple" edifice, as a picture of Houston's Carnegie Library, which had "Greek columns" on each of the building's eight sides.[9]

There is an old joke that goes around military circles that the U.S. Air Force first builds an officer's club and golf course, and then asks Congress for money to build runways. Well, the military did not invent that scheme, so perhaps city officials did. For example, Parkersburg, West Virginia had already been granted an increase from $25,000 to $34,000, but came back for $2,000 more. Bertram replied to Parkersburg, "...Glancing over the photographs you have sent, the carpets, easy chairs, reception room, etc. give one more the idea of a private house than a Free Public Library. In a busy city library one would expect more benches and tables and fewer carpets and arm chairs. In the newspaper room there only appears to be half a dozen newspapers. Why is a 'reception room' needed? Why should there be a 'boardroom?' Cannot the committee meet in the librarian's office?"[10] The more I read about James Bertram, the more I liked him. Of course, this author is not a city official trying to bleed as much money as possible from a rich source. Eufaula, Alabama added another floor to its library building as an unauthorized auditorium and then asked Carnegie for the additional $3,000 expense. Bertram replied NO![11]

The Carnegie Corporation became concerned about broken pledges and other abuses. It approached the problem in two ways. It sent out questionnaires to hear from the libraries themselves. It also hired Alvin Johnson, an economics professor at Cornell University, to make a study of the libraries. Johnson took a ten-week winding tour through the United States, visiting some 100 Carnegie libraries of various sizes. His report was presented to the Carnegie Corporation's board of trustees in 1916. The report was never publicly disseminated. Highlights of the report follow:

- Social Significance of the Free Library: It was a practical and cultural service of great value and offered instruction and entertainment to the whole *literate* community. [author's italics] Library service was essentially a public service closely related to popular education and equally deserving of public support. [It is difficult for us today to appreciate the situation in the early 1900s.] Johnson felt the role of the public library in the modern community was not sufficiently understood, which caused postponement of the start of library service and the lack of adequate appropriations after the library was established.

- Library Philanthropy: The free public library was a relatively new institution. Johnson found in his travels that many librarians were slow to perceive the idea that a library should actively engage in stimulating and directing the demand for books and to seek to cooperate with other forces in the community working for popular education and culture. The public recognized the benefits, but not sufficiently to compel the civil authorities to adequately support the library. The philanthropy was a key element to stimulate the process. "But the South was generally so backward in library service that the large cities offered the best promise for cultivation of libraries."

- Efficient Community Library Service: The library was not just to distribute printed matter. It needed to actively engage itself in creating a demand for reading and in directing the demand into the most profitable channels. Johnson suggested closer contact between the library and local schools. The library staff should have a systematic knowledge of the occupations and social conditions of the community. An active library would be able to gain support from the population, schools, employers, and workingmen's organizations, the better to be able to compete for financial resources. "It might be wise to attempt to win the support of other influences for the library through the sharing of clubrooms and lecture halls, particularly in areas where the reading habit had not been fully developed (as in the South and in many small towns throughout much of the country."

- Location of Carnegie Library Buildings: Johnson found that only about 10 percent of the 100 libraries he visited enjoyed the best possible location. In the majority of cases, the location appeared to be a distinct handicap to efficient service. The reasons for this were several: the site was donated; the site was purchased and a good central location could not be afforded; and the politics for a real estate motive. Johnson's general conclusion was a local failure to understand the requirements and potentialities of library service.

- Library Personnel: Johnson felt the efficiency of the library was largely dependent on the character and training of the librarian and on his or her ability to understand the community and cultivate the reading habit. In southern towns the librarian was generally found to be a 'decayed gentlewoman with the virtues and foibles of her class.' She had no special capacity to make good her lack of library experience through a careful study of the technical helps available in printed form to librarians.

- In other cases the office of the librarian was bestowed upon someone regarded as especially fitted by natural instinct: a local poet, a local authority on Confederate memoirs, or just someone who was popular and liked books. The prevailing view in small towns all over the country was that anyone who was fairly read, polite, and painstaking would make a satisfactory librarian. Since the community did not know what to expect from a library or its librarian, their shortcomings were often not recognized for a long time…."To Johnson nothing contributed more to the certainty of library inactivity than an untrained and unintelligent librarian."

- Facilities for Library Education: Johnson concluded that the number of trained librarians needed to be increased. At that time there were only thirteen schools providing library science education. The librarian needed to have knowledge of book selection, library resources, and a grasp of community and social conditions through education that would allow for professional recognition. [12]

Huntsville's Carnegie Grant approval in May 1914 was timely. The Carnegie library grants were terminated in November 1917.

"Prior to November 7, 1913, a Carnegie Library Board had been formed. Minutes of a meeting of the Board on that date, state that the Board met to consider the investment of $210.85, deposited to its account in the Huntsville Bank & Trust Company. The Board voted to invest the money in the purchase of such books as the purchasing committee of the Y.M.C.A. and a committee from the Carnegie Library Board might select. Mr. R.E. Spragins and Mrs. Felix Baldridge were placed on this committee. The books bought were to be placed in charge of the Y.M.C.A. for use in the Y.M.C.A. library. Should a Carnegie Library be established, the books would be withdrawn and placed in the Carnegie Library. One stipulation made by the Carnegie Library Board was that women as well as men be allowed to use the books on the Y.M.C.A. [Wonder how that worked?]

The officers of the Library Board were: Mr. W.T. Hutchens, President, Mrs. Felix Baldridge, Secretary, David Grayson, Treasurer. Mr. R.E. Spragins was the only other board member mentioned."[13]

On November 11, 1913, the Carnegie Board appeared before the city Commissioners to ask that they make an appropriation, for the support of a Carnegie Library. It was found that the city commissioners had already agreed to the usual conditions of supplying a suitable site for the library building and appropriating 10% of the cost of the building per annum for maintenance, $1500.[14]

On February 24, 1914, the Huntsville city commissioners met for their regular Tuesday morning meeting at 9:30 a.m. Commissioner Lanier offered the following ordinance, which was in writing and read as follows:

"AN ORDINANCE

WHEREAS in the opinion of the Commissioners of the City of Huntsville, the citizens of the City would appreciate the erection of a Carnegie Library, and are willing to pay the expense of maintaining the building, and the operation of a library therein, in accordance with the requirements of the Carnegie Corporation donating free library buildings.

BE IT NOW ORDAINED, that the sum of fifteen hundred dollars, annually, be appropriated, under the requirements and conditions of said Carnegie Corporation, for the purpose of maintaining the building and the operation of the library therein as foresaid.

BE IT FURTHER ORDAINED, that the City of Huntsville does hereby authorize the erection of the building to be used as the Carnegie Library on the South end of the lot recently purchased of W. L. Russell at the corner of Madison and Gates street, being on the North side of Gates street, and on the West side of Madison street, said building to cost $15,000.

And moved that unanimous consent be granted for the immediate consideration of the same. The motion being seconded and the roll being called on the adoption of the motion, the following vote was recorded:

AYES: -- Commissioners Humphrey, Lanier and O'Neal, total …3
NAYS: --…………………………………………………………………………0"

The President of the Commission, O'Neal, declared the motion adopted and the commissioners went on to approve the ordinance by the same vote.[15] The above ordinance closely followed the Carnegie Corporation verbiage set forth earlier in this chapter. The city's application had apparently asked for $15,000, and therefore the $1,500 was the 10 percent of the cost. James Bertram of the Carnegie Corporation eventually gave only $12,500 to Huntsville. Readers who might look in other histories of Huntsville could find the figure of $15,000, but the actual amount was $12,500, which will be in later documents.

At the City Commissioners' meeting on November 3, 1914, three representatives of the Carnegie Library committee, E.L. Love, W.T. Hutchens and D.A. Grayson, appeared before the Board of Commissioners and presented plans for the proposed library building. The Board approved Mr. Grayson as a committee of one to forward the plans to the Carnegie Corporation at New York for their approval, and to negotiate with them as they might see fit to secure the required funds to erect said building.[16] In retrospect, Grayson of Huntsville did not fare well in negotiations with Bertram of Carnegie! It was a mismatch, considering that Bertram did not negotiate, so Grayson came home with one-sixth less than he wanted. It would have been fascinating to hear what Grayson told the board upon his return to the little southern (hick) town of Huntsville.

The Library Board established several committees: Hutchens and Rev. Francis Tappey on the committee to inspect the new building and accept it when it was satisfactory; Grayson and Mrs. S.J. Mayhew were to agree which books would be acceptable; and Grayson, Baldridge and Mayhew were on the purchasing committee.[17]

On February 9, 1915 the city commissioners passed a resolution to accept the donation from the Carnegie Corporation:

"WHEREAS, Carnegie Corporation of New York has agreed to furnish twelve-thousand Five-Hundred Dollars, to the City of Huntsville, to erect a free Public Library Building, on condition that said City of Huntsville shall pledge itself by Resolution of Council to support a Free Public Library, at a cost of twelve-Hundred Fifty Dollars per year and Provide a suitable site for said building; now therefore

BE IT RESOLVED by the Council of the City of Huntsville that said City of Huntsville accept said donation, and it does hereby pledge itself to comply with the requirements of said Carnegie Corporation of New York.

RESOLVED that it will furnish a suitable site for said building, and will maintain a free public library in said building when erected, at a cost of twelve hundred fifty dollars per year.

RESOLVED that the following described lot is hereby set apart and devoted to the use of the Free Public Library, to-wit: --Beginning at the southern corner of the lot owned by Miss Sarah Lowe, on Madison Street, thence at right and with Madison Street, and along the south line of Miss Sarah Lowe's property in a westerly direction to the western boundary of the City's property, and to the east boundary of a lot owned by the estate of Charles E. Hutchens lot to the North side of Gates street; thence east along Gates street on the North side thereof to the intersection of Gates street with the western boundary of Madison street; thence North with Madison street on the west side thereof, to the place of beginning.

RESOLVED, that an annual levy shall hereafter be made upon the taxable property of said City of Huntsville, sufficient in amount to comply with the above requirements."[18]

Commissioner Laughlin had replaced O'Neal on the Board.

In April 1915, "Mr. Edgar L. Love appeared before the Board of Commissioners with plans and certificates for the proposed Carnegie Library Building. Said plans having been already approved by the Carnegie Corporation of New York. Upon motion of Commissioner Humphrey, it was directed by the Board that advertisements for bids for the construction of said Library building be placed in the Mercury Banner, and sealed bids be received by the Board on or before May 25th, 1915."[19] "It will be located on the city lot at the corner of Gates and Madison Streets near the City Hall. The commissioners have appropriated $1,250 per year for the maintenance of the library. Work will begin as soon after the contract is awarded as possible and the library will be open to the public, it is expected, during the next autumn."[20]

At the regular city commissioners meeting at 9:30 A.M., Tuesday, May 25, 1915, the sealed bids were opened and were as follows:

- Building construction:
  - Mr. Chapman...........$11,818.90
  - Rodgers Const. Co.....$11,885.00
  - Baxter Brothers.........$11,500.00
- Plumbing construction
  - W.T. Hutchens.............$950.00
  - D.R. London................$846.00
  - H.C. Blake...................$982.50

"BAXTER BROS. Submitted the following bid also to construct said building including heating and plumbing, provided a three inch stone veneer is used, at and for the total sum of $11,650.00. His bid being the lowest responsible bid received, the Board of Commissioners thereupon awarded said contract to construct said Carnegie Library in accordance with the plans, specifications etc. prepared by Ed L. Love, architect, and in accordance with the advertisements, notice for bids, bids, etc., to Baxter Bros., and directed the President of the Board of Commissioners of the City of Huntsville to proceed to enter into a contract with the said Baxter Bros. to so erect said building. Said contract was entered into by and between them, the original of which was filed with the Clerk of said City of Huntsville, and is now on file in his office."[21]

Note that two of the plumbing bids, W.T. Hutchens and H.C. Blake, are still familiar names in 2004 Huntsville. W. T. Hutchens was the great grandfather of Thomas Hutchens, an employee of the Huntsville Public Library in the Heritage Room. Thomas Hutchens was most helpful to this author in researching applicable information.

On October 11, 1915 the city commissioners approved Miss Caroline Burke as the Carnegie librarian at the salary of $50.00 per month.[22]

The building was completed by the end of November, 1915, and on December 3rd, 1915, the governing board of the Carnegie Library met at the office of Mr. David Grayson and accompanied by the architect, Mr. E.L. Lowe, went to inspect the new building.[23]

On December 7, 1915, the library board wrote a letter to the city commissioners asking that they be discharged, and that the city take over such funds as were now in the hands of the present existing library board, and that the board of city commissioners elect or appoint a governing board to be clothed with such authority as the board of city commissioners shall see fit to confer from time to time. The commissioners accepted the resignations and approved "an Advisory Board of ten members, to have duties and control of the New Carnegie Library, as the city commissioners may hereafter confer upon them, and that the following named persons shall constitute said Advisory Board, viz.,

Mrs. (James)Mayhew, Mrs. Paul Speake, Mrs. Ed Johnson, Mrs. D.A. Grayson, Mrs. A.C. Dillard, Mrs. Milton Humes, Mrs. Alice B. Baldridge, Rev. Francis Tappey, Mr. W.T. Hutchens, Hon. R.E. Spragins."[24]

One week after the city commissioners established the Library Advisory Board, they passed an ordinance, which established the powers and authority of that board:

1. "The Board shall be known as the Carnegie Library Board.
2. Said Board shall be authorized to solicit donations for the equiptment (sic) and maintenance of said Carnegie Library to be located in the Carnegie Library Building, located at the corner of Gates and Madison Streets on the West side of Madison and the North side of Gates Street.
3. The City by its Commissioners reserves the right to elect the Librarian.
4. The Carnegie Library Board, hereinafter referred to as the Board, shall controll (sic) the funds raised by it.
5. The Board shall elect its own officers.
6. The Board shall cause minutes of the proceedings of its meetings to be kept.
7. A strict account shall be kept of the receipts and expenditures of money.
8. The property shall, when donated to said Library, belong to the city of Huntsville and by it kept for the benefit of the library.
9. The board of City Commissioners shall fill vacancies occurring on Said Board.

10. The Officers and members of the Board shall serve without compensation, unless the Board shall determine to pay its Treasurer, and the Board shall fix the amount to be paid from raised by it.
11. The Board shall determine the number of officers needed, and shall elect its officers from its members.
12. The board shall determine when the library shall be used, and on what terms and conditions.
13. The board shall have control of the lecture room of the Carnegie Library Building, and shall grant permits for the use thereof, but the Board may, if it thinks proper, entrust this duty to the Librarian.
14. The Boadr (sic) shall on the first day of January and on the first day of July of each year, report in writing to the governing board of the City of Huntsville, the City Commissioners.
15. The Board shall adopt its own by-laws, rules and regulations, but they must not conflict with any of the powers reserved herein to the City Commissioners."[25]

On February 29, 1916, the Huntsville Carnegie Library was formally open to the public [whites only]. Miss Caroline Burke was the first librarian and the library was to remain open from 10:00 A.M. to 12:00 noon, 2:00 P.M. to 6:00 P.M. and 7:00 to 9:00 every weekday and Sunday 3:00 to 5:00. At the library board meeting, March 21, 1916, Dr. Humphrey objected to the hours, so Sunday was eliminated and the evening hours would be on Tuesday and Saturday evenings from 7:00 to 9:00 P.M.[26]

When the library opened, there was a set of rules which was placed in each book:
1. No person will be permitted to take out of the library more than one book at a time.
2. A book may be kept for two weeks and must be returned to the librarian before it could be renewed for one week.
3. Persons failing to report or return a book at the expiration date will be fined $0.02 per day, which must be paid to the librarian before another book is issued to such person.
4. No Reference Book can be taken from the library.
5. Any non-resident person will be permitted to take out a book upon the deposit of $2.00. This will be refunded upon return of the book.
6. Any resident of Huntsville will be permitted to take a book out of the library on presenting to the librarian a request to that effect signed by a taxpayer of the city.
7. Any person who injures a book unduly, to be determined by the Board of Control, shall pay the value of said book when new, as shown by the valuation list kept by the librarian.[27]

The library board required Baxter Brothers, the construction company, to fix a defect (nature unknown). Mrs. Hume was placed in charge of the children's story hour. The board paid $0.50 for cleaning and $1.75 for drayage.

At the regular meeting of the city commissioners on March 7, 1916, Mrs. Milton Humes and Mrs. F.E. Baldridge, representing the library board, asked the commissioners for a donation from the city to purchase tables, chairs, etc. for the New Library. The commissioners ordered the clerk to pay a sum of not more than $150.00 to library board.[28] Three tables and ten chairs were bought.

Mrs. Paul Speake, a member of the library board, resigned at the April 4, 1916 meeting of the city commissioners, and was replaced by Miss Grace Walker.[29] A dispute was brought before the city commissioners on April 11, 1916, which took over one year to resolve. Mrs.

Humes and Mrs. Baldridge came before the commissioners to ask that the commissioners secure from the City School certain books then in possession of Professor R.C. Johnson, Superintendent of the City School. Mrs. Humes stated that the books were the property of the Huntsville Library as it existed some years before, and were placed in the City School for use by the pupils for lack of suitable quarters elsewhere at the time. Now that the Carnegie Library was completed and in operation, the library board felt that the library was a better location for the books than the school building. The commissioners asked that members of the board of education meet with the commissioners at the next meeting on April 18, 1916.[30]

At the April 18, 1916 meeting, the city commissioners appointed Reverend Francis Tappey, Mr. W.T. Hutchens and Professor R.C. Johnson as a committee to visit the school building, examine and select from said books such as may have been purchased by the school children and such books as are essential in the school work, these books to be left at the City School. The remaining books as selected by the committee to be transferred to the Carnegie Library. The committee was given full power to settle the question as to where the books should be located.[31] Note that there were two members of the library board and only one from the City School.

At the library board meeting of April 20, 1916, Reverend Tappey tendered his resignation as president, which the board unanimously refused to accept. [poor guy] Mrs. Baldridge reported the sale of 20 sections of bookcases by transfer of money to the treasury: ($8.75, Mr. Goldsmith), (7.50, Mrs. Goldsmith), (Mr. Monroe, $6.250). Four more cases to be sold and $2.50 was due from Mr. Monroe.

May 4, 1916 was the regular meeting of the library board at the YMCA. The house committee reported defects in paneling, toilet room floor and paint on basement floor, which Mr. Baxter promised to repair during the summer.

At this time the children's library was located in the northeast corner of the main reading room. A Story Hour for children was started with Mrs. Milton Humes, Chairman, of this committee. Mrs. R.C. Bricknell offered her services. Later Mrs. Johnston reported that Miss Nona Allen had been engaged for three weeks for the children's hour, Miss Francis Jones for three weeks, and Miss Chapman for three weeks. Funds for books and materials for both adult and children's departments were raised by public subscription. 'BOOK DAYS' were held when house-to-house calls were made and books collected.[32]

Huntsville was full of graft, corruption and crime in 1916 and it makes one wonder how the library was built and actually opened. Another story was developing under the surface of high-minded and literary daily life. The sheriff and chief of police were openly involved in whiskey rings, while elected officials sold patronage and took kickbacks for city and county contracts.

February 1916 was a period of enlightenment, but the summer of 1916 turned sour. Recently elected County Probate Judge W.T. Lawler was under investigation for election fraud. He and his opponent, David Overton, had each spent over $20,000 in the last campaign when they had both pledged to limit it to $1,000. [Sound familiar?]

On the morning of June 15, 1916, Lawler's wife reported him missing to the sheriff, Bob Phillips. People thought Lawler left town to avoid testifying. The sheriff assured the wife that Lawler would show up. But in the middle of the night before, Overton had already told the sheriff that he had killed Lawler. A cover-up was organized. Later, an anonymous note to Deputy Sheriff Pierce said to look under the Whitesburg Bridge. The sheriff was told, but ignored it. The deputy investigated several days later and found Lawler's body. After more investigation, Deputy Pierce arrested Charles Nalls, Circuit Court Clerk and Percy Brooks, a part-time deputy, as accessories in the murder cover-up.

Events moved faster. Sheriff Phillips blew his brains out. An attorney, Shelby Pleasants, was implicated and killed himself with the alleged murder pistol. Nalls and Brooks decided to cooperate. A.D. Kirby, Huntsville police chief took over the investigation. He was implicated in the whiskey ring and resigned along with his chief deputy. The governor named a new sheriff. Overton escaped with help and was killed shortly afterward in a gunfight with police. Nalls died of a convenient "virus" several months later. The son of Sheriff Phillips was found dead, the victim of a "suicide." Brooks was run over by a train in Sheffield.[33] But somehow the Carnegie Library survived, even if some of the city officials did not.

A meeting of Carnegie Library Board was called Monday, June 19, 1916 to report results of soliciting contributions. Owing to a storm, no one was present except Mr. Humes and Mrs. Grayson.

During the July 6, meeting, the soliciting committee reported the following collections: Mrs. Humes, $5.00 from herself; Mrs. Johnston, $5.00 from the company; Rev. Tappy $146.00; Mrs. Grayson, $16.00; Mrs. Baldridge, $5.00 (promised) Ms. Burke, the librarian, reported $7.35 in receipts; $1.00 in gifts; and $6.35 in fines.

Mrs. Humes tendered her resignation at the meeting on July 25, 1916, but was asked to postpone it until September.

On August 29, 1916 the city commissioners gave the library board the authority to select and employ the librarian, after the term of the present librarian was completed. The city commissioners formerly held this authority.[34]

September 7, 1916 – The president read to the board the offer of Mr. Ed Bett to give to the library board the copyright of his history of Madison County, the board to assume the responsibility of publishing. The president was instructed to refuse Mr. Bett's offer, owing to lack of funds. The treasurer reported a balance of $177.09. The matter of the broken front step was taken up for consideration and it was agreed that Mr. Baxter be not asked to repair same, as he had already made repairs for which he was not responsible. A committee was formed to get up a course of free lectures at the library. Twenty-five dollars was appropriated for the purchase of books. A box was purchased for which citizens could drop in the names of books they wished in the library.

On October 2, 1916 there was a change in Huntsville's governmental structure. The *three city commissioners* were replaced by *nine* city *council* members.

Tuesday, October 3, 1916 – It was agreed that the library building should not be used for no purposes whatsoever where charges of any kind were made. The secretary was instructed to write letters of thanks to Mr. Baxter for his courtesies and for his gift of a bulletin board; also to Mr. Grayson for his kindness in having stenographic work done.

December 7, 1916 – Miss Burke, librarian, was re-elected for a term of six months.

January 4, 1917 – New material added to the library: Sets of Books, Message, and papers of the President; New Practical Reference Library, 6 Volumes; Spery's (?) Diplomatic correspondence of the American Revolution, 6 Volumes.

February 1, 1917 – A committee was appointed to try to get money from the city for books and free lights from the power company. The treasurer reported a balance of $144.34. Fifteen dollars was appropriated to buy book boxes for magazines.

March 1, 1917 – The book committee reported 19 new books purchased at a cost of $22.00.

It was now March 1917, and the almost one-year-old controversy over possession of library/school books had surfaced again.

"A committee from Carnegie Library, composed of Mrs. Ed Johnson and Mr. M.U. Griffin were present and addressed the (City) Council. The Board of Controll (sic), through their committee stated that there are some fifteen hundred books at the City High School which originally belonged to a Library Association. When the association disbanded they owed something like One Hundred Dollars, and this amount was paid by the city, at which time they took possession of the books. The Board of Controll (sic) of the Carnegie Library feel that these books would be of greater service to the public, if they were transferred to the Library building. They stated that it is not their desire to remove reference books, or such other books as would be of assistance to the pupils in their studies, but they would like to have to separate the books and use their judgment as to what books should be placed in the library. It was pointed out that during the three months when the school is not in session the public is deprived of the use of these books, while if they were in the Carnegie Library they would, at all times, be accessible both to the school children and the public at large. On motion of Councilman Betts, and seconded by Councilman Steele, this matter was referred to the Committee on Schools for investigation and report to the Council."[35]

It was almost a month later when the book issue returned to the city council during its regular meeting on Tuesday, April 17, 1917.

"Prof. Johnson (City School) was requested to make a statement regarding the books which the Carnegie Library Committee had asked be moved from the school to the Library. Whereupon he stated that more than a year ago they went through these books again and selected about 350 which were transferred, and later they went through again, and sent about 500 volumns (sic) to the Library. A third time a committee composed of Messrs Tappy, Hutchens and himself made a careful inspection and sent all the books to the Carnagie (sic) Library which were not absolutely necessary for school work, and it was hoped the matter was closed. Since that time the Teachers have catalogued all the books now at the school library. During each forty minute period, you will find an average of twenty pupils using these books in the school library, and if they were moved to the Carnagie (sic) Library, it would be impractical for them to use them as frequently as where they are now.

The Committee appointed to look into the matter of moving books from the school to the Carnagie (sic) Library, reported that they thought books would be of more service at the school library than at the Carnagie (sic) Library. Where –up-on Councilman Orgain moved that recommendation of the Committee be accepted, and that the books be left at the School Library. Motion was duly seconded and upon vote, unanimously carried."[36]

Well, that issue was finally settled. Doesn't it make you feel proud that the early library board fought to get as many books as they could? At least 850 volumes were returned to the library, which is more than this author would have suspected were in the old subscription library. Apparently there were even more originally.

April 5, 1917 – A new by-law was adopted. The librarian shall have the power and authority subject to the control of the governing board, to forbid the use of the library or books any person when in the opinion of the librarian such use by any person could be obnoxious to the general public using the library, and when the best interests of the library and the purpose for which it was established would be best advanced by so forbidding the use of the library or books to such person.

September 6, 1917 – The librarian was authorized to purchase the Dewey Decimal System, and pay for it out of fines collected. Mrs. Baldridge tendered her resignation as secretary and Mrs. M.U. Griffin was elected to succeed her.

The Huntsville Times came into existence in 1917 and had been a faithful supporter of the library ever since.

Mrs. James L. (Mattie) Darwin became the librarian in June 1917. She was 43 years old and a widow with three children.

November 1, 1917 – The treasurer reported income from fines and contributions of $473.02 and disbursements of #267.06, making the balance of $205.96. It was agreed to purchase children's books for $15 and adult books for $10.

December 6, 1917 – It was agreed to authorize the librarian to make a charge of $0.01 per day on new books for a period of three months, beginning at the time of the receipt of the books in the library. The secretary was to write a letter to the Civic League requesting it to renew its donation of $5.00 for magazine subscriptions. The librarian was authorized to take a subscription to the Birmingham (?) Herald when the present subscription expires.

January 3, 1918 – It was agreed to appropriate $30.00 for purchase of books in January, and thereafter not to exceed the amount accruing from the fines over charges in making book purchases. It was agreed to exempt the new children's books from the $0.01 per day charge. The librarian was authorized to publish in the daily papers the list of new books from time to time as they arrive.

A representative from the Christian Science Society visited the city council meeting on January 22, 1918. He stated that they had been negotiating with the library board to rent the library basement to hold services in. It was suggested that the matter be brought to the council's attention, since there was a question as to whether the authority rested with the library board or the city council. The council referred the matter to the council committee of library and the city attorney to investigate and confer with the library board.[37]

On February 12, 1918 the library committee reported that they had met with the library board and had agreed to allow them to rent the basement to the Christian Science Society, provided that no lease or contract be entered into, which might prevent termination of agreement should it become necessary for any reason.[38]

April 4, 1918 – Mrs. E.K. Johnston was appointed the new secretary. [This author certainly appreciated her handwriting as a huge improvement over that of Mrs. Griffin.] May 6, 1918 – books were purchased during May in the amount of $29.46. January 2, 1919 – It was reported during this semi-annual meeting that there were 1,385 visitors during the previous six months. June 5, 1919 – There were 1,396 books in circulation: adult fiction-797; non-fiction-53; and juvenile-546.

October 7, 1920 – The librarian was instructed to accept the offer of 50 books made by Mrs. Thomas M. Ocoece (?), Director of Archives and History in Montgomery. The Huntsville Library was to defray the expenses of parking and transportation. The problem of proper heat for the room selected by the Christian Science Society down stairs was under consideration.

December 2, 1920 – The librarian was instructed to see the city clerk about new light bulbs for the library. The treasurer's balance was $90.11.

March 3, 1921 – The librarian was instructed to write the libraries in Birmingham and Nashville to ascertain what method was used for disinfecting books, which had been in contagious diseases.

April 7, 1921 – The answers to the letters written to other libraries about disinfecting of books were read. Books in circulation now stand at 1501. Warren Harding was the twenty-ninth president of the United States.

May 5, 1921 – Mrs. Chase was asked to ask Mr. Chase to talk with the members of the Rotary Club about making a donation to the library fund for buying books. Mr. Addison White was authorized to ask the city for $250 for additional bookshelves. Books in circulation during the month were 1449.

June 2, 1921 - All members were asked to find out what they could about forming branch libraries. Any duplicate magazines and the New York Times were to be passed to Mrs. Layman in Maysville to form a branch circulating library in that town. Circulation in May was 1573. July 7, 1921 – June circulation was 1731. August 4, 1921 – Circulation was 1816.

November 3, 1921 – There was a need for an umbrella stand, a hat and coat rack, and a newspaper rack. Mrs. Grayson said she would put an article in the daily papers calling attention to the necessity for night closing unless the library was left warmer at night.

March 2, 1922 – Now that the winter was almost over, a bid for the needed heating plant for the library was submitted by the Hutchens Plumbing Company. April 6, 1922 – A bid on the building of a furnace place by Mr. Baxter was read.

May 4, 1922 – The subject of a clock for the library was discussed again, and it was decided to accept Mr. Moore's offer to give a clock to the library and he be permitted to place his name on the clock in small letters.

September 7, 1922 – Book circulation was 1722: adult 1302; juvenile 420. Balance in funds was $272.51. Two Board members were asked to see if the County Board could and would make a donation to the library. Circulation was 1279. The librarian reported that Mrs. Winston Garth wanted to place in the library Dr. Fearn's collection of medical books as a loan. Many of the books being in French and of long past editions. The loan was not considered suitable.

December 7, 1922 – Mrs. Pulley was asked to write an article for the papers about the winter closing hours on account of there being no heat at night. The librarian was to write to Mrs. Owens at the Archives and History in Montgomery to ask which counties in the state contribute to the libraries and what amount. Circulation was 1468: adult 1124 and juvenile 344.

February 2, 1923 – Mrs. Pulley was asked to see Mr. Pulley with regard to the monthly donation, which the county is to give to the library. This will not be the last time the county is delinquent in its contribution. Mrs. White proposed three gas heaters for night and Sunday use. It was agreed to spend $50 for the three heaters. The city would be asked to pay for the gas bill. Bad leaks in the roof were reported. January circulation was 1923.

March 1, 1923 – Plans were discussed for the yearly Book Day, which was scheduled for March 17. The treasurer reported a balance of $260.09. April 5, 1923 – The library hours were decided to be 12 o'clock to 8 P.M. Books given out on Book Day were 277.

May 3, 1923. – It was agreed to buy children's books in the amount of $30. Some adult books were also ordered. The matter of window screens was raised again. A committee would ask the city to give the screening.

July 5, 1923 – It was suggested that the heads of the various town clubs be asked to meet with the library to bring about a better understanding among them of the library's needs for help.

November 1, 1923 – The matter of a larger board was discussed, as apparently some decided that the existing 12 were not enough.

January 3, 1924 – Mrs. White was appointed to ask the city council if part of a janitress' wages would be given for a special janitress, to be under board control. Circulation was 1333. The bank balance was $161.51.

March 6, 1924 – Mrs. Pulley was asked to see if the new paper, *The Morning Star*, would be placed upon the reading table of the library free of charge as all the other local papers were. The present janitress, being unsatisfactory, to be dismissed and another one installed, to be under the control of the house committee of the library board.

April 3, 1924 – Mrs. Johnston reported that the mending committee had repaired 166 books during the month of March. Mrs. Bolling was asked to order or purchase books. A list of 25 of the favorite books was to be replaced. Some books were destroyed by the mending committee because of dilapidated condition. May 1, 1924 – The Mending Committee reported the mending of 50 books during April.

The library board journal of minutes from June 1924 through January 1929 apparently is missing from the library archives.

March 4, 1929 – The treasurer reported a balance of $318.10. The Grace Club and the Study Circle both gave $25 for children's books. Mr. Dewey Chase contributed $100 for children's books. Miss Mary Burns (sic, Beirne) Darwin was made the librarian of the children's room. [Mary was the daughter of Mattie Darwin. She is now Mrs. Robert Cook, a contributor to this history in 2004.] She was to be on duty from 2:30 to 6:00 on weekdays and from 3:00 to 5:00 on Sundays. She is not to be absent except for illness. In case of illness, she is to provide a competent substitute and pay her. The library had been closed for one month for repairs and was to be thoroughly cleaned before opening to the public. The children's room was to be offered to the Child's Conservatory League for their story hour on Saturday mornings. The question of Mrs. Darwin and Mary Burns Darwin (mother and daughter) taking their vacations at the same time was discussed and it was voted that they might arrange to do so. The Grace Club donated another $50.

June 3, 1929 – Three members of the board went before the county board and appealed for more money for the library. Mrs. E. T. Terry was requested to get a list of parallel reading by the city schools for the coming year. These books were to be ordered at once. Herbert Hoover was the thirty-first president of the United States.

August 5, 1929 – The treasurer's balance was $401.88, the first time over $400. Mrs. Darwin was requested to find out when the next Alabama State library meeting was to be held. It was agreed to spend $100 on children's books.

November 4, 1929 – It was agreed that hereafter the library would be closed on Sunday. This step was in line with other libraries of corresponding size all over the country. A report was read in regard to the tables and chairs lent to the city school by the library. No steps had been taken toward reclaiming them. Mrs. Pride was instructed to find if the tables and chairs are in use – if not – she is to ask for them.

The Alabama Library Act of 1919 permitted counties and municipalities to establish and operate free public libraries with tax monies under certain restrictions.[39]

The Carnegie questionnaires mentioned previously were sent out between 1915 and 1920. They provided valuable feedback to the corporation. Another source of information was the huge number of letters, reports, and clippings sent to the Carnegie group. One was an irate letter from Huntsville.

"Norah Davis, a well known author, reported in 1925 that the city government had shifted all library responsibility to the library board and paid only the salaries of the librarian plus heat and light bills. As a result, no funds were available for books and magazines. The library rented out books at two cents per day and was open only on weekday afternoons and two hours on Sunday afternoons. Needless to say, the building was little used and then only by a small group of people.

Norah Davis also had a personal complaint. She was upset because she had been expelled from the library for neglecting to give her chauffeur ten cents to pay for a library card renewal. She had always sent her chauffeur into the library because of the antagonistic attitude of the librarian. [That must have been Mrs. Mattie Darwin.] Her original complaint to the city did little good, as city officials merely told her to contact the Carnegie Corporation. [They really passed the buck on this one.]

James Bertram's reply was that the Corporation could not and would not interfere; instead, the state library commission should be contacted. This the complainant did, only to be informed that they had little power. The commission suggested that she contact the Carnegie Corporation. After writing to the Corporation again, she received a reply from Bertram indicating that the Corporation could not enter into any local library controversy. However, he sent her a copy of the original documents and implied that she could take action as a local citizen, since a library making a charge for regular library service was not really a free library."[40]

The Carnegie Libraries were assessed by historians as an important turning point in the democratization of American culture. The right to a free elementary school education was achieved earlier. The free library was a timely follow-on. Carnegie rightly deserves most of the credit for this. Federal, state, and local authorities had done little before Carnegie. The Carnegie grants gave a jump-start to the free library system. Carnegie had a passion for education and books. He believed that public libraries were the most democratic of all roads to learning. In Germany today there is a fee to belong to the "public" library.

Some people disbelieved Carnegie's motives. They thought he wanted monuments to his posterity. But Carnegie did not require his name be used on the buildings, but actually discouraged it. He did not suggest that pictures and busts of him placed in the buildings. Many criticize him for making money in the steel industry, but he was a man ahead of his time in the development of libraries. Carnegie did not buy books or to provide maintenance, because he believed that local government should be responsible for that. Carnegie's philanthropy made a significantly positive contribution to the advancement of American enlightened culture.[41] Earlier in this chapter I wrote that Huntsville was eleven years behind Decatur in its Carnegie Library. The Decatur Carnegie Library was built in 1904-5 and served the town until 1973. It then served the First Baptist Church across the street as a youth center for about 20 years. After $700,000 of renovations it opened in 2001 as the town's art museum. It was a stately, albeit small, structure at 207 Church Street, several blocks west of Route 31 / 6th Avenue, the main north-south road. Its interior was understated magnificence, structurally unchanged from the early days. It demonstrated a proud heritage and architectural excellence. The Decatur city fathers wisely preserved it for 100 years. It is worth a visit. Alabama A & M College received $12,000 from the Carnegie Foundation in 1906 to build an academic library. It later burned down and Carnegie sent replacement money. Despite Carnegie spreading library money within sight of Huntsville, our city fathers could not be accused about rushing to judgment to get some of Carnegie's money. I suppose ten years of dithering was about right for them.

The Decatur and Huntsville situations are worthy of comparison at this point. Decatur received a grant for $12,500, the same as Huntsville. Decatur received no architectural guidance from James Bertram, Carnegie executor, because that guidance was not started until 1908 when reports came in about extravagant architectures. Decatur's Carnegie design was up to the local officials. They created a lasting exquisite structure, which still exudes quality in 2004. Second, its placement in a residential area several blocks away from the central business area allowed it to weather the storms of creative destruction when modernity demanded more area for a growing population.

Huntsville was provided with six different architectural possibilities, although none were demanded, only guidelines. The Huntsville external architecture looked to be perfectly satisfactory, although not of the elegance of Decatur's. The second point became important, because apparently no one looked very far ahead in Huntsville, not even considering the space program, but just normal expected growth. But, in 1916 the city fathers had no reason to expect any growth. The Huntsville site was only one short block from the courthouse square, which made it vulnerable to even modest business expansion.

This chapter started with the creation of the Huntsville Public Library and ends with the creation of the Huntsville-Madison County Public Library. The following letter created the county half of the library:

"November 11th, 1926

TO ALL OFFICERS AND TEACHERS OF MADISON COUNTY SCHOOLS.

GREETINGS:

The Huntsville Carnegie Library is now open to all residents of Madison County. Heretofore the Library has been maintained by the City of Huntsville, and it was necessary to make a small charge to residents outside the City limits. Thanks to our Board of County Commissioners, the Library is now in fact a "free circulating Library," and its thousands of volumes are now available to all residents of Madison County. This change has been made possible by the action of the Board of County Commissioners who have appropriated $25.00 per month towards the maintenance of the Library with the understanding that if it is shown that the County residents really appreciate the Library and use it to the extent that their appropriation is warranted, it will be continued, otherwise, after a few month's trial it will be withdrawn.

In order to become a patron of the Library, it is only necessary that a card be signed by a tax payer in the County, and that the books be carefully handled and returned according to the rules in force.

The teachers of the County will find the Library a wonderful help in their research and reference work.

Please announce to your school that the children, as well as grown-ups, are welcome to the Library and invited to make use of it. To obtain a Library card entitling the holder to draw books, all that is necessary is to fill in an application form and have a tax payer sign same. These forms may be obtained from the Librarian at the Library which is open week days from 1 P.M. to 8 P.M. and on Sundays from 3 P.M. to 5 P.M.

We hope that you will cooperate in making the Huntsville Carnegie Library one of the most popular and useful institutions in North Alabama.

Cordially yours,
  Library board.

Mrs. Margaret Bolling	Mrs. James Pride
Mrs. Henry Chase	Mrs. Robert Pulley
Mrs. Amelia Dillard	Mrs. Harry Rhett
Mrs. David Grayson	Mrs. E.T. Terry
Mrs. Ed. Johnston	Mrs. W.I. Wellman
Mrs. Martin May	Mr. Addison White

Mrs. Mattie Darwin, Librarian

Mailed to 187 Madison County teachers and school officials."[42]

Since the American Library Association was founded in 1876, library professionalism was increasing, albeit slowly. "The Carnegie Foundation established a school for research in librarianship which opened as the graduate Library School at the University of Chicago in 1928. The research program began to spread to other schools. Librarianship began to reach out into studies of mass communication, intellectual and institutional history, the contemporary social culture, statistics and epistemology—applying appropriate concepts to the study of the library as an institution. This resulted in scholarly journals of librarianship, the *Library Quarterly* and *Library Trends*"[43]

Library professionalism would come to Huntsville in the next decade, but from an unsuspected source. Three letters, TVA, would be the impetus for change in the scope and operation of the Carnegie Public Library in the future.

Chapter 3

Regional Library

*"Had I the power, I would scatter libraries over the whole land,
as the sower sows his wheat-field."*

Horace Mann, American educator
Foundations of the Public Library (Shera)

January 5, 1930 – Mrs. Pride reported that the tables and chairs were in proper usage in the first grade and kindergarten

August 4, 1930 – Money in the amount of $200 was set aside in a special fund for the painting of the library walls and $26 for the children's room. September 1, 1930 – It was agreed that Mr. Baxter would refinish the library walls, clean woodwork and varnish the inside of the casements with two coats of varnish at a cost of $255. It was agreed that Miss Frances Jones be employed to mend the books. She was also to be allowed to take a course under Mrs. Darwin.

October 6, 1930 – The secretary was requested to write Mrs. Darwin in reference to her lack of co-operation in not keeping the board informed that she would not be here at the expiration of her leave of absence for vacation.

February 2, 1931 – It was agreed to reduce the size of the board to 10 members from the current 12. Remember back in November 1923 it was thought that 12 members were not enough. It was agreed to appoint Miss Frances Jones assistant and substitute librarian in addition to her job of mending books. She will be asked to mend books two days per week and act as assistant four days a week for a salary of $15 a month. In the absence of either librarian she will act as substitute with the salary of the librarian for whom she is substituting.

March 2, 1931 – It was agreed that Miss Frances Jones would be allowed two weeks vacation with pay, provided she took the vacation during the quiet season of the library. [That period was not identified]

May 4, 1931 – The secretary read a letter from Mrs. Johnson of the Birmingham Library in answer to one written to her in reference to the handling of books thought unfit for general circulation. The method used in Huntsville (keeping the books in the desk drawer and only allowing them to go to mature persons on request) is exactly the same one used in Birmingham. [The minutes did not explain which type of books qualified under such loose criteria. Should we allow our imaginations run wild on the "standards" applied in 1931, compared to 2004?]

The Board voted $50 for children's books and $50 for replacements in the adult area.

June 6, 1931 – It was decided to let Mrs. Darwin select the people she thinks best for her class in training at the library. The Board voted to close the library at 7 P.M. instead of 8 P.M. during the summer months.

August 3, 1931 – Mrs. Pride reported that Professor Boyd of Duke University had been written to in reference to certain rare books in the library, asking him to give us a price on them. Thirty-one books were purchased from Mrs. Knox Mullins. Mr. M.U. Griffin reported an offer of $2500 on the Lowndes' house. This would barely cover indebtedness, leaving nothing for the library.

34

January 4, 1932 – The library had received from the Government a beautiful portrait of George Washington, which was sent by courtesy of Senator Hugo Black. The library needed to find a suitable frame for the picture.

January 22, 1932 – The will of Mr. Lowndes read that after his debts were paid, the remainder of his estate was to be given to the Carnegie Library. The executor, Mr. Griffin, has been unable to sell the real estate and asked the library to sign a release of all claims in favor of Dr. Caldwell (?), who will pay all debts and take over the property. There was some objection to this. If the property was sold at public auction in March, if it was worth more to other bidders, and the property might bring more than the amount of the indebtedness, leaving something for the library. On the advice of Mr. and Mrs. Chase, the release was signed, giving up all claims on the estate. Mrs. Henry Chase was a member of the board, and Henry was the president of the Chase Nursery Company in Chase, an existing community just east of Alabama A&M University, which now contains the Chase Railroad Museum.

April 4, 1932 – The treasury balance is now $167.08. Circulation during March was 4,000 books. May 2, 1932 – The board accepted an offer from Mrs. Richard Walker for a large collection of narcissus bulbs that could be sold to raise money. September 5, 1932 – The librarian reported the gift of 22 assorted books from Mrs. Parks. January 2, 1933 – Miss Frances Jones thanked the board for sending her to the library conference in Chattanooga. Franklin D. Roosevelt was the thirty-second president of the United States.

In 1933 Congress passed the Tennessee Valley Authority (TVA) Act to build dams to control flooding of the Tennessee River. Navigation would be helped for river traffic to eventually find its way downstream to the Mississippi River and the Gulf of Mexico. Perhaps the most important reason was to provide the infrastructure for the rural electrification of the southern states, something badly needed if the South was to make economic progress. The TVA Act would later impact the Carnegie Public Library.

On June 14, 1933 the Twickenham Study Club was organized in Huntsville. It was limited to 20 people, all women, and its programs were reviews of good books: best sellers and classics. Once a year it held an open meeting. This activity may have been Huntsville's forerunner of today's book discussion groups hosted by the library.[1]

April 2, 1934 – The board granted Miss Francis Jones a $5 increased in pay, bringing her up to $20 per month. [I wonder what the employees in 2004 think of this.]

Throughout the minutes there were many references about the cleaning personnel and keeping the building clean. There is an old saying about cleanliness and godliness; perhaps the ladies on the board elevated cleanliness above godliness.

April 6, 1935 – There was a discussion about excavating another room in the basement, which the library surely needs. September 7, 1935 – The committee on an "Additional Room for the Library" reported that the work would cost $2,000 more than the city could afford at this time. It was decided to wait awhile before asking the city.

Mrs. Walker Bolling was urged to be active in the future. It was noted that members being absent twice in succession from the monthly board meetings without the excuse of illness or absence from town would be automatically dropped from the board.

March 6, 1937 – It was suggested that one room be furnished for Mrs. Darwin as a private sitting room. The room was to have a plate on the door with name.

May 1, 1937 – Mrs. Davis, President of the Library Board, related her experiences from attending the convention of the Alabama Library Association in Gadsden and her visit to the city's public library.

The Guntersville Dam was started in 1936 at a site where the eventual lake would narrow, about seven miles northwest of the town of Guntersville and 25 miles southeast of Huntsville. The Tennessee Valley Authority asked the Huntsville Library to cooperate with it to serve its workers.

December 5, 1936 – A letter was read from Mr. T.H. Ford, President of the Huntsville City Council, requesting the library board meet with the council on December 8 to discuss the educational program of the Tennessee Valley Authority and the feasibility of the work being carried through the library.

The Huntsville Public Library Board entered into contracts with the TVA, the county commissioners and the boards of education of Madison, Jackson, and Marshall counties. Mr. Hoyt Galvin, a trained librarian on the staff of the TVA, was put in charge of this regional program.[2] The Regional Library was an extension to the Huntsville Public Library. The librarian at the time was Mrs. Mattie Darwin.

My readers of the 21st century are asked to unleash their imaginations. First, ponder this Internet item making the rounds of cyberspace in October 2004: "A college student challenged a senior citizen, saying it was impossible for their generation to understand his. 'You grew up in a different world,' the student said. 'Today we have television, jet planes, space travel, nuclear energy. Computers…' Taking advantage of a pause in the student's litany, the geezer said, 'You're right. We didn't have those things when we were young; so we invented them! What are you doing for the next generation?'"

Second, try to imagine Northern Alabama in 1936. The entire country was in a severe depression for the last four years. North Alabama was primarily an agricultural area, with cotton being picked by hand. Most people were poor and uneducated. Electricity was not available in the rural parts of Madison, Jackson and Morgan Counties, which also applied to the rest of North Alabama. Roads were poor. There was railroad service through Scottsboro between Chattanooga and Huntsville. Telephones were "as scarce as hen's teeth." U.S. Senator John H. Bankhead, Alabama, and his brother, William B. Bankhead, U.S. Representative and Speaker of the House of Representatives, introduced legislation to reduce farm tenancy and provide guaranteed cotton prices for cotton and other farm products.[3] Those were hard times.

January 9, 1937 – Mr. Hoyt Galvin of the TVA explained to the library board about his work and the equipment necessary. He said a desk and office equipment would be $138. This amount was to be paid in monthly installments of $23.04. The board would be reimbursed for the amount by the T.V.A. The board agreed to the plan and equipment. Since Galvin was a trained librarian and a male, he conducted his operations largely independent of the female, not-formally-trained, librarians in the Carnegie Library. Hoyt Galvin's task was to create a network of library stops or branches across three counties to reach as wide a population as possible under difficult conditions described in the paragraph above. He went about the task with true missionary zeal, as will be demonstrated by correspondence provided in this chapter, which represents only a small portion of the available material in the library archives.

Three new rooms were excavated in the basement of the Carnegie Library building to house the TVA Regional Library. Works Progress Administration (WPA) [how many readers remember the WPA?] labor was secured to drive trucks and to handle other unskilled duties. [Readers, please note that "Works Progress" was later officially changed to "Work Projects," so both variations are in this history.]

Miss Frances Jones, head of the children's department, apparently had some questions on the TVA Regional Library Service. This seems strange since there were very few employees in the library, and communication should have easy and quick, but apparently not so. Hoyt

Galvin wrote a letter to Francis Jones with the letterhead, Regional Library Service, Carnegie Library Building, Huntsville, Alabama. It seems as if they were in different locations, instead of the same building. At any rate, the letter, dated April 6, 1937, provides an explanation of the Regional Library Service.

"Dear Miss Jones,

Confirming our conversation of this date I am setting down a few statements as a description of the Regional Library Service.

The Regional Library Service is an extension department of the Huntsville Carnegie Library which has been established as the central agency of a cooperative library project being conducted in Madison, Marshall and Jackson Counties in Alabama.

The Carnegie Library Board through the Regional Library Service has agreed by contract to provide a library program for the employees of the Tennessee Valley Authority in three named counties. They have further agreed to conduct the library program in cooperation with other local library groups in other centers in the three counties and to encourage and promote the establishment of a regional library service on a permanent basis, and to seek financial support from local services for normal community programs of library service.

It is my desire that public library centers may be established in Scottsboro, Guntersville, Albertville, Boaz, and other larger centers in the three counties and that deposits be placed in the smaller community centers and all of these library centers and deposits will be a part of one large circulating library system (a regional library system) with the central library located at Huntsville.

I hope that the above may help you to understand the program and I will be very glad to further describe any activities regarding which you may have question.

Very truly yours,

Hoyt R. Galvin"

The Steering committee of the Regional Library Service met on March 16, 1937. Members present were Mrs. Claude Davis, Chairman, Mrs. Florence Bolling, Miss Mary Rothrock, Mr. George Brown, Mr. I.N. Chiles and Hoyt Galvin, Secretary. Davis and Bolling were members of the Carnegie Library Board, while the others were apparently citizens of Huntsville. The committee: authorized the regional librarian to arrange for the necessary transportation in the regional library program at 6¢ per mile; authorized the expenditure of a maximum of $135.00 for assistance on an hourly basis at the Guntersville camp library to be employed on the recommendation of the regional librarian with the approval of the branch head of the TVA training section; authorized the purchase of books as selected by the librarians providing the total cost of such purchases did not exceed the balance of the book fund; and required the owner of any automobile used in transportation purposes for the regional library service be required to have 5-10 liability insurance for the automobile.[4]

June 5, 1937 – Mr. Hoyt Galvin, TVA Regional Librarian, invited the library board members to visit the libraries in Gadsden, Guntersville, Guntersville Dam, and Scottsboro.

On September 7, 1937 the library board sent the following letter to Hoyt Galvin,

"My dear Mr. Galvin,

At a meeting on September 6th, 1937, after consultation with Ms. Darwin [library director] and receiving her cordial approval of the suggestion, the Huntsville Library Board voted unanimously to request that you serve as Acting librarian in Charge during the absence now or in the future, of Mrs. Darwin.

The Board feels that your experienced and skilled assistance will be of great value to the Library and hopes that you will grant this request.

Very Cordially Yours,

Elizabeth Mastin, Secretary, Library Board"

The librarians of that era were usually nice ladies with an interest in books, but seldom had library training. Apparently Galvin's skills were obvious, since he was a trained librarian from the TVA and was moving rapidly to expand the number of localities provided library services.

October 4, 1937 – It was requested that Mrs. Bolling be the representative to meet with the Junior Grace Club, October 13th. Apparently her attendance at the board meetings picked up from the past. Mrs. Claude Davis, the President, told about her meeting with the Madison County Board of Commissioners. The additional amount given to the library was $50 for the coming year.

Hurrah! What a great day for the Carnegie Library. On October 9, 1937 it got its first telephone. The number was 477. Call in to reserve a book or to secure facts and information, which are needed hurriedly. This should be especially valuable to the business houses of the city. To publicize the new telephone, the library had printed 3 x 6-inch, yellow, thick-stock cards for distribution. The phone number was prominent in the upper right corner. The bold-faced title read, "**Offers Business Information By Phone."**

Available are: Business Law-Yearbooks-Dictionaries-Atlases-Buying Guides-Thomas Register-World Almanac-City Code-Code of Alabama-Van Nostrand's Scientific Encyclopedia, Etc. **Call 477,** or come in to browse while you rest in our lounge chairs with your favorite pipe… Business Week, Fortune, The National Horseman…63 other periodicals, as well as 3 out of town daily papers are available. This is but one of the many free services offered by YOUR Public Library from 9 A.M. to 9 P.M. every week day."[5]

New chairs and tables were also recently added to provide better accommodations. Some new non-fiction titles were added: *The Modern Parent*, by Myer; *Why Do You Talk Like That?*, by Burton; *Land of the Free*, by Agar; and *Youth Serves the Community*, by Hanna.

January 3, 1938 – It was agreed to charge one cent for each book reservation to cover the cost of the notification card. There was a discussion about the United Daughters of the Confederacy relics in the courthouse. It was thought that the relics would eventually be placed in the library museum, which did not exist at the time. The secretary was asked to write a note of appreciation to Mrs. Hoyt Galvin, the regional librarian's wife, for her splendid service rendered in the boy's and girl's library by the weekly story hour.

From this point through the 1940s, letters from and to Hoyt Galvin, director of the regional library system, will be quoted in full or in part. They are from librarians and citizens of Jackson County, mostly from the Scottsboro librarian, but also from other folks. Sometimes only one side of the correspondence is quoted. The intent is not to provide a complete picture, but to show the commitment by the local folks who wanted library service and the regional director to provide that service. As usual throughout this history, money was the driving factor. As you read the letter below, remember that it was January 9, 1937 that Hoyt Galvin explained his mission to the Huntsville library board. He did not let any grass grow below his feet in accomplishing his mission. Most of the incoming letters to Galvin were handwritten, reflecting the capabilities in the small communities. Galvin's outgoing letters were all typewritten and usually longer than the incoming. The letters reflect a prodigious output, of which only a small sample is provided.

Hoyt Galvin wrote the following letter to Miss Adele Rivers, Attendance Officer, Jackson County Board of Education, on January 6, 1938.

"I received your letter this morning and I must say you are to be congratulated on the Jackson County activity.

As you may remember, a County Library Board according to the Alabama Library Law consists of the Probate Judge as Chairman, the County Supt. of Education as Sect., and three other persons appointed by the Commissioners. It would be wise if a County Library Board could be formally established in this fashion so that there would be an official agency to whom the County Commissioners might appropriate if they choose to provide some funds for library work.

Also according to the Alabama Library Law, the County Library Boards may contract with any other library groups or agencies to conduct the programs of service for the county. Consequently with a County Library Board for Jackson County, contracts could be officially written in accordance to the Alabama Law for Jackson County to be part of a Regional System.

The following points have been receiving library service in Jackson County:

-Central. Located at the store. The store has changed hands recently and I do not know whether the new man will be interested in the Library. Service has been available at Central for over a year with about 50 books and the circulation has averaged about 90 books per month.

-Dutton. Service has been available at the Dutton Café for over a year. We have about 100 books at Dutton and the circulation has averaged about 175 per month. [Dutton is east of the Tennessee River and southeast of Scottsboro.]

-Flat Rock. Service has been available at Taylor's Store for only about 3 months. We have about 70 books with an average of about 75 circulations per month. [Flat Rock is east of the Tennessee River and northeast of Scottsboro.]

-Fackler. Seeber opened service at Fackler but it was apparently established in the wrong store as very [few] books have circulated and those that are there (about 20) are usually cover[ed] up in a corner.

-Tupelo. We had service at Tupelo but it was about like Fackler.

-Langston. Service has been available for over a year. About 80 books and 150 monthly circulation. [Langston is on the east side of the Tennessee River between Scottsboro and Guntersville, not an easy place to get to.]

-Macedonia. Service has been available at the School during the School terms for the past 18 months and at the Store during the summer months. About 100 books have been kept at Macedonia and the circulation has been quite high—about 200 per month. [Macedonia is about four miles east of Langston.]

-Pisgah. Service has been available at the Pisgah Café for about 18 months. We have had about 200 books at Pisgah and the monthly circulation has run as high as 500 but it has averaged about 400 per month. [Pisgah is six miles north of Dutton.]

-Paint Rock. Circulation has been at Rosseau's Store for about 10 months. About 110 books are kept at the store and the circulation has averaged about 180 per month.

-Rocky Springs. Books have been available at Mr. A.B. Adams home for about four months. It is one of the best library stations that we have anyplace in the area. Mr. & Mrs. Adams make everyone in the vicinity feel free to come to their home to get the books and the type of reading is somewhat higher than at most points since Mr. Adams encourages the reading of good books. We have about 70 books at Rocky Springs and the circulation has averaged about 120 books per month. [Rocky Springs is three miles west of downtown Bridgeport.] [Is there anyone in the 21st century willing to open his home as a book station?]

-Rosalie. Service has been at Chapman's Store (I think that is their name) for about 1 year. An average of 90 books have been stationed here and the reading has averaged about 90 books per month. [Rosalie is between Pisgah and Flat Rock.]

-Woodville. There has been a library committee in Woodville that has taken care of the library. During the school term the books have been at the school and in the summer the books have been at a store. About 100 books have been stationed at Woodville and the circulation has been about 200 books per month.

-Stevenson Public Library. We have assisted the book collection at the Stevenson Library and they say that we have caused the circulation to more that double by changing the collection of books periodically. This library is open only on Sat. and it should be open every day. Mrs. J.L. Armstrong is Pres. of the Stevenson Library Board.

-Section. About 100 books have been kept at Skeet's Place for over a year. The circulation is high being over 200 books per month. [Section is between Langston and Dutton.]

-Scottsboro Negro School. We have had from 100 to 125 books in the Negro School and a man by the name of Nelms has carried the books in his car to the homes of the Negro families in Scottsboro with an average of 250 circulations per month from the collection.

-Lim Rock. I have a request on my desk for services from Mr. Horace Maples. [Lim Rock is nine miles west of Scottsboro.]

-Bridgeport is planning to establish a Public Library and Miss Whitcher is taking the leadership. It will probably be located in the front of the News Office unless a better location is found.

There has been the special service to the men working in the TVA Reservoir Clearance Units which is in addition to the above. The Reservoir Clearance work is now over and the library service has been withdrawn, but you will not be interested in this service in talking with the Commissioners.

I forgot to mention that we have about 600 books at the Scottsboro Library at all times for the past year. Also we have mended about 600 of the Scottsboro Library Books.

The books located at the several stations have from 35 to 40% children's books depending upon the locality. Adult reading has been stressed a bit more than children's reading.

Should the Commissioners be in doubt, it is perfectly legal for them to appropriate funds to the County Library Board and it is their function rather than the School Board. The School Board's share is in relation to the service of the County Library to the Schools and the children. The Commissioners' share is for adult and non-school library service.

It might be mentioned that at Walker [County] where they have such an excellent County Library Service which serves both the Public and the Schools as a coordinated system, the Commissioners pay half and the School Board pays half which is $5000. each annually.

I trust that this part of the information that you needed and I will be glad to provide any other that you may need from time to time."[6]

The letter above mentioned numerous towns in Jackson County that had library stops. The population of Jackson County in 1940 was approximately 40,800, while in 2000 it was about 50,700, a gain of about 10,000 in 60 years. But the City of Scottsboro gained about 11,000 citizens during the same period, which means that rural Jackson County lost about 1,000 folks over the same 60 years. This data led me to conclude that the county population, minus Scottsboro, has remained essentially the same in numbers and distribution throughout the county. What you see in the rural county in 2004 was what you would have seen in 1940. For readers who have not driven in western Jackson County, it is like a different country from the large flat areas of

Madison County. The area is mostly hills and valleys, so travel is difficult when trying to move across the grain of the terrain.

February 7, 1938 – The treasurer's report for January follows: $66.12 in treasury; $175 from the county; $32.32 from fines; and $3.03 from juvenile. The budget for the coming year was: $30 for salaries; $48.48 for books; $30.38 for operations, per month. New mending amounted to $10.63.

Eliza Hackworth, of Scottsboro, will now be introduced. Her father was a probate judge in Jackson County and her mother was quiet and refined. Eliza was born in 1904. She grew up as a very independent person and was for women's liberty. In 1929 she volunteered to be the librarian in Scottsboro's first library in the northwest jury room of the courthouse. In 1932 the city gave the library an unfinished suite of rooms on the second floor of the town hall, and the building still stands in 2004 at the southwest corner of Courthouse Square. In 1934 the library was open two afternoons per week. According to her cousin, Nellie Hackworth, Eliza was never intimidated by anyone, and usually it was her intimidating others. Marie Garrett, librarian at Scottsboro in 2004, remembers going up the creaky dark stairs to the library and the smell of library paste upon arrival. "Miss Eliza" was strict with her patrons and enforced quietness, but they all learned respect for books. She steered many children in Scottsboro in the direction she thought they should go. She was zealous in following up to ensure they read what she gave them. Miss Eliza would also call the parents if children checked out a book that she thought was not good for them. Eliza was slim and slight of build. (Garrett) As you will see from her letters, Eliza was a stickler for statistics and doing things correctly. The stage has been set for Eliza's letters.

Eliza Hackworth, Scottsboro, wrote a letter to Hoyt Galvin, dated April or July 29, 1938:

"This note is my elation over 'my' pay shelf. It really takes salesmanship (a short review of the book I mean—I think that I'll start reading salesmanship psychology!) to get them going sometimes and I've taken two 'stickers' off and are facing having to take some more, but even so here is your check in full and I have $2.45 left. But, with the aid of my overdues, I can pay you for $5.+ now. So will you please send me the booklist again? [She wrote vertically in the left margin afterward, 'Don't you think that's all right?'] [and squeezed this between two lines 'and I'll get at least a $10 order because I'll have it by the time you need the bill.' *I'm ready and anxious. I know, there's danger in exuberance, but I really have my feet on the ground. Doesn't this prove it!* [This author's italics] There are so many people who have read the Sat. Post serial which I ordered, 'The Wall' by Rhinehart that I'm afraid of it, in a way. This time I don't want to get many serials—they have bothered me in 'Enchanted Oasis', 'Madame Curie', This Proud Heart' and some others. The serials in the Sat. Post and Cosmopolitan, I mean, for they are the most read.

Sorry to have bothered you with all of this, but aren't you feeling good about it, too?!

Say, I'm going to write an article on 'The Pay Shelf' and send it to the American Library Ass. Magazine (I'm laughing) so don't scoop me!

But seriously, I am sending it to my 'Will' papers and if they'll use it the locals.
Sincerely, Eliza H.

P.S. I have had the amount to send you longer than now, but it is hard to get—touch with treasurer—hope to remedy that right away.

Oh yes, we are cleaning the windows and putting up new curtains, so come to see me week after next and you'll se a more charming library—and it gets complimented occasionally as it is. E.H." [Don't you just love Eliza's enthusiasm and would like to have her for your librarian?]

One of the books in the Huntsville library archives was an official publication of the United States Army, *Designating Flags of the United States Army, 1861-1865*. The book was copyrighted in 1888 by Brig. Gen. S.B. Holobird, Quartermaster General, United States Army. It had the Library of Congress identification number LC#10-7976.

This next book in the library caught my attention for several reasons. First, the title is descriptive of its contents so you would know what you were going to read. Long and descriptive titles were the custom in the 17ᵗʰ and 18ᵗʰ centuries. Second, the subject and the publisher tell a little story. Third, there was a connection to Huntsville. The title filled the whole page and it will be compressed below, but retain the original layout.

"Ordinance Instructions for the Confederate States Navy

Relating to the

Preparation of Vessels of War for Battle

To the Duties of Officers and Others When at Quarters

to

Ordnance and Ordnance Stores

and to

Gunnery

Third Edition

Published by Order of the Navy Department

Confederate States of America

London

Saunders, Otley, & Co., 66 Brook Street W.

1864

Printed by Spottiswode and Co.

New Street Square"

This book belonged to 1ˢᵗ Lieutenant George A. Joiner, Steam Room, CS [Confederate States] Steamer Huntsville. So, Huntsville had a steamship named after it, only three years into the war. The book was printed in London, as the British were very pro-Southern during the Civil War. They probably hoped they could still teach those Colonists a lesson.

March 7, 1938 – The work of the museum committee was discussed, with the view of getting the idea before the public. It was decided to have a series of small teas, to which the invited people who might know of relics which might be placed there.

April 4, 1938 – Reports of Mr. Galvin's and Miss Jones' attendance at the state librarians' meeting in Mobile were provided.

Eliza Hackworth, the librarian at Scottsboro, sent the following letter to Hoyt Galvin on May 9, 1938.

"Enclosed is a check for the books you have sent me for the pay shelf with the exception of the amount for the extra bindings. I will pay you for these later, if that is alright. We also owe you for the book pockets and overdue slips, but can pay later. I mean that we have it, but I neglected to put it in the bill which I gave Mattie Lou [Darwin], and am sorry I have put this off for so long.

Could you please send me a list or catalog of the books listed by the company where you get them, as you said you would be glad for me to select my own list, then send it to you to order.

Thank you very much for this courtesy."

June 6, 1938 – The board voted unanimously to give Miss Frances Jones vacation starting August 1. The board chairman was authorized to sign a new contract with the TVA for regional service for another year.

The Guntersville Dam workers were housed in dormitories, 5 for white workers and 1 for Negroes, each with a capacity of 60 persons. There was a staff dormitory with a capacity of 52 and one for women that held 25. There were also 36 separate houses built for families. The construction village was a half-mile from the dam site and about 3.5 miles from U.S. Route 241, now 431, the main road connecting Huntsville and Guntersville. If you travel to the dam today on the access road, just before the road takes a sweeping left curve, there is an intersection. To the right is a road to the maintenance area. Immediately ahead is a vehicular gate. To the left is the road to the construction village. About 100 yards up the road is a vehicular gate, which bars further vehicular access. The road slopes slightly upward and on the left is a sign that identifies the private property belonging to the Blue and Gray Rifle and Pistol Club, of Huntsville, organized in 1961. The Club rents the property from the TVA. Another 50 yards up the road and to the left is a large flat area, which now functions as the shooting range for the gun club. That is where the community office, the staff dormitory and the single-family houses were located. The former road to the left is easily discernable when walking along it, which is on the right boundary of the long-distance rifle range.

The community building, for whites only, had a library room 18 x 25 feet, or 450 square feet. At first blush, that might not seem very big, but put in several shelves for books, and there was an adequate capacity for the number of potential patrons. In the 1930's the literacy among the white population was not very high. It was even lower among the laboring class that worked at the dam. The Negro recreation building had a 12.5 x 15.5 feet room that tripled as a living room, library and committee room. The literacy among Negroes was far lower than whites. Four-fifths of the Negroes in the South had poor or nonexistent library service.

There is just one remaining ramshackle building left from 1940. The building is not on the map at that specific location. This building has a garage, which occupies about fifty percent of the building, so I conclude that it was the original fire station that the builders put at a better location for easier access to all buildings. I digress from the library history, as it was more fun to analyze maps and building photos to try to uncover the secrets of the building that is not on the map.

But the Guntersville Dam was just a small part of the library service over the three counties. The regional bookmobile in 1938 made 53 rural stops in Madison, Jackson and Marshall Counties. The bookmobile circulated more books than the combined total circulation from the Huntsville, Scottsboro, Guntersville, and Guntersville Dam libraries. Library officials estimated that at least 100 stops were needed before a minimum program can be maintained. Stations were being set up as more books became available.

The Huntsville Carnegie Library may have been the first in Alabama to have a multi-county regional library, but it was not the first for rural bookmobiles. The Huntsville brochure compares itself to the standard set by Walker County, southwest of Madison County, in which Jasper is the county seat. Walker County served 60 rural stations, in addition to several public libraries in the county. In the 1930s the population of Walker County was 59,445, smaller than Madison's 66,000.[7] Eliza Hackworth, Scottsboro, sent another letter to Hoyt Galvin on August 12, 1938:

"This is the list of books I have chosen, although I do not have the money to pay for them at the present time I think I can get it by the time I get the books. I had an invoice from you about 'Rachel's Children' but I have not received the book, and I did not order it. ___ I don't mind having it, however. But I do not want to cancel the order for, 'The Wall', __ I think it will live after it gets off of the pay shelf.

- My Son, My Son   by Spring $2.50
- Southerner Discovers the South-Daniels $3.00
- Heartbroken Melody   Morris $2.00
                    Reprints
- Cards on the Table by Christie $0.75
- My Country and My People by Lin Yutang $1.39

According to this ten best of the rent shelves, I already have the most popular, but I have had requests for My Son – and am taking a chance, do you think that is alright?

Thank you very much for the magazines which I am returning."

September 4, 1938 – Mr. Galvin was given permission to have an exhibit at the fair and to buy a display case form Fowler Brothers. Miss Jones was asked to pay for magazine subscriptions out of her regular $10, this to be effective until January 1, this amount not to be repaid. A Huntsville Carnegie Library brochure of September 15, 1938 repeated the information above and added, "Madison County can also have good countywide library service. Funds are now available to operate the book truck over part of the County until June, 1939. The service will have to be discontinued at that date unless additional funds are provided. If you wish to see the County-wide book service continued on a permanent basis in Madison County, READ THE FOLLOWING:

WHAT
YOU
CAN
DO

1. Pass resolutions at your club meeting and at your Parent-Teacher meeting. (Send copies of these resolutions to the Huntsville Library Board and to the Madison County Court of Commissioners.)
2. Write to the Commissioner from your district urging him to support the County-wide library program.
3. Talk with your friends and neighbors about the library."[8]

During October 1-8, 1938 the Stevenson (northeast Jackson County) Library observed Library Book Week. The reading list more than doubled during the last year and the library started a drive to raise money. Through the courtesy of the regional library workers, additional books were made available. The library was open each Saturday afternoon from 2:30 to 4:30. The check out period was one week and the fine for overdue books was ten cents per week.[9]

A week later, Ida E. Maxwell, Stevenson, wrote a letter, October 14, 1938, to Hoyt Galvin:

"I am Adult Teacher here and the library is very inadequate. It only opens on Saturday and I usually go back to my mountain home late Friday afternoon and cannot be helped much by it. Could you people lend some reading matter for use among my pupils. I have several calls from men for books. I have no one above 8th and 10th, very few 10th. I have many 4th grade pupils.

May I hear from some one. I am not sure where to write but will try. Thank you for cooperation." Apparently she stayed in town during the weekdays. This points up the long-running division of support for public schools and the general public's reading. Dear reader, make a mental picture of Ida Maxwell going to her mountain home on weekends. We will hear more from her in the next chapter.

In 1938 the Madison County commissioners were annually contributing $325 to support the library. Mrs. Claude Davis, representing the library board asked the commissioners to increase their support. The number of rural readers increased by 2,019 over the last year. This number does not include those serviced by the TVA regional library. She also cited the 800 books repaired and 987 cleaned. The commissioners asked how much was needed. Mrs. Davis replied, "We could easily use $50 more per month," which is about 15 percent. It is a truism that every librarian could spend more money if they had it.[10]

Mr. Galvin gave his regional report. November 7, 1938 – Apparently Mr. Galvin and Miss Jones attended a Southeast Regional meeting in Atlanta.

Eliza Hackworth sent another letter to Hoyt Galvin, January 4, 1939, which covered a range of issues. She poignantly wrote, *"I'm tired of getting nowhere in such a hurry; I want to learn to be more efficient and know more of the science of management!"* [This author's italics.] Her thirst for knowledge was commendable and she rates high kudos in my book. The response from Hoyt Galvin was not found.

She sent another letter on February 25, 1939, which said in part, "How am I going to get books back when I send cards and they won't pay attention to me? I am still losing too many and still sending cards. Of course there are times when members of the club can help and recently did in one case, but that is just the exception. I can't refuse some children and give them to others because when I don't know about them my bet is as likely to be wrong as right because human beings are honest and nice when you don't expect it." Eliza was not only a librarian, but a philosopher as well.

A postcard from Eliza Hackworth, March 21, 1939, "If I do not have too many requests in already, will you please let me have these: 'The Trail of the Lonesome Pine' and two books of poems: 'White Buildings' and 'The Bridge' by Crone."

April 3, 1939 – The regional report on circulation was about 20,000. Mr. Galvin told of plans to attend the Alabama Library Association in Montgomery, where Huntsville's invitation for the next year's meeting would be extended.

May 1, 1939 – Mr. Galvin distributed copies of a tentative six-month contract with the TVA, calling for $66 in funds required from the three counties affected. Mr. Galvin made a report about his attendance at the state meeting, where he was elected president and Huntsville was selected for next year's meeting.

Eliza's postcard, May 6, 1939, "Will you please lend me a copy of 'How to Win Friends and Influence People' and also a 'History of Photography'? The new floor is looking better, won't you stop by to see it? Also a book on the theory and practice of wireless telegraphy?"

Well, let us try just one more of Eliza's postcards in this chapter, June 2, 1939, "My conscience has hurt a tiny bit about taking so many of your children's books and not returning them so here is my increased book circulation with the children making neat parallel: Sat – 139; Tues – 110; Thurs – 112. I have not been having quite a hundred even for Sat.s for last two weeks. The books have pepped talk up – the books are taken from the rack each day, too. Thank you."

Dear readers, this is the last Eliza letter to Galvin in this chapter, although we will meet her again in the next chapter.

"Will you please help me to learn the things in practical library science I do not know. Among those things the correct way to catalog books, more about indexing and arranging non-fiction section, better or best method of management. I send cards but I'm still having trouble.

I have completed a course, with the exception of the examination, from Peabody [College, Nashville] (Freshman English). This credit will be given on a B.S. and I plan to take others as soon as the Dean of Correspondence School sends me or marks the courses which she will credit and allow by correspondence. This may sound nearly hopeless to you but if anything nice happens and I get to go to Peabody in even six week sessions my credits by correspondence will help me that much. I also want to study the Dictionary and have been putting it off. How did you have to study it, please?

A very important item for the present is more salary. For three years – I believe its just two – I haven't made any progress toward improvement in this. I don't want to ask for something I don't deserve from the city, but don't you think that I do? Will you help me manage this – in the best way? Don't you think more afternoons a week are practical? I do. Because the people who come now will be here permanently probably and the growth is rather steady. Then I could have more time to fix my file (I've taken out the newspapers) and do some of the other things I want to do. It's hard to juggle two or three jobs and make nothing financially and in other senses but a failure. I would much rather have more time to myself + someone else to help me – except you to tell me – would be a tragic bother now it seems to me./ For I want to know and do first – I don't think this is selfish, do you?

I'd like to be a full time (and salaried) librarian and I can't learn any younger. I want to be good in it, try new things and keep up standards. But with no more time in it, I can't prove whether I have initiative – unless the fact that as I had gotten until you came was my idea even tho the ideas were the trial and error type – the club backed them, but I had to make and enforce most of the rules and did the work – can't initiative be developed anyways. And I know now that I had rather be a librarian – but a good one – than a news writer or reporter.

Can't we be cooperative in this sense? If you will and can help me now I'll be grateful forever. I am interested in the growth and success of your or our rural areas, too; and I want to know more and some better.

Mr. Robert D. England with the MacMillan Book Company came to see me yesterday. I told him that I order through you but when he knew that I make the selections he left me three catalogs. He says he knows you and you gave him an order recently. I was delighted with his sample book and have gotten a big kick out of the catalogs I've had time for. The club made some money last week and I believe they'll at least give me enough to order again. My payshelf is crying for more – Rebecca was a good buy but I failed in the most of the others this last time.

Circulation Tues was 139.

Thanks if you have not thrown this in the wastebasket and will please help me now. Sincerely, Eliza H." [Now folks, wasn't that a touching letter?]

The Second World War began on September 1, 1939 when Germany invaded Poland.

October 2, 1939 – The committee on by-laws recommended that the name of the library be changed from Carnegie Library to the Huntsville Public Library.

The Library Board in 1930 had the following membership:

- Mrs. Henry Chase, President
- Mrs. Martin May, Vice President
- Mrs. Thomas L. Patton, Secretary
- Mrs. Amelia Dillard, Treasurer
- Mrs. H. M. Rhett
- Mrs. Robert Pulley
- Addison White
- Mrs. John Mastin

- Mrs. W. I. Wellman
- Mrs. James Pride
- Mrs. E. T. Terry
- Mrs. E. D. Johnston (resigned)
- Mrs. Shelby White (replaced Mrs. Johnston)[11]

There were twelve members on the board, with only a "token" male among them. This certainly seems to be high number of board members considering the size of the library and circulation.

The Library Board in 1939 consisted of the following members:
- Mrs. Claude Davis, President
- Mrs. James Pride, Vice President
- Mrs. W. G. Hamm, Secretary
- Mrs. E. T. Terry, Treasurer
- Mrs. Henry Chase
- Mrs. Shelby White
- Mrs. J. B. Woodall
- Mrs. John Mastin
- Mrs. W. E. Butler
- Mrs. Walker Bolling
- Mrs. Robert F. Proctor[12]

There were now eleven members, and the lone man departed in 1931 after seven years on the board. Enough is enough.

The decade of the 1930s was devoid of much library significance except that the regional library was formed in cooperation with the Tennessee Valley Authority. The country was in the throes of the Great Depression. The southern states, to include Alabama, did not have much going for them before and during the depression days. The economic outlook was bleak. There was no hint of how the future might change. The War to End all Wars, World War I, was well in the past and future war was nowhere on the horizon for the United States, even though Germany had annexed Austria and Czechoslovakia, and invaded Poland on September 1, 1939, but that was on a different continent and of no concern to the United States. There was little hope for a better Alabama. People would continue to exist at low ebb. The population of Huntsville rose from 8,018 in 1920 to 13,050 in 1940. The town of Madison's population rose from 435 to 455 during the same 20 years.

The country outside the South was in a depression also, but hopeful thinking was taking place. Perhaps some of it would rub off onto Alabama. Let us leave the Huntsville library history of the 1930s with the following quotation.

"There Is No Past As Long As Books Shall Live

With a well-filled shelf of books, the reader of today is enabled to know the past even better that the people who lived in it. Outstanding events, like mountains, need to be viewed from a distance in order that their true proportions may appear. Biographies, when well and carefully written, often render their subjects more approachable than they were in real life. Great men are frequently surrounded by a veil of mystery, and are remote from the majority of their contemporaries. But through books they may become intimates in many a household.

Books are messengers of the past, not only in the biographical and historical realms, but in science and other fields as well. A wise man once said that by means of books the men of the present could stand on the shoulders of their predecessors and continue the building from the place where those earlier workers had left it. The student of electricity does not have to begin where Edison did, but rather where Edison finished, because books will give him the knowledge of the science up to the present time. His original work can rest on the foundations built in the past. This is true also of economics, sociology, and the other sciences.

As few men can possess all the books in even a very restricted field, it is the function of the public library to make available to each of its patrons all the books he needs or wants for the development of his talents and abilities. This is easily possible because public libraries nowadays are not isolated institutions serving a group of people who happen to live in the vicinity. On the contrary, they are parts of a great library system that covers the whole country and even reaches into foreign lands. Books may be interchanged as readily between libraries as between the branches of a single library system. Consequently the past may live for each inquirer through the books he can obtain in his own library, and no one can excuse his failures on the ground that he is ignorant of what has happened in the past."

Sabra W. Vought, Chief, Library Division, Office of Education, In *School Life*, January, 1937.[13]

Chapter 4

World War II Comes to Huntsville

*"The time was when a library was very like a museum,
and a librarian was a mouser in musty books,
and visitors looked with curious eyes at ancient tomes
and manuscripts. The time is when a library is a school,
and the librarian is in the highest sense a teacher,
and the visitor is a reader among the books as a workman
among his tools. Will any man deny to the high calling of such a
librarianship the title of profession?*

Melvil Dewey, 1851-1931
American educator and innovator in library science

The quotation above was selected because professionally trained librarians assumed leadership roles in the Huntsville-Madison County Public Library for the first time in this decade.

On February 8, 1940 the Huntsville City Council passed an ordinance, Number 477-A, which changed the name of the Carnegie Library to the Huntsville Library. The change was not an overt statement, but the adoption of a new ordinance that used the name, Huntsville Public Library. Andrew Carnegie made no conditions that the libraries should carry his name, so each town was free to choose any name it desired.

The ordinance provided for the creation of a five-member board to govern and supervise the library. The council would appoint the board, but the officers would be chosen by the board members and they would adopt its by-laws. The terms of the membership shall be for four years, except as first elected when one member shall be elected for one year; one member shall be elected for two years; one member shall be elected for three years; and two members shall be elected for four years. The ordinance established the powers and the duties of the library board:

1. It shall have full power and authority to control the expenditures of all funds received or appropriated for the Huntsville Public Library.
2. It shall have the power to erect or rent buildings, with the approval of the city council, to cost not in excess of the funds available to it.
3. It shall be authorized to purchase books and equipment, and to provide a system of library services to be made to all citizens of the City through the central library, branches, stations, book truck service, or other appropriate means.
4. It shall be authorized to elect a librarian and other employees, and such librarian shall be a professionally trained librarian when a vacancy occurs after the adoption of this ordinance.
5. It shall be authorized to receive gifts and administer trusts.
6. It shall be authorized to borrow books from and lend books to other libraries.

7. It shall be authorized to make contracts with other agencies for the providing of library service outside the City of Huntsville, subject to the approval of the city council.

8. Any property donated to said library shall immediately become property of the city and by said board kept for the benefit of the said Library.

9. The library shall keep accurate minutes of each meeting of said board and said minutes shall be available at the library building for inspection by the mayor or any member of the city council at all times such building is open.

10. The library board shall prepare a written financial and administrative report at the end of each fiscal year of the city (September 30th of each year) and the same shall be presented to the city council immediately thereafter.

11. The right and authority to amend or repeal any part of this ordinance or any other ordinance relating to said library "Library Board" is hereby reserved by the city council.

12. That sections 227 to 243, both inclusive, of Chapter 14 of the 1924 Code of Ordinances of the City of Huntsville be and the same hereby are repealed.

13. That any other ordinances or resolutions or parts of ordinances or resolutions in conflict herewith are hereby repealed.

Resolution 478-A stated the board members and their terms: Mrs. C.H. Davis and Mrs. E.T. Terry were elected for four year terms ending on the 10th day of February, 1944; Mrs. H.B. Chase was elected for the three year term ending February 10, 1943; Mrs. Robert F. Proctor was elected for the two year term ending February 10, 1942; and Mrs. S.I. White was elected for the term ending February 10, 1941.[1]

In 1939 it was apparent that the Guntersville Dam was nearly finished so a committee of permanency was formed to study the possibility of continuing the regional library on a permanent basis after the TVA withdrew. On January 1, 1940 the Regional Library Service of the Huntsville Public Library became a self-sustaining organization, drawing its support from the city, the county governing boards of the three participating counties and the boards of education of the three counties. On July 1, 1940 the TVA withdrew funds from the Regional Library because Guntersville Dam was finished.

Hoyt Galvin sent a status report of the Regional library service to the Huntsville Carnegie Library Board on January 4, 1940.

"The following is the December 1939 progress report for the total rural and urban cooperative library service program which is being conducted on a contract basis in Madison, Marshall and Jackson. Counties:

I. STAFF

The following tabulation shows the number and locations of persons working in the Regional Library Service program:

-Regional Library Service Office & Book
1 Full-time, Regional Librarian
2 Half-time, NYA Assistants
-Albertville Public Library
2 Half-time NYA Attendants
Guntersville Public Library
1 Three-fourths-time Librarian
Guntersville Dam Library
1 Full-time, Library Attendant

-Gurley Library Station
1 Half-time, NYA Attendant
-Huntsville Carnegie Library
1 Full-time, Librarian
1 Half-time, Children's Librarian
4 Half-time, NYA Attendants
-Buggs Chapel & Owens X Rds.
1 Half-time, NYA Attendant
-Scottsboro Public Library
1 Half-time, Librarian
-Stevenson Library
1 Part-time, Librarian,
-Bridgeport public
Library 1 Half-time

Volunteers, storekeepers, school principals and school teachers serve as library attendants at the several other points in the three-county area where service is available.

The closing of the Guntersville Dam Library has made possible the opening of several new points of service in the area and books are available for the opening of approximately two additional points in each county within the coming month. On the following page is a list of the points now receiving library service.

Madison County

1. Big Cove Store
2. Big Cove School
3. Buggs Chapel Store
4. Cedar Gap (Wiley's store)
5. Gurley Library Station
6. Hazel Green School
7. Hazel Green Store
8. Harvest School
9. Huntsville Carnegie Library
10. Huntsville Negro Recreation
11. Merrimack Recreation Ball
12. New Hope School
13. New Hope Recreation Hall
14. New Market Recreation Hall
15. Owen's X Rds. Store
16. Owen's X Rds. School
17. Pulaski School
18. Colburn's Store
19. Riverton (Riverside Ill)
20. Walnut Grove School
21. Monrovia School
22. Madison High School

Marshall County

1. Albertville Public Library

2. Arab High School
3. Arab Elementary School
4. Asbury School
5. Asbury Store
6. Boaz Drug Store Library
7. Boaz Elementary School
8. Boaz High School Library
9. Guntersville Public Library
10.Guntersville Dam Library
11.Claysville Jr. High
12.Hebron School
13.Whitaker's Store
14.Y Filling Station
15.High Point School
16.Grant H. S. & Community
17.Union Grove High School
18.Douglas High School
19. Douglas Elementary School

Jackson County

1. Bridgeport Public Library
2. Dutton Cafe (Across Road from School)
3. Flat Rock Store
4. Flat Rock School
5. Hollywood School
6. Paint Rock School
7. Rocky Springs Community Deposit
8. Rocky Springs School
9. Rosalie School
10. Rosalie (Bowman's Store)
12. Scottsboro Public Library
13. Scottsboro Negro School
13. Stevenson Public Library
14. Princeton High School
15. Woodville High School
16. Macedonia High School
17. Pisgah High School
18. Pisgah Library Club
19. Central
20. Section

The complete pamphlet and clipping file from the Guntersville Dam Library was transferred to the Scottsboro Public Library where it will fill a much felt need. The book collection from the Guntersville Dam Library has been distributed throughout the area. All dormitories, the cafeteria, the grocery store, the Community Bldg and the gasoline station at the Dam have been closed. A few families are still living in the houses at the Village, but it is reported that they were only waiting until after the holiday season to move. All library service was discontinued on Dec. 15 at which time the Community Building was closed and locked. The Library had been located in the Community Building.

The holiday season slowed the work of the library program since about half of the points of library service are located in schools, and it was not possible to service these library stations. The Regional Librarian attended the Mid-Winter Conference of the American Library Association in Chicago from Dec. 27 to 30, returning to work in Huntsville on Jan. 2.

Progress is being made toward the proposed WPA [Work Projects Administration] Library Project for this Three-county area. The Project will be completely coordinated with the Regional Library Service program. It will not be a separate library project operating in this area, and it undoubtedly will greatly increase the usefulness of the Regional program. It will be probably be 30 days yet before the project is in operation since the approval of such projects is a slow process.

A collection of new books has been received in the Regional Office. The order amounted to about $650.00. About half of this amount went for children's books that were selected from approved Alabama library lists. The adult books represented copies of new popular titles and some of the older popular titles. These new books together with the collection from Guntersville Dam have been most popular throughout the area. The eager look in the eyes of the elementary teachers of the area is most gratifying when they see the children's books on the truck that they have been needing so badly for their classrooms. Ten times the number of books which we have would not begin to fill the needs of books for this area.

The New Market School fire destroyed a collection of about 50 books. It is hoped however that many of these books may have been charged out to students at the time of the fire and that we will get the books. The charge records were also destroyed and the return of books will depend upon the conscience of the students. Books have also been available in New Market at the Recreation Hall that were not destroyed.

The NYA Book Mending Project has been continued during the month. Large book collections from the School Libraries at New Hope and Pisgah have been repaired in addition to smaller collections from other points in the area. This part of the library program is very popular since the book truck picks up worn books and delivers them back to the school completely repaired without cost to the school. The cost of mending supplies is furnished jointly between the Regional Library Service and the NYA."[2] Bravo, Hoyt Galvin, you have shown great initiative and professionalism!

Before time moves forward, refer back several pages to the part of Hoyt Galvin's long letter to the part where he described the staffing at several branches. Some of the branches have an NYA Attendant. NYA stands for National Youth Administration. Eleanor Roosevelt, the activist wife of President Franklin D. Roosevelt, helped establish the NYA in June 1935. The NYA helped more than 2 million high school and college students stay in school by giving them grants in exchange for work. They worked in libraries and college labs, and on farms. The NYA also found work for 2.5 million young people who were not in school and not working. As World War II approached, NYA youths worked in defense industries where they gained useful job skills. The NYA was an equal opportunity agency, providing aid to women and minorities. This feature of the program was very important to Mrs. Roosevelt. *"It is a question of the right to work,"* she said, *"and the right to work should know no color lines."*[3] Now notice that there was not an NYA Attendant at the Scottsboro branch.

Readers, do you remember Eliza Hackworth from the last chapter? Well, she's back. Her March 13, 1940 letter to Hoyt Galvin:

"...I am also sending the accession sheet back to you and aplogize(sic) for keeping it so long__the delay was in the fact that my typewriter won't hold the sheet so I have to use Parker Campbell's at the *Sentinel* and I can't always be at the *Sentinel* at the right time....Next time I will try to do a better job.

Miss Powell came and talked to me to-day about WPA helpers. Since she says it is your idea and that your idea was sponsored in an effort to help me, please listen and wait a minute. Right now Mattie Lou [Darwin] and I are working on a plan to get the Board more interested in keeping the library open each day and of course that means asking for money which I hate to have to mention but which is VERY NECESSARY, especially now to me. But we are also planning to try the library committee or board plan with representatives from each club and we hope this will work. Miss Powell told me that this method had worked so well in another place and we are willing to try something. Can't we please wait until the library is open each afternoon_then I can have more time and peace to teach the person. Right now I am almost sick_a nervous condition resulting from a cold (was in bed all of one day last week but am much better) and believe if you'll just be patient with me and give me a little more time I'll be all right.

How are "Douger" and Mrs. Galvin? I hope you will come back some time soon. Would you or do you think it advisable for you to meet with our new board when we get it organized and would you consider a talk to the City Board?"[4]

Two days after the letter above, March 15, 1940, Liza H. sent another letter:

"...Mr. Galvin, if you really want to help me; please do not push any worker on me _ I mean WPA NYA or what not until we can get the library fixed so that I can have the full hours in the afternoons. To have it open only a few minutes or hours would be practically impossible because I have to work over time as it is and then that would ruin me _ wreck each afternoon. I have had a helper before and I know how terrible it is _ not only doing mine but thinking out for her or him. I don't want to break physically and don't believe I will if you just won't push this on me and will help me. The more I think of it the slicker the idea of mentioning three so that the shock would make one seem desirable. I'm laughing, aren't you? But please don't do it.

You see I really am not completely well, so things have been absorbed in relays and thus you have two long letters when you didn't want one. Please help me instead of torturing me. Thanks. Sincerely, Eliza."[5]

April 1, 1940 – Mr. Galvin reported on his attendance at the Southeast Regional Library Conference in Knoxville, for which his expenses were paid by the Huntsville Library. It was agreed the new library hours would be 9 A.M to 7 P.M. April 18, 1940 was the opening of the state meeting in Huntsville.

On May 20, 1940 Eliza Hackworth sent another letter to Hoyt Galvin:

"I am sorry but it was not possible, I guess, for us to completely talk things out Thursday. So in the friendliest spirit ever will you please discuss it with me now and frankly tell me what your plans and hopes are for this particular unit in our library area.

You said, you remember, that you would give us until July to see if the City will give me full time and then you sounded threatening and that you were going to see it open regardless – you put it in a very nice manner, but that was your idea was it not?

Did you mean by that that you are trying to put in a WPA worker for three days and me for three days and that that would eventually mean _ possibly or definitely _ that the WPA worker would be give full time or all of the time gives as was the way you told me you worked it with Mr. Johnson at the Guntersville Dam? Or do you have some one who has a degree as librarian or did you mean that you could or would consider me as the WPA worker or help to get it or be it _ however it is managed – and let me be full time under your employ.

If your objection is to me and the work I have been and am trying to do please tell me frankly in what ways you consider me ill fitted, inefficient or what.

You know, as you said, doing many things makes it hard to either on every well _ and I am trying two or more things. If it could be managed so that I could be settled for full time I believe I could be a good librarian _ do you or not and why not?

I believe your method of helping is to discuss the flaws or neglects and you have done it in a very nice and appreciated manner _ or there isn't anything that I do or manage about the library in a praiseworthy way _ and I am nor seeking praise but I want to face the facts of what you are planning and thinking and I am asking you to do this as a kindness because I would rather face facts than have an uncertainty in the offing. … We have been too busy to ask, I suppose, but how are Mrs. Galvin and young Galvin _ I still want to see him, before he gets grown."[6]

Hoyt Galvin answered Eliza Hackworth's letter on May 22, 1940:

It appears that I have unintentionally worried you during our conversation last Thursday. I will try to answer your letter paragraph by paragraph. It is my sincere hope that every library in this area can be open both morning and afternoon every day of the week. Naturally I included Scottsboro in such hopes for as a matter of fact it is the only one now that is not open every day in the week. A few are open only in the afternoons.

It was not my intention to set July definitely as the final goal for achieving more cooperation from the city. It would seem however that after three years we should be able to secure it now or never. I would like very much to put a W.P.A. worker in your library to assist you, even though the library might be open as at present. There are many things such as clipping and picture files that you are not able to develop alone as they keep you too busy at the desk. I would be happy if it is possible for you to become a W.P.A. Librarian but your economic status would be too high for you to convince Miss Gunter that you are qualified. If I am wrong in this matter you may certainly see Miss Gunter about it. Miss Powell is the only uncertified person that we have and all uncertified persons must have a college degree with library training.

You have asked me for a frank comment on your ability. You have performed most satisfactory in my opinion in the Scottsboro Library for a person who does not have library training. I consider you equal to Mrs. Huckaby in the Guntersville Library. Your defense has been to oppose most new ideas until after you had been entirely convinced. This is a normal reaction however and I would not care to criticize you about it when I realize that you have not had the advantage of Library training and the advantage of working in other successful libraries. You may be sure that I am not working behind the scenes to have you replaced by another person, but you may be also sure that I sincerely desire to see the Scottsboro Library open during more days and more hours of the week. My first hope is that your new board might be able to secure a sufficient increase in your salary to allow you to work full time. Even if this is possible however I would desire to place a W.P.A. worker with you in order that a fuller and more complete library program could be conducted.

I believe you will agree with me that, if within the next few months, the city is not willing to increase your salary, it is doubtful that they will for a good many years to come. In such cases I would hope to accomplish something for Scottsboro with the assistance of a W.P.A. worker."[7]

Eliza H. of Scottsboro wrote another letter to Hoyt Galvin, May 30, 1940:

"…you promised also, I believe, not to help us get a WPA worker until we settled on more days with the City Board _ at least settled something. Can't we tactfully arrange to have someone that we could like to have and who would be a help instead of a pain? There is a person, confidentially, who we believe is trying to get employed in this capacity who we also feel sure would not prove satisfactory for several reasons. Some members of the board know her and agree on that point. I'm not fixing to be a gossip, but I can and will be glad to give our reasons confidentially _ its not social prejudice either.

Mr. Galvin, you have been and are being very grand and I appreciate it much more than I can express _ and that is not flattery, so don't get disgusted _ and the club appreciates you, too.

…I don't want to stay in the class of myself and Mrs. Huckaby _ although I never heard of the woman until you mentioned her _ but be as good as you and Miss [Frances] Jones. You needn't tell Miss Jones and you may laugh a lot, but at least I suppose you will confess that I'm ambitious?"[8]

In June 1940 library activities were discontinued in Marshall County because of its failure to make the appropriation for 1940-41. The library continued to operate as a two-county system with a branch in Scottsboro and the rural areas being served from the 12,000-volume store of books earmarked for regional circulation.

On May 31, 1940, the first Negro library in Huntsville was started in the basement of the Lakeside Methodist Church on Jefferson Street. Hoyt Galvin, library director, gave Mrs. Dulcina DeBerry a key to the church basement and told her to see what she could make of it, if she could. Mrs. DeBerry was well qualified for this position, as she had been a teacher in North Carolina and was active in the Lakeside Church. She started to be paid by the Works Progress Administration from that first day, May 31, 1940, until April 27, 1943. A total of 79 people were employed in the regional library system paid by the W.P.A. during 1940-1943.

She found in the basement two unpainted tables, two rough benches and a schoolroom desk with no chair. This was not a promising beginning. The holdings, 27 juvenile volumes, 39 books for adults and 10 used magazines, were stored in a large unpainted dry goods box.

Ten days later the library opened. DeBerry and two high school boys cleaned the basement and painted the furniture. Mrs. Z.K. Jackson, the minister's wife, donated a chair for the librarian to use. During those ten days, the main library had delivered additional books and magazines. The holdings on opening day consisted of 60 books for young readers, 79 adult books and 20 used magazines.

In a few weeks the number of patron increased from 10 to 30. Every two weeks the main library exchanged books and delivered special requests.

Heating became a problem in the basement, and on November 30, 1940 the library was moved to the Winston Street School. That school was demolished in 1980 for the construction of Interstate 565.

The library moved to Pelham Street, near Councill High School and the current main library building, in 1947 in a building owned by the Huntsville Board of Education. Soon after the move, the name of the branch became the Dulcina DeBerry Branch.[9]

August 5, 1940 – Mrs. Robert Proctor was declared to be no longer a member of the board, having failed to attend any of the last five meetings. September 3, 1940 – Mrs Bolling is back on the board. You remember she was dropped earlier for non-attendance.

In September 1940, Hoyt Galvin resigned the position as Director of Regional activities, and was replaced by Horace Moses effective November 1, 1940. Hoyt Galvin moved on to become the Director of the Charlotte Public Library in North Carolina and other library positions. In 1955 he was chairman of the American Library Association Buildings Committee. In that position he was the editor of a pamphlet, *Planning a Library Building,* which recorded the proceedings of an institute for planning a library building sponsored by the American Library Association.[10]

When Hoyt Galvin became TVA Regional Library Director in 1936, he was subordinate to the Huntsville Public Library Board, but not the Huntsville Library. His office was in the basement of the Carnegie Library building. When Horace Moses replaced Galvin, the Library Board minutes of September 11, 1940 reflect that the "Regional Director shall be in complete charge of the Huntsville Public Library and its extension services under the direction of the Huntsville Public Library Board." Mattie Darwin was the Librarian and Head of the Adult Department. Since there was a smaller library board installed, Moses became the Secretary of the Board. The tenor and style of the minutes henceforth reflect Hoyt Galvin's dominance in making changes and initiating many activities. Apparently he was persuasive and dominated with superior knowledge and professionalism. Remember the comments earlier that the early librarians were nice old ladies interested in books, but with no professional training.

November 11, 1940 –The city council approved the new salaries for Mrs. Darwin ($75 per month) and Miss Jones ($50 per month). The Board approved the program presented by Mr. Moses to unify the business organization of the library and the Regional program. All monies due the library from its various sources of income are to be carried in one account, and are to be disbursed through the office of the director. The board empowered Mr. Moses to make a survey of the adult department and its services. The survey was to be used by the director and the board for guidance in a plan of reorganization. Horace Moses assumed the job of secretary to the library board as signer of the minutes for the first time.

December 9, 1940 – The board voted to accept the proposed co-operative purchase plan as presented by the Julius Rosenwald Fund of Chicago for development of library service to Negro readers. These unit library collections to be purchased from Regional funds and to be distributed through the region by our custodians with the cooperation of the Jeanes (?) workers. The Julius Rosenwald Fund was created by Sears, Roebuck and Company magnate Julius Rosenwald (1917-1948) to coordinate his contributions for African American education. He was guided by Booker T. Washington and had Washington administer a program through Tuskegee Institute from 1913-1920 for the construction of new school facilities for black children in the South. In 1928 the Rosenwald Fund revamped its programs to address broader issues of education and health for African Americans and race relations.

February 10, 1941 - "The Director having withdrawn from the meeting, it was moved, seconded and voted that the salary of the Director should be raised from $2,000 per year to $2,400, as agreed upon at the time of his acceptance, and that the future increases of salary should be made at such times as additions to the Regional department were made." Back on November 11, 1940, the library board raised Mrs. Darwin's salary to $75 per month, the equivalent of $900 per year, so there were obvious differences in responsibility and salary between Darwin and Moses.

Mr. Alex B. Adams, the same Adams mentioned in the previous chapter as having a book stop in his home in Rocky Springs, prepared a speech, circa late 1941, which gave a perspective of the regional library system and rural northeast Alabama. My readers should prepare for a wise and insightful document. Adams was a worker for the W.P.A., June 1,1940 to April 27, 1943, but he was concurrently a social observer, philosopher, educator, economist and excellent writer. Ponder his thoughts and transfer them into our 21st century.

"In April I wrote asking a job of H.R. Galvin, I began work June 3, 1940 for Regional Library under W.P.A.

The first month I spent in installing books in Rural Communities, 6 in all, comprising the following: Mt. Carmel, 3 miles, Union Hill, 7 miles, Concord, 3&1/2 miles, Hog Jaw, 5 miles, Bryant, 11 miles, Long Island, 7 miles, these communities Rocky Springs included have a population of more that 3,500.

I worked in cooperation with community workers and teachers trying where possible to get books in the homes of people who had lived in the communities for several generations, also with families who liked to read as they would be sure to know all in the community who also liked to read and thus the work of advertising was cut in half.

For the first six months there was a gradual increase in circulation until in Dec. 1940 it showed a rise from 600 in June 1940, to over 2200 in Nov. 1940, it is now 2500. Circulation will vary some at different Seasons reaching a high in the winter and also late summer and early Fall, to drop again in Spring and early Summer during the period of planting and cultivating crops, canning and other such work.

Our High School System is available to all according to theory, but, the cost of the last two or three years in High School makes it prohibitive to many. Here is where the Library plays an important part to those who will avail themselves of the opportunity. For instance, in Feb. 1939, two boys, of 14 and 15 years respectfully began to check books, averaging from two to four a week showing a preference for Zane Grey's novel and other Western authors, both of those boys were about ready to enter High School.

Howard Jordan was in the 9th grade, he read for about 18 months but mostly for the thrill he would get from reading. There was a noticeable improvement in his Language and better Company.

Albert Prince began to read at the same time, his people were much poorer than Jordan's. He passed to the 8th grade. His father could neither read nor write and was W.P.A. worker and had been on relief work since 1933 and is still on W/P/A. and has a family of 7 children. The mother has probably a 2nd grade education and doesn't read but little.

They seem to have no aspiration beyond a mere existence and raising a bunch of children as fast as possible, allowing the children to raise themselves as they pleased and best could. Albert for one year read nothing but Western books, then a few non-fiction works such as, "Gentlemen are not Sissies", and books on other subjects. Today he continues to read, there is a very marked improvement in Albert from a boy of almost furtive, hang-dog actions. He is today welcomed in the best homes, is invited to any and all social gatherings, attends Church Services, bringing up his brothers and sisters with him. There is a marked improvement in his speech, personal appearance and personal conduct. He is the oldest child and so is able to a great extent to influence his younger brothers and sisters and to some extent his parents. The improvement in this boy is noticed and commented on by all who know him. His father on July 22, 1941 told me, "I thought at first his reading was foolishness but it sure helped him and I will tell anyone so." Here is where the library fills a very important place.

Last year I placed books in 4 schools, all having an enrollment of about 250, teaching up to the 8th grade in one, 6th in two, 4th grade in one. All the teachers were outspoken in praise of the service rendered them by the Regional Library Service. They all agreed that the children who read regularly were from 50 to 100 percent more efficient in their studies. At Long Island there were over 100 children enrolled, they would not read much before school. At the beginning of school circulation was 50 per month until Nov. and Dec. but little increase was shown – but by the time of school closing the teachers reported a circulation of 600 per month.

The circulation of the 4 schools was 9400. All of the teachers tell me that the child who reads during vacation goes ahead at once at the beginning of school while it takes from 2 to 4 weeks to start those who haven't read, giving the child who reads a month start of those who do not.

Readers range in age from 6 years to over 80. At Union there lives an old couple, the old lady is blind, the man's sight is badly affected by age, he is reading the book "Gone With The Wind" aloud to his wife, this will take in all at least two months. This would be impossible almost in a City Library as he is not able to go and recheck the book every 7 or 14 days. Each Librarian in each rural community has known each person for years, some of them are life long neighbors and friends and if it takes one week, two weeks or more for them to read a book they keep the book until it is read then return it.

In carrying books from one station to another my load is 10 to 12 Adult books and 15 Juvenile books, this gives each station an exchange of 10 Adult and 15 juvenile books every 14 days or in all 50 books per month. Each station has an average of 75 books per station.

In exchanging books I always allow the person in charge to pick whatever books from those on hand who would want to read it, also any book or books not being read. I take those books in and go over them carefully and get them ready for the next station being careful to have books that have not been there before. By working it this way and by exchanging books with the Truck once a month any one person can keep a number of stations supplied with new material if they will try and will work. It takes work and plenty of it but it can be done if one has the determination to go ahead.

What prominent farmers think of the Library Program:

-Henry Caperton, Stevenson, master farmer and member of Board of Education says, "The fact that the Library supplies Rural Schools with books the county is unable to supply one reason we want to keep it."

-Cal McFarlane, Bridgeport, says, "if the renters and others would avail themselves of the advantages of the library it is one of the best programs the W.P.A. has engaged in yet."

-W.W. Wicher, Bridgeport, says, "The people get more for the money invested than any other program."

By moving 25 books per load making 12 loads every 28 days you move 300 books per month or 2600 books per year. I walk 140 miles per month or a total of 1680 miles per year. This does not take in to account extra trips of which I make 20 or more during the year.

I also cooperate with the county agent and obtain from him, Bulletins and place them in the hands of farmers who ask for them. From the Home Demonstration Agents I obtain recipe books, also books on clothing and food preservation and pass them over to those who need them, the great trouble is getting enough to go around. In every way possible I cooperate with all programs that I can for I consider any one in the library Service as a servant of the public and as such to serve the public in any way possible, by doing so you gain the confidence of the people, this is very important rural work of any kind. Many rural programs sound in theory and fact have failed because of too much red tape and your rural citizen has scant patience with red tape of any kind. He lives close to nature in the raw, if you please a whole years effort depends on the seasons if they are normal all well, but wind, hail, rain, insects of all kinds, market conditions, all over which he has little or no control are to be considered.

The more anyone reads the more intelligently he can consider any question. So again in this the Library can play an important part in the prosperity of the rural communities. Prosperity calls for better homes and improved farms and this in turn paves the way for larger tax return – thus the rural Library Service is a paying investment for any County or State."[11]
[What a mouthful from Mr. Adams! Bravo!] He was a man of all seasons.

Scottsboro apparently was filled with readers and philosophers in the early 1940's. The following item was found in the Regional Library files, circa 1942. The author was Horace P. Snodgrass, a Negro W.P.A.-paid, library worker from December 7, 1940 until January 19, 1943, with an address of Post Office Box 289, Scottsboro. He had some trouble spelling and mastering the typewriter, but his thoughts were right on the money:

"THE JOY OF READING

To all cultivated person the joy of reading is so natural and neccessarry a fuction of their daily living that they suffer as acutely by being deprived of the kind of literture they are a accustomed to read as they would suffer from being deprived of noufishing foods.

Isn't It fortunate, then, during these portentous times we who live in America are able to enrich our lives and obtain the lasting pleasure derived from reading the out standing books we have in our libraries.

Our leading men of the day know that good reading enable a man to work more freely and sanguinely and rapidly. Good reading nourishes and builds up the worn tissues of the mind. Men and women who read and enjoy good books are released from fear and imbued with an exalted and revgrent courage. We know that we are in a wor and paper is being used for wor purpose we can't get new books from the publishing company every month, But we can get books brought to us monthly from the regional library in Huntsville by the books truck free of charge. Let us prove to them that we appreciate these books by coming to the library and use them. Some of these books may have been use once but they are still new to us if we haven't seem them.

We are proud of our country and the liberty for which we are fighting your membership in our club will help to make better citizen with the freedom of thought and expression in books. Come to see us. Librarian, Horace P. Snodgrass"[12] **Bravo, Horace Snodgrass.**

March 10, 1941 – There was a discussion about the status of the regional library, and with the advice of an invited lawyer, it was agreed that the probate judges and the county superintendents of education be instructed to form library boards in Marshall and Jackson Counties.

May 12 1941 – There was discussion about extending the activities of the Regional Library Service into four Tennessee counties. The director was authorized to make further investigation of the procedures necessary. [As a retired Army officer, the following item tickled my funny bone, my italics.] The supervisor of the Tennessee statewide library service wrote a letter to Horace Moses, Huntsville library director, about the above-cited lack of action to establish the service from Huntsville into Tennessee. "I feel that Mr. Horder and Major Hayes would cooperate and be interested in any program we might develop. We have talked with Mr. Horder quite a bit, and find him definitely interested in Library Service. He has been a great help to us in planning our program in and round Tullahoma. We have found *Major Hayes an interesting person, very willing to cooperate, but with not the slightest idea of what Library Service is.*"[13] The Tennessee expansion idea was not successful because the state representatives decided state laws and variations made it too difficult.[14]

On June 8, 1941 some folks from the United States Army visited Huntsville in search of a site for a weapons plant. On July 3, 1941 the Army selected 30,000 acres in Huntsville for Huntsville Arsenal. Why was it selected? Perhaps they were attracted to the red clay. Maybe they liked the useless ground on the Tennessee River. Thirty-two days later they broke ground for the arsenal. On October 25, 1941 ground was broken for the Redstone Ordnance Plant. Apparently they did like the color of the ground, as well as being on the Tennessee River for transportation accessibility. The United States would not be at war for another 44 days, but war in Europe was well established for 23 months, as Germany forcibly invaded Poland on September 1, 1939. France and the Benelux countries had fallen to Germany in less than two months by the end of June 1940. England was threatened. The handwriting was on the wall for America, despite the voices of many to stay out of the fighting.

August 11, 1941 – The principal problem confronting the Huntsville Public Library was the increased demands for service made upon it by the building of an arsenal near the city by the Chemical Warfare Service of the War Department.

September 8, 1941 – It was agreed to empower the director to further develop the remodeling of the circulation room of the regional department. October 13, 1941 – It was reported that the contract with the Marshall County Board of Education had been approved and signed

Sep 13, 1941 – The director presented a schedule for classification of staff, to include rules and regulations governing vacations, sick leave, leaves of absences and appointments, which were approved.

The Japanese sneak attack on the Hawaiian Islands, December 7, 1941 started the United States on the path to being a world power, and dragged Huntsville along with it, to include our public library.

December 8, 1941, the day after the Japanese attack on Pearl Harbor, a "Non-Expansion Policy of the Regional Department" was presented by the director and approved by the board. The director gave a report on progress and conditions in the entire system with particular emphasis upon community co-operation, which was shown to be necessary for building toward the permanency of the library.

January 12, 1942 – It was approved by the board that the director could assume the local chairmanship of the Victory Book Drive in Madison and Jackson. The drive for books was a joint effort of the American Library Association, Red Cross, and the United Services Organization (U.S.O.). It was approved that the Huntsville Public Library should submit an application for membership in the American Library Association.

On March 6, 1942 the Huntsville Chemical Warfare Depot was established. From nothing, in less than one year Huntsville became a modest home to a small part of the Federal government. It would grow dramatically for the next 63 years, far beyond what anyone could have possibly imagined in our little town of 13,050 people, or among the Madison County population of 66,317. We did not know we were on our way. We only knew we were making chemical artillery shells, not a very glamorous business. At the peak of the war, there were about 11,000 people employed on the Arsenal, about half of them women. The change was dramatic, from 13,050 Huntsvillians to 11,000 workers just in the southwestern corner of Huntsville. The jobs were better paying than the cotton mills that dominated Huntsville industry.

March 9, 1942 – A request from Mrs. Marie Bankhead Owen of the Department of Archives and History in Montgomery for information about bombing and incendiary fires was presented. Action for protection against such disasters was discussed, and the director was instructed to make a report to the office requesting information.

April 13, 1942 – It was agreed that as many as two members of the library staff be sent to the meeting of the Alabama Library Association at Auburn, May 1-2.

June 9, 1942 – The Board approved the expenses of the director, Horace Moses, to attend the annual conference of the American Library Association to be held in Milwaukee, Wisconsin, June 22-27. October 13, 1942 – Horace Moses reported on the Conference in Milwaukee, at which he gave a paper, "A Regional Library in Transition," which was reprinted as four pages in the "Library Journal". A gift of books from the Fort Wayne, Indiana Public Library was reported by the director, the gift consisted of duplicates and over-stock from that library amounted to about 10,000 volumes.

The following letter from Horace Moses to the Superintendent of the Jackson County Schools demonstrated the contribution of the Regional Library System to the public schools in Jackson County, which was in addition to the services to the public libraries and book stops.

"June 15, 1942

I should like to make the following report to your Board of Education on the library work carried on in Jackson County with your schools.

During the school year 1941-1942 the Regional Library has served 21 rural schools in the County. The schools are:

Bryant	Long Island
Central	Macedonia
Dean's Chapel	Mt. Carmel
Dutton	Pisgah
Fackler	Pleasant View
Flat Rock	Princeton
Freedom	Rosalie
Hale's Cove	Trenton
Hollywood	Tupelo
Larkinsville	Woodville
Limrock	

The library truck has called every four weeks at each school during the school year, where books have been exchanged. Each teacher has been supplied with a classroom library, for the use of her pupils.

During each of the school months more than 2,000 books from the Regional Library have been read by the children of Jackson County distributed by the schools. In addition to this number there have been 35,609 books read by children drawn from the 18 public libraries of the County also maintained by the Regional Library. In all approximately 50,000 books have been read by the children of Jackson County since July 1941.

During the summer months the libraries operate reading clubs for the children to further encourage reading of good books. Last fall teachers and principals reported to us that the general reading ability of their children had greatly improved through this summer reading. Throughout the year the Regional Library with its books and services extends its work further along to the benefit of the schools, teachers and pupils of Jackson County. During these days of war, we are doing all we can to aid the government in bringing facts and figures before the public. This Library has been selected as one of 2,000 all over the country to act as an information center. We are bringing vital war information into every community of Jackson County. There were 39 locations provided library service in Jackson County. I certainly hope that no one in the county complained about the lack of book service.

We appreciate the fine co-operation given us by the officials of Jackson County, and shall look forward to a bigger and more profitable year in 1943, working together."[15]

On September 17, 1942 Mrs. A.J. Armstrong, of Stevenson, Alabama wrote a letter to the Regional Library director. She complained that the library was closed since April because the librarian left for a better-paying job. "It distresses me to see it closed so long when our people want the books so much. This is a project close to my heart because I was largely instrumental in getting it started. There were only two or three interested enough to help with the work of getting books donated & help collect and catalogue them. I am handicapped now with long sickness in the house & can't get out & work at things of this nature but I am still deeply interested & sorry to see the library closed so long." She went on to say that many people are anxious to have the library reopened, since the Bridgeport library is still open and the regional book truck passes through Stevenson on the way to Bridgeport. Mrs. Armstrong made several other points in her letter, and these will be covered by way of the letter to follow.[16]

Horace Moses, the director of the regional library, wrote back to Mrs. Armstrong in a letter, dated September 17, 1942. [Why the return letter was dated the same day as the incoming letter cannot be explained.] Moses' letter points out one of the basic facts about the library business, the locals may want the library, but it does not happen until they make commitments to make it happen. Libraries do not fall from heaven as some people might hope, they take money and commitment. Let me digress to make the point by an oft-told military speech-makers' anecdote. The difference between dedication and commitment? You want ham and eggs for breakfast? The chicken is dedicated to providing the egg. The pig is committed to provide the ham. After that short interlude, we return to Moses' letter.

"I was very happy to receive your letter in regard to the library at Stevenson. It is encouraging to us to know that the work we carried on was appreciated, and that the Library has been missed.

The Stevenson Library has long been a puzzle to us. From all indications it should have been an excellent little library. It was well housed, and we considered Miss Bogart one of the very best persons we had working for us. We supplied a larger number of books to Stevenson, in proportion to either Bridgeport or Scottsboro. In spite of these factors, the circulation record of Stevenson fell far behind any of the major stations which we were serving. We tried a number of inducements to raise this record with Miss Bogart's help, but none seemed to work out.

Over a year ago we made a particular effort to again arouse local interest in the Library. We are ever fearful of the continued existence of WPA, which furnishes our workers. Should this organization cease to function as a governmental agency, we wish to be in a position to carry on the library work independently. With this in mind, I sent Mr. Joseph Benson, acting then as my assistant to Stevenson, to interview a number of people. He met with a group of ladies, and it was our impression that one of the clubs was to act as sponsor for the Library. That was the last we heard of the movement.

When Miss Bogart was removed from the WPA Library Project, it seemed that our last personal contact with Stevenson was lost. We have had a number of letters from Stevenson people, recommending Mrs. McGuffy for the position. Yours is the first in which real concern has been shown in regard to the Library itself, and its continuance. That is the reason I am writing in such detail. We cannot open and operate a library, merely to give some worthy person employment through WPA. We are building for the future betterment of Stevenson, Jackson County, and this entire region.

We are vitally interested in re-opening the Stevenson Library. It has had a good start. We have always considered it as "temporarily" closed. We have not withdrawn the stock of books which we furnished. What we need now is the active interest of the people of the town, and upon this rests the future of the Library.

As I understand Stevenson is an incorporated town, with mayor and council. It has been our hope that all such towns would gain the official recognition of the town by the appointment of a Library Board, by the mayor and council. This, for instance, has been done at Bridgeport. It is true that there must be some sponsoring body in the community to bring this about. In Bridgeport a ladies club was responsible.

We will be happy to make every effort to secure Mrs. McGuffey or any eligible person, whom this Board may select to serve the Library. At the present time however we feel that some definite action must be taken by Stevenson, itself, as a community to make the Library a going institution. We will do all in our power to help this along but it should not evolve upon this organization to promote civic action in Stevenson.

Thank you so much for your letter. I hope that I have helped clarify the situation, and I want to again express our intention to help Stevenson have the finest little library in Northern Alabama, if that is what Stevenson wants."[17]

December 21, 1942 – There was discussion about the elimination of the Works Progress Administration (WPA), which was closed by April 24, 1943.

January 11, 1943 – A gift of $32.83 from the Lowndes' bequest was accepted by the board. Remember the Lowndes' fund from 1932?

February 16, 1943 – It was voted that with the conclusion of the Works Progress Administration, the hours of the adult department be established from 1 P.M. to 9 P.M. daily except Sunday. The hours for the children's department were established at 2:30 to 6 P.M.

Mrs. Mattie Darwin, the second librarian of the Huntsville Carnegie Library, retired after 25 years of service in March 1943. The library had several hundred books in 1917, which grew to 26,000-27,000 when Mattie Darwin retired. She was credited with helping the Daughters of the American Revolution (DAR) to establish their lineage more than any other person in Huntsville. Mrs. Darwin was a widow with three children in 1917, and was placed in charge of the library, which she ran for several years without help. She had been a teacher at the old private Butler school, so she had a strong interest in education and reading. The Darwin children spent most of their time at the library, as they and volunteers assisted much in marking books and doing other jobs for several years. How wonderful it must have been to grow up inside a library. Mattie Darwin started a whole generation of Huntsville children on the right road to reading.[18]

There was more to Mrs. Darwin's resignation than meets the eye. At the February 16, 1943 meeting, the board requested the director to investigate, and report a suitable standard for guidance in establishing an age limit for service in the Huntsville Public Library.

Yet, in a letter from Mrs. Darwin, which will be quoted below, she refers to a letter she received from the board dated February 23, 1943. Here is Mattie Darwin's letter of resignation:

"Huntsville, Ala, Feb 26th, 1943

To The Board of the Huntsville Public Library,

Dear Members of the Library Board,

I have today received your letter of Feb 23rd, 1943 and am herewith handing in my resignation as librarian to take effect March 1st, 1943 if that date meets with the pleasure of the Board.

I should like to express my thanks to each member of the Board for my twenty five years of service in the Library and for their unfailing consideration at all times.

These have been years of pleasure and satisfaction in service to my fellow citizens

I realize the *gravity of changing conditions* [This author's italics] which must take place in the Library, and its welfare will always be uppermost in my interests.

Very Truly Yours, Mattie P. Darwin"[19]

Back on September 13, 1941, there was an item about a new library staffing classification document. On April 13, 1943, six weeks after Mattie Darwin's resignation, the library board approved a revised classification document, which had generally the same information, but with the added statement, "Retirement. The board of the Huntsville Public Library, with other educational, industrial and governmental agencies, recognizes the age 65 as that of retirement. Upon attaining the age 65, it becomes necessary for the individual to notify the Board, if no record of age is evident. The board at such time may request retirement, or extend employment for a definite period, not to exceed 12 months. Continuous employment by the Huntsville Public Library ceases at age 65." Since there is no copy of the letter received by Mrs. Darwin, it is assumed that she received the news about the retirement at age 65 in that letter. She was probably shocked when those "changing conditions" were thrust upon her, but her graciousness was demonstrated.

Evidence points to age discrimination on the part of the aggressive director, Horace Moses, with the board's concurrence. A chronology of related events follows:

- September 13, 1941: A staffing classification document was introduced. There was no mention of mandatory retirement age. Mattie Darwin was 64 years and 9 months old.
- February 16, 1943: The director was requested by the board to investigate mandatory retirement ages.
- February 23, 1943: The board sent a letter to Mrs. Darwin, contents unknown.
- February 26, 1943: Mattie Darwin "resigned", citing "gravity of changing condition" (italics in her letter) in the above letter. She was now 67 years and 2 months old.
- April 13, 1943: Board approved a policy of mandatory retirement at age 65.

Mrs. Robert Cook (Mary Beirne Darwin), Mattie Darwin's daughter, said that her mother was suffering from chronic asthma and bronchitis during those years and was ready to "resign." Moses and the board were determined to be rid of the long-time librarian and they cleverly pressured her to resign before the new policy was implemented so they did not have to "grandfather" her. Some readers may not understand "grandfather," which means not retroactively enforcing a new policy. Mattie Darwin died in Huntsville on September 5, 1966.[20]

March 2, 1943 – The board was to request an appropriation of $150 per month to the city council for the employment of a trained librarian in compliance with the Code of the City of Huntsville: Chapter 27, Sec. 8-(d). The city council approved the amount requested. The possibility of a branch in West Huntsville in conjunction with the United Services Organization (USO) was discussed. It was voted to allow $35 in expenses for Miss Ethel Sauders of Louisiana State University Library School to visit Huntsville as a candidate for the librarian's job.

May 13, 1943. – Miss Ethel Sauders accepted the job of assistant director and head of the adult department.

June 15, 1943 – The library board agreed that the library should accept gifts of books only upon the understanding that such books should be made a part of the general library collection, and should not be shelved separately. The director was instructed to investigate a suitable bookplate to mark such books as might be given the library.

Eleven months after Horace Moses wrote a letter to the town of Stevenson about the library closure, he wrote another letter, but this one was to the principal of Bridgeport High School, Mr. D.L. Bell.

"I am writing you again concerning the future of the Bridgeport Library, as I understand that you were elected as Chairman of the Board of trustees.

It has come to my attention that the library is closed, and that its future seems doubtful. I am very sorry to hear this, as we have had great hopes for that library. This organization has maintained the library in Bridgeport for several years, as you know. We have made every effort to provide every assistance possible to continue its existence, growth and prosperity. If our efforts have failed we feel it has been through lack of local cooperation rather than negligence on our part.

We, through the regional program, can supply you with books and printed materials in sufficient quantities to far surpass your present needs. Individuals in the community have provided an excellent location for the library. All that remains is for the community itself to provide for the maintenance of the library. To continue this must be done. After five years hard work and interest on our part, we are loath to be faced with failure.

I shall visit Bridgeport Friday morning August 20th, and will call on you at the High School. I will appreciate it if you can bring together the interested members of your Board to discuss this situation. I feel that the failure of your library at Bridgeport would be tragic, but also it may well jeopardize the entire library program in Jackson County.

Again, let me ask your help and cooperation in furthering a very worth-while public and community activity."[21]

September 14, 1943 – The director was authorized to open a branch of the Huntsville Public Library, to be located in the Winston Street School, and to be served by a faculty member of that school, would be qualified in the judgment of the director, for the use of the Negro population of the city; said branch to be under the control of the Huntsville Public Library and to be considered a branch of that system in all respects, the branch to be designated as The Winston Street Branch. Miss Ethel Sauders presented a plan to increase the present periodical holdings of the adult department. The board approved the plan and Miss Sauders was instructed to put the plan into effect.

Gussie S. Finley, Scottsboro, wrote a letter to Horace Moses, September 24, 1943:

"In our effort to secure a Librarian, we find that we must have certain information from your office. We must have a report showing the number of books, circulation, number of readers, etc. It is supposed that you have such information in your files, as reports from the former Librarian. Will you please send this report at your very earliest convenience? It is very important that I have this information in hand by Tuesday September 28, 1943. Please give this matter your immediate attention. Thanks in advance."[22]

Horace Moses replied the next day:

"Your communication of Sept. 24, received, and as you do not state which library you refer to, and as I know there has been some effort to start the Colored library, I am giving you the information requested on that library. Should I be in error please write again.

Books: The library for the colored at Scottsboro has charged against it approximately 700 books from the Regional collection. A number of these may be in rural stations at present, as Horace Snodgrass had five such stations. I never received definite word from Horace as to how many he brought back into the Library in Scottsboro. In addition to the Regional books there were approximately 500 other books which have been given the Library.

Circulation: We have had no reports on work since December 1942. During twelve months of 1942 there were 16,872 books reported as read from that library. This figure includes the books read in the county. It was not possible for him to keep a separate count of Scottsboro alone in his report to us.

Registered readers: On his last report December 1942, Horace [Snodgrass] reported 711 member readers, registered in the library. There were undoubtedly some readers who were not registered. Of the 711, 306 were children and 405 adults.

I hope this is the information you desire. We will be very happy to help you with the library at any time, if someway can be found to keep it open."[23]

November 9, 1943 – After a discussion by all five members of the library board, it was agreed that an executive committee consisting of the chairman, treasurer, and secretary-director be authorized to conduct business for the library in the absence of a quorum at a regular board meeting or in the conduct of emergency business in interim between meetings. All actions will be reported to the board at the next regular meeting.

February 15, 1944 – The board voted, in his absence, a bonus of $150 for the director, in lieu of a salary increase, to be judged semiannually, contingent of a satisfactory financial condition of the budget.

April 11, 1944 – The board authorized the director to make a trip to various library centers in a search for a new assistant librarian. The board interviewed Mrs. Elizabeth Parks Beamguard, informally, as an applicant for the position of head of the adult department and assistant to the director.

June 13, 1944 – The resignation of Miss Ethel Sauders as head of the adult department and assistant to the director was accepted. Apparently the resignation was expected. Mrs. Beamguard was hired at a salary of $1,800 per year, with a salary adjustment, to allow for increased living costs, of $240 per year, to be paid in four quarterly installments to begin after three months of service. The salary adjustment was to be contingent upon the financial ability of the board to allow such payments from the budget.

The director gave a report covering his recent trip to Indianapolis and Chicago with visits to library centers. As a result of this report it was agreed that the board would begin a series of studies on local library service standards. Mrs. Robert J. Lowe, who was just appointed to the board in March, 1944, was appointed chairman of a "Post-War Planning Committee," to develop plans toward the improvement of the Huntsville Public Library, its organization, personnel and services. This was the beginning of a long tenure on the board for Mrs. Lowe.

On June 22, 1944, President Franklin D. Roosevelt signed the Servicemen's Readjustment Act into law. Congress had passed the bill earlier in the spring. For long after World War I, the veterans of the war were unhappy about the lack of support by the Federal government for their service and interrupted lives. In 1932 General Douglas MacArthur ordered the Bonus Expeditionary Force, veterans demanding a bonus, routed from their tents along the Anacostia River in Washington, D.C. That lesson was not forgotten.

As early as 1942 studies were under way to preclude such problems as occurred after World War I. It was estimated there would be up to 15 million men and women who had been serving in the armed services would be unemployed when the war ended. From that fear, one of the greatest pieces of social engineering in American history was developed. It would dramatically and directly affect Huntsville, and indirectly the library.

The Servicemen's Readjustment Act, now commonly called the GI Bill of Rights (GI is short for Government Issue), would help the veterans adjust to civilian life. The act provided tuition, subsistence, books and supplies, equipment, and counseling services for veterans to continue their education in school or college. Within seven years, approximately eight million veterans received educational benefits. Approximately 2,300,000 attended colleges and universities, 3,500,000 received school training, and 3,400,000 received on-the-job training. The number of degrees awarded by U.S colleges doubled between 1940 and 1950, and the percentage of Americans with bachelor degrees, or advanced degrees, rose from 4.6 percent in 1945 to 25 percent 50 years later. Many of those degrees were engineering degrees.

The GI Bill provided subsistence to the veterans, so they could be educated, married, and have children all at the same time, not sequentially. That placed a demand for housing, cars, refrigerators, stoves, and other consumer goods. It provided an immediate jump-start to the American economy, which was sustained to this day.

Many of those engineers and others came to Huntsville to work at Redstone Arsenal in the rocket and missile programs, which spawned the space program even as the Army's missile programs increased. Many of those people came in uniform for 6 months or 2 years, and stayed for the good civilian jobs. They are still here! They were not from the South, but from all over the country. They changed the slow moving culture into a faster one, as the military needed to get things done quickly to meet the national threats. More details will be in the next chapter.

"At its present stage, [1945] the Huntsville Public Library bids well to assume a place of leadership in the plan for national library development. In the past four years, the rural service has been solidified into a regular coordinated feature of county school systems, and plans are being made, according to Director Moses, to broaden the base of operations from the center in Huntsville.

The plan first established here has already been copied by the state extension departments of Georgia, Tennessee, and Missouri in their development programs. Its main idea, the integration of the library and its resources into established educational agencies, has had an important effect on recent library legislation in neighborhood states.

Several library authorities in other states are in close contact with the officials of the Huntsville Library, following each new development with interest. It is a recognized fact that the local program is serving as a guinea pig in an experiment which may revolutionize all library growth in postwar years.

Despite the widespread professional attention to developments in Huntsville, few people here are aware of it as an outstanding institution flourishing within their reach.

Only a small minority in the city, Mr. Moses says, are taking advantage of library resources comparable to those found in some of the best cities of the nation. Though operations are now under the handicap of a small and inadequate budget (for the purchase of books there is only $350 a year, plus fines, rentals, and gifts), the director expects better provision as local interest increases.

In the future, he point out, the city may well be proud of having sponsored what may become commonly known as the 'Huntsville plan' for library services."[24]

"LIBRARY SERVICE IN MADISON COUNTY

During the operational year 1943-1944 the Huntsville Public Library has given service to twenty-one communities and schools in the county outside the Huntsville area. In the city of Huntsville the Library has maintained service on a high level through the adult and Children's Departments and the Winston Street Branch (Negro). The units of the library located in the city cooperate closely with the work carried on in the county.

In the following rural schools in Madison County approximately 3,600 children have access to books from the extension service of the Library. During 1943-1944 these children have read 51,325 books, or on the average of 14 selected books per pupil. The schools served:

Big Cove	Murphy Hill
Elkwood	New Hope
Farley	New Sharon
Harvest	Owens Crossroads
Hurricane	Plevna
Madison	Pulaski Pike
Meridianville	Riverton
Monrovia	Walnut Grove

In five communities of the county the Library maintains book deposits making books available to rural readers. During the year several community libraries principally those located at New Hope and Madison were moved to the High School where greater use could be made of the books. The Library at Gurley through the activity of Mrs. A. F. Reams and members of the Study Club has rendered an outstanding service to the community. The rural communities served are:

Gurley	Toney
Big Cove	Skinnem
Meridianville	

The Winston Street Branch, located in the Winston Street School has served the colored population of the county through the rural colored schools.

During the year 1943-1944 a total of 93,066 books have been read in Madison County. Of this number 70,454 have been read by children, under the supervision of teachers and librarians."[25]

"LIBRARY SERVICE IN JACKSON COUNTY

In the year 1943-1944 from April 1 to March 31 the Regional Library Service has served seventeen rural schools throughout the county. This is an increase of seven schools over the number given service in 1942-43. In addition to this number receiving service directly from the bookmobile the Library Station at Rocky Springs served the school in that community.

During the year reported 2,998 children in the seventeen rural schools have read 38,919 selected books outside of school textbooks, or approximately 13 volumes each. The following schools have been given library service:

Davistown	Pleasant View
Dutton	Princeton
Flat Rock	Rosalie
Langston	Section
Larkinsville	Skyline Farms
Limrock	Trenton
Macedonia	Tupelo
Mt. Carmel	Woodville
Pisgah	

The Regional Library Service operates seven community library stations in Jackson County through cooperation with local governmental bodies and citizens. Of these the libraries of Bridgeport and Scottsboro are supported by the city councils, and are constituted a part of the cities' municipal activities, the other libraries are maintained through the active interest of public minded citizens who cooperate with the officials of the Regional Library Service. The community libraries in Jackson County are located at:

Scottsboro	Stevenson
Bridgeport	Concord
Rocky Springs	Rosalie
Mt. Carmel	

In the community stations which serve both adult and juvenile readers 26,013 books were read in the past year. Of this number 14,895 were read by adults and 11,118 were read by children.

Throughout Jackson County a total of 64,932 books were supplied and read through the work of the Regional Library Service. Of this number 50,037 were read by the children of the county who are the citizens of tomorrow."[26]

September 12, 1944 – The board approved the purchase of a 50-volume set of the Yale Chronicles of America at the price of $55.25.

One of the old materials in the archives of the library was a document signed by President Zachary Taylor, the 12th President of the United States, which gave citizenship to Lit_ho_e, a member of the Creek Tribe, as part of a treaty, June 13, 1850, between the Creeks and the United States.[27]

November 14, 1944 – The library received $71.75 from the Lowndes' Bequest. Apparently the library was a periodic beneficiary of money from the Lowndes' Bequest.

February 13, 1945 – The board requested an increase of $300 per month from the city council. The council countered with $56.66 per month, to allow for staff salary increases. The library board refused to accept the proposal.

March 13, 1945 – The library hired two clerks at $35 per month, another at $65 per month on a basis of 30 hours and a fourth clerk at $0.35 per hour to allow for $30 per month. One of the new hires quit a month later. The salary of Mrs. Beamguard - Professional was raised from $1,800 to $2,000 per year. The salary adjustment was discontinued. The salary of Miss Frances T. Jones –Sub-professional, as children's librarian was increased from $50 to $70 per month in view of her years of faithful service and approaching retirement age.

May 15, 1945 – The board voted to bind the files of *The Huntsville Times.*

June 12, 1945 – The director, Horace Moses submitted his resignation, effective July 21, 1945. [This author will miss Horace Moses' clear handwriting.] He moved to Mobile as head librarian in the Mobile Public Library. During his tenure of five years, the city-county appropriation increased from $5,000 to $12,000. The total book stock rose from 20,507 to 27,436. By 1954 Horace Moses had moved again and was director of the Topeka, Kansas Public Library. He gave an oral presentation to the American Library Association Buildings Committee in June 1954 about the planning for the new Topeka library building.[28]

June 27, 1945 – Mrs. Beamguard was elected as "Acting Director" at an annual salary of $2,400 per year. She was a trained librarian and was educated at the University of Tennessee, University of Chattanooga and Emory University.

Mrs. Beamguard announced plans to improve the collection and organization of historical material. A filing cabinet was recently purchased, which was made possible by the donation of $50 from an unidentified patron. The new filing cabinet will allow the materials to be locked up. Many of the old rare volumes were kept on shelves in the director's office in the basement. Mrs. Bessie Russell was assigned the task of arranging and cataloguing the material on hand. As soon as space permits, a room will be set up for the historical collection. The material came from many sources: loans, people cleaning out their attics and cluttered rooms, and garbage cans.

January 15, 1946 – The Board finally selected Mrs. Beamguard as permanent director, after considering one other application. Mrs. Beamguard's handwriting, as secretary, was not much to brag about from the perspective of this author.

Do you remember Mr. A.B. Adams, who opened his Rocky Springs' home as a book stop in the 1930s and was quoted at length earlier in this chapter? In 1946 he was still around and interested in books. On March 7, 1946 Elizabeth Parks Beamguard, the new director, wrote Adams a letter that she had more visits in Jackson County and wanted his address so she could find and talk to him. "Tell me how I can reach you, and the state of the roads." Earlier he lived three miles west of Bridgeport, but now his address was Route #1, South Pittsburg, *Tennessee.* The letter implies that he might donate a collection of his books, but perhaps there was less there than I imagined.[29]

The Huntsville Library received a letter from the Tupelo, Alabama, School, dated March 8, 1946. Tupelo was about 6 miles north of downtown Scottsboro, as the crow flies, and probably at least 7 miles by road. A map inspection of the 2004 road network in the area of Tupelo almost qualifies it as, "You can't get there from here," so try to imagine it in the mid-1940s.

"The roads are all right to our school now and if you can arrange to get us some books we would appreciate it. If our school is too much off your route for you to come to it, would it be possible to leave the books at Scottsboro for us? Anyway that you suggest we will be glad to cooperate if at all possible.

We have missed the visits of the Library this year, but are looking forward to some more good books to read in the near future."[30]

March was apparently a good month to write letters to the Huntsville Library. It received one from Ida E. Maxwell, from Estillfork, dated March 30, 1946. We met Ida Maxwell in the last chapter when she was a teacher in Scottsboro who went to her mountain home on weekends. Apparently Estillfork was her home, which is 19 miles west of Scottsboro on a straight line. Mrs. Maxwell wrote:

"I wish I could visit Huntsville and meet you, but I do not seem to be able to get away from here except Saturday and presume you are not in then. After I close school, perhaps I will able to come your way.

This is a peculiar spot on the globe. The school building is on the east side of Estill Creek and the children on the west side, and there has been nothing but a foot-log on which to cross the stream. You can guess how often there days of "no school." If it rains in Tennessee the foot-log is covered over. An overnight rain, if it's a hard one, and the waters are everywhere, and sometimes a whole week is lost. So my lot is a vexing one. However, one pier has been built, presume before many moons there will be a bridge there here. Enough complaining, however.

Now, my school will not close before or about June 1st, or May 24th, but we will return the books at any date you state your truck will be in Princeton. [A town six miles down the Paint Rock River] If you can drop me a line, I will send the books to Princeton by bus so they will not lay over there a long spell before being taken up by you.

The children have done much recreational reading in your books. I have them read ?---? Readers in the A.M. and your books P.M. Of course, the older children take your books home and the family reads them. The adults have not read so much this time because springtime and gardening which takes up their time.

But my First, Second and Third Grades have thoroughly enjoyed your books of their level of reading. And the books of today are so colorful and every day factual. Children's experiences, animal life, flowers and fruits.

Well, the more I read the more I love books and I sincerely wish everyone could learn to love reading. It is very disappointing to find people who just can not find time for reading – I am an old person but have read much of my life. I find there is still so much to read and learn."[31]

Even in 2004 it was difficult to go from Stevenson to Estillfork, so it's hard to imagine what it was like in the 1940s. Estillfork was two mountains northwest of Tupelo, about 5.5 miles south of the Tennessee border and up the Estill Fork of the Paint Rock River. If you want to go Estillfork, there are two basic options: 1. Take great desire and a detailed map; 2. Go as far as you can, then go even farther. But the Estillfork school was not in Estillfork, but about two miles farther north to Gray's Chapel Church, which was at the intersection of County Roads 175 and 140. At that intersection go east on CR 140 for 100 yards and you will prepare to cross Burke Creek. I've used the term prepare, because there will be some reluctance when you see the creek. The crossing was a rough mass of concrete, concealing three one-foot diameter pipes carrying water under the crossing. If there is much rain, you may have to drive through a little, or a lot, of water. In that area, when they say the creek is rising, take it seriously. Mrs. Alice Sisk, who in 2004 lived a little up the hill on the east side above the crossing about 200 yards south of the former school site, pointed out that the cable, concrete abutment (mentioned by Ida Maxwell in letter above) and two vertical I-beams still remain from a swinging bridge for pedestrians. The swinging bridge was the successor to the foot-log mentioned in the letter above.[32]

If for some reason you decide to take a country drive and want to visit Gray's Chapel and the creek crossing, take Alabama Route 65 north through Princeton to Swaim, where it intersects with Alabama Route 146. A slight jog to the right and you will catch (I hope) County Road 9, go north about six miles and you will come up a rise and see on your right, Prince's General Merchandise, Est 1943, "If we ain't got it, You don't need it!" The door is always open at the store because the store is closed. Perhaps you will go there on a morning, as I did, because the local men play cards in the old store. I stopped in and said, "Excuse me for interrupting your card game. Did any of you go to Ida Maxwell's school?" One fellow replied, "He and I did." and played a card. He said, "I walked three and a half miles down from Dotson Cove, Franklin County, Tennessee to go to school," and played another card. No one else added anything. I thanked them and drove off, feeling good that I had not interrupted their card game. Very shortly after you pass Prince's, there will be a fork in the road. As the baseball player Yogi Berra said, "When you come to a fork in the road, take it." In this case, take the left fork, as the right fork goes down hill and crosses the creek at Freedom Baptist Church.

March 11, 1946 – The overdue book problem was hoped to be solved by furnishing a list of books six weeks overdue to the policemen who would pick up the books as they cruised about the city. The newspaper would have a story about the new approach.

People have also been giving books about genealogy as interest in the subject increases. Charles Leonard Nordyke gave *Old Homesteads and Historic Buildings, Genealogy and Family Lore*. Mrs. Thomas Hardie Seay gave *Francis Epps, Her Ancestors and Descendants*, by Eva Turner Clark. There were also many old Huntsville newspapers that were saved over the years. Other representative materials included three volumes of poetry by Miss Howard Weeden, a poem by Virginia Clay, and *Messages and Papers of the Confederacy*, complied by James D. Richardson.[33]

The library board minutes during the period mid-1946 to mid-1950 were not available in the Huntsville Public Library archives.

In 1946 the library had approximately 30,000 volumes, and the circulation was 168,836 items. There were 15,085 registered cardholders. In 1946 the library was open Monday through Saturday, 9 a.m. to 9 p.m. Mrs. Beamguard, in charge of the adult and regional departments, was assisted by Mrs. W.E. Haney and Mrs. C.E. Russell. Miss Frances T. Jones was in charge of the children's department, which was open only from 1:00 to 6:00, Monday through Friday, and 9:00 to 6:00 on Saturday. There was a story hour on Saturday afternoon and a vacation-reading club in the summer.[34]

The American Library Association (ALA) adopted a Library Bill of Rights in 1939. It was strengthened in 1941 and a broader version was adopted on June 16, 1948. It was amended on February 2, 1961 and January 23, 1980. The Bill of Rights was reaffirmed by the ALA Council on January 23, 1996, which is quoted below.

"Library Bill of Rights

The American Library Association affirms that all libraries are forums for information and ideas, and that the following basic policies should guide their services.

I. Books and other library resources should be provided for the interest, information, and enlightenment of all people of the community the library serves. Materials should not be excluded because of the origin, background, or views of those contributing to their creation.

II. Libraries should provide materials and information presenting all points of view on current and historical issues. Material should not be proscribed or removed because of partisan or doctrinal disapproval.

III. Libraries should challenge censorship in the fulfillment of their responsibility to provide information and enlightenment.

IV. Libraries should cooperate with all persons and groups concerned with resisting abridgement of free expression and free access to ideas.

V. A person's right to use a library should not be denied or abridged because of origin, age, background, or views.

VI. Libraries which make exhibit spaces and meeting rooms available to the public they serve should make such facilities available on an equitable basis, regardless of the beliefs or affiliations of individuals or groups requesting their use."[35]

Carl H. Milam, the librarian of Birmingham Library from 1913 to 1919, was elected executive secretary of the American Library Association from 1920 until 1948 and dominated the association as no other had done before or since. He was an effective spokesman for the organization and supported many library causes and laid the foundation for future ALA activities. Milam was instrumental in the ALA's involvement with the Tennessee Valley Authority and, therefore, indirectly influenced Huntsville's participation with the TVA.[36]

The folks in Jackson County continued to have trouble supporting libraries. On September 23, 1947, the regional and Huntsville library director, Elizabeth Parks Beamguard, sent a letter to the five Jackson County commissioners, chaired by Judge J.W. Stuart.

"As there had been no word from your Court concerning your appropriation for the incoming year, the Chairman of the Library Board, Mrs. Claude H. Davis, called yesterday during our Board meeting with the City Council.

We asked for an increase because we felt that increased cost of service and book purchase justified it; we stated adequate service could not be given to your county for less than last year's appropriation. To say that I am disappointed is to give a grave understatement; I am shocked that you should feel you could afford to cut the appropriation.

Your people need roads – I am the first to speak for that. Your people need schools, new buildings, and increased salary schedules. You, above others, should know, no people live by bread alone – and need for the education of our people to think straight, to live beyond petty personalities and local political squabbles, ranks high in the entire South, and gravely so in Mississippi, Alabama, and Georgia. Progress has been made, but not enough to make it stable, and it is with deep personal pride that I feel that I had a minute part in it. To retreat is unthinkable, and while it is impossible to give the service that I could take pride in, I shall make every effort to keep this part of our educational program as near the standard as possible.

It will be with sincere regret that I shall be forced to tell each of the schools on our next trip that we will not have the quality of books that they had been expecting, and that our service has been curtailed rather than expanded.

I appreciate the demands upon your court. I only hope that the next few years will not be as rocky as the past few have been, and that with your present Judge and your four men standing squarely together, will bring Jackson County to a firm and steady financial basis. You represent excellent communities and carry heavy responsibilities – I feel sure that as soon as you have steadied your resources, you will watch carefully for the best interests of your people. It has been a pleasure to work with your people. They are so appreciative and so eager that any undue effort is a reward within itself.

In spite of this disappointment and crippling handicap, you will have my utmost co-operation for this next year."[37]

Dear loyal readers, Eliza Hackworth was still at the Scottsboro library when she wrote the following letter to the regional director, now Elizabeth Parks Beamguard:

"Library_near closing time, January 5, 1948

Dear Eliza beth Beamguard"

(The typewriter don't write well for me, either.)

Since you didn't come, today, after re-reading your letter, did you want me to write you that it was alright to come to-day? I didn't get the letter until Saturday afternoon, so I didn't have time to write and I just took it for granted that you would come so I got ready for you....Then the other paragraph about the way Jackson County has acted. I didn't know anything about that and I don't know about the situation. I mean the reason and all, for you have never discussed that with me and Mattie Lou and I have both been so busy that she hasn't mentioned it to me either. But is there is any possible way for us to help in talking to the Commissioners or helping them to get 'Library minded' _ maybe that's one thing that they don't realize just how grand it is for us and how much a lot of us appreciate it...."[38] This was the last communication from Eliza Hackworth to the regional library directors that will be cited, as she was then on her third director.

Eliza was a determined librarian. Just read her letter of April 26, 1949:

"Miss Ophelia Little, **Astoria, Oregon** [at Columbia R. & Pacific Ocean]

Dear Miss Little,

You have failed to return to the Library two books which you checked out, The Home Book of Verse by B.E. Stevenson volume 1 and Tony's Scrap book by Wons. These were due March 8, 1949 which is seven weeks to-day or thirty-five days and at two cents a day this makes a total of one-dollar and forty cents for both books.

We are a part of the Regional Library Service of Madison and Jackson Counties. So the Regional Director and the Board of Revenue are backing me in giving you this choice of either returning the books at once (and if you do this we will not charge you and further overdue than today) with the overdues or paying with money order the full amount of the cost of both books which will be: six-dollars and ten cents for the volume of Poetry and One-seventy-five for Tony's Scrap Book, making the total seven-eighty-five.

I am very much disappointed in you that you would neglect a trust in this manner _ I have been by your boarding house and you did not leave them there _. However, we are giving you this chance now to redeem your reputation with us by returning the books immediately."[39]

There was no information on how the matter was resolved. You have to admire Eliza Hackworth for her persistence in all matters. Eliza resigned from the library in 1951. She worked as a features writer for the Scottsboro newspaper, did book reviews once a week and was active in book clubs and music clubs. Eliza told her cousin, Nellie, "I'm not like these people out there." She played the piano for the nursing home entertainment. She died on December 30, 1999 at the Jackson County Nursing Home at age 95.

April 10, 1948 – The board voted to contribute $40 to the American Library Association for its library fund.

The annual meeting of the Alabama Library Association (ALA) [notice we have 2 ALAs, but later in the century the Alabama version changed to ALLA] met in Huntsville in the spring of 1949. Mrs. Gretchen Schenk, president of the ALA, stated there were plans to establish scholarships for students wishing to study library science. Both the University of Alabama and Auburn offer minors in library study, but students wishing a major must go out of state. Mrs. Schenk pointed out that job openings in library work now far outnumber the number of applicants for such jobs. That statement was both good news and bad news. The number and size of libraries was on the increase, but the system was not producing enough qualified people to do the work.

On November 16, 1949, Elizabeth Parks Beamguard, the director of the Huntsville library and regional library service, wrote a letter, but without an addressee. The letter appears to be to the members of the board of education in Jackson County, and perhaps others. She tells them the facts of life regarding the bookmobile services.

"We had asked the Jackson County Commissioners to make their appropriation to the Regional Library Service for the usual $100.00 per month with an increase of $25.00 per month, and to meet Madison County in the buying of a new bookmobile. I feel that you, and the persons who understand the program should know what is facing the library program. It is understood by me, that at the present the County Commissioners plan to discontinue the program entirely.

I feel they do not know what a library program means to a county, and particularly where there is no county program of its own, nor library program in the school system. We have had the Madison County Department of Education to find out from the state just what credit is given to the schools with library service, but we do know that schools without service lose prestige, and professional rating. The loss to the children and the teachers is something that you folks would thoroughly understand, and could tell them better than I could.

We are sorry there has been no more personal contact, but were the facts and figures studied, we have gone beyond the call of duty for a long time. The program, of course could be dropped, and a county librarian employed, and in such case a county collection. This is an expense that the commissioners may not be aware of. A trained librarian, would expect $2,000.00 minimum, and then more, is my experience, for I have been trying to find one we could afford. A collection of books to serve a county runs about $5,000.00 for the initial collection, and there is the cost of binding, replacement, supplies, transportation, etc.

As you know, the book truck has been in a bad condition ever since I have been in the state, and it certainly has not improved with age, It has been operated at the expense of the City of Huntsville, and Madison County, been kept in condition at the City garage. We have long operated at a loss in Jackson County and only the interested and the need of the schools have kept us going. The increase in the school's appropriation helped defray the cost of books, but your departments $110.00 just can't keep the whole program going, nor is that your job alone. It is a county library, and the county needs to bear its share.

I have been told by authoritative sources that the county can afford to support the program, but evidently they do not realize what the program is, for they are planning to drop it.

If you folks want the service continued, you will have to see the commissioners on the idea. To them, I am an outsider. But as you know, it is your county program, I merely deliver the materials. Tell them, if you want it, tell them what it means to the schools and to the community."
I am sure they just do not understand. Will you let me hear from you, also?
Sincerely,
Elizabeth Parks Beamguard, Director"[40]

How to Use the Dewey Decimal System

The Dewey Decimal System organizes information into 10 broad areas, which are broken into smaller and smaller topics. Different topics are assigned numbers, known as "call numbers." For example, "Animals" are given the number 599. To see what books the library currently has in on animals, go to the non-fiction shelves and find the books that have a 599 as part of their call number. A list of some of the information you can find in the different Dewey Decimal areas, appears below.

You can learn more about the Dewey Decimal System and how it works in the book *The Dewey Decimal System* by Allan Fowler. The call number for this book is: J 025.431 Fo.

Dewey Decimal System

*000 General Knowledge

Almanacs, Encyclopedias, Libraries, Museums, Newspapers ---

*100 Psychology and Philosophy

Death & Dying, Ethics, Feelings, Logic, Making Friends, Optical Illusions, Superstitions-

*200 Religions and Mythology

Amish, Bible Stories, Christianity, Judaism, Islam, Quakers, Shakers ...

*300 Social Sciences and Folklore

Careers, Customs, Environment, Families, Government, Manners, Money, Recycling ...

*400 Languages and Grammar

Chinese, English, French, German, Italian, Japanese, Sign Language, Spanish ...

*500 Math and Science

Animals, Biology, Chemistry, Dinosaurs, Fish, Geology, Insects, Physics, Planets, Plants

*604 Medicine and Technology

Computers, Engineering, Farming, Health, Human Body, Manufacturing, Nutrition...

*700 Arts and Recreation

Architecture, Crafts, Drawing, Games, Jokes, Music, Puppets, Songbooks, Sports

*800 Literature

Children's Literature, Plays, Poetry, Shakespeare, Writing ...

*900 Geography and History

Biographies, Countries, Native Americans, States, Travel, Wars ...

The last decade provided the basic building blocks for an even greater library system in the future. Three professionally trained librarians made their mark in Huntsville, with both operational discipline and outreach services. The Carnegie Library did not physically expand, but the philosophy of greater service to the community was infused into the spirit of the personnel. The stage was set for the surprises of the next decade.

Chapter 5

Space Comes to Huntsville

*"Thou must have full knowledge of what is given to thy charge. The first duty of a librarian
is to strive, in his time, as far as possible, to increase the library committed to him.
Let him beware that the library does not diminish, that the books in his charge do not
in any way get lost or perish. Let him repair by binding books that are damaged by age.
Let him know the names of the authors."*

Unknown Medieval English librarian
A History of Libraries in the Western World
Elmer D. Johnson

The military activities at Redstone Arsenal during World War II gave no indication of the future of the military in Huntsville, and how it would transform the city and county in the years ahead. There was absolutely no truth to the rumor that in the mid-1950's the president of the Huntsville Chamber of Commerce said, "Thank God for the military-industrial complex."

The Huntsville Public Library circulated some 3,000 more books than Chattanooga during the year ending June 30, 1950, Mrs. Elizabeth Beamguard, head librarian, announced. The Huntsville total was 265,108 books. The total included the county branch service, the Negro branch, and the main circulation desk. The Dulcina DeBerry Negro branch issued 3,593 adult and 1,877 children's books. The county library service, which included Madison and Jackson counties, brought 186,325 volumes to 38 schools and 4 book stations. This total also included circulation branches in Stevenson and Bridgeport.[1]

"Library service in Jackson County has weathered six fires, five close-outs, poverty and rejection, but a new Bookmobile, new books and a stabilized schedule, shows what the interest of children and citizens is capable of doing. The new Bookmobile, which was made possible by an appropriation from Jackson and Madison Counties, is a reality.

Since November, 46,000 miles has been covered by the Bookmobile and 10,000 books passed through the hands of the Bookmobile Librarian and the school children of the two counties.

One only has to see the enthusiasm and eagerness in such communities as Flat Rock, Mount Olive, Princeton, Macedonia, Dutton and Trenton, to know what the books mean to them.

In January (1951), approximately 7,000 books were distributed in the two counties. Of this number, approximately 1,876 were non-fiction and 5,624 were fiction. This record is incomplete as no report has been received from three schools. The handicaps throughout Jackson County are typified by the incidents that occurred in Stevenson. Five different times the community started up a library in local quarters and five times the quarters had to be taken back by the owners for personal business. Finally it was housed in the City Hall through the courtesy of the City Fathers, so that 500 books were available for the people throughout the rural section, only to have a fire in November, only to have the library closed again. Hardly had plans been made for the bookmobile to be on hand when quarters were repaired for the library. The fact that through six movings and two fires, only 23 books were unaccounted for is most remarkable. In Bridgeport, the library burned twice. The people of the town housed the library in the basements of churches and finally found a place for it in the City Hall.

Because of this interest, the appropriation for library service was increased so that for this year the Jackson County Court of Revenue and the Department of Education set aside $1800.00 each, which together with the appropriation of $6,000.00 from Madison County, provided for the reorganization of library service. Now library service has been set up this year in an organized business manner, whereby fifty-six stops in the two counties are visited approximately every four weeks."[2]

The amount of historical material in the library was steadily increasing, and therefore, the collection drew more interest from the patrons. Miss Lucille Griffith, assistant professor of history at Alabama College in Montevallo, visited the archives to gather material for her book, *Yours to Death, the Civil War Letters of John W. Cotton*. Dr. Everett Dick, head of the history department at Union College in Lincoln, Nebraska, spent several hours looking through the material. He was the author of six books on Southern frontier life. Two of his books mentioned Huntsville, *The Sod House Frontier* and *The Dixie Frontier*. The name of the donor cited in 1945 who gave $50 was identified as John Fuller Trump of Springfield, Ohio. He also donated two copies of Cincinnati newspapers from 1861 and 1865.[3]

In June 1951, the Dulcina DeBerry Negro Library Branch moved to 224 Church Street, where it shared a building with the Church Street Community Center. The library was on the second floor.[4]

"The following bookmobile schedule [Madison County] is announced, with the time of arrival at each station given. People are urged to meet the bookmobile to make personal selections if they desire. TELL YOUR NEIGHBOR

A special book needed by an individual, or a school, may be requested by phone, or by post card. The book will be brought on the next trip, or mailed out from the office. PLEASE TELL YOUR NEIGHBOR. Address: Box 275, Phone: 477.

The following is the Bookmobile schedule for 1951-1952: [Times and days not shown.]
ROUTE STOPS

No.1	Redstone Park	No. 6	Farley School
	New Hope Station		New Hope School
	Cave Springs Station		Owens Crossroads School
	Big Cove Station		Big Cove School
No. 2	Meridianville Station	No. 7	Monrovia School
	Hazel Green Station		Harvest School
	Skinnum Station		Madison School
No. 3	Maysville Station	No. 8	Riverton School
	Harvest Station		New Market School
	New Market Station		Plevna School
No. 4	Madison Cross Roads Station	No. 9	Central School
	Harvest Station		Gurley School
	Madison Station	No. 10	Meridanville School
No. 5	Pulaski Pike Station		Hazel Green School
	Madison Crossroads School		Walnut Grove School
	New Sharon School"[5]		

The library's newsletter in late 1951 reported that the German rocket scientists and engineers, recently arrived from Fort Bliss, Texas, have been cultivated by the library through personal contacts, reading lists, and staff efforts. "We felt if we made good happy citizens of them we had won many points in being good citizens. Reading lists were based on local interests, and national holidays, food, thought, ideals. The response in use has been tremendous. Our work load in the adult department has almost doubled. The night load has doubled. As many as 38 men sit at night to read, or come in to browse, or 'just visit'. This is their headquarters. On rainy Saturday mornings by actual count 34 men came before noon to get books, to read, or reference. This is quite a load for so small a community, and so small a library. This does not include women and children."[6] The above situation should have warmed the hearts of the librarians, a full library! Based on the dominance of the German male, it is very possible that he would act as the "family reader" and sign out books to be read by his wife and children, rather than them coming in to make their own selection. This custom was practiced in Germany.[7]

The newsletter writer probably did not realize that most of the German men were university-trained engineers. They were men who understood the value of education. They later organized a symphony in Huntsville, because that was part of their culture, despite Americans' opinions of Germans during World War II. They organized a Lutheran Church, since that was the major religion in Germany but Huntsville did not have one. The German group, with their dependents, moved from El Paso, Texas to Huntsville between April and November 1950. Huntsville's population in 1950 was 16,437, but began to expand as the rocket program at Redstone Arsenal brought 500 military, 120 government civilians, and several hundred employees of General Electric, the prime contractor for the Army. The Germans joined organizations and put their children in local schools. They also hiked through the woods, because that was (and still is) a national custom in Germany. It is difficult to imagine ordinary Huntsvillians hiking through the woods on Sundays in 1950.[8]

The arrival of the Germans and the expanded federal government presence was an economical and social turning point for Huntsville and Madison County. The provincial society of the old conservative South was about to change in Huntsville. . The power of a few Alabama politicians to thrive by keeping the poor whites and Negroes from gaining an education and improving their economic conditions was about to change in Huntsville. The people who looked back to the Civil War, and why they lost it, as the focus of their lives were now faced with a rapidly changing world. The Germans and the federal government were now talking about going into space, a ridiculous idea to most Americans and totally foreign to Alabamians. Now the foreigners were in the community. The number of jobs was increasing and many of them paid well. Huntsville was about to separate itself economically and culturally from the rest of Alabama.

The population of Madison County increased from 66,317 in 1940 to 72,903 in 1950 as most of the workers at Redstone Arsenal were local folks. That will not be true in the 1950s as cited above, as the stage was set for the future by the GI Bill discussed in the previous chapter. Some statistics relating to the Huntsville library, circa 1950, but note that the census cited was for 1940 (the last available before the 1950 census), are shown below.

"Per Annum. income of the H.P.L. $1,500.00
City of Huntsville (Salaries)   500.00
City of Huntsville (Maintenance)   500.00
Madison Co. Bd. of Commissioners (Books)   350.00
Fines and rentals   300.00
Gifts (Individual and groups)   2,900.00
Population of Huntsville and Environs
1940 Census figures

City of Huntsville   13,171
Mill villages (Total)   <u>11,304</u>
Greater Huntsville   24,515
Book Stock of the Huntsville Public Library (Estimate)
Adult department
Fiction   4,378
Non-fiction   <u>2,600</u>
             6,978
Children's Department 1,000
Total   7,978
Registered Borrowers (Including children.)
City of Huntsville   4,320
Mill villages   <u>3,004</u>
Total   7,324
PERCENTAGES

Expenditure per capita		Circulation per capita 1940	
City of Huntsville	22¢	City of Huntsville	1.4
Greater Huntsville	11¢	Mill Villages	.9
		Greater Huntsville	1.1
Books owned per capita		Circulation per Reg. borrower	
City of Huntsville	.06	City of Huntsville	4.3
Greater Huntsville	.03	Mill Villages	3.1
		Greater Huntsville	3.8

Registration
City of Huntsville   3.1%
Mill villages   3.9%
Total   3.3%"[9]

"The loan of books from the Negro library to schools and communities has been set up. Good fellowship as well as other library values, has been created by this effort. Excellent attitudes and 'working together' feeling has come by this. Books can be mailed out from the DeBerry branch or called for by the schools needing classroom collections. A county-city integration of a reading program, book week and education week, is conducted by all white and Negro schools."[10]

September 5, 1950 – The library board issued the following statement regarding the Jackson County contract:

"The Library will make no further contacts for appropriation inasmuch as all that can be done has been done, and now it is the Court of Revenue that is to make the report. Only satisfactory amount of money, for instance, $300 per month from the entire county would make it satisfactory to continue relationships. The library office is not to contact the court of revenue.

The Board further suggested to the director that they stood on record as feeling all responsibility of continuing contacts rests with said county. If no word was heard, contact would be made to pick up books, having been worked out on some given basis of 25 60 3/5(?)"

The brouhaha between Madison County and Jackson County about library services and the payment of those services continued. The State Board of Education encouraged Mrs. Beamguard to help support the Jackson County attempts to receive better library service, both from public libraries and school libraries. She believed she offended Judge Stuart of the Jackson County Court of Revenue because she presented considerable evidence that the people of

Jackson County wanted the services, but the Judge and the commissioners did not provide adequate support, for which they were embarrassed. Mrs. Beamguard did not go to further meetings, so the disagreements did not become personal. There were further meetings, but no evidence was found of the results. This short synopsis is from a full-page description from Ms. Beamguard.[11]

The director, Elizabeth Parks Beamguard, wrote a letter to Roy Stone, Chairman, Madison County Board of Commissioners, on September 11, 1950:

"In submitting our request for 1950-1951 appropriation for operation of library service in Madison County we attach a copy of cost of operation, and a comparison of other counties and their appropriation. [not discovered in archives] We feel you should expect more of us than these counties expect of their library, for our county is so much ahead in every respect.

It has long been the habit of some institutions to ask for more than they expect to get, but that seems an insult to the intelligence of the appropriating Board; we have submitted actual cost. We show you that the cost is $4,126.00.

In the past years we have given what we consider skimpy service, and even at that the existing staff had to work overtime, and have lost two good workers because of inadequate salary. One cannot keep trained workers for $125 a month. The state has more requests for trained librarians than they can fill. The least a graduate librarian will accept is $2,820.00. You will see that we have asked for $4,000 to keep the program in action with adequate service to the people all over our county.

Thank you for all the fine things you have helped us do in the past.

We want you commissioners to help us plan the service in your areas, we want you to look over our reports. It is your contribution and service to your people."[12]

Bravo, Elizabeth.

Elizabeth Beamguard attended the Southeastern Library Association in Atlanta in the fall of 1950. She wrote a memo to the Board describing her experiences:

- Hoyt Galvin sent each of you his love, and to tell you he has baby girl. He is happy, and doing well. He remembered so many people and things, and so interested in how you folks are. He and I were on the Public Library Program, he debating and I the secretary.
- The librarian in any library has need of functioning as such, with clerks or untrained workers doing clerical tasks. They must know the economic backbone of the community in which they operate, and not how to file cards.
- A guest psychologist said that in the stress of living today it was much more important to know the factors behind housing than to know how to read Latin.
- The following needs were underlined over and over:
  - What is the living situation, the cost of overhead, the availability of housing and the reasons for each, in your own community?
  - What is the wage situation, what is the labor attitude? A country's security rests in a far greater manner than we realize upon the nation's paycheck, for therein lies health, mental peace, security, or the lack of these.
  - What is the health of the community? Why? Mental and physical well-being affect national security and international policy.
  - What of the moral quality of the community? Physical morality would take care of itself, if mental morality existed. Honesty of mind, spiritual quality of living. These affect the various mediums of propaganda. Mental honesty overshadows all the community welfare.[13]

These factors were stressed as things of local importance, but actually underlying the war shadows of the moment. The Korean War started 2 days short of 4 months before Beamguard dated her memo. International affairs, of whatever nature, were in reality based upon the community of all parts of the world. Librarians must realize and act upon the knowledge that they are one of many cogs in a wholesome propaganda machine for mental and physical health, kindly human relationships. Beamguard's conceptual and strategic thinking allowed her to move to greater positions of responsibility, and Huntsville's loss.

There were 14 outlying stations in the Regional Library Service in the summer of 1951. All of the stations in the two counties of Jackson and Madison were visited once in April and May. Two of the stations were added in May. One was located in Vandiver's store in New Market. The library was on the balcony and had more volumes than most of the stations located in a grocery store. Approximately 75 volumes were left there. The other station opened was at the Virginia McCormack Center in West Huntsville. Approximately 125 volumes were left there.[14]

July 17, 1951 – The director of the University of Alabama, Huntsville Center, wishes to say as a matter of record, were ever conditions such that it were possible, the Center wishes to be considered as an applicant for space.

Below is a report from the Regional Library Service, Huntsville Public Library, in Huntsville, to the Madison and Jackson county commissioners and boards of education:
"Report for the months of November and December, 1950 for the Regional Library Service in the counties of Jackson and Madison.
The bookmobile was not ready for operation until November 20.
14 routes covering the 56 stops were set up.
7 routes are Jackson County and 7 are in Madison County.
45 schools are serviced.
11 stations are serviced. This includes Scottsboro Public, Stevenson Public and Bridgeport Public.
3 of these stations were set up in the communities of Meridianville, Gurley and Hazel Green. These stations were serviced in the old W.P.A. days. Service was discontinued because there was no place to leave the books. Now, in each instance they are left in a prominent grocery store of the community.
3 stations were reopened. They have been closed for a short period because of no place to put the books. These books are also housed in grocery stores.
All of these schools and stations were visited once between Nov. 20 and Dec. 18. Christmas holidays followed. There are four to five weeks between each visit.
On the first visit a complete inventory was taken at each stop. This was quite difficult because of the loss of books due to fires in the past several years at the following places; Stevenson, Bridgeport, Woodville, Toney, Elkwood.
Library Service for Negroes within the 2 counties: *No direct book loan is offered from the bookmobile, because of state law.* [Author's italics] However, a separate library is maintained by the City of Huntsville as a branch of the Huntsville Public Library. This is called the Dulcina DeBerry, and occupies a building owned by the city. Through this Negro Library Branch, county library service is offered to any and all schools. The teachers may and do borrow classroom collections. A Negro library in Jackson County burned several years ago. It has not been replaced because of lack of funds.
In November approximately 5000 books were distributed among the stops in the two counties. In November a total of 6034 books were reported as being read. Of this number 2054 were read

in Jackson County and 3980 in Madison County. In December a total of 5377 books were reported as being read. Of this number 5203 were read in Jackson County and 3174 in Madison County. These figures are incomplete because 12 reports failed to arrive at this office."[15]

Excerpts from the December 1951 regional library report to the Madison County commissioners and board of education are below:

"...One of the lower grade teachers at Madison, Ala. Reported an almost unbelievable number of 1286 books read. This is quite remarkable but authentic as the lower grades children handle the books over and over during the month.

Number of books reported read:

County schools	12,780
County stations	977
Total	13,757

Where space is available in a store, filling station or home, books are used more because access to the books is possible at the personal convenience of the individual. No space is available yet in Maysville, Madison, Ala., or New Hope. Negroes in Madison have asked for books. We plan to select a collection from the Negro Library and put them on the truck, thus giving them books too; but books from their own collection. We want your approval of this. We have found that they really want to read. The city set up a Negro library, so there would be no confusion. Six individuals at Madison have asked about this. Experience has proven to us that the best service occurs with a stationary collection. We hope to have such a collection in the above mentioned communities when space is available...."[16]

January 8, 1952 – The director, one member of the board, and the library chairman of the city council met to discuss the inability of the library to carry its load under the present appropriation, which was much the same as four years ago. The library would be forced to close one day per week to get its work done. This was a wake-up call to the city.

May 13, 1952 – The city approved and sent an additional $150 per month, and the library replied that it would keep open six days per week until the end of the fiscal year. Interest was shown for new stations at Union Grove, Monrovia, New Sharon and Owens Cross Roads, with Negro service requested for consideration at Blutcher's Cove and Madison. It was reported that Negro library service from the book truck was possible by shelving one section with a collection from the DeBerry Library at Madison.

Some recent additions to the library's historical collection in 1952 are described. Three papers ready by Mrs. Lilie Bibb Greet on "War Days in Huntsville – 1862 to 1865." Copied from the originals, which are owned by Mrs. C.M. Stanley, Montgomery, who is Mrs. Greet's daughter, the papers tell about General Sherman and Bishop Lay, first rector of the Church of the Nativity; about Lilie Bibb's war experiences – the burning of the Limestone creek bridge and her subsequent arrest and trial; and about the fidelity of the Negroes to the white people of the South during the war. A reprint of a letter from Joseph Holt on the policies of the general government, the pending revolution, its objects, its probable results if successful, and the duty of Kentucky in the crisis. Included among the general historical and rare book items are two volumes of *Rural Life* contributed by Mrs. Jean Hall. Published in London in the early 1800s, these books contain more than 100 steel engraving prints, a complete system of "modern veterinary practices," as well as "authentic information on modern farming, shooting and angling." One other addition is noteworthy because it was published in London in 1928 and has a long title and subtitle, which was prevalent in that era. The author was Israel Worsley and title was a mouthful, *A View of the American Indian – Their General Character, Customs, Religious Rites and Traditions: Showing Them to be the Descendents of the Ten Tribes of Israel – The Language of*

Prophecy Concerning Them and the Course by Which They Traveled. Authors of the era wanted you to know the complete story, before they told it. Such long titles have a certain cachet to them, compared to the 3-4 word titles of today.[17]

The director wrote a memo to the library board members, which discussed the interaction of the library board and the city's board of education to provide books and libraries in schools. "It is so good that two Boards, so friendly, with mutual respect may discuss our policy. This is the result of splendid professional relations throughout the year. We have now have a program that has grown from a state of apathy to the point where every school community in the county is requesting a library of their own. This is a tremendous compliment to our influence, and it is certainly a tribute to the Library Board that growth of this service, and the execution of it has been left entirely to the Public Library...the Department of Education has just left it to us. Of course this has only made us work harder...and the staff of the entire Library has felt the professional and moral responsibility of doing everything possible to serve."[18]

Libraries, and library buildings, are not just places to go to read or checkout books. They are also community centers recognized for other purposes. For example, in September 1952, the Carnegie Library was the location for a display of Bibles, which are not normally maintained in a library. Two pages from a 1613 edition of the King James Version of the Bible were displayed. The first edition was printed in 1611. The display was part of a community-wide observance sponsored by the Huntsville Ministerial Association of the publishing of the Revised Standard Version Bible.

The Bible is the most printed and published book in the world. It is also the most retranslated and revised book in the world. There have been thousands of versions in the over two thousand years of its existence. Each one claims to be the true meaning of the "Word." Each translated language has its unique meanings that are not always true translations. Each translator puts his own linguistic skills into his version. When translated back into the earlier language, new meanings and interpretations appear.

This display included a Norwegian Bible, a Norwegian New Testament for children, German and French Bibles, two Jewish Bibles (1866 & 1917 versions), a Douai Version of the Bible, an American Standard Version of 1901, a Revised Standard Version of the New Testament of 1946, and The Bible Designed To Be Read As Living Literature (1936).[19]

The library's local history collection continues to grow. Mrs. Elizabeth Parks Beamguard, library director, described some of the holdings. The library obtained photostats of some 30 letters from John W. Walker. Walker was president of the assembly that met in Huntsville on July 5, 1819, to form the state's first constitution. He was later elected Alabama's first U.S. senator.

Mrs. Bessie Russell, custodian of the historical collection, donated a copy of *The Douglas Register* as a memorial to the late J.D. Humphrey. *The Douglas Register* was one of the most important tools in tracing Southeastern genealogy during the period 1750 to 1797. It was rarely found except in larger libraries.

The New Hope library station was re-established in August 1952, this time in Cooper's Café. The library station was first established in 1947 but was changed to a bookmobile stop in 1950 when store space became unavailable due to the town's growth. This brings the total number of stations in Madison County to 14. The bookmobile would leave books there every first and third Monday. More than 100 books were normally left in New Hope.[20]

September 24, 1952 – Mrs. Beamguard, a member of the Executive Council of the Alabama Library Association, said that the Alabama Library Association had requested to hold the annual meeting in Huntsville in the spring of 1953. Huntsville had not hosted the event in about ten years.

September 30, 1952 – Silver fish have invaded the Library again. When they were evicted several years ago there was no sign until fall, now they even walk out at the loan desk.

The Huntsville Library received a letter, dated October 20, 1952, from George Parmly Day, Director, Bureau of School and Community Service, University Extension Division, Department of Education, Yale University. The letter's first two paragraphs are quoted:

"I am happy to tell you that the Yale University Press is forwarding to you on our instructions as a gift which we trust you will welcome for your Library, copies of two of its publications that will, we believe, be of interest to readers concerned with the fate of Europe and of European civilization, since these books are, in the opinion of competent critics, "invaluable for an understanding of the past and of the troubled present." For each may well be described as "an authoritative analysis of the deeper causes and meanings of World War II and European development": and for this reason should, we feel, be made available for use in libraries throughout the United States.

It is our hope then that, as I have said, you will welcome our gift of a copy of the LAST DAYS OF EUROPE, by Grigore Gafencu, Minister of Foreign Affairs of Romania from 1938 to 1940, whose "picture of the road to catastrophe is vivid and convincing": and of a copy of Professor Alfred Weber's FAREWELL TO EUROPEAN HISTORY - a title indicating his belief that the old political system based on the free competition of large and small relatively loosely-knit contiguous states which we have known is definitely gone, and his surmise that what is to take its place may be some kind of a new World Syndicate based on two or three overwhelmingly great states."[21]

Apparently this was a gift out of the blue, as the wording seems to indicate that many libraries were receiving the same books. Weber's book was published by Yale University Press, while the other book was published by Archon Books in Hamden, Connecticut, a suburb of New Haven, the home of Yale. Neither one of the two books are still in the Huntsville Library. The Salmon Library, University of Alabama in Huntsville has a copy of Gafencu's book, and both are available on the Internet at www.abebooks.com. It is hard to imagine that many folks in 1952 Huntsville read the books, but possibly some of the German scientists might have done so, as they had first hand knowledge of some of the people in the book, such as Hitler, Goering, Mussolini, Neville Chamberlain and Winston Churchill.

Weber's book provides an opportunity to reflect upon writings 56 years afterward to check the outcomes of predictions of political scientists. "Weber was deprived of his Heidelberg (Germany) professorship as soon as the Nazis came to power, and he returned to the university in 1945 after the German defeat....Professor Weber sees history as an interplay of conquest, of the appearance of one dominant power after another, and he now considers that period now at an end....A new use of man's power is called for in a time when the separate nations have played out their historical parts entirely, and fresh world concepts are now essential for man's survival." (http://dogbert.abebooks.com) I think Weber would be disappointed his vision did not come true.

October 28, 1952 – The Library received a gift of some 250 books from the McDonald home and it is expected that out of this number there are pieces of real value to a collection of old books.

Mrs. Beamguard attended another Executive Council Meeting of the Alabama Library Association, and reported the group accepted with "enthusiastic alacrity" the opportunity to hold their annual meeting in Huntsville in April, 1953. The Huntsville of 1953 was vastly different from the 1930's. Huntsville now had a large Federal installation and a contingent of foreigners, called Germans, who were the leaders in the Army's missile and rocket programs. We were internationally known, and those central and southern Alabamians were anxious to see the big-time stuff going on in Huntsville. Hosting the convention was to put a joyful strain on the library staff for the next few months to make everything go smoothly. Many of the internal meeting activities were arranged by committees from the Alabama Library Association.

Elizabeth Parks Beamguard further reported to the Board in writing:

"The Southeastern Library Meeting which I discussed with you folks sometime ago, is this weekend. When I asked to participate in the program, we noted it was included last fall in our permissive trips – my part of the program is to discuss the Reference Service of this library in relation to our county and the schools. Mr. Camberon, head of the division, feels that the relationship here of our office with other libraries has been an example of goodwill and would like it brought out how the reference with the high school and University Center works....We seem to have things pretty well in order, so may I request that Miss Frances go? It may be her last meeting as she is of course rather frail. She can stay with Miss Wheatcroft, so she will not cost the library anything. The Children's Library is expected to be exceptionally good. She has been so industrious and so faithful I'd like to see her get to do it. I have made out the schedule as attached. You will note the schedule which will show she can go without upsetting anything. (This week Mrs. Herrin is in the office, next week she is on the road everyday.)"[22]

"900 Kiddies Find 'Reading Is Fun,'" was the column heading of a story about National Book Week activities at the library. Miss Frances T. Jones, children's librarian for more than 25 years, said, "we feel it was one of the most satisfactory Book Weeks we have ever had, because the children not only had fun, but learned what books can offer in the way of serious information. The large number of children reflected the growth of the library in this growing town. We have always had big crowds before for Book Week, but never 900 before." Each day had a different topic, leading into the over-all theme, "Reading is Fun." Monday featured art in books to show information, and to design and make things. Tuesday was about Southern folklore and local heroes in history. Wednesday was about recreation and featured fairy tale dances. Thursday was puppet day by Mrs. Mathew Weber. Friday was music day, with demonstrations of various musical instruments, stories of operas, and lives of famous musicians. Saturday climaxed the activities with a filmstrip of old fairy tales and favorite childhood stories shown by Mrs. Bessie Russell.[23] How many readers of this history have ever seen a filmstrip?

November 11, 1952 – There was an arrangement with Dr. Otis Gay in Triana to have a collection of books left with his nurse, Dant, to help form a branch library. There was also a plan to place a collection of books in the county health building, to be open on clinic days. The books will be part of the Negro library collection.

The library board minutes in the early 1950's contain a disconcerting number that do not have a date, wholly or the year. The following two paragraphs came from one such set of minutes.

The Alabama State Public Library Service requested Mrs. Beamguard to fill a temporary position in Montgomery for one year. This was to replace a woman who took military leave of absence and the office needed an experienced librarian. Mrs. Beamguard would travel throughout the state representing the Public Library Service. Her reputation in the cooperation of the Library and the community was well known in Montgomery. They wanted to build up public libraries in the state and create prestige with the legislature.

Mrs. Beamguard requested a one-year leave of absence with the possibility of returning in 12 months. A trained librarian with a degree in library science, Miss Dorothy Webb, would be available until the school term started.[24] The leave of absence was delayed for one year, in 1954.

In February 1953 the library received the following letter from the Union Pacific Railroad:

"Please accept with our compliments this beautifully lithographed portrait of Abraham Lincoln.

It was Abraham Lincoln who first realized that a rail link between the east coast and the west coast was vitally necessary, and it was through his efforts that the necessary legislation was finally passed in Congress so that the Union Pacific could be built.

Union Pacific today serves eleven western states, nearly all our western National Parks, and Sun Valley, Idaho. If you or any of your friends are planning a trip into the Union Pacific West, we would consider it a privilege to serve you."[25] Looked like a promotional giveaway, but possibly the old Carnegie Library had a spare wall. Well, probably not.

In April 1953 the Huntsville Library hosted the Alabama Library Association at the Russel Erskine Hotel. The Friends of the Library hosted a luncheon, which featured a speech by Charles G. Bolte, executive secretary of the American Book Publishers Council, New York. Panel discussions were conducted covering a variety of subjects.[26]

Mrs. Grace Stevenson, executive secretary of the American Library Association and principal speaker, told the 240 Alabama librarians at the state convention that, "Our democratic society is predicated upon the ability of the people to govern themselves wisely, and in order to do that they must be well informed." She further discussed the continuing problem that librarians must continue toward increasing professionalism. They must have continuing self-education in order to be more than just caretakers of books.[27]

The conventions featured speaker at the annual banquet was Miss Virginia Kirkus of New York. Miss Kirkus was the founder and director of the Book Shop Service, which forecast the success or failure of forthcoming books on publishers' advance lists not yet available to the public. She and her associates screened approximately 4,000 books each year from 70 of the most important publishers in the country. She personally reads and evaluates about 1,000.[28] [Try that in your spare time.]

Miss Kirkus spoke about such "good" war stories as *The Naked and the Dead* and *The Caine Mutiny*, which "are written with honesty and a good grasp of people at every level." She also said there was a returning trend toward historical novels, because in times of stress, people turn to diversionary reading rather than think about tough issues and "they feel a little more virtuous about it if they are reading history." Does that apply to the readers of the 21st century? She also asserted that it is not the job of the librarian to force books upon people. "You should know the books yourselves and be able to decide which books will capture the imagination of the people." Membership in the Alabama Library Association was at 340, with 51 of Alabama's 61 counties represented.[29]

The Redstone Park Library opened in Redstone Park on Thursday, July 23, 1953. The library was started at the urging of citizens of the area. The Huntsville Housing Authority provided a room in the community house. The library was staffed by volunteers only.

The bookmobile stop at Redstone Park was terminated in 1967. Why did the bookmobile stop? Remember commentator Paul Harvey's radio items and his books, *The Rest of the Story*? Now for the rest of the story. If this history book was not about the library, the title of this vignette would be "The Rise and Fall of Redstone Park." But since this is about libraries, the title shall be "The Library Went to Redstone Park, but Redstone Park Moved Its Houses Away from the Library."

Redstone Park was located at the northwest corner of the intersection of South Memorial Parkway of Green Cove Road (Buxton Road on Redstone Arsenal). As you turn west on Green Cove Road, stop immediately and imagine Redstone Park to your right front. Redstone Park was a cluster of small wooden houses, which started about 50 yards from the Parkway. The houses would have been where the Farley School now has a large grassy field with a running track in the center. The community continued west along the right side of Green Cove where the PALCO Manufacturing plant now exists. Drive to the entrance to PALCO and notice the back of the PALCO building. That distance represents the approximate depth of Redstone Park from Green Cove Road. Ninety yards west of the PALCO entrance is an old road, and culvert over the drainage ditch, which goes nowhere today. Park on the culvert and you can see and walk on an old road without much trouble. That road curves slightly to the right and intersects the PALCO parking lot near the rear of the building. That road represents approximately one-half of the length of Redstone Park from the Parkway. The rest of the community extended approximately to the U.S. Army Engineer building to the west. In the back middle of the area described is a tall tree, which is probably close to the north boundary of Redstone Park.

The War Housing Authority built Redstone Park in 1942-43 for rental to Redstone Arsenal workers. Imagine 300 housing units crowded into the area described above, which was approximately 65 acres. The workers traveled to their work locations on a special train consisting of an engine and three railway cars. The ownership of the units were transferred to Redstone Arsenal in 1956 and renovated for military use. The military later started to build housing on the north part of the Arsenal, at the existing (2004) housing areas. The buildings at Redstone Park gradually were used less. A storm in 1966 tore off shingles and damaged roofs. Other maintenance costs rose significantly. The houses were sold to private companies and hauled off to locations in Alabama, Tennessee, Mississippi and Georgia. "Goodbye, Redstone Park, we loved you dearly," the former occupants.[30]

September 8, 1953 – There were some activities to be cut to save money. About 6-8 periodicals will be eliminated. The staff curtailment would consist of the elimination for the next six months, or longer, of a bookmobile driver and an assistant for circulation. Replacement of two vacancies would be discussed at the end of the month. It is expected that the saving of the $165 and $135 per month would amount to something of a backlog that would give security to the library in the event of a curtailed appropriation.

November 17, 1953 – Mrs. Henry B. Chase resigned from the library board because of her physical inability to get to the library and to attend meetings regularly. Some of the meetings were held in her home. She served on the board from 1918 until November 1953, 35 years, which is the second longest tenure by a board member. She was elected an honorary life member of the board. She had demonstrated a keen mind and objective viewpoint, her opinions were of continuous value, and she contributed to wholesome community relationships.

Redstone Arsenal was making its presence known by paying more competitive salaries than the library. Several employees left the library for better paying jobs.

During National Book Week in 1954, members of Girl Scout Troop 39 presented a play at the Huntsville Public Library. The play was named, "Bookworms Don't Have to Bite." People who read a lot and seem to always have their nose in a book are called, deservedly, bookworms. Are there really such things as bookworms? Yes and no. Many books in the days long ago there were cylindrical holes bored in books. Because the hole was round, the natural assumption was that a round worm did the damage. There are several insects that qualify as bookworms, but the most common is the silverfish (*Lepisma saccharina*). The silverfish feeds on mould, so the worst damage is done in moist conditions. A bookworm of early times was the deathwatch beetle that laid its eggs near a source of food. The larvae would feed on the books and it could take up to ten years before it turned into a beetle. They obviously enjoyed the books' contents.[31]

August 5, 1954 – The library board thoroughly discussed that if Mrs. Beamguard's term of service to the state department be terminated at such time as to send her back to Madison County, would the library be in a position to retain Miss Webb and Mrs. Beamguard. Several members of the board pointed out that such a staff of two trained librarians had been the original plan in bringing Mrs. Beamguard to Huntsville, and with the departure of the director at that time, Mrs. Beamguard was moved up to replace that director, and she had never been replaced. The time had come when perhaps such a staff was not only the aim, but an actuality of this system. Having dropped two staff members last fiscal year at $150 each per month, and having continued in growth of population, it might be well be the step of having an adequate staff.

The financial details were aimed at, for in giving the staff members a $10 raise, it would leave the budget pressed. Mrs. Amis pointed out, and the rest of the board agreed, that having acquired a back-log purely for operation, she was certain that to continue holding back $300 per month would be frowned upon by the appropriating bodies. It was now the time to throw into active operation most of it, if not all of that $300, as the retrenchment could be continued too long not only for the morale of the institution but for the support of the city and county. They could say they supplied the funds, and full use was not made of them. The result was that if Mrs. Beamguard came back earlier than Miss Webb had to return to school, the services of both librarians will be retained, even if it means to go into the saving fund. In that way it will be determined whether the board will do better to have two full-timed professionally trained people, or go along with training clerical help.

Miss Dorothy Webb arrived in Huntsville Friday, September 17, 1954, just in time to be taken to the meeting of the Union Grove Library in the Union Grove Church. Eight members of the community, under the chairmanship of Rev. McQuiston, met with members of the staff of the library, and held an instructional meeting on the care of the community library. The community church wished to have: Rev. Elvie Stewart, Concord Presbyterian Church; Homer Hall, Principal, Walnut Grove School; Mr. Ricketts, Plevna School; and Rev. McQuiston as the library committee.

Monday morning, September 21, 1954, Mrs. Davis, Mrs. Herrin, Miss Webb and Mrs. Beamguard paid a courtesy visit to the county commissioners to introduce Miss Webb, to thank them for their past support and assure them a definite and stable extension program the ensuing months.

September 21, 1954 – Miss Dorothy Webb was appointed to be the acting director during Mrs. Beamguard's leave of absence. The library board suggested the librarian not accept loans of personal material without the owner accepting the complete responsibility of the possible loss of the material. The library has not storage space, and to prevent any hard feelings with the public, it is better to have a gift or a temporary loan of something of value, that can be returned at once, rather than linger in the building unclaimed.

The Library acquired ten new books in February 1955 through its "Memorial Books" program, said Miss Dorothy Webb, acting director. Four of the books were in honor of Miss Annie Merts, former assistant principal at Huntsville High School, who died recently. The Huntsville city schools main office in 2004 is in the Annie Merts Center at 200 White Street. The program was started in World War II by the Acme Club, which donated a book for each serviceman killed in the war. Since then, the Acme Club had given about 202 books, and other individuals and groups have given another 175.[32] When a donor notifies the library of his intention to buy a memorial book, he is shown a list of volumes of long-term value, which the library needs. They are grouped by subject matter, in case the owner wishes to choose a book reflecting the interests of the deceased. His choice is not restricted to the list. He may state what book he wishes to give, or he may even give one to the library; but the public library prefers that he check first for duplication. If he chooses the book, the library will order it for him. The library then sends a card to the family of the deceased, stating the name of the book given, and identifying the donor.

When the book arrives, a memorial plate is put inside the cover, and it is shelved in its proper place. No "special collections" will be kept separate from the regular shelves. The system was still in existence at the library in 2004.

February 15, 1955 – The acting director, Dorothy Webb, said a vacuum cleaner was seriously needed in the library.

March 15, 1955 – The Board agreed to purchase a vacuum cleaner from Montgomery-Ward for $69.95, plus tax, on the condition it shall be only used for cleaning the Huntsville Public Library.

One of the books acquired in the library's earliest years was *History of the United States from their First Settlement as English Colonies in 1607, to the year 1808, or The Thirty Third of their Sovereignty and Independence*, by David Ramsey, M.D., Volume III of 3, 2nd Edition, Revised and Corrected, Philadelphia, published by M. Carey & Son, No. 126 Chestnut Street, for the benefit of the heirs of the author. May 1st, 1814. It carried a Huntsville Library bookplate, 1818 Lib # ___ and Hermatherian Lib # 627, $1.00. It was once loaned by the Huntsville library to the University of Alabama library.[33]

April 19, 1955 – The New Hope Library Station was moved from Cooper's Café to Mr. Moon's Feed Store. A new station would be opened in Walnut Grove on August 22.

Elizabeth Parks Beamguard resigned from the library directorship on December 1, 1955 to work as a field representative for the Alabama State library Service. She eventually became director of the Alabama State Library, and retired from that position in 1974. She was one of the grande dames of the library profession, who lobbied for federal money to support libraries, which had been traditionally been financed by local revenue. Donna Schremser, director in 2004, who met Beamguard in the early 1970s said, "She was so regal. She could wear lovely suits and hats and gloves. But she could really get in there and fight for libraries." Elizabeth Beamguard died July 19, 2003 in Montgomery.[34]

Miss Dorothy Webb replaced Beamguard as permanent head librarian.

There were in 1955, and probably still are in the current era, people who did not realize that they could borrow books from all across the United States. *The Huntsville Times*, March 17, 1955, had a two-column article explaining the borrowing system through a series of past examples of such borrowing. Each book ordered from another location required a $2 deposit. When the book was returned to the local library, the postage fees were deducted and the borrower received the remaining money.[35] Remember, we are talking about $2 in 1955 with the postal rates of that era considerably lower than today. In 2004 the fee for getting an interlibrary loan was $3 per book, which was the United States Postal Service book rate for a round trip by one book. With today's Internet search services, it is quite easy to search libraries to find the book you want to borrow.

July 19, 1955 – A new bookshelf was placed in each of the following locations: Skinnum, Big Cove, Hurricane, Meridanville, Cave Springs and Harvest.

During Huntsville's 150th year anniversary in 1955 some folks boldly predicted that the city's population of 50,000 might double to 100,000 by the year 2000. Little did they know about the future.

March 27, 1956 – Reverend Snodgrass had taken over the position of librarian of the Dulcina DeBerry Branch on March 1, replacing Mrs. Fannie Jackson. Rev. Snodgrass had undertaken the redecoration of the two rooms; the walls had been painted; the ceiling papered; the bookcases stained; arrangements made for polishing the floor. The library will assume all expenses of the redecoration and purchase venetian blinds for the four windows.

June 19, 1956 – New stations were opened in the county at Sulphur Springs and Quick's Store, while the station at Union Grove Baptist Church was discontinued.

March 19, 1957 – There was a discussion about starting a Friends of the Library organization for the purpose of promoting interest in and means for, a new library building.

Miss Frances Jones retired from the library on April 30, 1957 after 26 years with the library. She was specially recognized by the of directors for serving as the head of the children's room for 20 years. "Miss Frances," as she was known, was born, lived, and died in the same quaint, gray, gingerbread house at 524 Madison Street, just a block and a half from where she worked in the Carnegie Library Building. "She was a loving and gracious lady who took a possessive and personal interest in the gaggle of tykes who peopled the wonderful world in the basement of the old, domed library." She started the countywide summer reading club and story hour in 1952. Miss Frances died at the age of 91 years young on June 12, 1973.[36]

Judy Purinton, head of adult services in 2004, remembers going to the Longfellow Children's Room in the basement of the Carnegie Library when she was eight years old. Miss Frances found a book for her, *Judy and the Golden Horse*, by Faye King and printed in 1947 by Caxton Press. Purinton grew attached to the book and forty years later purchased the book on E-Bay for $30 so she could read it to her grandchildren. That is a classic love of books and how much they mean to us. Judy Purinton also remembers that she and a friend went to the children's room immediately after swimming in the Big Spring. Miss Frances let them know that wet hair was not appropriate attire for the library.

The Longfellow Room was for children up to age fourteen, one then graduated to the upstairs. The small Carnegie Library was usually crowded on the weekends as students were trying the research the same thing at the same time. The basement had the children's room, the librarian's office, the catalogue, and the bookmobile area.[37]

The library loaned nearly a quarter-million books in 1957, as there were more than 26,000 registered readers. Bravo. The bookmobile served 26 stations in the county, including two new ones: Plevna and Monte Sano. The one on Monte Sano was in the basement of the home of Mrs. James L. Studdard. There were 4,465 volumes added to the library in 1957, to include donations of 800 books, as well as donations of innumerable magazines and 25 recordings. Examples of the distribution of accessions include: history and travel-268; applied science-227; social science-382; religion-119; biographies-196; fine arts-116; language-47; literature-173; and children's-418. The library continued to be a popular place for local organizations to utilize the meeting rooms.[38]

November 19, 1957 – The director, Dorothy Webb, "requested an increase of salary for herself, stating that her salary was fifty dollars a month less than the amount paid to the former director and that the work necessary to operate the library had greatly increased during the three years she had been here and that living expenses had also greatly increased."

December 17, 1957 – "Minutes of the regular meeting held on November 17, 1957, were read. The chairman felt that additional data should be included in the last paragraph [quoted above] – but since this included what the director considered a misquotation of the director, she objected to writing the statement into the minutes."

January 21, 1958 – The director, Dorothy Webb, presented a letter stating that her services to the library be terminated on June 1, 1958. The letter was accepted with regrets. [Apparently the salary increase request was not approved.]

In January 1958 a seminal event occurred in the history of the Huntsville-Madison County Public Library, the incorporation of the Friends of the Library. This act provided structure and legal and fiduciary responsibility to this key library support group in accordance with the laws of the State of Alabama. The group's stated purpose was to promote the interests of the Huntsville Public Library and to work for enlarged facilities, through cooperation with the library board, the city council, and the board of county commissioners. The Huntsville Chapter of the American Association of University Women was the organizer of the Friends organization and deserves all the credit. They left a strong legacy in Huntsville.[39]

All participants are worthy of mention in this history. Directors with three-year terms were: Claude H. Davis, Mrs. A.L. Ferranti, Stuart Jones, Nathan F.S. Porter, Jeff D. Smith, Mrs. Addison White, and William Mickle. Two-year directors were: Allen R. Deschere, James R. Record, Dr. Frances Roberts, Neil F. Roberts, Roscoe Roberts Jr., Dr. Martin Schilling, and Miss Dorothy Webb. One-year directors were: A.D. Elliott, Angelo Ferranti, Mrs. Edith Johnson, Alvin Blackwell, Dr. Dennis M. Nead, Mrs. Howard A. Slayden, and Mrs. H.L. Green.[40]

The first public meeting of the Friends of the Library was held March 28, 1958. The speaker was Mr. Robert S. Alvarez, Director, Nashville Public Library, who spoke on the subject, "The Library in the Growing Community."[41]

Mrs. Patrick Pruitt was elected president of the state Friends of the Library organization at the annual meeting of the Alabama Library Association in Albertville on April 17, 1958.[42]

May 20, 1958 – Three members of the Friends of the Library, Dr. Dennis Nead, President; Mr. Roscoe Roberts, Chairman of the Facilities Committee; and Mr. Allan Deschere, Chairman of the Public Relations Committee, met with the library board. The meeting was for the purpose of deciding what steps should first be taken towards having a survey of Huntsville made in the interest of formulating definite plans for a new library building for the Huntsville Public Library.

Dr. Nead stated that the Friends of the Library had been organized for the purpose of bringing together individuals of the community who would be interested in promoting the interests of the library. This organization could offer an opportunity for discussion of interests and needs of the library and it could assist in promoting the interests of the library by giving the library a strong popular backing.

Mrs. Davis had received the supporting statement of the new library in Auburn, Alabama, she supplied each member with a copy of this stating that she felt that it would be very helpful in guiding the efforts in Huntsville. She also stated the three functions of the survey would be to make an analysis of the community, to define the services which the library could render to the community, and the survey would be an aid in estimating the space required for the services of the library.

Mr. Roberts stated that the facilities committee of the Friends of the Library would endeavor to formulate a picture of an adequate library to serve the community, that a survey would be necessary and in order to correctly inform the people concerned with the responsibility of promoting such a proposed building, that a survey would serve to further interest of the public, and to define something specific to work for. He stated that if the committee could help in the survey that the guidance and direction from the library board and the city planning commission would be welcome at all times.

It was agreed by all present that a survey of the community was of foremost importance and that it would be advisable for the library board and the board of directors of the Friends of the Library hold a joint meeting for the purpose of discussing such a survey, at a time when Mr. Dean Matthews, chairman of the city planning commission; Miss Emily Wheelock Reed, Director of the Alabama Public Library Service; and Mrs. Harold E. Klontz of Auburn, Alabama, who could meet with them as councilors. Mrs. Klontz was recommended to Mrs. Davis, by Miss Reed, as a person who had been very efficient in her efforts in connection with the new library at Auburn. The tentative date for this meeting was June 14. It was agreed that the Friends of the Library would defray the expenses of the two out of town guests.

Mr. Deschere stated that the members of the Friends of the Library could be an articulate force for the library, and he and Mr. Roberts agreed to visit the city council, with a member of the library board, and request a sum of $300 for making the survey if the city was agreeable to the plan. Mr. James Record had offered to present such a request to the county commissioners. This money would be used for the fees and expenses of the survey.

In July 1958 Mrs. James L. Murphy became head librarian, replacing Miss Dorothy Webb, who resigned after four years as head librarian. Mrs. Murphy, the head cataloguer for four years, had a bachelor of science degree in library science from Emory University and an A. B. degree in English literature from the University of Georgia. She was the librarian at Butler High School for one year, and had worked on the staffs of the Washington Memorial Library in Macon, Georgia, the Atlanta Public Library, the Georgia Institute of Technology Library, the University of Georgia Library and the Pennsylvania State College Library.[43]

August 19, 1958 – Five 12-minute parking meters were placed around the Library.

Mrs. Gretchen Schenk, a well-known library authority and consultant, visited Huntsville August 11-16, 1958 and conducted a survey and analysis of the city and county library needs. She had been president of the Alabama Library Association and director of the Alabama Public Library Division and had an extensive background in library activities. She came at the request of the Huntsville-Madison County Library Board and the local Friends of the Library. The cost of the project was shared equally between the city and the county. Mrs. Schenk's report made the key points:

- Huntsville was growing rapidly, with a population of 68,000, but the Carnegie Library was built in 1916 for a population of 8,000.
- The infrastructure was growing also, for example, electricity customers rose from 6,375 in 1941 to 28,714 in 1958 and people with telephones went from 2,564 in 1941 to 26,743 in 1958.
- Postal receipts went from $73.484.52 in 1935 to $532,490.65 in 1957.
- The property evaluation for Madison County rose from $17,591,414 in 1940 to $52,252,380 in 1957.
- The library's organization was marked by stability, continuity and conservation administration.
- The financial support history of the library was appalling. The conservation administration during the depression years enabled the library to continue, but growth since that time was hampered by adequate financial support.
- Reference and circulation services were barely adequate because of low salaries and part-time staff.

Mrs. Schenk identified factors influencing service: continued population growth; more functional organizations; better trained personnel; more cooperative projects; more financing options and efficient spending; and multi-faceted service opportunities. She also described the growing professional standards toward libraries cooperating together. The twenty-page typed report contained a wealth of other definitive analyses and recommendations. She was prescient, because most of her analyses and recommendations were gradually implemented in some form over the years. Our library evolution into 2004 reflected the step-by-step movement toward the standards and goals, which she notably identified in 1958. Gretchen Schenk's study represents a "before and after" history of the Huntsville-Madison County Public Library.[44]

In September 1958 it was announced that a second Negro library would be established. It is expected to open in November in the new Cavalry Hill Junior High School. The library would have a separate entrance and one into the school. It would be available to the students during school hours and to the public from 3 to 9 p.m. daily. It was expected to begin with 1,000 books. There would be one full time librarian supported by one assistant.[45]

September 16, 1958 – There was general discussion about appropriate sites for the proposed new library building. Three sites were proposed to the city and county officials; Laughlin Funeral Service lot, diagonally across from the present library building; the Schiffman garage lot on the corner of Gates and Franklin; and the corner occupied by Sample Shoes and other small businesses.

The library completed 1958 with another banner year of accomplishments. Almost 260,000 books were circulated and registered 2,196 new adults and 2,192 new children. The big news was the purchase of land for $100,000, possibly for a new library, diagonally across the street from the current building. The land was currently occupied by a funeral home and owned by the Liberty National Life Insurance Company of Birmingham.[46]

In 1958 the library came into possession of five documents from Hugh Lawson Clay, a Huntsville native and local lawyer, who was appointed as a captain at the age 24 during the Mexican War of 1946-48. He was directed to raise a fighting force. A document dated July 15, 1948 showed him commanding a 62-man company that included 4 sergeants, 1 corporal, and 24 privates from Huntsville.

The documents had been the property of Paul F. Hammond, a certified public accountant and operator of a plantation near Cheraw, South Carolina. Hammond's niece was Mrs. Emile Joffrion, whose husband was the rector of Huntsville's Church of the Nativity, an Episcopal church. The documents were sought by the University of Alabama and the Alabama Department of History and Archives. The items were microfilmed for the University and then preserved under glass.

The signature of President James K. Polk appears on the commission naming Clay a captain of infantry, dated May 24, 1847. The document was on parchment and in good condition. It was also signed by William L. Marcy, Polk's secretary of war. Clay was appointed a captain two and a half months before the commission. The appointment, dated March 5, 1847 gave authority for Clay to round up troops wherever he thought he would have the most success. It instructed him to report the names, ages, and residences of his men to the Department of War, and advised: "The recruiting service will be conducted agreeably to the Regulations, which are to be carefully observed." The men who served under Clay are listed in meticulous script on a muster roll.

The muster roll, dated July 15, 1848, lists Clay's unit as Company H of the 13th Infantry Regiment. The unit's first sergeant was Walter V. Jones from Huntsville. Under Clay were First Lieutenant John W. Perkins, and second lieutenants, William F. Rives and Philander Morgan.

There were also two books in the collection, which was brought to the attention of the Joffrions by Hammond and obtained for the Huntsville library at the suggestion of Dr. Frances Roberts, then a history teacher at the University Center in Huntsville (this was the name of what is now the University of Alabama in Huntsville).

Hugh Clay's brother was Clement Claiborne Clay, a United States Senator. Their father, Clement Comer Clay, was at various times governor of Alabama, member of the House of Representatives and U.S. Senator.[47] In those days, military officers were not selected on the basis of military skill or training, but strictly on political connections.

January 18, 1959 – The library board agreed not to accept any new library site which involved an existing structure, such as the Laughlin building across the intersection from the current library. Such a building would cause too many building maintenance problems. Hoyt Galvin, former director of the regional library and now director of the Charlotte-Mecklenburg County Libraries, sent a letter expressing his interest in the possibility of a new library and indicated his willingness to be employed as a consultant for it because of his former connection with Huntsville. The county shed serviced the bookmobile, the roof leak and gas tank repaired and the heater adjusted. Two telephones were installed at the DeBerry Branch instead of one as requested. The director had the extra line removed. Mr. John Rison Jones, Jr. recently gave the library valuable genealogical material.

February 17, 1959 – On Saturday, February 14, 1959, the library checked out 600 books from the adult department and 300 from the children's department, which broke by a large margin all previous circulation records. The library also bought a new 1959 Encyclopedia Britannica and renewed its subscription to the Junior Literary Guild for the children's room.

March 17, 1959 – Mr. Allan Deschere, a director and vice-president of the Friends of the Library, and also general manager of the Redstone Division of Rohm and Haas, spoke to the board about microfilming and its uses in the Library. He pointed out the unlimited possibilities for the use of microfilms in the library and its usefulness in the preservation of newspapers. He suggested possible ways of financing a microfilm cabinet, and the microfilming of back issues of Huntsville newspapers. He suggested putting in a request for it in next year's budget, or getting civic clubs or the Friends of the Library to take it over as a project.

May 19, 1959 – The Board discussed the possible employment of Hoyt Galvin as a consultant on the new library building. They thought it would be easier to get funds appropriated if concrete plans for a building had been made. The library board voted to use emergency funds to hire Mr. Galvin to come to work immediately on plans for the new building.

June 16, 1959 – Hoyt Galvin made his initial visit to Huntsville June 12-14 and gathered information and statistics to begin drawing up the program. He hoped to have it ready to send to the board in August.

July 21, 1959 – Mrs. Davis, Chairman of the Library Board, and Mrs. Murphy, Director, had a meeting with Mr. Goodson, Chairman of the Library Committee of the City Council, about hiring an architect for a new library building. Mr. Goodson suggested the board needed to meet with the city council to discern its position before discussion about an architect went further. Mrs. Murphy, director, submitted a letter to the Board requesting the board consider the hiring of a director who could give more wholeheartedly of his time to the building of a new library and directing of same. Mrs. Murphy's letter is quoted below:

"The Huntsville Public Library should start construction of a new building within the next few years the way things are shaping up now. In view of the time, talent, and whole-hearted pre-occupation with details this project will demand from the librarian, I feel that in fairness to the Board, the library and my family, the Board should begin looking for a librarian who will be able to devote his entire energies and total interest to this enormous undertaking. The overall supervision, organization and planning for this building will require much more time than one could give it in the normal working hours of 9 till 5.

I am well aware that the selection of a new librarian is one that you will want to give time and thought to and that is why I am bringing the matter up now. I will be happy to continue to work in my present capacity until you find a replacement that is entirely satisfactory to the Board. I do feel though, that it would be wise to hire some one as soon as possible in order for them to be in on the ground floor of this undertaking.

The possibilities for expansion of the library system in Huntsville are so great and such a challenge that I do not feel you will have any trouble getting the vigorous, dynamic person you will need. I have two suggestions to make of librarians you might wish to interview, both of whom I understand are very capable young men. I have listed them below. (Richard J. Covey, Gadsden Public Library; and John Hyatt, Anniston Carnegie Library)

I have thoroughly enjoyed working with Board and have found them progressive and cooperative. I have greatly appreciated their support and confidence and would have no objection to continuing this relationship if I did not so sincerely feel it would be doing them an injustice. I hope that when a new head librarian is selected they will let me continue to work for the library in some lesser capacity if there is an opening that I could fill."

September 15, 1959 – The folks that live in Decatur and Athens who work at Redstone Arsenal asked to join the library without paying the non-resident fee. The Board voted, NO.

Almuth Gessner, who was living in the home of Wernher von Braun for a year on a visitor's permit, volunteered to work in the library in April 1959. In August she applied for a job at the library in order to get a visa to stay in the United States for another year. There were no openings. In October, Miss Gessner had to leave the country and return to her home in Spain. Since she had worked so faithfully from 9 to 1 daily in the catalog department, but could not be paid because she was on a visitor's visa, the library board awarded her a cash gift of $100 in token of the board's appreciation.

December 15, 1959 – Mrs. H.B. Chase, a board member for 35 years, passed away earlier in the year and her husband donated $1,000 to the library, hopefully for the children's department of the new library. It was decided to buy plaques honoring the recently deceased Mrs. Chase and the still living Miss Frances Jones.

The growth of Huntsville and Madison County during the 1950s, fueled by the large Federal programs at Redstone Arsenal, was ready to spring forward in dramatic fashion during the next decade. University engineering graduates continued to be drafted into the Army and sent to Redstone Arsenal to put their talents to work. When their two-year commitments were up, many were immediately employed by the Arsenal at a much higher salary than their Army enlisted pay. Some married local girls and stayed in town. The higher education of the work force produced children more likely to value education, which placed greater demand on the schools and the public library. The influx of non-Alabamians continued into the 1960's and beyond. I came here in 1979 and stayed. Anecdotal evidence from my neighbor, Jack Bissinger, who came to Redstone in 1962, suggests that 60-80 percent of the 400 Army-drafted engineers came from locations outside the South. Many of them stayed in Huntsville. They brought different cultural values to Huntsville and helped turn sleepy Huntsville into a progressive and cosmopolitan city. Little did they realize that we were on the way to the moon.

Chapter 6

Finally, A Bigger Building

"Judged by every standard and measured by every criterion, the public library is revealed as a social agency dependent upon the objectives of society. It followed – did not create – social change. It was an outward and visible manifestation of the spirit and ideals of the people."

Jesse Shera
Foundations of the Public Library, 1965[1]

The Federal census of 1960 showed that the population of Madison County was at 117,348, up from 72,903 in 1950, an increase of 61 percent in 10 years. Huntsville's population was 72,365 in 1960, up from 16,437 in 1950, an increase of 440 percent. The demand on the old Carnegie Library was in place.

March 15, 1960 – The city council members seem to think that the new library building should be financed with a new city hall and police department, the latter two in an earlier stage of planning than the library.

The 3rd of May 1960 brought forth a needed improvement to the Carnegie Library. A drive-up book deposit metal container was put into operation. It was on the south side of the library on Gates Street.[2] The building's front was toward Madison Street. Sorry folks, a drive-up deposit container will not solve our library problems.

June 21, 1960 – In July 1959, Mrs. Murphy suggested that the library needed a more dynamic director for the era of the new building. The board did not act on that suggestion. One year later, Mrs. Murphy announced to the board that it was necessary for her to step down as director because of family obligations. She would like to continue in a less responsible capacity. The Board finally acted, and instructed her to write the two candidates mentioned a year earlier. If one was suitable, the opening salary offer would be $6,000.

In June 1960 it was announced that Brown Engineering was selected to be the architect for the proposed $750,000 library to replace the Carnegie building. Two sites were under consideration, one on the southeast corner of Gates Avenue and Madison Street and one in the Heart of Huntsville area.[3] The Hundley House, built in 1900, was on the southeast corner of Gates and Madison. It housed the Laughlin Funeral Home from 1930 until 1958. The city bought it in 1959 and converted it into the police station and also some city offices. It was used for that purpose until 1976, and it suffered considerable damage through lack of proper maintenance for such an old building. It was such a wonderful edifice in 2004 that it was hard to imagine that it was once a utilitarian police station.

July 18, 1960 – John Hyatt, Director, Anniston Library, indicated he was not interested in the position. The Board interviewed Richard Covey, Director, Gadsden Library.

August 16, 1960 – The Board reviewed Richard Covey's references and set his salary at $7,500, 25 percent higher than earlier.

On the First of October 1960, Richard J. Covey assumed the position of director of the library. He saw a tripling of usage during his four-year tenure at Gadsden. His philosophy was to make people feel welcome and provide an atmosphere of brightness and cheerfulness. He believed that increased patronage would follow public relations work and refurbishment of the physical facilities. Richard Covey had an undergraduate degree in library science from the University of Oklahoma and his master's degree in political science from the same school. He worked for the Oklahoma Library Commission and was director of the Muskogee, Oklahoma public library.

Covey found a great need for a new library in Huntsville, as the current one was built in 1916 and was adequate for a population of about 5,000. The influx of people associated with Redstone Arsenal's rocket and missile programs, coupled with a high enrollment at the University of Alabama Huntsville Center, produced a lively spirit in Huntsville that needed a larger library. The proposed new library would be adequate for a population of 100,000. Covey said that the new library must last for a generation or more. He missed the prediction by a little because the new library, to be built, only lasted a short generation before it too was replaced.

Richard Covey also discussed that modern libraries must offer more than books. Libraries are information centers with people from all walks of life searching for information. Libraries are not just "silence," but workshops instead of storage. Libraries should be prepared to offer files on microfilm, a collection of framed reproductions of art for lending, and a stock of phonograph records.[4]

The New Hope library stop opened again after it found a new home in the New Hope Feed and Seed Store. The previous store host closed his store. The bookmobile made a stop every second and fourth Wednesday from 1 p.m. until 2 p.m.[5]

In February 1961 a special Civil War shelf was started. Many new titles, plus the present collection of books, were placed on the shelf.[6]

March 21, 1961 – The board decided to eliminate the holding of group meetings in the library due to crowded facilities and the impossibility of doing library work during the hours when the children's room was not open to the public.

During the 1961 legislative session, the Alabama Legislature passed a bill, which provided for construction of libraries through public building authorities. The Huntsville City Council in September 1961 gave approval for the incorporation of a Library Building Authority. A.D. Elliott and Enoch Sparks prompted the action, as they had addressed the council as representatives of the Friends of the Huntsville Public Library.[7]

Also during 1961 the Alabama Legislature passed a bill establishing library scholarships. Scholarship recipients desiring to acquire a masters degree in library science at an accredited library school must agree to return to work for two years in the state's rural library program. The executive board of the state service will award an annual scholarship and seven study grants for 10-week study periods. Up to $5,500 annually may be spent for the two types of scholarships under a federal-aid program for which Alabama could not qualify until passage of the state library scholarship act.[8]

The often-violent civil rights demonstrations that convulsed Alabama, particularly 1961-63, were largely muted in Huntsville. Federal officials quietly informed the city officials that the millions of dollars coming to Redstone Arsenal were in jeopardy if the violence in the southern two-thirds of the state occurred in Huntsville. That subtle threat had a calming effect in Huntsville. On September 9, 1963, four Negro children enrolled in Huntsville city schools, making the system the first in Alabama to integrate. In April 2004 a marker was placed at the corner of Governor's Drive and Gallatin Street, marking the location of the former Fifth Avenue Elementary School, which was demolished in 2003.

In 1964 the national Civil Rights Act was passed by Congress and signed by President Lyndon Johnson. The Huntsville-Madison County Public Library and its customer base undoubtedly benefited from those two events, one a positive event and the other the absence of a negative event.

President Lyndon B. Johnson signed the Library Services and Construction Act (LSCA) on February 11, 1964. This act was to provide long lasting assistance to libraries across the nation.[9]

In June 1962 the library board agreed on the location of the new library at the corner of Fountain Circle and Williams Street. The cost of the land was expected to be $250,000 and the building $750,000, for a grand total of $1,000,000.

In 1962 the Oak Park Branch was established in the Oak Park Shopping Center on the southwest corner of North Memorial Parkway and Oakwood Drive. It was started by the American Association of University Women (AAUW) and staffed by them during the first year. In 1975 the branch was moved to a leased modular structure in the parking lot of the North Parkway K-Mart. At that time it was renamed to the Bessie Russell Branch, in honor of the lady who was head of the Heritage Room. She started part time nights in the library in 1947, and retired in 1980. She was an institution by herself and was always friendly and helpful, while keeping a sharp eye on old material she could get for the library.

In April 1963 Miss Carolyn Burke passed away in Richmond, Virginia, and was be buried in Maple Hill Cemetery. Miss Burke was the first librarian in the new Carnegie Library in 1915 and served until 1917.[10]

The History of Ancient Greece, Its Colonies and Conquests, by John Gilles, L.L.D., was another early accession by the library. The front cover's verso carried the Huntsville Library # 41 bookplate, it could be checked out for three weeks and cost 18 & ¾ cents for the first week, and subsequent week, of overdue. The book was published by F.R.S. and A.S., London, F.R.S. Edinburgh and Histographer to his Majesty for Scotland. First American from the Last London Edition, Volume I of 4, New York, 1814.[11]

The Huntsville City Council filed a loan application for $1.1 million with the Federal Housing and Home Finance Agency to construct a public library. Construction was expected to begin in 1964 and be completed in 1965. The council had agreed to provide the additional capital should the project exceed the Federal loan amount. Huntsville's Public Building Authority would construct the library and lease the facility to the city until the indebtedness is retired, hopefully in less than 30 years.[12] The population of Huntsville and Madison County grew from 117,348 in 1960 to 178,285 in 1964. A new and larger library was certainly an overdue problem to be dealt with because the old Carnegie Library was too small for that population.

Bids on the new library were opened on August 11, 1964, with O'Donnell Construction Company of Atlanta getting the job with its low bid of $665,000. That was just for the building; the cost of land, equipment and other expenses brought the total price to well over $1 million.[13] Huntsville's new "million dollar library" ($1,093,000) was dedicated on Sunday afternoon, January 16, 1966, although it officially opened its doors to the public on December 18, 1965. Key personnel attending the dedication ceremony were: Richard Covey, Director, Huntsville Public Library; Glenn Hearn, Mayor, City of Huntsville; Dr. Leslie Wright, President, Samford University; Mrs. Mattie Darwin, first "official librarian" for the Huntsville Public Libraries who served as director from 1917-1943; and Mrs. Elizabeth Parks Beamguard, state director of libraries and Huntsville librarian from 1944-55.[14]

The library had 134,460 volumes, more than 1,000 records, and 56 art reproductions, which may be checked out by the public. The ground level contained 31,460 volumes for adults and young adult readers. The second floor, which had the children's room and the local history section, contained 18,000 volumes. The basement contained 85,000 volumes used in the county bookmobiles. The new building also contained an auditorium, conference room, magazines, a Bible in Braille, out-size print editions, and the Wernher von Braun collection of papers. The new facility also had five incoming telephone lines, which would dramatically improve service. The steps to the second floor were carpeted and a selectively-directed public address system was installed.[15]

Mrs. Roscoe Roberts was appointed to the library board to fill the unexpired term caused by the resignation of Mrs. E.T. Terry and attended her first meeting on October 19, 1965. She was to have a long tenure on the board, and as chairman led the library through many changes and some controversies. Mrs. Terry was voted an honorary board member for life, having served for 42 years, longest in the history of the library.[16]

The library employed 44 persons, 13 of which were full-time staff members. In 1918, the library possessed only 1,236 books and employed 2 persons.[17]

In the 1960s Huntsville received considerable federal money under Urban Renewal Legislation. Mayor Glenn Hearn, City Council President Houston Goodson and Councilmen Dark, McNaron, Pearsall and Rodenhauser embraced urban renewal, slightly regretted (a little) tearing down historical buildings and said it was "in the public interest." Many old areas of downtown Huntsville were demolished. Thus, when a large public parking garage was built close to the courthouse area, our Carnegie Library was on the block that was chosen, and it was leveled. It was unanimous, and there was no Huntsville Historic Association to protect "Our Carnegie." The Public Building Authority records of that era could not be found by this author to see if there was even a passing discussion about preserving the Carnegie Building

Goodbye, Carnegie, we loved you, but you just had to go into oblivion and banished from our memories of past, present, and future generations. You could have been one of the wonderful old relics still in existence along with many others in downtown Huntsville. We were saddened by your demise.

In February 1966, *The Huntsville Times* took on a new writer, Carolyn Callahan. She started a once-a-week column on Sunday titled *Ex Libris,* (from the library). Her cheerful picture in the column made library research easier by looking for her picture. The first column I identified was on March 6, 1966.

In her second article Ms. Callahan informed readers about the facilities in the library, to include microfilmed *The Huntsville Times* since 1929. She talked with the librarian, Mrs. Bessie Russell, who recounted her sorrow when a local resident chose to burn a trunk full of letters from a Confederate soldier rather than donate them to the library. That is truly a sad story because those memories are gone forever, and some local genealogists might have overjoyed to find such a treasure trove. Mrs. Russell begged people to give up their old diaries and letters to the library, or let her make copies of them.[18]

How Best to Spend $37,500 Is Problem of Librarian was the title of Carolyn Callahan's weekly column, Ex Libris, in *The Huntsville Times*, March 27, 1966. The article provided a case study of how books were selected for accession to the library. Eleanor Murphy, librarian in charge of book acquisition, had a June 30 deadline to spend $37,500 from a federal-state grant to the library. The total of the grant was $43,321.25, but $5,821.25 must be spent for a station wagon as a condition of the grant. This was intended to promote the reaching out to communities beyond Madison County. The remaining money must be evenly divided between adult and children's books.

The library board determines basic policy for book selection: Know the community, avoid overlapping other libraries in the area, present both sides of an issue without prejudice, and no censorship. With those basic guidelines in mind, Eleanor Murphy consulted annotated lists in *The Library Journal, The American Library Association Book List, Publishers' Weekly Book Buyers' Guide,* and the *Standard Catalogue Annual,* plus magazine and newspapers reviews. The popular books (best sellers) were selected from The American Lending Library lists and rented on a contract basis for the duration of their popularity. Those books, which were judged to have some lasting value, were purchased by the library at a 75 percent discount after six months.

Department heads' desires and suggestions from the reading public are integrated into the list of potential candidates. The recommendations of specialists who are well informed in their particular field of interest are welcome, since one person could not sample all the books published each year – some 30,000 in 1965. The technically oriented community does look for books that are light and entertaining. The tremendous demand for current fiction kept the collection constantly depleted. The wail of frustrated readers, "But you never have any books!" must echo through Eleanor Murphy's dreams.[19]

A story hour was conducted at the library under the auspices of the American Association for Childhood Education. This was a trial program to develop techniques to help children learn. Twenty kindergarten youngsters listened to stories, joined in exercise games and even dramatized some of the stories. Mrs. Barbara Harris, administrative assistant to the library director, had a regular Friday morning discussion period for five minutes on radio station WFIX at 10:30 a.m.[20]

In May 1966, the Huntsville Chapter, Telephone Pioneers of America donated a 16 mm movie projector to the library.[21]

The Huntsville Public Library was eager to help students who decided on a library career. The library gave preference to high school juniors to work part-time in the library. Boys had a slight edge over girls as prospective employees, because a boy might be better able to maintain order in the library and because the handling of large numbers of books was hard, physical work. Carolyn Callahan, *The Huntsville Times,* wrote those words in 1966. They seem to fly in the face of the casual observations that most library employees were women. A young person must have graduated from an accredited college in order to enter a graduate library science program. Alabama had no accredited library science programs in those days, so students usually went to Peabody College in Nashville, Emory in Atlanta, Louisiana State, North Carolina, or Kentucky Universities. The Alabama Library Association recently instituted out-of-state tuition assistance programs to help Alabamians, if they promised to work in the state. Richard Covey, library director, said a library science graduate could expect a beginning salary somewhere between $5,000 and $6,000 per year. For readers who were not in the job market in 1966, they might not be impressed. This author was an Army officer during that time, so that was a fair salary for someone dedicated to serving others and willing to work hard. It did not compare favorably with many other jobs, but someone could find satisfaction in the sharing of his enthusiasm for books and reading.[22]

The American Library Association (ALA) standards recommended that there be a full time staff member for every 2,500 people in the served area. This would require a staff of 70 personnel for the Huntsville Public Library. In August 1966 there were 55 full time employees. The library staff underwent a fifty percent turnover each year. There were many hours lost of more efficient operations during the training required for the new employees. Another ALA minimum standard specified 15 staff members with a master of library science degree to head the various departments that handle a collection of 100,000 books. Huntsville had three staff members, plus the director, who had library science degrees.[23]

"August 11, 1966

Mrs. Roscoe Roberts…

Dear Mrs. Roberts:

On August 7, the staff of the Huntsville Public Library met to discuss taking action regarding the unrealistic salary structure in the library. A committee was formed to present a statement of the feelings of the staff to the Library Board. The staff would appreciate your reviewing the enclosed statement for discussion at the August 16 Library Board meeting.

Very truly yours,

HUNTSVILLE PUBLIC LIBRARY

Pauline Wright Murray

Committee Spokesman"[24]

In November 1966, Richard Covey, director, prepared an application for federal matching funds to finance a new bookmobile. Eight Alabama communities would be selected to receive the federal grants. It would be in early 1967 before the grants are announced. This bookmobile would be considerably larger than the one the library operated in the county. This vehicle would be for city operations. The grant is limited to $7,500, which the library will have to match. Additional funds might also be required. The van would look more like a bus, with air conditioning and its own generators.[25]

In March 1967 the bookmobile grant had not been awarded. The cost was now estimated to be about $25,000, so a federal grant of $7,500 leaves a big remainder to be raised. A fund drive was started.

Covey also pointed out that the Huntsville per capita allocation from the city was $0.75 when he came to Huntsville in 1960. It is now $1.35 for the city, and less for the county, but the ideal number is $3-4. His sights slipped some, now he hoped to have the bookmobile in hand when Huntsville hosts the April, 1968 Alabama State Library Association Annual Convention.

By May 1967 the bookmobile fund raising was expanded. Operation Bookmobile barrels were placed in front of the library and several department stores around town. The Exchange Club and Woman's Club had taken on the leadership roles. Southern Bell Telephone Company put donation forms in their monthly bills and all local banks put donation forms in their monthly statements.[26]

May 16, 1967 – Mr. Covey recounted the high turnover of personnel in the library and suggested that action be taken as soon as possible to adjust salaries of those who had contributed over a long period of time to the operation of the library. It was agreed that a report of the pay scale for selected employees be developed and a special board meeting be called to consider it.

The fund drive was lagging in September 1967, but Richard Covey announced that the federal government would provide 60 percent of the cost, double the previous amount. The fundraisers redoubled their efforts.[27]

It is now February 1968, and Carolyn Callahan wrote in her regular Sunday Ex Libris column on the 26th that the bookmobile would arrive in Huntsville the next day. That was an exciting day. The vehicle cost $24,130.22, and the fund raising was still short $6,619.20. The fundraisers had just sent out another round of requests for donations, as the bookmobile was expected to arrive two months later. **It's here now!** Wish we had used the term "urgent" in our last mailing mumbled the fundraisers. Ten percent of the cost must be paid the day the unit was delivered, and the balance in twenty days.[28]

The bookmobile was in town for two days and there was still a shortfall of $2,800, to be raised in the next 18 days. The city may be asked for the money, or it may come from private library endowments, said Richard Covey. But, private endowment donors would have to be asked if they agree to change the purpose. The city was not supposed to pay, based on the agreement with federal government.[28] Isn't there someone who can shake his sleeves for the $2,800? Huntsville Public Library was painted on the sides, so it must belong to us, if we could only pay for it.

On March 11, the General Electric Employees Federated Fund came through with $600, but we still need $1,500. Please, Please.[30] Apparently there was a little slippage in the system, as the final $250 was donated by the Huntsville Woman's Club in September 1968. Bravo to the Woman's Club, who started the project – and finished it!

The bookmobile was carpeted, heated, air conditioned and carried 3500 to 4000 books. It contained special shelving for record albums. It still needed a driver and a librarian. There were still not enough books to fill the shelves, but were being ordered. The route was being planned, as the Mountain Gap area had asked for the service several months ago.[31] And it was ready for the state convention in April.

Eleanor Murphy, of the library staff, wrote the Ex Libris column on March 19, 1967. She highlighted some of the libraries accomplishments during the first fourteen months in the new building. "Seven hundred thousand books were taken out and returned (well, most of them were), causing quite a bit of wear and tear on the more than 100,000 volumes now owned by the library, 30,000 of which were added during 1966."[32] The problem of some books not being returned had been in existence for at least 2,000 years, going back to the ancient libraries of Alexandria, Egypt and Pergamun, Turkey. Some things never change.

In August 1967 a library branch was established at 7920 Charlotte Drive, just west of South Memorial Parkway. Cecil Clowers, a real estate owner, volunteered the facility. There were 1,500 square feet of floor space. The Civic Association of Parkway Estates and Fleming Hills had the responsibility of staffing the new library. Mrs. Clifford Jones, of that organization, had some 90 volunteers for the job. The association also had to build shelves for the books. This was an outstanding example of civic determination to provide more convenient book-borrowing opportunities for the families in that area and further south. Bravo.[33]

Mrs. Wayne L. (Joyce) Smith joined the Huntsville-Madison County Public Library on October 2, 1967. That was an important day for the library, because you must be blind if you know the reason. The Huntsville Subregional Library for the Blind and Physically Handicapped was officially started. The project was set up under the Library Services Act as a pilot project. The library worked with the Library of Congress, Division of the Blind, and the Alabama Institute for the Deaf and the Blind at Talladega, Alabama. Materials such as Braille books, talking books and recorded tapes were available.

Joyce Smith was a qualified Braille transcriber, so she was able to transcribe selections from texts and local history items that would not be available from the Library of Congress. Joyce Smith became interested in the plight of the visually impaired as a girl scout in Wisconsin after watching a troop of blind girl scouts function. Years later, she took a class in Braille transcribing as part of a mission works program at her church.[34]

Louis Braille was a Frenchman born in 1809. He was blind at age three, with a disease in one eye and an awl in the other eye. At age 15, at the Blind Institute in Paris, he heard about a French Army captain who invented dots on paper to communicate at night. Braille developed his own system of six raised dots. He died in 1852. The system did not achieve worldwide acceptance until 1932, 80 years after Braille died. The march of progress crawls slowly.

But now, the rest of the story behind the Subregional Library. Richard Covey was the library director in 1967. He had dealt with blind library clients in Oklahoma before coming to Huntsville, and had a "soft spot" for them that caught his eye when Congress changed a law in

1967. The new law allowed libraries to design special departments for the blind, deaf and physically disabled, thus allowing all citizens access to research and knowledge.

Covey flew to Washington, D.C., where he hoped to appear before Congress and get in on the ground floor. He was not in town two hours when a knife-wielding mugger jumped him and a fearful fight ensued. The mugger had one of those curved linoleum knives. The struggle was fierce and one arm of Covey's jacket was cut off, but he came through intact. On the next day, battered and bruised but undaunted, Covey stated his case for the first of these new facilities to be established in Huntsville. He won. The nation's original subregional library for the blind and disabled was opened in the Huntsville Library in Fountain Row. Bravo Richard Covey! Bravo Joyce Smith!

Richard Covey saw a space problem as soon as the area was set up. Braille books take up to 20 times more storage space than regular books. The library was responsible to get books and periodicals printed in oversize type for the person with impaired sight. The library had the New Testament in Braille and received two religious periodicals in Braille.[35]

A book published in 1996, in conjunction with the opening of the new main San Francisco Public Library, titled *A Free Library in this City*, by Peter Booth Wiley, claimed that in 1974 the San Francisco library pioneered blind and physically handicapped services. It seems as if that "pioneering" took seven years to move from Huntsville to San Francisco.[36]

Sometime during the 1960's the Dulcina DeBerry Negro Library Branch was moved to a private dwelling in the Edmonton Heights area when the Church Street building was demolished for urban renewal. In August 1968 the library board decided to use the bookmobile more and on October 1, 1968, the Dulcina DeBerry Branch ceased to be, after eighteen years in existence at six different locations. Huntsville's schools were desegregated in 1963.[37] The Negro library was pushed around, as was the Negro population, but it was arguably better in Huntsville than the remainder of Alabama.

In May 1968 the Lee High School Red Cross Youth bought a subscription to the American Junior Red Cross News in Braille for use within the library.[38]

In June 1968, Carolyn Callahan, in her Ex Libris column, described the bookmobile's stop at the Sherwood Park shopping center off Madison Pike in West Huntsville. One thousand books were borrowed during two days. Many new cards were issued, mostly to children looking for summer reading now that school is out. Summer reading programs were important as it was estimated that children lose 30 percent of their knowledge over the summer. Reading was a fun way to keep children's minds active for those long days of summer. Perhaps mothers also enjoyed reading with their children. Reading to young children, starting at a very early age, to include infancy, is a critical factor in a child's development.

Richard Covey, the library director, was a busy man during the summer of 1968. He was arranging for more Bookmobile stops, as each one had to have an outlet for 220- volt current in order to run the air conditioning unit. He was also functioning as the children's book-buyer in the absence of a full-time children's librarian.[39]

In August 1968, Carolyn Callahan, in her *The Huntsville Times* Ex Libris column, provided a ten-month update on the Library's facility for the blind and physically handicapped. Joyce Smith, director, had extended a "lifeline" to over 100 North Alabamians whose physical conditions make them eligible for the services. Twenty-five of them came in on a regular basis. The collection now had 700 titles in the talking book section, *The Readers Digest* in Braille, plus about 20 books in large type for the partially sighted.

Joyce Smith, director, corresponded with several people in Braille and was teaching Braille to five sighted Huntsvillians. She is also waiting for a $25,000 grant to come in, principally for shelves. She continued to work with Talladega's Regional Library for the Blind and the local office of the Alabama Vocational Rehabilitation Service to inform North Alabama residents of the lifeline available to them at the Huntsville Public Library.[40]

The library, with local bookstores and the Huntsville Literary Association, distributed bookmarks with a William Shakespeare sketch on them. Also included was Emilie Poulsson's poem, "Books are keys to wisdom's treasure; Books are gates to the lands of pleasure; Books are friends. Come and let us read." What a marvelous and simple poem that tells everything that needs to be said about books.[41]

The library granted amnesty for overdue books during the week of March 3-9. 1968. Readers of *The Huntsville Times* article on March 3 were encouraged to look in their cars, behind refrigerators, under davenports, and even in their bookcases (a strange place for a library book) for overdue books. There will be NO overdue fines under this one-week program.[42]

Carolyn Callahan's Ex Libris weekly articles in *The Huntsville Times* were worthy of emulation and quotation. The article she wrote on March 24, 1968 would lose much of its value if it were only paraphrased, so it shall be quoted in full because it captured the spirit of the dedicated genealogist.

"**Library Acquiring Mass of Material For Genealogy.** The funeral was hardly over when Bessie Russell set out to acquire the 'most extensive collection of genealogical papers in existence' from the estate of Mrs. Howard Jones of Huntsville for the local history room of the Huntsville Public Library.

Mrs. Jones and her sister, Mrs. Pauline Gandrud, had spent years scouring county records, tombstones, letters and newspapers and recording the data. They has amassed nearly 300 volumes of records, many of them the only ones in existence.

This treasure trove has tongues hanging out as far east as Virginia, as news of Mrs. Russell's coup spreads among those whose passion is climbing their ancestral tree. The local genealogical buffs are so thrilled at the prospect of having this material available at the public library, that they have quietly gone about raising $772.78 to date, to help the library pay for the papers.

However, according to library director, Richard Covey, the papers as yet do not belong to the library and therefore are not available to anyone. Probate proceeding must be completed before the sale can take place. In the meantime, the papers are being housed at the library under Mrs. Russell's fiercely protective gaze.

Even after completion of the sale, it may be some time before the papers are ready for public perusal.

A number of them may require retyping or being put in some more lasting form. They are currently typewritten papers in Manila folders separated according to counties. Some of the pages are copies and are readily legible.

Still and all, Mrs. Russell calls it, 'A feather in our cap! This is the sort of collection one generally finds only in large libraries.' Judging by the letters of congratulations pouring into the library, there are plenty of others who think so, too. More than one person has ruefully admitted that he wishes he had gotten there first, and if the library (heaven forbid) should decide not to purchase the papers after all, let him know."[43]

The local history room actually began when Mrs. Martha (Mattie) Darwin willed her private library to the Huntsville Library. She was the Huntsville Library's librarian from 1917 to 1943. Mrs. H.C. "Bessie" Russell, director of the local history room since 1945, was warm, witty, interesting, and interested in everything.[44] [Writers are not supposed to overuse "interesting" without saying why by use of another word. But, interesting covers a multitude of writing sins, because it is not always possible to discover or make up a reason why a person or thing is interesting. A person is attracted to it, by sight, sound, or touch, perhaps without knowing why at the time. It is just a good descriptive word. That is interesting.]

Bessie Russell was always on the lookout for any papers, books, letters, and other material that might be thrown out of attics or because of moving. She wanted to look at it to determine if it had historical value. In this business, history and historical value are in the eye of the beholder. She started as a night librarian in 1947 in the old Carnegie Library. There was no local history room as such, but she collected newspaper clippings. She said, "People laughed and said that wasn't history but I told them that anything that happened yesterday is history. Things that happened around '47 and on up to the coming of Redstone Arsenal is what people are vitally interested in."[45]

Bessie Russell imparted three jewels of wisdom to folks who visit a library:
- Children need tradition, and they need to know where it came from.
- Do not get started with your family tree and its history unless you want to get addicted.
- Finding one small fact about an ancestor can send you off on a great new historical adventure.[46]

The oldest book held in the Huntsville-Madison Public Library was a Holy Bible, printed in 1580 by Jacob Stoer. It was printed in French and was a Huguenot Bible, that is, a French Protestant. Huguenots were adherents of a Swiss political movement named after Besancon Hugues, 1532. The Bible was 11 x 15 &1/2 x 4 inches. The stiff cover was loose, as were many of the pages. The verso of the cover had the handwritten words, "Catherine Trachy 1787," which was assumed to be one of the probably many owners over time. The cover and pages are raggedy and well worn, as you would be if you were 424 years old. The cover still had one of the two metal latches that were used to keep the Bible closed. Jacob Stoer was best known for inheriting Jacques Dupuys *Dictionaire François-Latin* of 1573 and republishing it as *Grand Dictionaire François-Latin* several times between 1593 and 1606.[47]

The Alabama Library Association once again convened in Huntsville for its annual convention, which was held April 25-27, 1968 at the Sheraton Motor Inn. There were over 400 librarians in attendance to listen, to attend meetings and see the latest in library equipment, binding techniques, encyclopedias and other published materials. The keynote speaker at the first general assembly was Carl Elliott, former representative from Alabama's Seventh Congressional District. When in Congress, Elliott was instrumental in the enactment of legislation benefiting libraries. He was on the President's Commission on Public Libraries and was an honorary life member of the Alabama Library Association. The theme of the conference was LSD – Library Services Daring, Distinctive, and Dynamic. That was also the era when LSD meant more than library services.

Amidst the state activities, two local events were featured, the dedication of the new Joseph F. Drake Memorial Library at Alabama A&M College and the dedication of the new bookmobile of the Huntsville Public Library. Lieutenant Governor Albert Brewer made the dedication address at Alabama A&M.[48]

"Library Facing Personnel Crisis
By Carolyn Callahan, Ex Libris
The Huntsville Times, May 5, 1968

The operation of the Oak Park Branch is on a day-to-day basis. An agreement to staff Oak Park with A.A.U.W. volunteers during the first year of operation expired since April 27. Since then, public library personnel have alternated shifts and days. The rent-free lease with Oak Park developers stipulates that the branch station must be open from noon to 8 p.m. Mondays through Saturdays.

Despite the drain on the library staff, which is making it impossible to put the bookmobile on the street immediately, library director Richard Covey expects to keep the branch station open as long as the developer will allow him to stay. The lease is now on a month-to-month basis, and could be terminated if the developer needs the space.

Circulation at Oak Park runs about 100 books withdrawn a day, plus returns, reference questions and requests – enough to make it worth keeping Oak Park open, according to Covey.

Down at the other end of the Parkway, the Charlotte Drive branch station faces a similar crisis when volunteers from Fleming Hills Estates Civic Association complete their commitment to the library in August. The lease of that facility, which is not rent-free, has another year to run.

In the meantime, the main library has lost eight staff members, for various reasons, in the past 30 days, according to Covey. He sees no prospect of an influx of experienced summer help at this point. In fact, he knows of only one student returning to the staff when school ends, and he's keeping his fingers crossed about that one.

People are being interviewed, but so far they are asking about 40 per cent more salary than the library can pay, says Covey. Is he looking for volunteers? No. **He's looking for qualified personnel who are willing to work for peanuts!** The prospects are not encouraging."[49] [This author's bold.]

The Friends of the Library had another used book sale on Friday and Saturday, June 7-8, 1968. Mrs. A.L. Ferranti of the Friends issued a call several weeks earlier for the membership to bring in books suitable for sale. As one satisfied buyer explained, she would read the armload of books she carried out, and the return them next year for resale again. That is the spirit of the book, nothing was changed in the book from reading it, so it can be read again by new readers. Each person will gain new enjoyment and learning from the device that keeps on giving and advances our civilization.[50]

Storytelling was one of the most basic methods of instruction, from the beginning of human endeavors. Storytelling was still the best way to introduce preschool children to books. The Huntsville Public Library had long depended on volunteers to undertake most of the storytelling activities. The job required a love of children and books, and some storytelling skill. Throughout the library's history, such dedicated and skilled volunteers have made significant contributions to our children's learning processes and instilled a love of books that will last a lifetime. If volunteers were not available, then staff members performed the task. Books were the memories of our culture and it was necessary that the cultural tradition continued.

Richard Covey, Director, Huntsville/Madison County Public Library, left the city on December 31, 1968 after eight years in the position. His wife would work on the staff of newly elected United States Senator James Allen. Richard Covey expected to find work at one of the many libraries in Washington, D.C. On his departure, he reflected upon some of the library's accomplishments during his tenure. The annual book circulation increased from 270,000 to 610,000, an increase of 125 percent. The book inventory doubled to 123,000 and the budget quadrupled to $200,000.

Many readers, including the author, have dreamed of working in a library to be around books all day. Richard Covey put that dream into reality as he reminisced about his early life. Reading books on the job was forbidden in that profession. But he knew he just liked spending his working hours surrounded by books, so he went back to school to get a degree in library science.[51]

Richard Covey, asked about his replacement, replied that the board would prefer someone with a degree in library science, although the state of Alabama does not require it. "Actually, the ability to fill in any capacity in an emergency is a prime requisite for a library director." During his first years in Huntsville he often had to act as night librarian at the front desk after a full day as director. One aspect of the director's job is salesmanship, which includes "the ability to extract allocations from governing bodies. You have to be persuasive without hurting your library with high pressure tactics."[52]

Mrs. Robert J. Lowe, chairman of the Huntsville Public Library Board, said, "The board is working on finding a replacement but no action has been taken." Mrs. Eleanor Murphy, assistant librarian, was selected to serve as interim director during any period of transition.[53]

For the second time, Eleanor Murphy assumed the title of interim director of the Huntsville-Madison County Public Library. The first time was in 1958-60. She hopes the interim position will be shorter this time because she prefers her job as adult book selector to that of administrator. She first came to the library in 1954.

"Nothing much will change," she said in her interim position. Her job is to provide continuity with the help of the department heads: Mrs. Ann Gooch, "one of the best reference librarians in the country"; Mrs. Bessie Russell, "who has more local history in her head than in all the books in the local history room"; Mrs. Helen Moore, "a newcomer, but very experienced in circulation"; Mrs. Elizabeth Abercrombie, "who has done a masterful of holding the children's department"; Mrs. Eugenia Morelock, the only other degreed librarian on the staff full-time who is in charge of book processing; Mrs. Joyce Smith, who with Covey created the department for the blind and physically handicapped, the only one in the state; and Floyd Tidwell, longtime county bookmobile driver and librarian.

Carolyn Callahan was back at her reporting in *The Huntsville Times* Ex Libris column of April 13, 1969 with a fine bit of research as an opener. "In July, 1964, Mr. Frederick Smith found in his possession a book overdue from the library at Bishop's Stortford, Herefordshire, England. The accumulated fines were estimated to be 550 pounds sterling or $1,540," says Guinness Book of World Records. The Huntsville library would always rather to have the book than the overdue fine. Amnesty will be granted to anyone returning library property of whatever nature during National Library Week, April 12-26, 1969. No fines will be imposed, no questions asked. Please return it to any library branch, bookmobiles, or school libraries.[54]

Mrs. R.J. Lowe, chairman of the library board of trustees, announced that Elbert J. Watson, director of the Anniston-Calhoun County Public Library System, would be appointed direction of the Huntsville-Madison County Public Library, effective, July 1, 1969. Watson, a native of Birmingham, has been with the Anniston-Calhoun County library system since 1966. He had a master's degree in history from the University of Oklahoma and a master of library science from George Peabody College in Nashville, Tennessee. His salary was $12,500 per year and he was furnished a car.

He had done extensive historical writing, as his articles have appeared in various journals including the *Alabama Review, Alabama Historical Quarterly, Chronicles of Oklahoma, and Tennessee Historical Review*. He was a member of the Alabama Library Association, Southeastern Library Association, and American Library Association.

Watson regarded the Huntsville-Madison County system as "one of the most challenging opportunities for library service in the Southeast today. It is obvious that the Huntsville-Madison County system is part of the spirited movement for expanded library service sweeping the South today. We will endeavor to meet the challenging opportunities which are ours in this great North Alabama area."[55]

The following editorial was printed in the *Anniston Star* on May 5, 1969:

"Elbert Watson in his stay with us here gave a full measure of himself as director of the Anniston-Calhoun County Public Library, and the news reports of his resignation detailed the many accomplishments of his tenure.

His professional achievements, however, are but a partial inventory of the works of the man, for Mr. Watson and his wife joined fully in the life of the community and participated usefully and enthusiastically in the efforts and programs of local life.

Good citizens are treasured assets and are sorely lost, but we take comfort that in moving to Huntsville the Watson family is not lost to Alabama. As director of the Huntsville-Madison County Public Library, we expect to continue hearing of the effective work of Elbert Watson."

The Charlotte Drive Library Branch will now be completely staffed by paid personnel, after almost a year of a mix of volunteers and paid people. It was staffed by only volunteers during its first year.[56]

During the summer of 1969 five metropolitan newspapers were added to the library's subscription list: *The Washington Post, The Montgomery Advertiser, The Houston Post, The Los Angeles Times*, and *The Chicago Tribune*. Mrs. Bessie Russell, the local historian librarian, continued her search for a picture of Green Academy, "one of the earliest academies of higher learning east of the Alleghenies," which stood on the land which is now the location of East Clinton Street School.[57]

Elbert Watson's first five months as director was marked by expansion in the library's programs: story telling for youngsters in the Heritage Room; in the art, movies, slide, and record collections; in ready reference materials; and in all phases of the library's activities.

Watson expressed some definite goals for the library, "A progressive library should reflect the personality of the community. It must be involved in the mainstream of community activities...not an island set apart. I want the public to think of the library as a place keeping pace with the times."

Watson established a collection of 8- and 16-millimeter films to be circulated like books. Some of the 8 mm films include Laurel and Hardy movies, the Tunney vs Dempsey fights, and the moon landing. Color 35-millimeter slides have been collected also.

The department for the blind and physically handicapped was popular and was constantly being added to. Braille and large print books as well as talking books have opened a new world for the area's visually handicapped.

Watson also added $4,000 of microfilm, to include the Federal Census records for Alabama from 1820 through 1880, several historical publications and *The New York Times.*

The library's "Peppermint Princess" entertained pre-schoolers on Monday afternoons from 4 to 4:30 and children 6 to 8 years old on Thursdays at the same time. Advance reservations for these periods must be made at the main desk. Library volunteers tell stories to 4 to 6 year olds on Wednesdays between 10 and 11 a.m. and on Fridays from 11 to noon.

Watson predicted that in spite of the library's progress, the central building would be unable to provide all of the services which require the community requires. "We need a strong library system. We now have two branches to serve the more than 204,000 people of Huntsville-Madison County. We need more than that. Ultimately, if the population continues to grow methodically, we will need at least six branches. This won't come overnight, but it should be the aim of the community."

The state standard is two books available for each person in a county. Madison County should have approximately 400,000 books, but has about 123,000.

Various women's organizations have helped the library to obtain a bookmobile, to open the Oak Park Branch in the shopping center at the intersection of Memorial Parkway and Oakwood Avenue, and to buy books. The Friends of the Library sponsored the Peppermint Princess program and purchased an outside drop recently.

Watson feels the library had received "broad community support from various community groups. There is a wholesome attitude on the part of the city fathers, and we have a very cooperative board."[57]

Story hours were offered at the main library and the Oak Park Branch in November 1969. The weekly schedule at the main library consisted of the Peppermint Princess telling stories to children 4-6 years, 10-11 a.m. on Monday; Thursday it was Sara McDaris at 10-11 a.m. for 4-6 years old; and Peppermint Princess for ages 6-8 from 4-4:40 p.m. At Oak Park, Mrs. Wallace Jones held sway for ages 4-6 every Wednesday at 10-11 a.m.

The library director, Elbert Watson gave capsule book reviews on radio station WFIX, 5 days a week at 10:05 a.m., 1:05 and 10:05 p.m.

The Friends of the Library conducted a successful annual membership drive, as 331 supporters contributed $1152 in fees. The fees were the contributions above the $2 membership, as the money goes for the purchase of books. The friends' executive board supplied and decorated, with the staff's help, the library's first float for the annual Christmas parade which introduced the Peppermint Princess to the children of Huntsville, The board also paid for one of the library's two new drops.[59]

A typical bookmobile schedule for August 1969 follows:
"County Bookmobile
- Tuesday: Hubert's Store, 11 a.m.
  - New Market checkoff truck, noon
  - Plevna, Johnson's store, 2:30 p.m.
  - Moore's Mill Road, M&M Supermarket. 3 p.m.
- Wednesday: Gurley, Hewlett's Store, 10 a.m.
  - Hurricane, Bragg's Store. 11 a.m.
  - Maysville, Harbin and Sharpe, noon
- Thursday: Madison, Humphrey's Store, 9:30-10:30 a.m.
  - Madison Center, 10:30 a.m.-noon
  - Harvest, Mrs. Durham's Grocery, 1 p.m.
- Friday: Monte Sano, 2:30-3:30 p.m.

City Bookmobile
- Monday: Northwest YMCA, 1 to 5:30 p.m.
  - Harris Home, 6 to 7 p.m.
- Tuesday: Triana Boulevard and Drake Avenue, 1 to 4:30 p.m.
  - Rose and Ninth Avenue, 5 to 7 p.m.
- Wednesday: Limon and Gunnison Swimming Pool, 1 to 5 p.m.
  - TP Grocery, Mountain Gap, 5:50 to 7:30 p.m.
- Thursday: Sherwood Park Swimming Pool, 1 to 7 p.m.
- Friday: St, Barkley Day Care Center, Norwood, 1 to 4: 30 p.m.
  - Lincoln Boys Club, 4:30 to 7:30 p.m."[60]

On December 12, 1969, Elbert Watson, library director, officially changed the name of the local history room to the Heritage Room. Watson gave an impressive talk on the importance of our heritage. He emphasized our collective responsibility for preserving and transmitting American ideals. He stressed the pronoun "we" in our documents such as, "We hold these truths to be self-evident." And "We the people of the United States." Attending the ceremony were mayor Joe Davis, county commissioner James Record's representative, Mrs. Richard Gilliam, Mrs. R.J. Lowe, chairman of the library board, members of the library staff, the Historical Society, and several Friends of the Library who served refreshments. Watson was prescient, because he added many materials, but he recognized that an increasing number of Huntsville residents were not born in Alabama. Today the genealogical materials cover much of the United States and the early immigration years.[61]

The heritage room procedures were written out so it helped the employees to better serve the customers. They are repeated here because they also identify the holdings of that era. Perhaps they will help future visitors to the heritage room find their way around it easier.

"Historical

(a) Alabama

(b) Confederate

(c) Indians

(d) Other States

All books are catalogued and filed by number and author within the number. Look in catalogue files for name and author of book to find location on shelf.

Owen's History of Alabama is a quick reference. Vols. I & II are for non-biographical subjects and Vols. III & IV are biographical.

Alabama Encyclopedia is a quick reference for most Alabama subjects.

Pickett's History is for quick reference on Alabama Indians.

Betts History of Huntsville and Taylors History of Madison County reference for this area.

Files are arranged alphabetically on Alabama, Madison County and Huntsville materials. Index to material is in front of "Madison County" drawer.

Genealogical

Have books containing genealogical material from many states. Look in catalogue files.

If a person wishes to start his family search: ask how much he knows? Who were his grandparents? Where did they live? See if they are in the census of that county. (Book showing how to put reel on machine is in front of desk drawer.)

If the ancestor lived in Alabama give them the Jones books for that county or look in Alabama County book. Can find number by looking in files.

If family has been traced back to early 1800s look in 1790 census books and find which county this family lived in. Search books of that county.

In files have Huntsville Times from 1928. Some very early 1800 newspapers, located in last cabinet by window.

Census records in cabinets labeled with state and year.

In cabinet behind desk are found early newspapers from other states; Cherokee newspaper, Ala. Confederate Soldiers, Church records & etc.

Index Books

Index to Confederate Military and Naval Records is in second drawer from top in gray filing cabinets at end of files.

Swem's Index to Virginia Records is filed with Virginia books. (Dr. E.G. Swem's Index is the authoritative record of all family names in the United States)

Most all books have index in back.

Nothing in room checks out without Mr. Watson's permission. (author's italics) If he gives permission it may be checked out, write in checkout book author, title and accession number, date checked out, name, address and telephone of borrowers

Nothing in files checks out.

Memorial Books

Take name of person giving the book, name of person given in memory of, name and address of person to whom the card is to be sent. Ask how much they wish to pay for book. Refer to Mrs. Murphy's office.

Interlibrary Loan

Take the person's name, address and telephone number. Write down the film or book (author and title.) Turn information over to Mrs. Talbert."[61]

The room arrangement and size have changed from the 1970s era if you go into the heritage room of the year 2000 era.

A workshop on local history and genealogy was held at the library November 8, 1969. It was sponsored jointly by the Huntsville Historical Society, the Tennessee Valley Genealogical Society, and the library. There were two speakers in the morning. Milo Howard, director of the Alabama Department of Archives and History spoke of "The State Agency's Role in Preserving Historical and Genealogical Records." Walter Jordan, Director of Archives and Records Management for the State of Tennessee, discussed "The Tennessee County Records Microfilming Program – the Preservation of Genealogy and Local History." W. Warner Floyd, executive director of the Alabama Historical Commission, addressed the group over lunch on "Historic Preservation Projects in Alabama." The afternoon session featured Wilbur Hembold, director, Harwell Goodwin Davis Library, Samford University, on the subject, "The Library as a Repository in Genealogy and Local History."[63]

The 1960s was a good decade for the Huntsville-Madison County Public Library. A new and larger main library building was now in place and two single-purpose branch library buildings were instituted. Two energetic professional librarians led the way toward increased public support of the library system. A higher plateau of library services was available to the surrounding area.

Chapter 7

Cooperized?

"To forbid us anything is to make us have a mind for it."

Montaigne, 16th century essayist
100 Banned Books, Censorship Histories of World Literature

"Cooperizing the Library Stirs Immediate Storm" read the title to *The Huntsville Times'* Letters to the Editor section on December 3, 1967. E. Cantey Cooper, Assistant City Attorney, recently asked Richard Covey, Director, Huntsville-Madison County Public Library, to remove from circulation Norman Mailer's book, *Why We Are In Vietnam?* [Author's note: I played tennis doubles weekly with Cantey Cooper during 1985-6, with no knowledge of this event.]

The Book Bombshell hit Huntsville in the Friday, December 1, 1967 issue of *The Huntsville Times*. "Book Banned By Attorney" was the column heading of a story broken by Jim Wooten, *Times* Staff Writer. Cooper, now deceased, received a call from the police department and a complaint from a city employee about the book. Cooper found the book to be "objectionable, vulgar, obscene and unfit for public consumption." Acting on his own without the knowledge of either the mayor or the city attorney, Cooper took the action after a city employee brought him a copy.

Mayor Glenn Hearn discussed the situation with Cooper and decided to give him the "the full backing of the city." Hearn said the matter had not been brought to him prior to the Cooper's action because he did not believe it was important enough to do so. That was a serious misjudgment.

Mayor Hearn was asked if that was "censorship" and he replied, "it is no way a matter of censoring the library books. It is a matter of cooperation. Mr. Cooper has done a fine job in keeping the shelves of our book stores and magazine shops clean and I'm behind him 100 percent in this situation, too." The mayor also said that if there are other questionable books on library shelves that they should also be removed.

Mayor Hearn characterized the book as "...nothing but trash according to everyone I've talked to about it." Hearn admitted that he had not read the book. Cooper said that he had not read the book but "skimmed it enough to know it isn't the kind of thing we want in our library."

Richard Covey, the librarian, said he complied with Cooper's request because, "...the library is an agency of the city, financed by the city and controlled by the city." Covey also said he would not have removed the book on the basis of his own judgments, but he agreed with Cooper that it contains "unnecessarily shocking language." Covey cited two books that have been taken from the shelves of many libraries because someone objected to the content: Mark Twain's *Huckleberry Finn* and Pearl Buck's *The Good Earth*.

Covey further cited several controversial books currently in the library: *The Tropic of Cancer, The Tropic of Capricorn, Catcher in the Rye, Lolita, Lady Chatterly's Lover, Fanny Hill, Peyton Place,* and *Battle Cry*.[1] *Times* writer Jim Wooten's article the next day had a quote from an interview with Norman Mailer, "One instant of that war in Vietnam where we're burning children is more obscene than all the books pulled off all the library shelves by all the city attorneys, greedy for publicity, in the U.S.A."

Mrs. Jane K. Lowe, Chairman, Huntsville Public Library Board, said she was surprised and shocked by the removal of the book. The board does not make decisions on what books shall or shall not be offered for circulation in the library. "That is Mr. Covey's job and we have complete confidence in his ability. I believe we are most fortunate to have him at the head of our library program." Covey said that if there were a demand for the book he would return it to the shelves to be as equally responsive to the public opinion as he had been to Cooper's opinion.[2] Thus ended the second day of the controversy, featured by Jim Wooten's stories on December 1&2, 1967.

The third day of the banned book issue was Sunday, December 3, a traditional day for greater length articles by newspapers and editorials. Jim Wooten's article headlined that Cantey Cooper was studying the possibility of a movie review board for Huntsville. Cooper had helped draft an obscenity ordinance last summer and spearheaded a crackdown on the sale of girlie magazines at local shops and stores. Cooper said he believed a citizen's group is preparing to approach the city council about the establishment of a movie review board. Mayor Glenn Hearn described Cooper as "the city's expert on obscene literature." It is assumed that Hearn was only referring to those employed by the city that he knew of. Norman Mailer, in his earlier interview, had described Cooper as "greedy for publicity."[3]

The Huntsville Times Sunday editorial for December 3, 1967 will be quoted in its entirety. Under its byline on the editorial page were the following words: *"For Truth, Progress and Independence."*
"Mauling Mailer

Faulty judgment rather than book-burning is the issue, at this moment, in the case of Norman Mailer's controversial *"Why We Are In Vietnam?"* But the issue needs to be illuminated here and now and the point made bluntly that no city official – neither Assistant City Attorney Cantey Cooper, who requested the book's removal, nor Mayor Glenn Hearn, who said he approves of Cooper's action – has the authority or the competence to decide what Huntsvillians shall read and what they shall not read.

The city has a competent professional librarian whose responsibility it is to provide the broadest possible literary fare for the patrons of the public library. In discussing the case of the Mailer opus, Mr. Richard Covey pointed out that books for the library are selected, not on the basis of his personal preferences but upon criteria of literary value and popular appeal.

The preferences of individual readers, Mr. Cooper and Mr. Hearn included, certainly are proper subjects for discussion with Mr. Covey, if they wish to bring them to his attention – as sometime users of the library.

But their likes and dislikes should carry no more weight with the librarian in the exercise of his professional judgment than mine or thine. And he certainly ought not be subjected to the kind of inferred official pressure that was represented in Cooper's request for removal of the Mailer volume.

This, of course, is not to recommend Mr. Mailer's latest screed to the casual reader. The language is foul from the first page to the last and will repulse many readers; but in the context it is plausible. Mr. Mailer is, nonetheless, a talented and compelling literary figure whose works belong in any good library. This one, however, would require special handling and circulation to a mature audience only.

The danger inherent in this episode was stressed in Mayor Hearn's assertion that 'other questionable' books should be removed from the library shelves, too, if they are any there. "Questionable" is hardly a precise evaluation of the literary worth of a book.

And the question that must immediately arise is who shall make the determination.

The answer simply is that the librarian, the professional the city employed for this purpose, shall make the decisions. And he should be allowed to make them free of extraneous pressures. He has, over the past seven years, demonstrated the soundness of his judgment and will, we may be sure, continue to do so, despite the momentary lapses that caused him to put Mailer's latest on the shelf in the first place and then to succumb to the urging of an official who was acting out of turn."

The Sunday Letters to the Editor contained the results of two quick-acting citizen respondents. E.A. Worden, Huntsville, sent the following telegram to Mayor Hearn, "RECOMMEND YOU AND OTHER CITY EMPLOYES (sic) SPEND MORE TIME BALANCING BUDGET THAN CENSORING LITERATURE."

Thomas E. Loughead, Huntsville, wrote an open letter to the mayor, "...Who are you, Mr. Mayor, to decide what I am to obtain to read? By what criteria do you and Mr. Cooper decide what is fit and unfit for my consumption?"[4]

Monday, December 4, brought new information. Richard Covey, Librarian, announced that Mailer's book would go back on the shelf. Another citizen's (anonymous) response to the controversy was printed in Monday's paper:

"The Question

A BALLAD OF CANTEY COOPER

A four-lettered word is a **** **** thing, And though I'm self-appointed
I'm well equipped to judge a book. For I am self-annointed.
How many four letters may one book have, And still stay on the shelf?
That's a blank blank thing to ask of me, Who am only a righteous self.
One small d—n and a low-key darn, Are, some hold, quite emulsive,
But three blanks in a row plus asterisks Are (delete) (delete) repulsive."[5]

The dawning of yet another day in this controversy brought new information in Jim Wooten's column for Wednesday, December 5. Huntsville's bookstores are sold out of Mailer's book, and the public is asking for more copies. Richard Covey said he will return the book to circulation when he receives 25 letters demanding that it be done, and he knows of at least 25 folks who are doing so. It was not clear where the number 25 came from, or whether there is anything magical about it or whether it comes library standard procedures.

Cooper now feels he was acting more as a private citizen than a representative of the city when he made the request. But he admitted that "in practical terms" he supposed what he did was an official act. He continued to backpedal saying his request could be considered as nothing more than the expression of any other Huntsville citizen. Well, which is it??? Cooper then said it was, he supposed, more personal than professional. He had no plans to keep the book from being sold in bookstores.[6]

The Huntsville Times on December 5 printed nine letters to the editor, the section called "Go Tell It on The Mountain." At the bottom was this item:

"Essays for Contemplation

THE LETTERS to the editor appearing on this page represent every mailed communication on the subject concerned which *The Times* has received at deadline time for today's editorial page.

We cannot recall a case where a similar number of letters has exhibited a percentage so predominantly backing the *pro* or *con* of such a forum topic.

The letters seem to speak forcefully enough.

They should provide plenty for contemplation and soul-searching by those who feel that Huntsville is in dire need of spoon-feeding."

The letters printed were 7 to 2 against Cooper's solution to the issue. Only one of those letters will be quoted here.

"Mr. Editor, please tell this one to the mountain.

At the tender age of 13, my fellow-students and I contributed to a 'clean-sing' public bonfire fed by books from our junior high school library. The German government had decided what was 'good' for us.

At the age of 25, I came to the United States and had an opportunity to slowly grasp the meaning of this fire. Now that I am nearly twice the 25, I do not require the least bit of governmental assistance on such matters.

If there is a need in Huntsville refresher courses on the subject of 'Free Country,' there are quite a few immigrants qualified and available to teach graduate-level evening classes.

WALTER WEISMAN, Huntsville"

Walter Weisman was a member of the Wernher von Braun rocket team, which came from Germany to the United States and eventually ended up in Huntsville

For the benefit of the majority of the readers of this history who think World War II is ancient history, I offer this important explanation of Walter Weisman's letter. The following is a quotation from William L. Shirer's book, *The Rise and Fall of the Third Reich*:

"On the evening of May 10, 1933, some four and a half months after Hitler became Chancellor, there occurred in Berlin a scene which had not been witnessed in the Western world since the late Middle Ages. At about midnight a torchlight parade of thousands of students ended at a square on Unter den Linden opposite the University of Berlin. Torches were put to a huge pile of books that had been gathered there, and as the flames enveloped them more books were thrown on the fire until some twenty thousand books had been consumed. Similar scenes took place in several other cities. The book burning had begun.

Many of the books tossed into the flames in Berlin that night by the joyous students under the approving eye of Dr. Goebbels had been written by authors of world reputation. They included, among German writers, Thomas and Heinrich Mann, Leon Feuchtwanger, Jacob Wassermann, Arnold and Stefan Zweig, Erich Maria Remarque, Walther Rathenau, Albert Einstein, Alfred Kerr and Hugo Preuss, the last named being the scholar who had drafted the Weimar Constitution. But not only the works of dozens of German writers were burned. A good many foreign authors were also included: Jack London, Margaret Sanger, H.G. Wells, Havelock Ellis, Arthur Schnitzler, Freud, Gide, Zola, Proust. In the words of a student proclamation, any book was condemned to the flames 'which acts subversively on our future or strikes at the root of German thought, the German home and the driving forces of our people..'

Dr. Goebbels, the new Propaganda Minister, who from now on was to put German culture into a Nazi straitjacket, addressed the students as the burning books turned to ashes. 'The soul of the German people can again express itself. These flames not only illuminate the final end of an old era; they also light up the new.'

The new Nazi era of German culture was illuminated not only by the bonfires of books *and the more effective, if less symbolic, measures of proscribing the sale or library circulation of hundreds of volumes and the publishing of many new ones,* but the regimentation of culture on a scale which no modern Western nation had ever experienced." [7] (author's italics)

On Thursday December 6, another letter to the editor: "LET THEM REMEMBER. Hear Ye, Hear Ye, Hear Ye and shades of *Mein Kampf.* (My Struggle, by Adolf Hitler) ...I sentence these gentlemen (Cooper and Hearn) to review recent Supreme Court decisions and to sit for hour on end viewing newsreels of the 1930s showing Fascist and Communist book burning. B.L.TICKLIN, Huntsville"[9] Book burning has a long history as one of the ways to subjugate populations by destroying their culture. Emperor Qin Shi Huang burned books in 213 B.C. Qin, pronounced "chin", was the first man to unify China (221 B.C.), which takes his name. He was also responsible for the renowned Terra-cotta warriors, which were his soldiers. The Vikings, who invaded the British Isles during the second half of the first millennium C.E., destroyed books in the monasteries and killed monks because they resented a culture superior to the Viking's.

During the Enlightenment period in Europe during the 17th and 18th centuries, conquerors became interested in liberating (stealing) the books of the losers. They became prized possessions of the winners, and many of the finest libraries in Europe today take pride in their core holdings that came from another country and in a foreign language.

In the middle of the 19th century, Heinrich Heine, the famous German poet, wrote, "Where books are burned, people will be burned." His prophetic words preceded the Nazi Holocaust of the Jews by 100 years.

Book banning was usually in one of four general categories, political, religious, sexual, or social. Religious books have been banned since the beginning of Christianity. The Catholic Church maintained *An Index of Forbidden Books* from 1559 until 1966. Further reading on the subject can be found in *100 Banned Books,* by Nicholas J. Karolides, et al., 1999, although there are other books on the subject.

On December 8, 1967 *The Huntsville Times* had this to say:

"In an almost unprecedented stream, letter(s) from readers concerning the case of the book removed from the public library have arrived at *The Times.*

It speaks well indeed for the community concern of every one who has written, no matter whether he has defended or protested removal of the volume. Many have phrased their opinions well, and the time spent in earnest attempts to make their points obviously has been considerable.

The time seems overdue, however, to dispense with further publication of letters on this topic. Even the most spirited of debates grows wearisome to the readers, and the basic issues appear to have been well established by now.

A tally made yesterday indicates that the ratio of letters objecting to book-removals and-or the wisdom of censorship at the municipal level has been approximately five to one."[9]

On December 10, *The Times* printed one more letter of the subject. This letter was from the Friends of the Huntsville Public Library to Mrs. Jane K. Lowe, chairman of the library board of the Huntsville Public Library:

"Dear Mrs. Lowe,

The Friends of the Huntsville Public Library are a volunteer organization whose purposes are 'to promote the interest of the Public Library and thereby, the people it serves; to enlarge the facilities and expand the services of the Library; to work, counsel and cooperate with the Library Board, the City Council of Huntsville and the Board of County Commissioners and thereby, foster the progress and goals of the Library.'

We, the board of directors, regret the recent controversy over a book in the Huntsville Public Library. We strongly believe that the operation of the Huntsville Public Library should be the sole responsibility of the director of the library in conjunction with the library board.

We, the Friends, support the above statement and wish to exert every effort to unite the members of this community to aid in preventing any individual or groups of individuals from hampering the operations of the Huntsville Public Library in fulfilling its duty to the citizens of Huntsville and Madison County.

Sincerely yours,

ROBERT B. SMITH, President

Friends of the Huntsville Public Library"[10]

Well, Folks, I've saved the best to last, but that is also the way it came out chronologically. It's Sunday, December 10, 1967, and time for Carolyn Callahan's Sunday column, Ex Libris, in *The Huntsville Times*. Remember, the book banning issue broke in the afternoon paper on a Friday, nine days ago. Carolyn's column probably got scrubbed at that time. But she more than makes up for it. My favorite Ex Libris columnist has outdone herself with this effort. For my younger readers, she wrote a parody on the main theme of The Music Man, which came out only five years before. I hope you enjoy it as much as I did quoting it.

"Dirtiest Word For a Reader: 'Censorship'

Well, Folks, we got trouble in River City. Yes, Sir, we got dirty books; books like Chaucer, Rabelais, and Balzac! And Lawrence, Miller and Mailer. Yes, Sir, we got Trouble, and that starts with T and rhymes with C, and that stands for Censorship. And that, Folks, is a dirty word!

Yes, we got Trouble. We got an assistant district attorney and the mayor banning books they ain't even read. Course no politician can afford to admit he's read a book that ain't fit to read. Not many of 'em want it known they've read ANY books, 'cept maybe the Bible. There are those who think the Bible gets a bit earthy in places. I've even heard some authors say that they quote from the Bible in cases where they're trying to establish in court whether or not a book's fit for the library or the local bookstores.

Yes, Sir, we got Trouble. We got people clamoring to read a book that's all over the front pages of the press and on TV without having to go out and buy it for $4.95. We've got a library director who can't get his work done for answering telephone calls from people who want to get the book back on the shelves before the assistant city attorney and the mayor start making it a habit to ban every 'questionable' book they ain't read. We've got an author rubbing his hands with glee because his 'trashy' book is getting thousands of dollars worth of free publicity. The whole mess'll probably be in TIME next week.

Yes, Sir, we got Trouble. How we gonna keep the old ones moral after school if we 'low these dirty books to creep into our public library? Don't somebody read all 30,000 books published every year? Can't they put all those 'questionable' ones on a certain shelf and let honest, upright, men of good character who ain't likely to be tainted by 'shocking language' take'em out? Course there is a little red band on the back of some of the books to show that somebody over at the American Lending Library Company thought these books might offend somebody. But maybe not everybody knows about that little red band, and then that's only on the new books for a few months while so many people want to read 'em.

There's lots of old books in the library that don't have anything on the cover 'cept the author's name and title. You'd just about have to READ them to know whether or not they're offensive. Most people probably have forgotten when Mark Twain and Dickens used to raise some eyebrows. I even had a librarian tell me one time I was too young to read "Heidi."

Yes, we got Trouble. The question is, are we gonna let the mayor, the assistant city attorney or any other aspiring politician tell what we can and what we can't read? Or are we gonna be our own censors?

Are we gonna get Mr. Mailer back on the library shelf so he don't make a fortune on book sales in Huntsville, Ala.?

Yes, Sir, the question is: who's saving us from what, and for how long? And what's he gonna save us from next?"[11]

Bravo, Carolyn.

Chapter 8

Outreach and Controversy

"A true university of these days is a collection of books"

Thomas Carlyle, "The Hero as Man of Letters"
On Heroes and Hero Worship (1841)

The decade of the 1970s began with the director's assessment of the state of the library. As stated in the introduction, each director was in a different position from his/her predecessor and had different motivations and professional goals. They cannot be compared with each other easily. Elbert Watson's six-month assessment quoted below tells many stories, and was the only one of its type that this author found. I have italicized some words for special attention by the readers, in order to highlight elements of Watson's words that provide clues to his tenure as director.

"SIX MONTHS REPORT TO THE LIBRARY BOARD

Having concluded six months of service as Director of the Huntsville-Madison County Public Library System, it seems that this is a good time to report on the various accomplishments and changes which have taken place in the library system during this period, and also to *project our thinking ahead* to see what might yet be accomplished

PUBLIC RELATIONS

Thus far I have placed *Public Relations at the top of my priority list*, because it seemed that the Board was vitally interested in a better community-wide image of the library. These are some of the things which I feel constitute solid accomplishments. Your Director has personally addressed a dozen or more local clubs such as the Kiwanis Club, Lions Club, Exchange Club, Sertoma, Tennessee Valley Genealogical Society, Huntsville Historical Society, Twickenham DAR, Virginia Clay Clopton UDC Chapter, and various smaller clubs and organizations.

I have dealt directly with both local newspapers, radio station WFIX, and all three television stations. Out of these contacts have come, I feel, improved coverage of the library through the news media. Both the "Times" and the "News" have given us ample coverage upon request and sometimes without it. The state edition of the Birmingham "Post Herald" has carried feature stories on the library twice and the Birmingham "News" once. WFIX gives us free time for a daily capsule book review. I have been interviewed on all three television stations and appeared once statewide on the ETV channel.

From the very beginning, I have conscientiously tried to *build an image in this community of your Library Director as a professional citizen*. As time and ability have permitted me, *I do not recall one instance when I backed away from an opportunity to enlarge my own sphere of influence,* and to thus represent the library as an integral part of community life.

IMPROVEMENTS ON THE BUILDING

A glaring need last spring was the deteriorating appearance of our library building, and the general displacement of certain departments and portions of the library collections. Most of the fiction material is now concentrated near the main entrance to the building, thus providing easier accessibility to the general readers who wish to spend only a few minutes in the library. The unsightly periodical racks, with the magazines hanging limply in them, have been moved to the western side of the main reading room where, at least, it is possible to eliminate some of the cluttered up appearance which once greeted patrons upon entering the library. Plastic binders have been added to most of the periodicals to keep them in an upright position. Three racks were eliminated by simply placing the magazines closer together.

On the second floor of the building, the former conference room is now the story hour room. The Local History Room was moved from the northeastern corner of the building to the southeast and renamed the Huntsville Heritage Room. The Children's Department, formerly located in this room, was moved to the Technical Services Department and renamed the Young Readers Room. The Technical Services Department was moved downstairs to the basement. As a result of these changes the following improvements have been noted:

The Huntsville Heritage Room is provided with 80% more floor space and is more accessible to its patrons; the Young Readers Department is provided with 50% more floor space and is more accessible to its patrons; the Technical Services Department, although its quarters are not impressive in appearance, is more accessible to the arrival of library materials which must be processed.

Other building improvements include the following:
(1) The downstairs area and the Young Readers Department have been given new coats of paint.
(2) Vinyl wall fabric of an impressive quality has been placed in the upstairs hallways, the story hour room, auditorium, and the Huntsville Heritage Room.
(3) Wall paneling has been added to the Director's and Assistant Director's offices.
(4) Orders have also been placed for lounge furniture and additional shelving. Once this equipment arrives, the general appearance of the building will be further enhanced.

EXTENSION DEPARTMENT ADDED

Previously, our organizational structure had several interesting arrangements, one of which was placing of bookmobile, branches, reference, and circulation under one heading. In September an Extension Department became a separate entity in the library organization. A weakness in our earlier extension work is noted by the fact that last year we only circulated approximately 5,000 books through our county deposit stations. For this small service, we paid one employee $4,500, which, combined with other expenses, meant that we spent over $5,000 to circulate 5,000 books. This seems to be a rather small return on our investment. *In assessing the county situation, we decided to eliminate the deposit stations in favor of regular bookmobile stops.* Although a few county patrons will be inconvenienced by this change, it is believed that in time they will realize the value in having a much wider selection of library materials available from the bookmobile. The extension department is presently investigating the possibility of placing a book deposit in the Juvenile Detention Home and Harris Home. *It is hoped that branch libraries will one day constitute one of the strong arms of our public library service.*

LIBRARY STAFF

On a whole, I feel we have a public library staff which is above average. I have endeavored to *bring new people into the organization who are intellectually alert and personally attractive in their appearance.* Although a salary schedule was adopted by the Board last fall, we are not, as yet, in a position to be competitive with other professional library salaries in the area. But I feel that overall we have a staff that is professionally competent and resourceful in their duties.

MISCELLANEOUS ITEMS

(1) Audiovisual materials -- We are building a large and versatile collection of microfilm, which will be one of the best to be found in any public library in Alabama. Faced with a serious space problem, more libraries will turn to microfilm as a solution. We are in the vanguard in this important area with our growing collection of Huntsville "Times", New York "Times", Federal Census Records and other important holdings. Recently we have begun adding 8mm films, which can be circulated to library patrons and clubs for various programs and activities.

(2) Peppermint Princess -- Through the Peppermint Princess we have effected a good contact with children, some of whom have had no previous experience with the public library. The Peppermint Princess has appeared four times on television, visited several elementary schools, and spoken to children of members of the Huntsville Literary Association.

WHAT OF THE FUTURE?

I strongly feel today, as I did last spring during my interview, that this library system can have an outstanding future. I am glad that you gave me the opportunity to come here and be a part of it. *Naturally, I am a human being and I have certain hopes and aspirations for myself.* When I think of the flexibility, which you members of the Board have exercised in this time of transition, I feel confident that the future bodes well for all of us who are interested and concerned for the public library. *Here are some of the things which I hope to continue to work on in the future:*
(1) To build a strong reference collection in subject areas which will go beyond the fine ready reference collection which we have at the present.
(2) To focus attention upon the great need for a strong branch library system.
(3) To impress upon the citizens of the county, as well as the city, how important public library service can be to them.
(4) To build a dedicated professional staff with sufficient incentive in salary and related benefits so that we will be second to none anywhere among our sister public libraries.
(5) To make this entire community aware of the fact that the public library is entitled to a place in the mainstream of community activity if it is given the opportunity.
Respectfully Submitted
Elbert Watson, Director"[1]

In February 1970 the library board approved a "no smoking" policy in the heritage room of the Huntsville Public Library. This policy was long overdue for anyone who has looked into the various means by which books and papers are degraded over time. Even second-hand smoke will coat the top edges and spines of shelved books significantly over time. Presumably this policy did not affect smoking in the rest of the library.[2]

April 14, 1970 – Mrs. Roberts was elected chairman of the library board, and she would have a long tenure in that position.

The library reached a new plateau of activities during the 1970's and 1980's, although there were many new events and activities in the future. I discovered there was less of interest to write up from the board minutes than in the 1940's through the 1960's. During those three decades, the board focus was more on getting books on a small budget and trying to build up the library services and community outreach. The 1970's and 1980's cited above had 20-25 items on the agenda each month, many were old business that just went on and on, but the issues were such things as health and dental insurance, salaries, retirement, other personnel issues, boiler problems, building maintenance, and internal environmental control. Those items were important to the board and the library personnel, as the number of employees increased and the work became more stratified and bureaucratic.

Sherlock Holmes, where are you when we need you? In May 1970 the library reported that over 2,500 books have been "lost" from the main library building. From October 1969 to May 1970, 477 books were taken and not returned from the extension department, 213 from the Charlotte Drive Branch and 264 from the Oak Park Branch. About 1,000 of the books taken from the main building were from the children's department. But non-returners are equal opportunity folks. More expensive books such as reference volumes on world records, law, medical dictionaries, investment handbooks, and works on Shakespeare were not returned, because they were not loaned out. They were just plain stolen. All of the above books must be replaced at additional cost, which is borne by the taxpayer, instead of adding new ones. At $4-5 per average book, that adds up to a considerable amount of money. In 1970 books were loaned for three weeks, with no renewal program.[3]

The Library opened a branch at 2500 Brahan Street in the Huntsville Model Cities Area II facility in June 1970. Mary Nichols, Coordinator of Library Services rode the bookmobile to the area and then knocked on doors to gather children for the weekly story hour. In the first two months of operation, the library had 695 visitors and 864 books were withdrawn, as enthusiasm was apparent by the response. The collection was heavy in black biography and history, and had a great many paperbacks. The small reading room had one adult size table and chairs and another small set for children. An overdue list was posted and a patron could not make any more withdrawals until his name was removed from the list. That solution should be remembered, as overdue problems are surfaced in the later years.

The Brahan Street library was the brainchild of Mrs. Elizabeth Beamguard, Director of Alabama Public Services, and Elbert Watson, Director, Huntsville Public Library. Mrs. Beamguard, head librarian, 1945-54, knew Huntsville well. The two approached John Bracey, Director, Model Cities Program, to see how they could help. Since transportation was a chronic problem, the best solution was to take the books to the readers' neighborhoods. Huntsville was fortunate to have such forward-looking individuals coalesce into an innovative solution for the benefit of the citizens.

Mary Nichols had previous experience in library extension service and was assigned the task. She toured three Model Cities libraries in Atlanta, then came back to implement the ideas in Huntsville. She only provided 2-3 hours of service per day, but volunteer high school students staffed the library during the summer.[4] The Brahan Street site in 2004 was a vacant gray building at the northwest corner of Governor's Avenue and Brahan Street, across Brahan from a Conoco gasoline station.

The library's blind and physically handicapped department continued to improve its services in 1970. Only one blind person out of eight learns to read Braille, but talking books can take provide a substitute. The library maintained a steadily increasing inventory of 1,000 talking books. Joyce Smith said, "We presently have about 70 active users, but based upon the size of Huntsville, there are probably about 650 blind persons in the area who are eligible. There are probably three times as many handicapped eligible."

The average talking book takes about eight ten-inch discs recorded at 16 2/3 rpm. Magazines are recorded at 8 1/3 rpm, a speed not on ordinary record players. The perennial favorite, "Gone With the Wind" takes 27 records and the marathon work, "War and Peace" requires 43 records to convert it into a talking book.

About 20 talking magazines are available at the Huntsville Library. American Heritage, Newsweek, Look, Atlantic, Harpers, Readers' Digest, Saturday Review, and Jack and Jill are favorites.[5]

The Oak Park Branch was named after Miss Bessie Russell, currently the head of the Heritage Room. The 1970 summer reading program was named, "Summer Reading is Out of This World," in consonance with Huntsville being the home of the space program under the leadership of Wernher von Braun. Each reader had a space-age motif membership card to keep track of the number of books read over the summer. A UFO signified 5 books, a space capsule represented 10, an American flag 15 and 2 short book reports, and an astronaut indicated 20 books and 5 short reports. Elbert Watson, library director, indicated that books were flying off the shelves in the children's department at a rate of nearly 1,000 per day.[6]

Venture, the monthly two-page newsletter published by the Friends of the Library, in November 1970 reported a total of $935.05 netted from the fall used book sale, which brought the total for the spring and fall sales to $1,635.06. Marelle Pruitt was chairman, with Christel McCanless as co-chairman. Helen Akens handled the publicity through local spot announcements on television and radio stations. Articles and pictures were in *The Huntsville Times, Huntsville News*, and even the *Birmingham News*. Prices were reduced as the sale progressed, with many books going for one cent and magazines five for a penny.

Also reported in the Venture was the establishment of a long range planning committee to formulate a master plan for orderly growth of the library with special emphasis on the creation of permanent branches in the city and county. The committee had 2 members from the library board, 2 from the library, and 2 from the friends.[7]

Elbert Watson, library director, was the author of two books, *The History of Etowah County* and *Tennessee at the Battle of New Orleans*, and in 1971 was working on another to be titled, *Tell Me About America.* In addition to belonging to state and national library associations, Watson was a member of the Alabama Historical Association and on the Board of Directors of the Huntsville Historical Association. His avocation as an amateur historian was instrumental to the library from two perspectives. First, he continued to increase the holding of the Heritage Room, particularly of genealogical material and Southern memorabilia. Second, he was aware of the historical development of the American library system and he took a long view of the future roles of public libraries. He addressed the Huntsville Rotary club in January 1971 with this primary theme: knowledge of both the past and present provides society with a sense of direction it sorely needs. He believed that a library is a university of learning and ideas, which should be accessible to the general public providing them with both knowledge and ideas. It is not enough for a library to exist as an edifice; contents give it character and a library's personality is part of its character."

Watson told the Rotarians he was concerned with making the public aware that libraries as a storehouse of learning and ideas are an integral part of the growth processes in society, a necessary tool in lending perspective and balance to society. "I believe in history and the lessons derived from it, and I'm a firm believer in the American dream. But I fear the American dream will perish if ever the American heritage dies."

Watson disclosed plans for an extended outreach program designed to bring the library within reach of everybody in Madison County. This would entail increased emphasis on branch libraries and bookmobiles, even an institutional outreach program for hospitals, nursing homes, and jails beginning in February 1971.

He said that the Huntsville Public Library now has one of the largest, most comprehensive community service library sections in the state, to include nearly 4,000 books and magazines for the blind and physically handicapped.[8]

Sunday, January 10, 1971, was a disappointing day for this author, although I did not know it for 33 years. That was the day Carolyn Callahan, the Ex Libris column writer, wrote her last column for *The Huntsville Times*.[9] She dug out the facts and wrote with style. She was a great asset to the Huntsville Public Library and *The Huntsville Times*.

The Library of Congress opened its first reading room for the blind in 1897. There are now over 200,000 persons across the country enrolled in the Library of Congress service for the blind and handicapped. The outreach service celebrated its 40th anniversary in 1971, and the Huntsville Public Library was proud of its affiliation. The Library of Congress estimated there were 500,000 blind persons in the United States and 1,500,000 more who are physically handicapped so that they are unable to handle, hold or turn the pages of printed books and magazines in 1971. They were eligible for the service, which was free, including postage. Imagine yourself being one of them. More than 2,500 titles were recorded on discs and tapes. Playboy magazine was printed in Braille, imagine that.[10]

In July 1971 the community services department of the library began sending out a bi-monthly newsletter to about 300 blind, visually limited and physically handicapped persons. The newsletter was in Braille, large type, and tape recordings. Articles included announcements and explanation of benefits, new books, organizations, tips on new procedures for the handicapped and a listing of libraries that served the blind.[11] Harold Wilson "read" 3,000 books over the last eight years, and he's blind. He used talking books supplied by the Huntsville Library and the Library of Congress. Upon request, the Huntsville Library would supply a record player or tape recorder with headsets and pillow phones attachable. He kept a constant supply at home and in the mail coming in and going back out.[12] The Cavalry Hill Friendship Center had an extension of the Huntsville Public Library in January 1971. This was apparently the same location as the second Negro library, which was started in 1958. The friendship center was part of the Huntsville Model Cities Area II at 7900 Fairbanks Street, which is on the western side of the 2004 Academy for Academics and Arts. The extension was open Monday through Friday from 11:00 a.m. until 6:p.m. Barbara Weaver, librarian, said that approximately 300 children and adults had used the library within the first three weeks it was opened and more than 430 books were checked out. The reading material had a wide selection for all ages, books, magazines, periodicals, reference books, etc.[13] By November 1971, the library's project outreach was in full swing. The project was the brainchild of Elbert Watson, library director, and Judy Tate (Mrs. Doug Tate) was the coordinator. The project started in February 1971, when the Huntsville Library became the first public library in Alabama to undertake a full-time, full-scale outreach program, whereby library personnel take books and materials to hospitals, day care centers, nursing and retirement homes.

Judy Tate said, "Reading is a habit. Some people get out of the habit after they get out of school." Her job was to reintroduce them to the habit. Her approach was a one-on-one personal attempt to make it easy and fun to read. Each person is different, and has different reading desires. One woman told Judy she will only read nonfiction selections because she doesn't "care for lying in any form." {My wife reads fiction and I read nonfiction. Perhaps I should try that "lying" description for her favorites.]

Hospitals and homes participating were Crestwood Hospital, Huntsville Hospital, Fifth Avenue Hospital, Extendicare Nursing Home, Big Spring Manor Nursing Home, Madison Manor Nursing Home and Todd Towers Retirement Home.

Hospitals were visited twice a week. Nursing and retirement homes were visited once every two weeks. Hospital administrators have supported project outreach because it helped make the participants stay more pleasant. Judy Tate noticed that many people really do judge a book by its cover. She also found that patients expecting a short stay in the hospital are particularly inclined to read a paperback because they don't expect to be hospitalized long enough to read a hardback novel. The hospital outreach faded out in the 1990s as hospitals apparently prefer their patients buy reading material at the hospital's gift shop.

The elderly like the large print books. For patients who must lie flat on their backs, the Heritage Junior Women's Club gave the library prism glasses and book stands for the large print books. Talking books were also popular.

Judy Tate told the story [remember we are back in 1971] that she was wearing a short skirt and boots, an elderly woman she saw on her route in a local retirement home warned her, "You better get those knees covered up or you're gonna have rheumatism in 'em for sure."[14]

In January 1972 there was a vote on a state constitutional amendment to allow voters in any single county to decide on additional taxes for public libraries. It would allow the local governments to impose an additional property tax of not more than five mills with the consent of the voters in that governmental area. This was not a directed tax by the state, but only allowed the folks in a county to vote for it. An identical amendment was defeated two years ago statewide and in Madison County. Would it pass this time?[15] The vote on the amendment is in. The results were best described in the following editorial by the *Huntsville News* on January 28, 1972.

"A slim vote for literacy

Huntsville and Madison County voters who passed Amendment No. 1, the Alabama constitutional issue in the recent election, can today be semi-proud that the rest of the state agreed with our county that libraries are important enough to justify giving each county's electorate the option to vote a very small additional property tax upon themselves to improve, expand, and more fully stock these vital storehouses of information, stimulation, and recreation.

Note that we qualify our statement: semi-proud seems the just word in this connotation. For it was a slim vote for literacy – far, in fact, too slender for comfort.

An absolutely reliable source here late Wednesday that Alabama Secretary of State Mabel Amos has confirmed that the controversial amendment, defeated the last time it was presented to the electorate, narrowly became law by a very minimal two to three hundred vote margin.

Margins in favor of the constitutional amendment, which is in reality enabling legislation which permits a county to call a tax referendum if it so desires, were comfortable only in Madison, Jefferson, and Montgomery Counties – three of the state's four major urban areas. The prime reason for defeat of the amendment in Mobile County was a lack of leadership; the central library there had no chief executive during the crucial six months advocates of the measure were working for its passage.

The primarily rural counties, however, in the main opposed it. **As usual**. [Author's bold.]

WE DO NOT PAY that much attention to spurious national ratings, but any perceptive person must realize Alabama must by now certainly stand to climb in national esteem and achievement. Fuel for such an operation bootstrap is education, and education's most vital tool is the printed word – storehouse of man's slow exploration and analysis of himself and his environment.

The functional illiterate condemns himself to a half-life more related to animal sensation than the full glory of the human experience.

It somewhat saddens us to observe that those who would seem to most need libraries and the wealth of knowledge they house are the least interested. But the amendment has passed, no matter how barely. The opportunity now exists for increased statewide literacy and its accompanying enrichment.

It is our sincerest hope that the option will be embraced."[16]

The slim vote cited in the Newspaper editorial was actually 55.5 percent in favor of the amendment. The second and third paragraphs from the end are telling statements about the long-term problem with the lack of education in Alabama. Alabamians are apparently proud of being ignorant, and doing their best to remain so. The situation is reminiscent of a statement by Thomas Paine in his *Rights of Man*, 1791, "Ignorance is of a peculiar nature; once dispelled, it is impossible to re-establish it. It is not originally a thing of itself, but is only the absence of knowledge; and though man may be *kept* ignorant, he cannot be *made* ignorant." (Paine's italics)[17] To Paine's statement must be added the statement from the comic strip character Pogo, "We have met the enemy, and he is us."

The need for a state constitutional amendment on this issue was a legacy of the infamous 1901 Alabama Constitution. One of its numerous faults was that it does not give home rule to counties and large cities. Huntsville and Madison could not even vote on the opportunity to allow a tax, except that the entire state must vote for it. The legislators in Montgomery keep the power in their hands. But there was more to this process. There was an old saying, "from the ridiculous to the sublime." The 1901 Alabama Constitution was far beyond the sublime. The county commissioners wanted to move a graveyard. They had to convince the state delegates representing Madison County that the need exists. The delegates then introduced a bill in the legislature for a constitutional amendment. The full legislature had to approve the amendment to be put before a statewide vote. All of this takes time. Of course, the dead people were in no hurry to be moved, but whatever progress might be underway can be stymied any place along the way. A statewide vote was required on a typical single-county amendment such as Amendment 520, approved on June 5, 1990. It authorized the Madison County Commission to excavate graves.

The United States Constitution has 7,482 words. The 1901 Alabama Constitution has over 315,000 words and over 660 amendments, and still counting. Dare to say the process is beyond ridiculous! That is the reason progress comes so slow to Alabama, to include improved library facilities and services. We have met the enemy and he is us!

A *Huntsville News* editorial from March 25, 1972 was worth quoting:
"Libraries, rights, & diligence

Books and libraries are among mankind's greatest sources of enlightenment. They contain the cultural inheritance of our forefathers and the core of our educational system. In the words of Thomas Carlyle: 'All of Mankind has done, thought, gained, or been; it is lying as in magic preservation in the pages of books.'

'Rights' is a word which has generated most of the major movements relevant to man's present and future on this troubled orb, but little is heard of the right to read. While many avail themselves of the opportunity, few reflect upon the unavoidable fact that like any other right, this one must be preserved and protected by active effort.

The Huntsville Public Library did not spring like mythical Camelot from the machinations of a Merlin; it was built with no little effort and is preserved, as so many institutions of ultimate worth, precariously at best through the diligent efforts of the few who care. Are you among them?"[18]

The above was just one more demonstration of the strong support of Huntsville libraries and the right to read for everybody. Sixty years ago that was not true in Alabama, and 100 years ago it was even worse. The statistics in 1900 were not significantly changed from the 1880 numbers, which show that the 25 percent of the white children could not read or write, and 80 percent of the Negro children could not read or write. Both figures were for children ten years of age and older. No Southern state had a compulsory school law in 1900, while only two Northern states did *not* a compulsory attendance law at the time. [Author's italics.] The demand for better public education came out of "white" counties. The Educational Apportionment Act of 1891 provided for the apportionment of funds to all counties in the state according to the number of children of school age. Township trustees were allowed to divide the money as they deemed "just and equitable." They paid Negro teachers less than white teachers and less money was spent on building and equipment for Negroes. More money became available for white children. School money was spent to send white students to private academies and colleges. If you are not allowed to go to school to learn to read and write, then you probably do not need a library. Such was the apparent thinking of Alabama's white leadership.[19]

Project outreach was in jail, literally. The library was providing books to the Madison County jail March 1, 1972. Judy Tate, outreach coordinator did not go to jail, but filled reading requests from the prisoners. Members of the Weatherly Heights Baptist Church did the delivering. Naturally, law books have a high priority, but requests covered a broad range of topics, from atomic theory to comic books. Travel materials were very popular, perhaps many wanted to travel a long way from Huntsville when they were released. Religious books were also requested. Sex books, those heavy with profanity and blood, and how-to-escape books were not allowed.

The prisoners could keep the books for two weeks and then turn them in to the matron, leave them with a buddy or trade during the next delivery. Books were checked out by name and cell number. No mention was made of a library card. The book cart circulated every Saturday, with about 100 books distributed every week. The cart took 4-5 hours to make the rounds.[20]

April 12, 1972 – A noncommercial FM radio station operated by the library such as WPLN in Nashville was presented to the board as a possibility for the Huntsville Public Library. The director began investigating this after Councilman Wall gave him a letter he had received suggesting the library look into it. Elbert Watson went to Nashville to talk with the director of WPLN and to see its station in operation. The Board authorized Watson to continue his investigation. The rest of the story will be told in Chapter 9.

"The Apt man for the Hour

Elbert Watson, director of the Huntsville-Madison County Library, is to be congratulated upon election Friday as first vice-president and president-elect of the Alabama Library Association.

It couldn't happen to a more capable person, but it must also be noted that, in his eyes at least, we feel sure the honor is almost overshadowed by the responsibility as the state – as well as our community – enters into a time of crisis which will effect everyone's right to read as a public service unless something is done.

While all the facts have not yet been made available to us, we have discovered that the state seems to face a severe cutback in federal funding which will effect (sic) all library systems.

As soon as we can document the facts, we'll present them to you. But Watson and other library officials here tell us that right now it looks like a rough year for Alabama libraries in fiscal terms.

Watson enters the number two spot at an opportune time, even though the responsibility is great. He has proven himself capable of directing a very urban and progressive library system. His election honors not merely him but Huntsville as well; it, however, also serves the entire state at a time when expertise is most needed."[21]

Every year a National Library Week is celebrated. This week is an important time to reflect upon the wonderful public library system we have in the United States of America. We are blessed in that regard, compared to almost all the other countries in the world. But Americans made the country what it is, no one gave it to us. We worked and fought for it. *The Huntsville Times* can be depended upon to provide appropriate editorials. Its editorial from Library Week 1972 is quoted below. It is long, but it covers a lot of ideas that need to be kept in the eyes of Huntsvillians, and reinforced each year.

"Library: You are involved

This is national library week's conclusion, a good time to capsule not what most libraries are, but what they ought to be.

Is a library merely a repository of reading matter made available on a limited basis to the person who walks in the door? Or should it be more?

What about persons who lack transport: who have no way of reaching that lovely building in our city core or the rather meager branches the Huntsville Public Library is currently able to maintain only by squeezing every nickel in appropriations or other funding until it bleeds? What about the sick, the disabled, the handicapped, the blind, the poor, the disadvantaged who have never been advised of their right to use what Elbert Watson, library director, so aptly terms 'this arsenal of ideas, this people's university?'

Under Watson's direction, the Huntsville Public Library has elected to try and go out into the community and provide what is needed rather than merely sitting and waiting for the community to come to it.

Project Outreach and other programs currently maintained by our library have caused a national stir in library circles; yet the average Huntsvillian is neither informed nor involved in this crucial area of community service.

Such projects are not made possible by city funding alone. The library this year received $280,000 from the City of Huntsville, $14,000 from Madison County, $45,000 from federal Library Services and Construction Act funding, $11,500 from gifts, donations, memorials, and fines – an operating budget of about $400,000.

Sound like a lot of money? It doesn't go far when you consider this progressive library system, certainly a model for Alabama if not the entire region, is maintaining fairly respectable book, magazine, film, music, and document holdings while also serving economically disadvantaged, maintaining early childhood education, environmental education, career education, and taking the library to the city slums, the homes for the aged, the jail, and to individuals who are blind or otherwise physically handicapped.

Quite frankly, we are proud of what the library has achieved and we think we have a right to be. Watson and his capable staff have maintained this broad program of community service only by hiring almost entirely non-degree personnel so committed to the community as a whole's right to read that they work long hours at low pay to serve you as you deserve to be.

But even with a pinch-penny approach, money can only spread so far. All the personal dedication in the world – and this the library staff and its unpaid volunteers who assist it in abundance – cannot compensate for inadequate operating funds. Federal funds and gifts are intended to supplement – not provide – basic operating moneys.

Huntsville's current book holdings amount to only .8 books per capita. Alabama standards – poor by national standards which establish **six** books per capita as a norm – demand only **two** per head, and we have less than half that. (author's bold)

We know there are many areas of concern in the community, widely differing causes and interests. But the right to read – to be educated, to be exposed to new ideas and to compare them with the rich heritage of the past – this basic right is the one upon which this United States was founded.

For our Constitution itself and our Declaration of Independence, documents which have literally transformed half the world and had an immeasurable impact on the other half, come to us in the form of the printed word.

If the words in print are freedom's standing army, then libraries are the citadels from which they are sent forth.

Let's do more than merely appreciate or even use our community library; let's get behind it and help it perform its true mission – providing the right to read to every citizen in Madison County."[22]

In August 1972, President Richard M. Nixon vetoed the Health, Education, and Welfare Department's budget request and subsequent action by the U.S. House of Representatives to uphold the veto. That action put federal library funds in jeopardy and the *Huntsville News* editorialized about the potential negative impact. It pointed out that elevated funding is needed if the library is to carry out the broad scope of services to the surrounding area.[23]

James J. Kilpatrick was a nationally syndicated conservative columnist. In Huntsville we know him as the author of The Writer's Art, which appears Saturday morning in *The Huntsville Times* in 2004. I am a fan of this column, because I try to learn to be a better writer, and he has an inviting style. He was also a curmudgeon. In 1973, after Nixon's veto (above), Kilpatrick wrote a column on the subject, which is offered below for your consideration.

"Federal Aid to Libraries? Why?

A considerable effort is being mounted on Capital Hill in support of continued direct federal aid to libraries. President Nixon has recommended that such aid be stopped at the end of this fiscal year. Dearly as I love libraries and librarians – and I love 'em all – Nixon's position is soundly based and merits support.

The liberal position in support of library aid was eloquently defended – perhaps over defended – in a recent column by Coleman McCarthy of the *Washington Post*. McCarthy is a topnotch prose stylist and an able exponent of the liberal view, but in common with many of his colleagues he tends to weep easy. In this piece he weeps 10 gallons.

Because of Nixon's proposal, he writes, libraries 'are now on the endangered species list.' He applauds a protest planned for May 8 by the American Library Association, when libraries across the country will dim their lights by way of accusing Nixon of 'dimming the light on the public's right to know.'

'The association speaks with precision,' says McCarthy, 'when it says the public's right to know is at stake.' After all, people go to libraries to read magazines, newspapers, and other sources of information, and Nixon's goal is nothing less than 'the smothering of information.' He conjures up a vision of the President chortling with pleasure at the closing of libraries that spend money for publication critical of administration policies. 'Can any other way of silencing critics be more effective than closing down libraries?'

Horsefeathers! The current program of federal aid to libraries, like the recently halted program of federal aid to small-town water and sewer systems, provides one more case of Big Government come down with a bad case of bloat. It all started with the Rural Library Services Act of 1956, in Eisenhower's day, a modest little $7.5 million program to aid in providing library facilities in communities of less than 10,000 population. It seemed a happy idea.

One trouble with happy ideas is that in Congress they get to be hilarious ideas. In 1964, the program was extended to all public libraries under the Library Services and Construction Act. The following year brought further expansion, in the form of federal aid to elementary and secondary school libraries. Still another act provided $5,000 grants for college and university libraries. The program now has swollen to $140 million a year.

Now, it would be useful if Congress has paused, back in 1956, to consider a threshold question: Does it have the power, under the constitution, to appropriate public funds for rural libraries? It may be that South Carolina's Strom Thurmond and Iowa's H.R. Gross raised the question – they are about the only ones who ever do – but theirs are voices crying in the wilderness. The answer, in my own strict-constructionist view, is no: Libraries, desirable as they are, even essential as they are, are not the responsibility of the federal government.

Put principle to one side, which is where principle often gets put. On the merits, it is nonsense to argue that termination of the $140 million aid will 'close down libraries,' or 'smother information,' or put the public's right to know at stake. Heavens to Betsy, McCarthy! Dry your eyes!

About $54 million now is allocated for aid to public libraries. The sum represents roughly 5 percent of their budgets. If an institution must 'close down' because of a 5 percent cut, it can't be much of a public institution. And what is wrong with replacing the 5 percent through local appropriations or local fund drives? Must we walk forever on federal crutches?

Under Nixon's proposed Better Schools Act, intended to replace categorical grants with broad revenues-sharing, school libraries will have available the same potential aid they have enjoyed in recent years. They will have to compete for the money before local governing bodies, but so what? They won't get 'smothered.'
Up the lights, you librarians! You can live without Big Daddy, if you try."[24]
James Kilpatrick was asked via e-mail to comment on his old column, but he did not reply.

Sometimes interest in rare books cause them to be reprinted. Two such books are now in the Heritage Room.

"*Memories of Old Cahaba* is a 1905 book by Anna M. Gayle Fry, an author who names many names as she writes of her recollections of Alabama's first capital and its people and events. There are sketches and photographs of some of the old Cahaba buildings, and the book includes some of the author's poetry reminiscent of the era a half century ago." [25]
Cahaba, a small settlement about ten miles southwest of Selma at the confluence of the Alabama and Cahaba Rivers, was chosen as the site of the new Capital of Alabama, which it was from 1820 to 1825. It was a bad choice, as the two rivers flooded the low ground. During the 1825 legislative session, one of the highest floods on record inundated the area. Legislators

had to be rowed in boats to the second story of the building in order to hold their session. There were also fevers during the summer months. It was moved to Tuscaloosa.[26]

"Probably the most popular book in the Huntsville Heritage Room, and certainly the rarest, is the 'Huntsville Directory of 1859-60.' Purporting to contain the names of everyone who was anyone in 1859-60 Huntsville, this 166-page book also features illustrated advertisements of many of the types of merchandise of the day, ranging from metallic burial cases to fashionable millinery and photographic and ambrotype gallery equipment. The last part of this book contains a complete list of all United States post offices in 1859, including the territories of Oregon, Utah, New Mexico, Washington, Nebraska, and Kansas, as well as post offices in the mining regions."[27]

"The first Alabama library to break into the cable television picture was the Huntsville Public Library. Their library program was first begun in July 1971, and its new television series, Adventures in Library Land, a program for children, is broadcast Mondays through Thursdays, from 3:30 to 4:00 p.m. on Channel 9, CATV, Huntsville. This program is Director Elbert Watson's newest effort to put the Library back into life, 1970's style instead of a still shot from the 1930's.

The television program hostess, Sara McDaris, is assisted by comedian Sandra McNabb (Buffy, the florescent pink hand-puppet bookworm, and Sirocenie the Genie), and for each program she has about five pre-school (usually kindergarten) children on the show."[28]

"Razors, water, dogs; many methods used to ruin books," was the title of an article in the *Huntsville News* of January 29, 1973. The article continued, "Slashed with razor blades, ripped by hand, submerged in puddles, mauled by dogs; it almost seems that a segment of Huntsville's population is waging a vicious war on the books housed in the public," wrote Linda Cornett. Apparently many students find it much easier to rip a page out of the book to insert in their term paper than make a copy. But it not just students, as recipes, house plans, and diets are ripped out. It is equal opportunity destruction, because those people really don't care since the material does not belong to them. Of course, their tax dollars eventually have to foot the bill for repair or replacement. The library's technical services' staff are the ones to make decisions about repair, replacement, or destruction. Mrs. Elizabeth Herrin devoted 12 of her 22 years at the library in the repair shop. Her skill returns many books to the shelves, as she uses glue, tape, string, scraps of colored paper, pages from old copies, and reproduced copies from books in other libraries to make the repairs.[29]

The 69th annual convention of the Alabama Library Association was held in Huntsville, April 18-20, 1973. The convention center was the Sheraton Inn, with about 500 delegates in attendance. The theme of the convention was "Crisis or Challenge." The "crisis" referred to the Nixon veto in August 1972 cited above. The "challenge" referred to the need for librarians, library boards, and friends of the library to write to their congressmen to get the funds restored. There needs to be a constant battle to influence state and national representatives to secure funding for library projects.

Considering that National Library Week is in April, Huntsville was indeed fortunate to have the president of the American Library Association, Miss Katherine Laich, in town to address the convention. She said, "Money isn't everything, but everything takes money. Therefore, I was happy to see your frank acknowledgement of this fact in the slogan of your legislative workshop. If the most important thing in the world for libraries isn't money, it's who has the money and how to see them about it."

Miss Laich praised Elbert Watson, director of the Huntsville Public Library, who was the new president of the Alabama Library Association. She also noted that Watson was the representative for a seven-state southeastern area to the American Library Association. Also praised by Miss Laich was former Alabama Senator Lister B. Hill, who was one of "the American Library Association's staunchest friends and was the sponsor of our first federal library legislation in 1956. Let us never forget this."

Mrs. Virginia Cooke, director of the American Library Association, said, "Remember it took 10 years to get that first library funding bill passed by the 79th Congress in 1946. Many of you here helped in that struggle, and it finally culminated in a victory with President Eisenhower signing the Library Services Act in 1956." Mrs. Cooke also quoted a 1968 speech by Senator Hill, "you should have a great sense of pride for the service you have rendered all our people in this country. Let this be an hour of renewed dedicated to continue this battle and to continue to go forward in building our libraries so our country may be better prepared to meet the issues of the day."

State Senator Eugene McLain of Huntsville said the Alabama was faced with two humiliating issues in the next session of the legislature – mental health and prison reform. A lady in the audience told McLain that if "funding had been available for libraries when they were children, we wouldn't have all these people in our mental institutions and prisons."[30]

Governor George Wallace officially launched the State's 1974 Smoky Bear Summer Vacation Reading Program on May 1st. The Alabama Public Library Service and the Alabama Forestry Commission cooperated to assist Alabama children to learn more about nature and the environment. Smoky Bear visited libraries throughout the summer.[31]

On November 4, 1974 the Elbert H. Parsons Sr. Law Library opened in the old J.C. Penney store at 205 East Side Square. This law library was a branch of the Huntsville-Madison County Public Library. James Record, Chairman, Madison County Commissioners, was told by the American Library Association that the facility was the first truly public law library in the nation.

The county maintained a one-room law library in the Courthouse beginning in 1963. It was always cramped and disorganized, and about 1970 county officials, at Record's urging, began planning a move to a new space. Record did more than that. He donated one of Alabama's only two known complete sets of state and territorial acts, dating back to 1811.

At this point a word must be said about James Record, Chairman, Madison County Commissioners. He was probably the greatest maker and recorder (pun intended) of history that Madison County has seen. He made history in the county with his progressive personality and activities. But he also wrote a lengthy history of the county. The county bought the first sets of legal references and court reports with a $20,000 federal Law Enforcement Planning Agency (LEPA) grant; the main library then had an annual budget of about $26,000 and was having growing pains. Robert Sellers Smith, the chairman of the Huntsville Bar Association's committee in charge of the law library said they needed $4,000 or $5,000 more to get some really good things in there. Smith believed the city should help, even if it is just $2,000. Record said he was not bothered about the lack of city money, because it was a logical county function.

The Madison County Commission paid the salary of $6,380 for the librarian, Mrs. Cleo Cason. The county also provided the maintenance and security guard. Another $14,000 for the library's 1977-78 budget came from the county trial fees. The Huntsville Bar Association contributed $5,000 from membership dues.[32]

The American Library Association was concerned for the free flow of information and ideas. In January 1975, the following Statement on Professional Ethics was approved by the ALA Council:

"A librarian

- Has a special responsibility to maintain the principles of the Library Bill of Rights.
- Should learn and faithfully execute the policies of the institution of which one is a part and should endeavor to change those which conflict with the spirit of the Library Bill of Rights.
- Must protect the essential confidential relationship which exists between a library user and the library.
- Must avoid any possibility of personal financial gain at the expense of the employing institution.
- Has an obligation to insure equality of opportunity and fair judgment of competence in actions dealing with staff appointments, retentions, and promotions.
- Has an obligation when making appraisals of the qualifications of any individual to report the facts clearly, accurately, and without prejudice, according to generally accepted guidelines concerning the disclosing of personal information."[33]

"Libraries PLUS (People for Libraries Urging Support) is a nonprofit organization working to 'insure for Alabama citizens their right to education, personal enrichment and achievement through public library services...and to raise funds by subscription, sponsorships and other means to help assure continued operation of the corporation, and thereby the public libraries in Alabama.'

PLUS was formed in June 1975 to represent the more than 70 libraries in Alabama. Twenty-eight counties were in active support of the group at year's end.

Lobbying efforts go back to the legislative session of 1973 under the sponsorship of an umbrella group, the Alabama Library Association. The Association backed away from lobbying in 1975, leading to the formation of PLUS. (PLUS President Elbert Watson, Director of the Huntsville-Madison County Public Library, was president of the Alabama Library Association in 1973.)"[34]

In 1973 Governor George Wallace committed the first Revenue Sharing Grant to public libraries, amounting to $272,000 in addition to the annual appropriation of $254,000. The legislature was then prompted to grant an additional $400,000 for public libraries over the 1973-73 biennium appropriation of $614,000. Libraries PLUS, with Virginia Tomme as lobbyist, gained $828,000 in appropriations from the legislature—a far cry from the allotment of $247,000 three years ago. Alabama's record of allotment to libraries was **$0.09** a year per citizen, while the average amount set aside in other states was **$0.80**."[35] [author's bold]

The Oak Park/Bessie Russell Branch was in leased facilities no more. It was replaced by a new facility, which was three times as large. The new building was semi-mobile (the first in Alabama), and will hold 17,000 volumes. It opened on February 27, 1975 at the northern end of the K-Mart shopping center parking lot on North Parkway. The property was donated by S.S. Kresge Company, the parent corporation of K-Mart. The building was designed by Herrin and Jones and constructed by Hereford Construction Company. The building was named after Miss Bessie Russell. Mrs. Nevada Easley would continue to serve as the librarian of the branch. This was the first building to be owned outright by the Huntsville Public Library System. In 1986 the building was moved to its current location at 3011-C Sparkman Drive.[36]

In 1975, the Committee of the American Library Association assumed responsibility for the National Library Week. The funds provided by libraries through their purchase of ALA's National Library Week materials made a year-round library public relations program a reality.[37]

"America's heritage was dramatized on June 8, 1975, as the Huntsville-Madison County Public Library became the stage for living history in a tribute to the Spirit of '76 and great moments in the nation's history. Called 'Reflection of Yesterday,' the program comprised an afternoon of music, character portrayals, films, and displays. The Friends of the Library paid expenses."[38]

The heritage room continued to be one of the favorite spots in the library. The amount of materials was increasing, and the more there is, the more folks came in to search for their ancestors. Genealogy was just like eating peanuts. You cannot eat just one peanut. You cannot uncover just one generation. That raises many questions: who, when, and where did that generation come into existence? Where did those people live and die, and what did they do for a profession?

The Henry B. Zeitler Historical Room was dedicated on March 28, 1976. The Zeitler collection of some 5,000 items was donated by George Lawrence McCrary, Jr., Henry Zeitler McCrary and Frank Boykin Haggard. The Zeitlers, a distinguished family of Mooresville, Alabama, about 17 miles west of Huntsville, endowed their library with a wealth of knowledge by collecting books on America's social, political, religious, and military histories. The collection emphasized the Civil War, with material from both sides of the issue. Combined with the library's present holdings, the Henry B. Zeitler Historical Collection became one of the most valuable collections housed in any library in the state of Alabama.

A former Alabama governor and his family were highlighted in the Clement Comer Clay division of the Zeitler Room. Found here were books and documents of the Huntsville family, which rose to political fame in the 1800s. Clement Clay was governor of Alabama, 1835-37. The collection was donated by Dr. Clement C. Clay of Durham, North Carolina, and Misses Emily and Mary S. Clay of Southern Pines, North Carolina. The donors were grandchildren of John Withers Clay, former editor of the *Huntsville Democrat*.[39]

The Friends of the Library donated $8,150 toward library services during the fiscal year, July 1, 1975-June 30, 1976. The money was distributed as follows: Building directory, $50; Carpet replacement, $1,600; WLRH public radio, $5,000; Records for audio-visual department, $400; Living History Program, $200; Libraries PLUS, $100; Newspapers, $300; and Printing cost of "Venture," library newsletter, $500. There were 13,877 borrower's cards issued during fiscal year 1975-1976, bringing the total number of cardholders to 75,015 adults (over 14 years of age). The bookmobile circulated 28,810 books during the same period. The heritage room was used by 130 persons from 25 states outside Alabama, in addition to one person from England. Five hundred interlibrary loans were secured through the heritage room during the fiscal year.[40]

Go to jail for 30 days because you, yes, I mean you, failed to return a book to the Huntsville Public Library? No? Okay then, how about a fine of $100? The library board asked the city council to adopt an ordinance that would do just that in May 1977. The library lost more than 4,000 volumes a year because some patrons do not return the books they check out. Yes, I mean you! National figures put the cost of replacing a book at $16, an estimate that includes the ordering and processing costs and the purchase price.

A person who failed to return a book or other borrowed library material after receiving a written notice would be in violation of the proposed ordinance. The violation would occur 10 days after the library mails an overdue notice. Under the proposal, failure to return the book on time would be considered evidence that the borrower does not intend to return it. The library charges five cents a day for an overdue book, up to a $2 maximum. City Attorney Charles Younger said, "Just putting someone in jail for a civil debt has been unlawful since the Magna Carta" was signed in England in 1215, however, "that ordinance comes as close (as possible) to meeting constitutional muster."[41] The library installed an electronic detective sensor device in August 1976 to catch those who take them out without checking out.[42]

Two days later *The Huntsville Times* editorialized that the council probably would not support such an ordinance. The library does need to get tough. Not returning a book after 2-3 warnings is stealing, and that should be a punishable offense. The library could act by swearing out warrants for non-returners. It could not lend again to offenders. If the council does not act, then the library needs to find solutions on its own. *The Times* editorial ended with its usual bit of logic. "Hurt your feelings? Trod on your rights? Those other patrons waiting for your delinquent books have feelings and rights too."

Finally!! The city council approved a contract for $35,000 for the repair of the library's leaky roof. The firm that posted bond for the construction was no longer in business, so the city had to cover the repair cost. Improved insulation was also in the contract.[43]

In 1976 the library board established the archives and rare books department.

In 1977 the American Library Association had 28,754 personal members and 4,762 organizational members. The ALA cited the following 12 universities in the Southeast as having accredited masters of library science, or the equivalent: University of Alabama; Alabama Agricultural & Mechanical University; Atlanta University; Emory University; Florida State University; University of Kentucky; University of North Carolina; North Carolina Central University; George Peabody College for Teachers; University of South Carolina; University of South Florida; and University of Tennessee.[44] There are now sufficient schools in the Southeast to provide an opportunity to become a professional librarian and raise the level of the management of libraries, which are considerably more complex than they were 50 years before.

On Wednesday and Thursday, November 9 and 10, 1977, the library board held two executive sessions the week before the regular board meeting on the third Wednesday of every month. Elbert Watson, the library director, was in attendance. The next day, Friday, November 11, Watson submitted a letter of resignation to the board. He had been forced out! Watson's last day of work was to be November 11, but the resignation would be effective January 15, 1978. The reasons behind this action were not identified. There were apparently "irreconcilable differences" with the board over library management. Mrs. Roscoe Roberts, chairman of the Huntsville-Madison County Public Library, declined comment to *The Huntsville Times*, only saying that the circumstances would have to come from Watson.

On Tuesday, November 15, Watson submitted a letter to the board, stating that he was withdrawing his resignation because he had been denied due process because of "the improperly constituted library board." He called for a hearing on charges against him. Watson said the library board bylaws called for annual election of officers in March and said no such elections had been held in recent years. Watson further said the board did not inform him of some of the meetings and denied him access to others although the bylaws called for him to attend all board meetings.

Wednesday, November 16, 1977 was a busy day in this saga. Councilman Leon Crawford called a meeting of the city council and the library board jointly to discuss the situation. He wanted to know how this situation came up in such a hurry. There were three council members in attendance, Crawford, Jane Mabry, and John Glenn. City Attorney Charles Younger told Crawford the council had no jurisdiction over the library board's dealing with its employees since the appointed board is an independent body. Crawford attempted to close the meeting to the press, but Younger said neither he nor the council had the authority to do so. Mabry and Glenn favored keeping out of the situation, so the three council members departed.

The library board then met in closed executive session for one hour before the regularly planned monthly meeting. During the regular meeting, the board, by 4-1, voted to suspend Watson pending a formal hearing November 30 on charges against the director. Mrs. Roberts said the board did not know the bylaws even existed. In the regular meeting, however, she said board member Maurice Deal had seen the bylaws. Deal voted against the board on both the suspension and the follow-on motion, which named assistant director Eleanor Murphy as acting director.

Councilman Crawford raised the issue that library board member Harold Herring, an attorney, received $8,000 for legal involved in preparing the library's application for a license for public radio WLRH-FM. Documents showed that Herring had received $6,968 for that work. Whether Crawford had received that information from Watson or someone else seemed to be in doubt. Mrs. Robert said that City Attorney Younger and the federal auditors said those payments were not improper.

Mrs. Roberts told the three council members that the board's position on Watson had nothing to do with the financially troubled radio station. Most of the information that led to the board's request for Watson's resignation surfaced within the last two weeks.

Mrs. Roberts said that Watson had ordered the library's staff not to talk to her about library operations. "What kind of place is he operating?" she asked Crawford. Crawford replied that it sounded like a "distinct personality conflict" to him between Roberts and Watson.

Council Crawford said on Thursday, November 17, that he may well call for a complete audit of the Huntsville-Madison County Public Library because he believes the recent suspension of Watson was directly related to the information he had recently received regarding library operations. Also on Thursday, the Huntsville-Madison County Chamber of Commerce jumped into the fray, questioning, incredibly enough, the authority of the library board to select its own director.[45]

More than 26 years after November 1977, Mrs. Roberts spoke about the events of that month. Elbert Watson was a very dynamic director and accomplished many things. But he also lacked respect for the females within the library, most of whom were not trained librarians. Over a dozen of them left the library because he was demeaning to them. The women were freer to obtain employment in other fields, than had they been professional librarians with limited other opportunities in Huntsville. Mrs. Roberts decided that the specific reasons for Watson's departure needed to be handled discreetly to avoid embarrassment to Watson and his family. Some of the employees came back after Watson departed.[46]

The departure of Elbert Watson provided an opportunity to look at the advertised job description for library director.

"JOB DESCRIPTION

Huntsville-Madison County Public Library - December 14, 1977

JOB TITLE:

Director (Professional)

QUALIFICATIONS:

The following minimum requirements are established for the position of Director:

1. A Master's Degree in the field of Library Science

2. A minimum of five years of experience in the field of professional librarianship, with a minimum of three years in administration

RESPONSIBILITIES AND DUTIES:

The Director is responsible to the Huntsville-Madison County Public Library Board of Trustees for the following activities:

1. Establishing goals for the growth and development of library service to this area and making long range step-by-step plans for their implementation.

2. Establishing procedures, policies and systems that make for efficient library operation and provide the best possible library service to the community.

3. Hiring, organizing, coordinating and supervising all library personnel; representing the staff in contacts with the Board of Trustees, and assuming overall accountability for work performed in all areas of the library.

4. Preparing an annual budget for approval by the Board of Trustees. Overseeing all financial operations of the library in order that funds are disbursed and accounted for according to established accounting procedures.

5. Acting in an advisory capacity, as a professional expert, to the Board of Trustees, preparing the agenda for and attending Board meetings, with the right to speak on all matters under consideration.

6. Keeping the public, and governing agencies aware of the materials, projects and activities available at the Library by means of a comprehensive and continuing public relations program.

7. Cooperating as a team member with the library staff in performing any professional or non-professional duty essential to the achievement of efficient library operations.[47]

In January 1978 the Huntsville City Council voted to ask the State Examiners of Public Records to audit the financial records of the Huntsville-Madison County Public Library. This action was taken following a recommendation by the Madison County Grand Jury for state examiners to audit the library's accounts. The grand jury report for January 1978 cited an investigation by the grand jury, but the underlying initiative for the investigation could not be determined. The report stated, "such an audit is considered to be prudent action at the time of key personnel changes. We further recommend that there be an annual detailed audit of the Huntsville Public Library, which is the case in other autonomous boards. Such annual audits are considered by this Grand Jury to be in the best interest of the membership of the various boards and the public as a whole."[48]

Councilman Leon Crawford said that enough doubts were raised that it was in the best interests of the library board to look at the books. The Council agreed during a pre-council meeting to ask for the state audit rather than one by a private certified public accounting firm, which council president Dr. Jimmy Wall suggested. City Attorney Charles Younger said that it might be sometime before the state could get to the audit, and the state might not do it unless there is probable cause of a great displacement of funds.[49]

January 16, 1978 – Eleanor Murphy was selected as director at a salary of $18,000 per year, which was a 44 percent increase in the director's salary in the 9 years since Elbert Watson came to Huntsville.

In 1978 the Huntsville-Madison County Public Library joined the North Alabama Cooperative Library System (NACLS). It was a federation of autonomous libraries in DeKalb, Marshall, Madison and Jackson Counties. The coordinator of NACLS was in Huntsville and various members of the local staff provided the leadership.[50]

The audit of the library was conducted by B.R. Smith, certified public accountant, and covered the year, which ended September 30, 1977. The audit was dated May 9, 1978. The library's general fund budget that year totaled $453,338, of which the largest amount, $272,276 went to salaries. Book purchases were allocated $28,000. The following items were noted and in some cases remedial action was accomplished.

- No listing of capitalized assets was available. Each library department is now listing fixed assets and all will be tagged for depreciation identification.

- Only one person was needed to open the library's safe deposit box, and it was recommended that two or more persons be needed for access to library securities.
- No city ordinance existed in regard to overdue books. Smith recommended the council study such an ordinance.
- The library had no formal requirements regarding part of the director's and business manager's salary to be reimbursed by the North Alabama Cooperative System. Smith suggested verbal board approval on certain percentages be put in writing.
- Bank statements were not filed in an orderly way, and voided checks were kept too long. Proper approval was not received for all disbursements, but an approval stamp was obtained for incoming invoices.
- The library had no accounting manual or procedures, but one was now implemented.[51]

Martin Towery started working in the library as a volunteer at the tender age of 17 in 1973. A year later he was working part time shelving books and doing the mail run. Later on he was a full time employee in circulation, mostly nights and weekends, and the bookmobile. He reminisced about the days in the Fountain Circle building. A group of German and American engineers came into the library frequently and settled around a small round table to talk and play chess for about an hour. There were also boys in the library playing Dungeons and Dragons. There were only three library locations in those days, Fountain Circle, Oak Park and Charlotte Drive, therefore, most of the city children gathered at the main library to do their research homework. The place was not noisy because some rooms had doors and the layout helped muffle noise from one section to another. That arrangement was later contrasted with the way noise carries in the three-floor and even higher ceiling openness of Fort Book to built in 1987.[52]

The library building on Fountain Circle was bursting at the seams in 1978. The building was occupied in January 1966 and had 40,000 square feet of space. It housed 193,000 books, several thousand magazines, a staff of 67 and several services. The library board and the library director, Eleanor Murphy, were looking for additional space in other locations. They would like to house the historical collections in the Hundley House at the southeast corner of Madison Street and Gates Avenue. The Hundley House was circa 1900 and was diagonally across the intersection from the old Carnegie Library. The house was owned by the City of Huntsville. The Huntsville Historic Preservation Board offered the house to the library, but Mrs. Jane Roberts, chairman of the library board, said that the board was interested but could not afford the renovations or the additional operations. The house had been used as a police station from 1959 to 1976, and not well maintained, to put it delicately as seen by a later buyer, attorney Doug Fees. The library was also looking at the chamber of commerce building on Church Street just behind the library. The chamber had not decided to move, but the closeness of the two buildings made it an attractive expansion option.

The most likely course of action to obtain more library space would be to build a mezzanine level in the library's high-ceiling basement. The elevators were already designed to include the interim floor. At that time, the board did not have sufficient money for the mezzanine project.[53]

For many years, the only local library service to the town of Madison was provided by the county bookmobile, which stopped to drop off and pick books at the old Humphrey's General Store on Main Street at the railroad tracks. There were bookshelves on the stairs, and people could check out or return books using the honor system. In 1978, with the support of the Huntsville-Madison County Public Library staff, a group of 40 interested citizens organized the library at the recreation center at 1282 Hughes Road.

The Madison branch library opened in September 1978. The city officials and the citizens had worked for seven years to finally get their own library. But even at the opening, they started to look to the future to find a permanent library in another location. They had demonstrated the teamwork that characterizes the Madison County area. The library collection consisted of some 7,000 volumes, most from the main library in Huntsville, and a few were donated. For some time the branch was manned entirely by volunteers and was open for only 22 and ½ hours per week. The first paid staff member was funded by a Comprehensive Employment and Training Act (CETA) grant.

For decades the staff of the Huntsville-Madison County Public Library has sought additional funding wherever it might be found. They have been diligent and creative. Below is an example of a letter of intent to request a grant:

"December 13, 1978

NEH Challenge Grants

Mail Stop 800

National Endowment for the Humanities Washington, D.C. 20506

Gentlemen:

The Huntsville-Madison County Public Library intends to apply for an NEH Challenge Grant in the amount of $9,000, through the Division of Public Programs/Library Program. The non-federal match will be $27,000 for a total of $36,000. $7,500 in gifts is expected to be in hand by June 30, 1979. Funds for the non-federal match are to be raised by an enlarged and expanded membership drive and other fund-raising activities by the Friends of the Library, over and above their current activities and donations, and by a request for additional funding for this specific purpose from the City and County appropriating bodies.

The Challenge Grant will be used to construct a Periodicals Room in the existing main library building. The Library has a collection of bound and unbound periodical material, primarily in the humanities, which is not readily available to the public due to space limitations. The building of the Periodicals Room in the basement of the Library will enable students, scholars and the general public to have easy access to this material for the study of the humanities. Huntsville-Madison County Public Library serves as resource center for the northern third of the state. The Periodicals Room would also make it possible for the Library to acquire additional materials in the humanities by providing space to house an expanding collection.

The official who will authorize the application is Jane G. Roberts, Chairman, Library Board of Trustees. Those responsible for the preparation of the grant application are Eleanor E. Murphy, Director and Donna Barrett, Administrative Assistant. The telephone number is 205-536-0025.

Very truly yours, Eleanor Murphy, Director"[54]

September 17, 1979 – The Board approved a new position title. Donna T. Barrett, Administrative Assistant, will have the title of Assistant Director with added duties. The change of title was important in the corporate world as denoting far more responsibility and authority than the previous title.

This chapter will end with a subject that is near and dear to all our hearts – money. The 1979 library budget is provided below as a typical budget of that era to allow readers a sense of the funding support needed to keep our library going and provide the services the customers want. Of course, we all want more, but that is usually not possible. We have to live within our means, unless we have a credit card, but the library does not have a credit card. Below is a breakout of the sources of income at the end of the 1970s.

LIBRARY SOURCES OF INCOME – October 1, 1979-September 30, 1980

Source	Amount	% of Total Budget
City of Huntsville	$500,000	76.2
CETA*	31,581	
Madison County	46,581	7.6
Law Library	6,786	
State and Federal		9.6
LSCA	27,525	
State of Alabama	31,859	
Major Urban Resource	7,676	
Library Grant		
Gifts, Bequests, Interest	9,000	1.2
Fines, Xerox reimbursement	35,500	4.8
Other Grants	2,875	.4

The above is the amount of money the library had to distribute toward the various facets of the library. The largest slice, about 62%, went to salaries, payroll taxes & benefits. The collections of books, periodicals, newspapers, records, microfilm, etc. received about 16%. Operating expenses such as bookmobile, building maintenance, equipment repair and maintenance, furniture, insurance and bonds, postage, equipment rental, consumable supplies, and utilities received about 22%. *Comprehensive Employment and Training Act (CETA)[55]

The decade of the 1970s was one of continuing outreach to all citizens of Madison County and providing improved service in all aspects of library operations. This continued improvement set the stage for an even more dramatic outreach in the next decade.

1. Huntsville Library–1819 J.N.S. Jones law office   2. Huntsville Library - 1819 Book cabinet

3. Huntsville Carnegie Library

4. Decatur Carnegie Library – Outside

5. Decatur Carnegie Library - Inside

6. Huntsville Library – Fountain Circle

7. Huntsville Library – Monroe Street (Fort Book)

8. Eleanor E. Murphy Library

9. Elbert H. Parsons Public Law Library

10. Bailey Cove Library

11. Bessie K. Russell Library

12. Madison Library

13. Tillman Hill Library

14. New Hope Library – First Building on Highway 431

15. New Hope Library – Main Street

16. Monrovia Library

17. Gurley Library

18. Oscar Mason Center Library

19. Richard Showers Center Library

20. Triana Youth Center Library

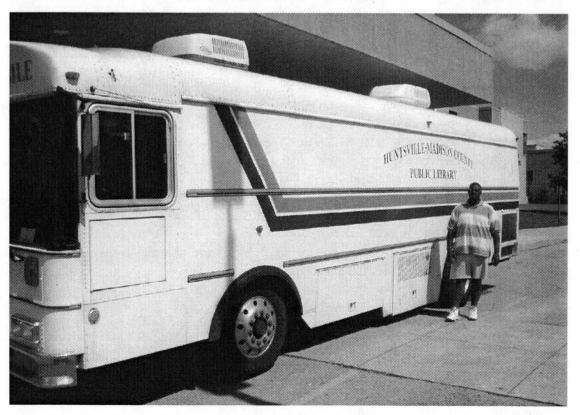

21. Huntsville Library Bookmobile - 2004

Chapter 9

Public Radio

A Bridge Too Far
Cornelius Ryan, 1974

On Friday, October 27, 1972 the Huntsville-Madison County Library Board, led by Mrs. Roscoe Roberts, Chairman, gave its approval to apply to the Federal Communication Commission (FCC) for a license to operate a non-commercial FM radio station. The radio proposal was the idea of Elbert Watson, the library's director. He and the board had been working on the idea for about eight months, and earlier in October the word leaked out. Petitions and letters streamed into the library supporting the idea.

The station would offer classical music, information programs and in-depth studies of what was going on in the community. Plans were for the broadcasting studio to be located in the main library and it was hoped that, if the license was approved, broadcasting could start in the fall of 1973. It would take six to eight weeks to file the proposal and four to six months for the FCC to take action.

Board members and friends of the Library made several trips to Nashville to visit WPLN-FM sponsored by the Nashville Public Library. WPLN was started in 1962 and had a staff of fifteen in 1972. Its facilities included two control rooms and three sound studios. It had a 100,000-watt transmitter with an 85-mile radius. It broadcast eighteen hours per day, featuring educational, informational or cultural programs.

WPLN was a member of the National Public Radio Network, which had 132 member stations across the nation that feed locally-produced programs to other stations. Twenty to 25 percent of WPLN's programming was produced locally.

The station was seen as an extension of library services. Grants totaling about 75 percent of the construction were available from the federal government and community organizations would have to raise the remainder. If the station were established, Huntsville would have been the third city in the country to have a library-sponsored public service radio station.[1]

The library's application to the Federal Communications Commission was forwarded in April 1973. In December 1973, the library asked the Department of Health, Education, and Welfare for $137,000 to be used for purchase and installation of the necessary broadcasting equipment and tower. The library, in turn, had to put up $35,000 in cash and services as matching funds. Mrs. Virginia Thomme, the library coordinator, said the grant and construction permit would probably come at the same time.

The operating costs would amount to an estimated $45,000 per year. The staff would include a station manager and four other full-time and three part-time employees. The studio would be located in the basement of the library and the transmitting tower on Monte Sano at the Burritt Museum.

The library board changed the operating hours from 14 to 18 hours, which would result in the station receiving between $16,000 and $18,000 from the Corporation for Public Broadcasting. Library officials said that donations of $30,000 would be sought, but no funds would be required from the city council nor the library.

The station was expected to broadcast on 89.3 megahertz. Programming would feature classical music, interspersed with book reviews, poetry readings, health topics, national and local news, children's books, travel features, legal information, folk music by local artists, Fantasy Playhouse, the Arts Council, women's news, Senior Citizens, and a "Huntsville Forum" for call-in listeners.[2]

On February 8, 1974, Elbert Watson, Director, Huntsville Public Library, and the initiator of the radio project, wrote the following letter to the president of the city council,

"The Library Board would like to investigate the possibility of acquiring the old Jeremiah Clemens home on the corner of Church and Clinton Streets. We understand that the structure is still basically sound and can be renovated into a useable facility. We feel the building can be utilized for various kinds of historical programs which we envision for the library.

Of course, our budget at this time is a prohibitive facture (sic) in our ability to purchase the building. But we did want you to know of our interest in doing something to preserve this historic structure for the community...."[3]

By coincidence, exactly 30 years and 1 day later, on February 9, 2004, *The Huntsville Times* carried an article that the Clemens House was going to be moved to a new site at Pratt Avenue and Meridian Street. The house was more than 170 years old and was on the National Register of Historic Places. The records suggest the house was built between 1825 and 1835. Jeremiah Clemens was a colonel in the Mexican War, a U.S. senator for Alabama, a newspaper editor, and a peace activist during the Civil War. The house in 2004 belonged to Huntsville Utilities, which wanted the space for a parking lot.[4] Now parking lots are big. In the 1830's, one could tie up many horses in the space that two of today's monstrous sports utility vehicles (SUV) take to park, and block other drivers' vision.

In July 1975 it was announced that the $137,000 grant from Department of Health, Education, and Welfare and a $50,000 grant from the Corporation for Public Broadcasting were approved. The station will have the letters WHPL on 89.3 megahertz and will be associated with the National Public Radio Network. For readers who might not be familiar with the U.S. radio designation system, "W' is for stations east of the Mississippi River and "K" is for stations west of the dividing line. The "HPL" appropriately stands for Huntsville Public Library. George Dickerson, of WFIX radio in Huntsville, was named station manager. The radio will operate from two suites in the old Times Building on Holmes Avenue in downtown Huntsville and the antennas will be on Green Mountain. The station was expected to reach over 500,000 listeners with 100,000 watts of power over a 100-mile radius. Making the announcement was Elbert Watson, library director, Mrs. Roscoe Roberts, chairman of the library board, and Walt Weisman, chairman of the Friends of the Library, which raised money to support the station.[5]

In August 1975 the library released news that a new organization, Friends of the Public Radio, Inc. was formed to support the new public radio with financial donations and audience development. Officers were: Walt Weisman, President; Walter Linde, Vice-president; James Bush, Secretary; and Abner McNaron, Treasurer.[6]

Sometime between July and November 1975, the radio's call letters changed from WHPL to WLRH, which is what it is to this day. Walt Weisman was to fly to Washington, D.C. to tell other organizations how Huntsville organized public support for its station. The Friends of the Public Radio had a goal to raise $150,000 to get the station on the air and keep it there. There were 24 personal on the board of directors of the Friends. Their goal was for each to contact 10 others to join the Friends, and those 10 contact 10 more.[7]

The Friends of the Radio and Friends of the Library sponsored a breakfast meeting on Friday, January 16, 1976. The guest of honor was Joe McCorquodale, speaker of the Alabama House of Representatives, who warned that raising taxes was not likely, and the legislature was hunting for ways to reduce expenses. The message seemed to be, don't look for any increase in funds. Marelle Pruitt, president of the Friends of the Library, presented a check for $5,000 to Walt Weisman, president of the Friends of the Public Radio.[8]

"Governor George Wallace allocated $40,000 to establish a broadcast service to 19,000 blind and handicapped persons in 22 North Alabama counties, according to Representative Hartwell Lutz, chairman of the Madison County delegation.

The $40,000 in state revenue sharing funds is the first "score" on the Friends of the Public Radio campaign to raise $100,000 to establish the station.

The station, WLRH, becomes the second public radio station in the nation to receive revenue sharing funds.

'Reading the newspaper grocery ads is a simple act for the sighted,' Lutz said. 'This grant to station WLRH-FM will make it possible for the print handicapped to hear – and take advantage of – weekly grocery 'specials,' hear best sellers read over the air, and learn of services beneficial to them.'

Elbert Watson, library director, said that by his action establishing Alabama first broadcast station to the blind and handicapped, Governor Wallace has earned 'the sincere appreciation of those who care for their fellow man.'"[9]

A Day to Remember – October 13, 1976 – WLRH On-the-Air The station was officially opened when James Record, Chairman, Madison County Commission, cut the ribbon at 2:15 P.M. A 40-seat auditorium was dedicated to Dr. Eberhard Rees and James Record. There was a reception from 2-4 P.M. That evening there was an invitation dinner at the Carriage Inn. The special guest for the dinner was Chester "Lum" Lauck of radio's early classic "Lum and Abner" series. [I hope some of my readers remember Lum and Abner.] Other popular radio shows of that era were The Shadow and The Great Gildersleeve. "Lum" was an appropriate guest because WLRH-FM set aside Saturdays and Sundays for replays of "old-time" radio shows. The studio was open for public tours on October 13-14, the Saturday and Sunday after the opening.[10] It needs to be reemphasized that the station received neither library nor local tax money.

On December 17, 1976, Elbert Watson, library director, sent the following memo to the library and radio staff:

"FUND RAISING SPECIAL FOR LIBRARY AND RADIO STAFF
Full time, part-time and pages will individually receive:
1 day off for the first $100.00 given to the radio station through your fund raising activities.
4 hours will be given for the second and subsequent $100.00.
No more than five days may be accumulated for this special.
RULES:
1. No partial days will be given. ($25.00 does not entitle you to 2 hours off.
2. The money must be turned in to Mr. Watson as you receive it.
3. This offer expires January 15th. All money must be turned in by that date.
4. Full-time and part-time staff must take their days off by February 28, 1977.
5. Pages must take their day off by March 31, 1977
6. Time off must be approved by the department head.

7. Fund raising that is to be applied to this time off special cannot be done during your regularly scheduled work day.
8. These contacts should be personal and not business or civic groups. These should be cleared through Margie Weisman.
9. Those people who give $10.00 or more will receive the WLRH Program Guide for 1 year.
10. *You may not tell your prospects of the incentive for participating in this funding effort.* [Author's italics.]
11. Administrative staff is excluded from participating."[11]

In April 1977 the radio station was running out of money. Virginia Tomme, station director, said the station would run out of money in May sometime, and the station board decided not to borrow any money with no money coming in. A committee was formed to consider taking the station's Federal Communications Commission license from the library and giving it to a "consortium" of business and government leaders and private citizens. The cash flow was not there and there was only enough money to pay part of the bills in May.

Audience response to the station had been good, but management and money problems plagued the station since the beginning. The grant of $50,000 from the Corporation for Public Broadcasting apparently had strings attached from the very beginning. The community must match each grant dollar with three dollars, which equates to $150,000 by the end of the fiscal year July 31.

The grant was also conditional on the stations using expensive programming from National Public Radio, programming such as concert performances and current events discussions, which are predictable monthly drains on the available cash.

The station set up with three arms of control: the library, which had legal license responsibility, an advisory group on programming, and the Friends of Public Radio, the prime local fundraising group. Experts who reviewed this system after it was formed told the locals it "is not a matter of if the problems will occur, but when they will occur," Mrs. Tomme said, She said they were right. The fundraisers did bring in well over $125,000 for the first-year operations.[12]

The news about the public radio station continued to worsen, 'but now the rest of the story,' ala Paul Harvey, the noted radio commentator. But before the rest of the story is told, it is appropriate to introduce *Augustine's Laws,* by Norman Augustine, 1982. Norman Augustine held multiple management positions in the Department of Defense (DoD) Research, Development, and Acquisition structure in the 1970's. Later he was chief executive officer of Martin Marietta Corporation. While in the DoD, he collected many statistics about the cost, schedule, and other facets of developing military hardware. From that data of dozens of systems over 40-year periods, he prepared graphs depicting trends. He then drew conclusions from the trends and developed Augustine's laws, which were whimsical and satirical statements about the conclusions. The data support his conclusions, but people in that business do not like to hear them because their job of getting more money from D0D and Congress depends upon optimism, not historic realism.

This brings us to the juncture of public radio and Augustine's laws. Augustine's Law Number XIII states, "If a sufficient number of management layers are superimposed on top of each other, it can be assured that disaster is not left to chance."[13] And now the rest of the story. In April 1977 the money problems of the public radio operation started to surface. Jack Hartsfield, *The Huntsville Times,* wrote a comprehensive story on May 1, 1977. Virginia Tomme, previously quoted, said, "Up to now, its been like sitting in a rowboat trying to tug the Queen

Mary off a sandbar." The managerial turnover at the top was one factor contributing to the problem. Newman Milwee, a Huntsvillian with local commercial experience stayed only a short time. Kim Hodgson, from Minnesota, stayed for only six days. Tomme is the head because the higher management cannot find a professional who would do the job for the salary that was available. The Friends of Public Radio, the volunteers expected to keep the donations rolling in to sustain the operations have become almost nonexistent. There was always hope for future grants, but that had mostly faded.

Bob Loren was chairman of a citizens committee seeking help for the station. The committee was trying to one, or several, of the local colleges to take over the operations. Those schools were Alabama A&M University. The University of Alabama in Huntsville, Oakwood College, Athens College, and Calhoun Community College.

Managerial problems, technical difficulties, disputes among the staffers, and lack of know-how became evident not long after the station opened. Within the first month of operation, expenses soared beyond the estimated income from both grants and donations. Elbert Watson, the library director and station originator said the concept of grants and public donations just did not happen.

The Friends of Public Radio did have 600 members, but the group splintered when the Friends did not have a say in the programming. Walt Weisman, who headed the Friends group from the beginning, resigned when the station began operating. He believed that the station should have had a university connection from the beginning. He believed that was still the needed affiliation to help the station survive.

The public radio station in Birmingham operated under the wing of the University of Alabama in Birmingham. The station in Nashville, under which pattern Huntsville was organized, operated under the public library, but obtained annual funding from the city's general fund. Huntsville's was not established on that basis, even as a contingency.

Elbert Watson continued to take the heat, but everyone admitted that the station would not have started had it not been for Watson's initiative.

The station would like to reduce the number of employees to six and cut out the expensive syndicated pre-taped programs such as the Philadelphia Orchestra and the Boston Symphony. But hope was fading for someone to step forward with significant donations or to take control of the station.[14]

The woes of WLRH were laid before the city council Thursday night, May 5, 1977. The station obtained a loan for $8,000 from the library, with the station's unencumbered equipment put up as collateral. This only met the January 1977 payroll. The station had nine employees in May, but had 14 or 15 earlier. Mrs. Tomme, on the hot seat in front of the council, responded to questions by Councilman Leon Crawford. Crawford thought that 3-4 people could operate the station. Mrs. Tomme replied that 3-4 could not do what the station intended to do. The public broadcasting folks in Washington told them that no station had set out to do what WLRH wanted to do with less than 14 people.

The station's operations manager, George Dickerson, had 10 years experience and another employee, Jonathan Potkin, was in radio for 3 years in Oregon. Unsaid were the experiences of the other employees, so no experience was the presumed answer. Mrs. Toome, labeled a director, admitted that her background included no radio work, but that her primary duty was in the area of fund-raising. If the station was closed down, the $50,000 grant from the Corporation for Public Broadcasting would have to be returned.[15] In July 1977 the library board decided to continue operating the station after the July 31 end of contract with the Corporation for Public Broadcasting. The radio would only broadcast 12 hour per day instead of the original

156

18. The state Educational Television (ETV) had expressed interest in taking over the station, but had no guarantees that they would have the money when their fiscal year began on October 1. The library board determined it would close the station before October 1 if the ETV people lost interest in the project.

The city council, by a 3-2 vote, had earlier approved the sum of $35,000 to keep the station afloat until October 1. This action occurred after the University of Alabama in Huntsville officials failed to get permission from university trustees to take over the station.[16] The library and its friends had only raised $122,000 of the $150,000 required by the CPB. If everything collapsed, $56,000 would have to be repaid to the CPB.[17] Everything finally collapsed and the radio license eventually wound up at The University of Alabama in Huntsville, continuing as WLRH-FM and part of the national public radio system as of 2004.

The library radio sounded like a noble and worthwhile opportunity, but as usually happens, a lack of money can easily sink the greatest of projects. This project was analogous to the World War II Allied offensive of seizing key bridges told in Ryan's book, the idea was good but it led to overreach of capabilities. The failure laid the foundation for future success and led to the public radio still in Huntsville in 2004, so all's well that ends well.

Chapter 10

The Golden Decade Begins

*"Libraries are reservoirs of strength, grace and wit, reminders of order,
calm and continuity, lakes of mental energy, neither warm nor cold, light nor dark.
The pleasure they give is steady, unorgastic, reliable, deep and long-lasting. In any
library in the world, I am at home, unselfconscious, still and absorbed."*

Germaine Greer
Daddy, We Hardly Knew You (1989)
The Quotable Book Lover

Have a question and are too lazy to chase down the answer? Ask the library, specifically the reference desk of the Huntsville-Madison County Public Library, which was in the basement. The folks there were specialists in knowing where to find the answer, and maybe would chase down the answer for you. The reference island was surrounded by answers, some may be in the books on the second floor, some may be in archives on other floors and some may be found in other libraries across Alabama and beyond which can be accessed by computer.

In the spring of 1980 the Huntsville Public Library took the initiative to write a grant proposal to the state library service to develop a cooperative program to make it easier for customers in North Alabama to access documents from multiple libraries. The grant of $250,000 was for the first year of a three-year pilot program to allow 25 public, school, and specialized libraries in eight counties across North Alabama to access and share collections. Lee Pike of Evergreen, Colorado was hired as a full-time coordinator of the program.

Mrs. Bessie K. Russell, director of the local history room for 33 years, retired in July 1980 and went to live with her son in California.[1]

The Comprehensive Employment and Training Act (CETA) was a U.S. government program designed to assist economically disadvantaged, unemployed, or underemployed persons. Enacted in 1973, CETA provided block grants to state and local governments to support public and private job training and such youth programs as the Job Corps and Summer Youth Employment. In 1982, CETA was superseded by the Job Training Partnership Act, which established the Office of Job Training Programs.

The Huntsville-Madison Public Library was highly dependent on CETA positions in the early 1980s as supplements to understaffed areas. The funding of these positions provided the minimum needed to fulfill commitments to the public. Without CETA positions it would have been imperative to request additional funds from sponsoring agencies or reduce current levels of services.

In 1980 the library employed four people from the CETA program. Mrs. Joan Baretta worked as a circulation assistant in the Young Readers Department; Mrs. Jeris Hill was a Reader Advisor in the Subregional Library for the Blind and Physically Handicapped; Mr. Brian Moore was a Maintenance Assistant; and Mrs. Vivian Richardson as a Film Technician in the Audio-Visual department.

What kind of person steals books from a library? What is stealing? *Webster's Dictionary* defines it as "to take the property of another wrongfully and esp. as a habitual or regular practice." If you check a book out of the library and forget to return it, that is not stealing. If you fail to return the book after being notified that it is overdue, what is that? You have the book knowingly, but fail to return it. Seems as that might qualify as stealing. What kind of person does that? Probably people from many walks of life.

What kind of person steals a rare book from a library? Undoubtedly it would not be one of the homeless persons who inhabit the library sometimes. It probably would be someone who likes books, maybe even loves books, and has a good appreciation of the rarity or value. Stealing books, with great purposefulness, has a lengthy history. Two examples are below.

In the middle of the 17th century a fellow by the name of Giambattista Pamfili, a member of the Catholic Church, inspected a well-endowed private library in Paris with some of his colleagues. The owner noticed a book was missing. Cardinal Barberini, who had assembled the group and vouched for them, locked the door and insisted that everyone be searched. Pamfili protested, there was a struggle, and the book fell from his robes. Pamfili later became Pope Innocent X. As pope he drove the Barberini family out of Rome. Pope Innocent X was a book thief and not so innocent. But people eventually stole from his Vatican Library.[2]

During the 1970s – 80s, Steven Blumberg stole 23,600 books from 268 libraries in 45 states and 2 Canadian provinces. He stole from America's finest libraries, and they did not realize it until he was caught and the police searched for the rightful owners. He liked books, and liked to steal. What a combination! He selected his books carefully.[3]

The Huntsville Library was not fortunate enough to have someone famous steal a book from it. But book lovers are candidates, because they know value. Who would know such value better than a friend? A friend of the library, that is.

In late 1980, John Pannick of 3613 Conger Road, Huntsville, stole a document from the Huntsville Public Library. Pannick was a "regular" patron of the library who helped set prices for books at benefit sales. He was vice president of the Civil War Roundtable, a local historical group. The stolen document was a printed, undated "broadside" from the library's Zeitler Collection. The broadside, large paper printed on only one side, was valued at between $500 and $750.

The document was, "Letter From The Ladies Of The South To The Soldiers Of The Confederate Army." Pannick, 36 years old, had represented himself as the owner of "The Sword and Saber," a home business, and mailed the document to a rare-book dealer in Boston at "Goodspeed Bookshop." Bailey Bishop, the dealer, checked it in a standard national bibliography and saw it listed as part of the Huntsville Library's collection. Ranee' Pruitt, library archivist, confirmed that it was missing. It was identified by a watermark, printing details, and other features visible on a library photocopy.

The library called the local police, who called Mr. Bishop in Boston, and he mailed it back. Assistant Library Director Donna Barrett said the incident marks the first apparent theft of an historical document from the library.[4] "First apparent theft" is a deceptive phrase. As in Blumberg's case above, no one knew about the missing books until notified. Some books were not returned because there was not sufficient identification to determine the owner. Rare documents are not usually inventoried, but only found to be missing when someone looks for them.

On March 25, 1981, Robert E. Cramer, Jr., District Attorney, sent the following letter to Ms. Barrett at the library.

"Our files indicate that on the 12th day of December, 1980, the Huntsville Public Library was victimized. This office has successfully concluded the prosecution of the defendant in this case, and he has pleaded guilty to the amended charge of Attempted Theft of Lost Property.

Punishment meted out by the District Court Judge was a sentence of six months in jail in the Madison County Jail. The sentence was suspended, and the defendant was placed on probation for a period of 12 months. The defendant was also ordered to pay a fine of $500 and court costs.

Should this office or any member of my staff be able to assist you in any way in the future, we will consider it an honor to do so."[5]

The weekend after Pannick was sentenced, the library took in hundreds of dollars in fines, as people were dumping so many books in the book depository that library personnel had to empty the depository six times in one day.

Martin Towery, who worked in the adult department in 2004, remembered the early days of his 30-year tenure with the library, when back in the Fountain Circle location he worked mostly nights and weekends. He closed up on a Friday night after he had done his security checks. The next morning he opened the building and there was a homeless man reading a magazine, who had been missed the night before and enjoyed his night of solitude. After all, which homeless person will call the police to get them out of the library at night when locked in. It was quiet, he had his choice of sleeping arrangements and there was no one to bother him.[6]

March 19, 1981 – Eleanor Murphy, Director of the Huntsville-Madison County Public Library announced to the library board that she would resign, at a date that would give the board time to select a replacement. It was time for her to retire after 28 years with the library. Since the North Alabama Cooperative Library System would likely dissolve at the end of the fiscal year and more state aid money would be coming directly to the library, there would be an opportunity for new programs and projects. A new director would be able to be involved in the new programs from the beginning.

On May 12, 1981, Donna T. Barrett, Assistant Director, submitted her name and resume to the library board for the job of director: "I have ten years of library experience, seven of which have been in direct public service and three of which have been in administrative work in this library. I have, during my library career, done everything from typing overdue notices and performing puppet shows to making presentations and undertaking sophisticated research projects. I am proud of our library, its staff, and its potential. I would be honored to have the opportunity to be its Director."[7]

Donna Barrett received a Master of Library Science from the University of Alabama in 1976, which she earned on a part-time basis while working full-time at the Birmingham Public Library. She received a Bachelor of Arts Degree in history and political science from Mississippi State College for Women, Columbus, Mississippi. She was selected as the director in May 1981.

Eleanor Murphy officially retired from the library on July 31, 1981. She worked for the library for 28 years. She was head librarian, 1958-60, and assistant director, 1961-77. Upon Elbert Watson's resignation in 1977, she became acting director and then director until her retirement.

October 1, 1981 – The friends of the Charlotte Drive Branch requested that the branch be renamed the Eleanor Murphy Branch in honor of Mrs. Murphy and her long contributions to the Huntsville-Madison County Public Library. The library board approved the action.

November 18, 1981 – The friends of the library made almost $10,000 on their book sale in October and $3,500 on the mini-sale in September. The friends have raised $34,000 for the library between 1973 and 1981.

The Huntsville Times editorial, February 17, 1982 criticized the library for closing on President's Day. The Chairman of the Library Board, Mrs. Jane G. Roberts, sent the following letter to the *Times*:

"Being criticized for closing the library in observance of President's Day is a mixed blessing. While we dislike inconvenience to the public because of closing, it is reassuring to see that our citizens consider the Huntsville Public Library an essential service.

Holidays for library employees are set each year by the library Board. The board tries to align the library's holidays with those observed by city hall as much as possible. We felt justified is allowing our employees a holiday that many other citizens enjoy. Our library serves the community 68 hours a week, including service on Saturday and Sunday afternoons. Very few governmental agencies could boast that. During 1981 our library was open for service 353 out of 365 days.

We feel that one of the reasons for the Huntsville Public Library's continued growth and success in an age when other public libraries around the country facing cutbacks in collections and services is due to our responsiveness to the needs of our community. The board will certainly re-evaluate its policy of closing in observance of President's Day, and all other holidays observed by the library. We're sorry for the inconvenience, but we're glad you missed us."[8]

The Alabama Library Association annual convention was back in Huntsville in April 28-30, 1982. Donna Barrett, Director, Huntsville Public Library, was chair of the event. The event hosted 700 Alabama librarians in the Von Braun Civic Center. In 1953 Huntsville hosted 240 state librarians at the state convention. The difference between 240 and 700 in 29 years reflects the growth of Alabama libraries. There may be other reasons for the larger numbers in Huntsville. In 1953 there were hardly any tourist attractions in town, and travel was not as easy as in 1982 with the interstate highways.

The keynote speaker at the first general session was Robert Theobald, author and social critic. He was the author of *An Alternative Future for America's Third Century, Beyond Despair, Social Policies for America in the Seventies, and Economizing Abundance.* He challenged state librarians to accept that their mission in the modern world is "to convince people that they are not going crazy. ...You have a self-interest in assuming that the public is ill-informed. ...It is a professional tic, and the same is shared by educators."[9]

The luncheon on the first day of the convention honored former United States Congressman Carl A. Elliott, Sr. Elliott, 1913-1999, was a native of Jasper, Alabama in Walker County about 75 miles southwest of Huntsville. He was the son of a tenant farmer and worked his way through the University of Alabama, graduating in 1933 and from the University's Law School in 1936. He was in Congress from 1949 to 1965, representing the Seventh District. "In 1956, Elliott authored the Library Services Act, which brought bookmobiles and library service to millions of rural Americans. In 1958, he co-authored the National Defense Education Act, which improved science, foreign language and technology education nationwide and provided low-interest loans for college and graduate school for needy students. Both laws have been extended; more than 30,000,000 loans have been made for students nationwide.

Elliott campaigned for Alabama governor in 1966 on a platform of federal assistance to the needy, better education, and racial tolerance. He lost the election to Lurleen Wallace and slipped into political obscurity, practicing law, writing books about local history, producing columns and book reviews for area newspapers, and publishing books by local authors. His books included five volumes of *Annals of Northwest Alabama*, a history of Red Bay, and seven volumes of histories of coal miners.

Elliott received new recognition of his achievements in 1990, when he became the first recipient of the John F. Kennedy Profile in Courage Award. His autobiography, *The Cost of Courage: The Journey of An American Congressman*, was published in 1992."[10]

The American Library Association approved a resolution honoring Carl Elliott during its midwinter meeting in Denver, January 22-28, 1982. The Huntsville library director, Donna Barrett, was one of three people active in the effort to secure the honor for Elliott.

After the convention in Huntsville, Carl Elliott sent the following letter to Donna Barrett:
"May 5, 1982

Dear Donna,

Never in my life have I been so honored so completely and in such detail and good taste as was done by the Alabama Library Association on April 27th. To you, as chairperson of the convention, and as a friend, I tender my most hearty, yet humble, thanks. Both resolutions were beautiful and well written, though as we both understand grossly overstated. I think if that kind of praise was bestowed on me very often it would take hold. Before you all were finished I could feel stirrings which might eventually lead to a delusion of belief. I might be one of those people who couldn't ever stand much praise. First, I fear I'd believe, then start quoting all the beautiful things that were said and read.

The book ends were beautiful and useful, and something I personally needed. I think of them being somewhat symbolic of my life with books.

I thought the pictorial presentation was outstanding. It surprised me. It had never occurred to me that it would be done and had I known it was being done I wouldn't have expected the high quality of its craftsmanship. I thought it bore the attributes of professional excellence.

Now, I'm sure one of the best things that ever happened to my career was Bob Schremser becoming interested in it. He's making my little place in history glisten with such importance as to be unreal. I guess that's what the fable meant when it spoke of making mountains out of molehills.

It was very thoughtful, and to me most meaningful occasion. It was that in contemplation I'll gain strength and encouragement from a long time.

Thanks, Donna.

With admiration for you, and esteem, always, I am

Your friend,

/s/ CARL ELLIOTT, SR."[11]

After the convention in Huntsville, Anthony W. Miele, Director, Alabama Public Library Service, sent the following letter to Donna Barrett:
"Dear Donna,

Just wanted to take this opportunity to congratulate you on an excellent conference. There is no doubt in my mind that this is the best Alabama Library Association Conference I've attended since I've been in Alabama.

Your hard work and good planning were very apparent in making the conference successful.

Congratulations to you and your committee for a job well done! Montgomery will be hard pressed to equal your performance."[12]

In April 1982 the library had a "Free Fine Week", when 4,000 books were returned. One lady brought back 30 books at one time. A second patron returned a book that had been out since 1942. The library tried to call borrowers on the phone to arrange for the books to be picked up. Ms. Barrett, Library Director, said, "We get to their house and find no one at home." Ms. Barrett said the library lost 15,470 books between 1979 and 1982. It was not just forgetfulness, as books turned up at garage sales and flea markets. One woman refused to return almost $1,000 worth of audio-visual material she had checked out. Only a letter threatening to turn her case over to the city attorney's office prompted the woman to get right with the library.[13]

The replacement cost of lost library materials was approximately $120,000, and the annual budget for the purchase of materials for 1982 was only $147,000. That was a significant loss.[14]

Donna Barrett married Bob Schremser, also a librarian, at 2: P.M., August 7, 1982, so there will be a name change in this history from now on.

What kind of person fails to return books? Forgetful? Yes. Willful disregard for others people's property? Absolutely! Maybe those folks believe it is okay to steal from the public's treasury of books, but would they tolerate a government official stealing books? Probably not, but if they do it, they probably consider it a civic right to steal from government. What runs through their minds? Maybe not very much.

On September 2, 1982 the Huntsville City Council agreed to adopt an ordinance giving the Huntsville Public Library the authority to seek court action against those who "fail or refuse to return … any book, periodical, recording or other material borrowed" from the main library or its branches. Under the law, borrowers who refuse to return books can be fined up to $100 and/or be sentenced to up to 30 days in jail by the municipal judge. The borrower must be given at least 10 days written notice before he can be prosecuted.[15]

The activities of the Young Readers' Department for the first week of October 1982 was quoted in its entirety to demonstrate the breadth of the activities available to the children of Madison County. This week was repeated each week of October.

"Friday 10/1

1:30-2:00 Storytime at the Bookmobile stop in Madison.

Monday 10/4

1:00-1:30 Storytime at the Bookmobile stop in New Market.

Tuesday 10/5

9:00-10:00 Storytime at Bessie K. Russell Branch Library with Mrs. Green (preschool).
1:30-2:00 Storytime at the Bookmobile stop in Harvest.
4:00-4:30 Storytime at the Bookmobile stop at Madison Cross Roads.
4:40-5:00 Grunches and Grins ETV (Educational Television).
7:00-8:00 Family Night for all ages at the Bessie K. Russell Branch Library to enjoy films, puppet shows and crafts…

Wednesday 10/6

9:00-10-00 Storytime at Eleanor Murphy Branch Library. Crafts with Judy Bell (preschool).
10:15-11:00 Storytime at Huntsville Public Library with Sara McDaris
(preschool).
1:30-2:15 Storytime at Huntsville Public Library with Sara McDaris (preschool).
1:30-2:00 Storytime at the Bookmobile stop in New Hope.

3:30-4:00 Storytime at Bessie K. Russell Library with Ben Heiman (ages 7-10) Movies and a Puppet Show featuring "Misty Rainbow" and Ms. Anderson will follow Storytime.

Thursday 10/7

4:30-5:00 Grunches and Grins ETV."[16]

February 15, 1983 – A resident from Gurley requested that a branch library be started in that town. The Board requested that the director follow-up on the possibility of a branch. It took several years before Gurley got a branch. It does take more than the request of one person, it takes a whole community to work to achieve such a goal. The stories of several branches will be detailed later.

The city ordinance of September 1982 enforcing overdue library books received some attention of *The Huntsville Times* in March 1983. The paper ran articles on March 4 and 17 about people served summonses for failing to appear in court. Those receiving a summons had already received three letters from the library. Fourteen folks had their names in the paper, which probably provided a little embarrassment, as well as a little dent in their pocketbooks.[17] I tried to find their names in the 2004 telephone book, but was unsuccessful.

In 1983 Huntsville Public Library, Wheeler Basin Regional Library (Decatur), Gadsden Public Library and the Alabama Library Exchange Inc., together wrote a grant request to the Federal Library Services and Construction Act. The $100,000 that was received was equally matched by local money and a contract was made with CL Systems, a company that markets library computer systems. This system was called the Library Management Network Inc. (LMN). Ten other libraries and institutions subsequently joined the network. Members of the network pay additional fees to connect another terminal to the network, for maintenance and for additional software.

There were 12 terminals at the Huntsville libraries and 30 more were used by other members. In addition to the LMN was "ALEX", a term for the Alabama Library Exchange. It was six-year-old cooperative library system pilot project to improve and equalize library services in an eight-county area of northeast Alabama. There were 41 public, academic, school, and research libraries participating. This was the first interconnected system in the Huntsville library to allow a much wider electronic search for books and documents not held in the library. Since Huntsville had the most books, the other participants benefited from it perhaps more than Huntsvillians. The money was received and implemented in 1984.

Win some and lose some. That was the story in applying for grants. The letter quoted below was from the Alabama Public Library Service, June 22, 1983. It was a win.

"The Executive Board of the Alabama Public Library Service, the Alabama Advisory Council on Libraries, and the staff of the Alabama Public Library Service have reviewed your grant applications for FY1984 federal funds under the Library Services and Construction Act, Title I. We are pleased to notify you that the following application(s) have been approved, and contingent upon your library's acceptance of the terms of the grant and the availability of federal funds, you will receive FY1984 funds for the projects in the amount specified:

Collection Development $20,000

The local library must provide one dollar ($1.00) on collection development for every two dollars ($2.00) of LSCA funds received under the grant.

Computer Literacy $ 4,000

Service to Disadvantaged Children $ 3,000

Young Adult Service $ 6,000

Library materials purchased under this grant must be located in the public library and its branches, not in public schools.

When funds become available, your library will receive contracts which must be signed, notarized and returned to APLS. The grants will be in effect from January 1, 1984 until December 31, 1984."[18]

The next day, June 23, 1983, the APLS sent a letter disapproving a grant request.

"The Executive Board of the Alabama Public Library Service, the Alabama Advisory Council on Libraries, and the staff of Alabama Public Library Service have reviewed your grant application(s) for FY1984 federal funds under the Library Services and Construction Act, Title I. The following proposal which your library submitted was not approved for funding:

Local History/Genealogy

Microfiching $ 5,600

The project was not approved because the Advisory Council believed it to be local in nature and would not have statewide implications.

Thank you for your interest and cooperation in the continued development of public libraries in Alabama."[19]

Sue Royer was appointed Assistant Director in July 1983. She was still in that position in 2004.

A lease was signed in December 1983 to place a branch library in Madison Mall. The branch opened on August 1, 1984. One hundred new library cards were issued the first day. It was in a cubby hole beside the escalator at the west end of the first floor.

In 1984 the library initiated the ambitious project of automating the handling of books and materials. This was the bar-coding of all materials so that a computer can easily keep track of materials, checking out, checking in, maintenance, inventory, acquisition and de-accession. This action was related to the Library Management Network activity cited above. Patrons were issued bar-coded library cards also. The computer will keep up with overdue materials so tardy readers can be notified.[20]

The city ordinance about overdue books helped bring down the loss rate of books down to about 100 per year. In addition, the electronic theft-proof measures have also helped bring down rates. Another theft issue still continued. People tear pages out of reference books and take them home instead of making a copy of the pages at the library. When the losses are noted, a library employee has to track down the missing page in another document or location, make a copy, and paste it into the original document. This takes considerable time.[21]

February 19, 1985 – The board agreed with Mrs. Schremser's recommendation that the branch librarians be responsible for book selection at their branches, because they have more knowledge about what was needed in their collections.

November 19, 1985 – A patron complained that *George Washington's Expense Account*, by Marvin Kitman, cast a poor reflection on Washington's reputation as the father of our country. She thought it should be removed from the collection and the board agreed.

The fact that the board banned a book based on the say-so of one patron, and the flimsy reason, got this author's adrenaline flowing. I got on the Internet in September 2004, found the book, bought it and read it. My conclusions about the book were:

- George Washington's expense account in his own handwriting was reproduced from the archives.
- The author used other historical material to fill out the history of that era and provide the basis for his conclusions, which were well documented.

- The author's explanations were logical and his assumptions about other situations to explain Washington's expenses were solid.
- He drew parallels to later warfare and modern military-industrial complex relationships to support his conclusions. I spent 27 years active duty in the U.S. Army and another 8 years working for a defense contractor, so I have a base of knowledge that can fairly judge Kitman's statements.
- He had a sharp and sarcastic wit and style, but it was only applied to his logical conclusions and assumptions.

To ban the book because one person thought Washington should be considered a perfect God above all commentary about his life and decisions is a violation of the Library Bill of Rights, as promulgated by the American Library Association. I stand ready to debate anyone about Washington's expense account and its meaning.

I wrote a letter to Mrs. Roberts, the chairman of the library board during that period, asking for her response to my assessments above. She graciously responded by telephone. She remembered that the library patron was a member of the local chapter of the Daughters of the American Revolution (DAR). The person declared that the DAR chapter would not donate to the building fund for the current Fort Book if the book remained in the library.[22] This event occurred two years before the building was finished. Recalling the biblical verse about casting the first stone, who among us would not cast out a book for the sake of a nice donation for a new library building? Probably few people read the book or knew it existed anyway. We need to keep our perspective and paraphrase Marie Antoinette, of French Revolution fame, if they want to read it, let them buy it. On a personal note, I thank that patron, 19 years later, for introducing me to an amusing and enlightening book about the Revolutionary War.

Now, back to George Washington's reputation. The mainstream historians from about 1800 to about 1950 generally glorified the American experiment in democracy. They emphasized the white Anglo-Saxon heritage, made near-gods of our founding fathers and decided to barely mention women, Negroes and Indians, except in a diminutive sense. Parson Mason Locke Weems, an itinerant bookseller, was a biographer of Washington in the first decade of the 18th century. Weems was the popularizer of the "Cherry Tree" myth and wrote, "The *Life of George Washington with Curious Anecdotes, Equally Honourable to Himself and Exemplary to his Young Countrymen.*" The full title tells it all, and generations of historians following Weems perpetuated the glorious story of our first president.

Have you ever wondered what all the letters mean that are before the Dewey Decimal System number or the first three letters of the author's name? Here's your chance to memorize them, because most are obvious.

- F   Fiction
- B   Biography
- L   Large print
- YA Young adult
- J   Junior or juvenile
- E   Easy readers – picture books for small children
- PB Paperback
- R   Reference – cannot be checked out
- Z   Archives
- SF Science fiction
- M   Mystery

- W Western
- SC Story collection, by first author's name
- VT Video tape
- T Cassette tapes
- CD Compact disk
- 364.25 Nonfiction classification by Dewey Decimal System

The fourth annual "Banned Books Week" was observed by the library during 9-15 September 1985. The event was sponsored by the American Library Association; the American Booksellers Association; the American Society of Journalists and Authors; the Association of American Publishers; and the National Association of College Stores.

Mrs. Donna Schremser, who joined the library staff in 1977, was quoted by the *Huntsville News*, "We're very fortunate that we live in a progressive community that respects a person's right to read whatever he wishes to. We have not had any incidents (at the public library) that I recall." She was not in town in 1967 when the Assistant City Attorney, Cantey Cooper, decided to start a one-person crusade to ban a book by Norman Mailer.

According to the American Library Association, censorship rose from 300 in 1979 to about 1,000 targets in 1984, but most of those were in public schools.[23]

In 1986 the Bessie Russell Branch moved from the North Parkway K-Mart parking lot to 3011-C Sparkman Drive to place it in a more residential area. That was where it remained in 2004. It was in a very small building, which was stuffed like a sausage with books and videos. In 2004 it had four computers and one library search monitor. In 2004 it was staffed by 2 full-time and 1 part-time employee, and supplemented by a volunteer high school student. There was a small children's area about three feet from the computers. The librarian's desk was in the middle so the computers can be monitored, as they are only ten feet away. There was only one small reading table. On second thought, it may be stuffed even tighter than a sausage. It needs more community support. There was a vehicular drop-off box outside.

Susan Markham joined the library on May 20, 1986 and was promoted to Head of Outreach and Extension in July 1987. That was the start of the Golden Decade of branch expansion, 1988-1997, during which ten new branch locations were opened and the Madison Branch moved to upgraded locations twice. She was still with the library as of 2004.

"Reading Skills Are Nothing To Clown About

'Ringling Readers,' a nationwide campaign by Ringling Brothers and Barnum and Bailey Circus to encourage children to read, will be introduced here Monday and Tuesday. The special presentation will be conducted by circus clown James Wade on Monday at the auditorium of the Huntsville-Madison County Public Library downtown at 10 a.m. and 1 p.m. and again on Tuesday, June 10, (1986) at the Madison Square Mall at 10 a.m. and 1 p.m. 'Ringling Readers' is presented in cooperation with the Huntsville-Madison County Public Library and *The Huntsville Times*.

'Ringling Readers' is a motivational program designed and coordinated by the Circus in cooperation with Reading Is Fundamental (RIF), a national non-profit organization, the Urban League and local business and community organizations across the country. The highlight of the 'Ringling Readers' program is a 25-minute show presentation called 'Reading Is Three Rings of Fun,' which actively involves the children in the many adventures of reading.

Each youngster who attends the program will receive a copy of *The Ringling Reporter*, compliments of *The Huntsville Times*. This is a newly published eight-page newspaper containing stories about the Ringling Brothers and Barnum and Bailey Circus especially written and edited for children by Reading Is Fundamental (RIF).

James Wade, whose clown name is Patches, says, 'I enjoy using the magic of clowning to encourage children to read. By showing children how reading helps them grow, laugh and imagine, we hope to spark an interest that will last a lifetime.' James, a native of Charleston, W. Va., is a 1985 graduate of Ringling Brothers and Barnum and Bailey Circus College. He previously traveled with his own clowning and magic show and has taught as an artist-in-residence in the West Virginia public schools.

'Ringling Readers' is being initiated in response to the fact that an estimated 23 million Americans are unable to read well enough to cope adequately in modern society."[24] The 23 million cited above equates to 9.6 percent of our country's population of 239 million in 1986, which was a sad statistic.

January 27, 1987 – A City Council member from Gurley called and wanted the bookmobile back in Gurley. The town was willing to pay $1,000 if the bookmobile stop was reinstated. The town also wanted to discuss a branch in their area.

The 1987 Alabama Library Association annual meeting was conducted in Huntsville on April 1-3. Mrs. Jane Roberts, Chairman, Library Board, Huntsville-Madison County Public Library, received the Alabama Library Association's Public Service Award in 1987. She was the board's chairman for the last 21 years and had experienced the library's economic hardships during the 1960's, the steady growth in staff and services in the 1970's, and the construction of the new library building and its $1.9 million capital fund drive. The library had many achievements under Mrs. Robert's guidance to include the following:

- The opening of the first Sub-regional Library for the Blind and Physically Handicapped.
- First public library to establish a public radio station.
- Establishment of the Alabama Library Exchange in 1980 in Huntsville as a multi-type cooperative of all types of libraries in North Alabama.
- Start of the Library Management Network, a shared state-of-the-art automated system for nine North Alabama libraries, headquartered at the Huntsville Public Library.[25]

On April 26, 1987 the new Huntsville-Madison County Public Library was opened and dedicated. Librarian Cecil Beach, director of the Broward County, Florida library gave the dedication address. The local Daughters of the American Revolution presented a flag for the new building and a Grissom High School color guard team performed. More details about the new building are in the next chapter titled, "Fort Book." [This author calls it the Citadel of Knowledge, but my wife calls it Fort Book, as did many Huntsvillians]

In April 1987 the Library Board established two policies, which are quoted below:
"Policies Governing Donations of Historical Memorabilia

The mission of the Huntsville-Madison County Public Library is to provide excellent library service to the residents of its tax-support area. This will be achieved by providing residents with library materials and information services proportionate to levels of demand and use through local resources and through contacts outside the library system.

The Library collects and preserves specialized and historical materials (print, manuscript, and photographs), with special emphasis on Madison County and the Tennessee Valley. The Library prefers not to collect plaques, artifacts, or other museum-type pieces, unless they pertain directly to the collections of the Library or they have historic value for ongoing display purposes.

The Library has an Artistic and Historic Collection Evaluation Committee to determine whether or not such donations would be beneficial to the Library collection. Any donation becomes the exclusive property of the Library. Donors may request that gifts judged no longer appropriate for the Library shall be returned to the donor.

It is the responsibility of the donor to have such gifts appraised for tax purposes."
"Policies Governing Donations of Art Works

The Huntsville-Madison County Public Library is delighted to receive gifts of art for display within the Library. The Library has an Artistic and Historic Collection Evaluation Committee to determine whether or not donated artwork is appropriate for the Library. Art works will be evaluated by the committee, and a recommendation will be made to the Director to accept or refuse gifts.

Art works donated to the Library shall become the exclusive property of the Library. Donors may request that gifts judged no longer appropriate for the Library shall be returned to donor.

It is the responsibility of the donor to have art donations appraised for tax purposes."[26]

The total circulation at the Huntsville-Madison Public Library and its branches continued to increase since the new building was opened on April 26, 1987. The July 1987 circulation was 104,000 items, compared to the comparable time in July 1986 with 91,000 items. Circulation of children's items in June 1986 was 12,786, while it was 26,307 in June 1987, which is over 100 percent increase year to year in June. The July figure for children in July 1986 was 14,651, compared to the July 1987 number of 25,120. Those were most impressive increases. The new building was a pleasure just to visit, as well as browse and check out items.[27]

Money drives almost everything, and especially governmental services. An example follows for the fiscal year 1987-88. It is offered as an example of the interplay between our city officials and the library director, and the director then has to live and adjust with what she finally receives.

The budget submission for the Fiscal year 1987-88 is quoted:
"June 15, 1987
The Honorable Joe Davis, Mayor
City of Huntsville
P.O. Box 308
Huntsville, AL 35804
Dear Mayor Davis:

Enclosed is the Library Board's budget request for Fiscal Year 1987-88 in the amount of $1,850,000, compared to the current year's appropriation of $1,575,000. Most of that increase reflects the increases in operating costs for our new Main Library in utilities, maintenance costs for heating and cooling systems, insurance, and building maintenance.

This request reflects a 5% increase in employee salaries and funding for 3 additional employees for our current staff of 70 FTE to assist the more than 3,000 people who use the Main Library and its branches daily. We anticipate use of the Library to increase even more during the next year, as we now have the ability to offer many more services.

In addition to increases in operating costs and salaries, we have a vital need to significantly increase our book holdings, our primary mission to this community. We have included a statistical comparison of our library with other public libraries serving similar communities, which we hope will document our needs even further.

We thank you for your support in past years, and we are appreciative of our new facility. The continued success of our program depends upon the continued strong commitment of the City to support the Library adequately so that we can provide the quality service that our citizens demand.

Sincerely,

Jane G. Roberts, Chairman Library Board

I. Salaries and Benefits:

We are requesting a 5% salary increase for employees, 3 additional FTE salaries and continued funding for the 2 additional FTE we started at mid-year 1987.

We anticipate an additional 10% increase in group health insurance and coverage must also be extended to new employees.

Total increase for salaries and benefits for City Budget is $214,200.

II. Library Materials

The public continues to demand additional materials, and we are requesting an additional $42,800 over the current year. With our total materials budget of $379,000 we should add 16,000 volumes, 420 periodical subscriptions, 1500 records, tapes, and compact discs, 480 videocassettes, and 10 16mm films. We anticipate our circulation will top one million by the end of the fiscal year.

III. Building Operating Expenses

We are asking for an increase of $26,000 over the current year's funding for increases in utilities, maintenance of heating, air conditioning, elevators, increased insurance premiums, and grounds maintenance. Much of that increase reflects a full year in this building.

IV. Automated Services

The Library is decreasing the amount needed for automated services, due primarily to a decreased cost of our cataloging utility and its availability on a CD ROM disc, instead of an expensive online service. We are decreasing our request from $85,000 to $73,000.

V. General Operating Expenses

The Library is requesting $3,500 increase to cover costs primarily for office supplies and cataloging supplies.

I. SALARIES, PAYROLL TAXES, BENEFITS

Salaries	$868,000
Payroll Taxes	65,000
Group Insurance	53,000
Retirement	42,000
	$1,028,000

II. LIBRARY COLLECTION

Books	300,000
Periodicals	18,000
Newspapers	4,000
Records, Tapes, Comp. Discs	15,000
Videotapes and Discs	24,000
Microfilm	10,000
Film - 16 mm	5,000
Binding	2,500
Manuscripts and Photographs	500
Framed Art	500
	379,500

III. BUILDING OPERATING EXPENSES

Utilities	135,000
Janitorial Supplies	8,000
Building Maintenance	34,000

Grounds Maintenance 7,000
Telephone   16,000
Insurance and Bonds 30,000
Madison Square Branch 15,000
Building Security   5,000
                      250,000

IV. AUTCMATED SERVICES
Circ. System Support & Maintenance 60,000
Bibliofile   4,000
Online Searching   3,000
Software   6,000
                       73,000

V. GENERAL OPERATING EXPENSES
Accounting & Audit   4,500
Postage   16,500
Vehicle Expenses   2,500
Equipment   20,000
Equipment Maintenance 26,000
Printing   10,000
Office Supplies   20,000
Cataloging Supplies   12,000
Training & Conferences 8,000
                      119,500

TOTAL $1,850,000"[28]

Statistics of comparable Southern public libraries were attached to the budget request. Thirteen mid-size cities were compared. Huntsville was the fourth largest in population, but its total budget was only the ninth largest, which indicated it was below average per population. Huntsville rated ninth for total salaries, which was not good, but was rated tenth in percentage of budget for salaries at 51 percent. That was bad news for employees. Huntsville was fifth in the number of materials and second in percent of budget for materials, which were both good news for being effective stewards of the public money. Huntsville ranked below average for salaries for the director, assistant director and Masters in Library Science (MLS) professionals, which meant Huntsville had a harder time attracting professional librarians.

In September 1987 the library asked for $1,850,000, and the mayor's budget only allocated $1,560,000. The director, Donna Schremser, offered the things she would have to do to meet the shortfall. There would be cuts of $30,000 in employee salaries and benefits, $169,000 in library collection, $36,000 in building expenses, $14,000 in automated services, and $41,000 in general operating expenses. She said Huntsvillians were flocking to the new building and demanding more services. The larger facility led to increased operating expenses. Mrs. Schremser offered the following specific service reductions:

- Closing the main library on Thursday evenings, the facility's slowest night of the week;
- Closing the Eleanor Murphy Branch on Tuesday and Thursday evenings and Saturday nights;
- Discontinuing direct services to nursing homes, providing book deposits only;

- Reducing the materials appropriations to 1983 levels; this means no funds for 16-millimeter films, manuscripts and photographs and framed art. Newspaper subscriptions would be cut in half; and
- Closing library meeting rooms unless the library is open to save on utilities.[29]

August 19, 1987 – The U.S. Department of Education contacted the Huntsville Public Library for more information about the International Media Center, which was recently recognized as one of five exemplary programs in the United States for new citizens.

In 1987 the book lovers and citizen activists in southeastern Madison County decided that the bookmobile service was not adequate to serve their desire for books for their communities. In parallel, activists in both Gurley and New Hope decided that the local governments were not going to improve library services, so grass-roots agitators started to take matters into their own hands. Within a year both towns had library branches—in buildings! Gurley's story will be told now. New Hope's story is in a chapter of its own.

For several years some citizens of the little town of Gurley, population 900-1000, 16 miles east of Huntsville on U.S. Route 72, had pestered Mayor Bennett and the Gurley Town Council for a library in a building. The bookmobile stop at the local Piggly Wiggly grocery store was popular and had heavy usage. It was time for a building! In the spring of 1987 those agitators and other citizens met in the Gurley Cumberland Presbyterian Church Annex to discuss how to raise money for a library building. It was decided to hold a country fair and a committee was appointed to investigate. Most of the clubs and institutions participated and the town's enthusiasm netted $2,000. It was a start, but there was a long way to go. Hope springs eternal. The library's scrapbook had the following statement, "There were some dark days, some tears, and a lot of hard work to follow."

The Gurley Town Council met for its regular meeting on August 4, 1987. Each council member (name behind selectee) was allowed to select one person for the library board, with the following results: Frances Harless (1 year term) (McClendon); Sue James (2) (Thompson); Betty Smith (3) (Harless); Ernestine Shephard (4) (Putnam); and Jewel Pence (4) (Mitchell). The following Ex-Officio members were appointed: Betty George, Anthony Stone, Hayes Power, Frances Forhand and Billy Layne.

The minutes of the historical first meeting of the Gurley Library Board is quoted below in its entirety to give recognition to the participants and to demonstrate the community interaction necessary to get a difficult project on its path to success.

"The First meeting of the Gurley Public Library board was held at 7:00 p.m., August 31, 1987, at the Cumberland Presbyterian Church annex. Five members, appointed by the Gurley City Council, were all in attendance. The six ex-officio members were well represented with an attendance of four. Two interested citizens attended.

Meeting was called to order by Mrs. Sue James. First order of business was election of officers. Mrs. James asked for nominations. Mrs. Earnestine Shepard nominated Mrs. Sue James. Ms. Frances Ann Harless seconded. Vote was unanimous. Mrs. Jewel Pence was nominated for Vice-President by Mrs. Sue James. Seconded by Mrs. Earnestine Shepard. Vote was unanimous. Mrs. Betty Smith was nominated for Secretary by Mrs. Sue James. Seconded by Mrs. Jewel Pence. Vote was unanimous. Mrs. Sue James nominated Mrs. Earnestine Shepard for Treasurer. Seconded by Mrs. Betty Smith. Vote was unanimous. Mrs. Sue James nominated Ms. Frances Harless for Parliamentarian. Seconded by Mrs. Jewel Pence.

Formal business session was opened by Mrs. James, with a background of all ground work done so far.

It was unanimously agreed that the Board meet with the City Council September 1, 1987 at their regularly scheduled meeting to request their guidance, and request that the City Council and the Board meet with the Huntsville Public Library officials as soon as possible.

Possible locations and building costs was discussed, with many suggestions considered. It was noted that the old City Hall would, with some restoration and renovations, be one likely prospect, since it had suitable area and storage facilities. It was also pointed out that there might be a possibility of a Federal Grant to help restore an historic building.

Funding was the next issue. Federal and State grants being a possibility, decision was made to check into both. Mrs. Jewel Pence is to contact the League of Municipalities, Mr. Albert Hall and Mr. Lowell Barron [state legislators]. Mrs. Sue James is to contact Mr. Roy Stone and Mr. Jerry Craig for further guidance [county commissioners].

The decision was made to set the meeting date as the First Monday of the month at 6:30 p.m. at the Cumberland Presbyterian Church annex. The next meeting will be held November 5, 1987 because the first Monday is a holiday. Special meetings will be called as needed.

Fund-raising was next on our agenda. An open discussion was held, and it was apparent we needed a fund-raising committee. Mrs. Jewel Pence nominated the ex-officio members as the fund-raising committee. Seconded by Mrs. Sue James. Vote was unanimous. It was agreed that we would try to have one fund-raiser each quarter, starting with the Country Fair, handled so capably by Mr. Anthony Stone.

Suggestions for fund-raisers were solicited. Mrs. Earnestine Shepard suggested a street dance for all ages with entertainment to be held. It was decided we would try to have the street dance around the First of October. Mr. Kyle Davis was appointed chairman.

Mrs. Marty Stone suggested a combined auction, sit down dinner for invited guests only, to be held possibly in early March. Mrs. Frances Harless, chairman.

Mr. Anthony Stone suggested a community cook-out, picnic at the school parking lot in June 1988, as a thank you for all of their great support at the Country Fair. Mr. Stone was appointed to look into it.

The fund-raising committee will meet September 13, 1987 at 7:00 p.m. at the Cumberland Presbyterian annex. The Board is to meet in a special called work session September 13, 1987 at the Church annex. Time will be 4:30 p.m. The board encourages public participation in our meetings. The financial report was given by Mrs. Earnestine Shepard, Treasurer. We have at present $2079.04 in the bank, with no outstanding expenses. Meeting was adjourned. Mrs. Betty Smith, Secretary."[30]

The Gurley Branch finally opened on Sunday, March 27, 1988 in the former Shirley's Cafe building at 331 Walker Street. The rented building required months and plenty of work by volunteers to make the interior presentable as a library. The restroom could only be accessed from the outside. Brrr. The library was manned by volunteers, and is still manned only by volunteers in 2004. The branch volunteers are proud that their branch building was in first in Madison County outside of the City of Huntsville and it is the only branch library in the Huntsville-Madison County Public Library system that has no paid staff of the 11 branches.

The Huntsville Public Library Foundation was a separate organization established to raise money for the library. The agreement between the library and the foundation was signed in January 1988 and is provided below:

"RESOLUTION AND AGREEMENT BETWEEN THE HUNTSVILLE PUBLIC LIBRARY BOARD AND THE HUNTSVILLE PUBLIC LIBRARY FOUNDATION
WHEREAS, the establishment of the Huntsville Public Library Board, hereinafter referred to as the Board, was authorized by the State of Alabama in 1919; and

WHEREAS, the Board's primary purpose is the governance and supervision of the Huntsville Public Library including authority and control of all funds received or appropriated on behalf of the Huntsville Public Library;

WHEREAS, the Huntsville Public Library has funding needs over and above those funds provided by the various governments which it serves;

WHEREAS, there are numerous civic organizations, charitable organizations, corporations and private individuals that wish to support and further the interests of the Huntsville Public Library; and

WHEREAS, to assist in administering gifts from these sources, the Board has caused to be created the Huntsville Public Library Foundation, hereinafter referred to as the Foundation; and

WHEREAS, the Board desires that the Foundation be and is an autonomous and independent body;

WHEREAS, there exist a need for close coordination between the Board and the Foundation;

WHEREAS, the AGREEMENT below is intended to provide guidance to the parties for coordinating the activities of the Board and the Foundation.

NOW THEREFORE, be it resolved that the following AGREEMENT is entered into between the Huntsville Public Library Board and the Huntsville Public Library Foundation this 18th day of January 1988.

THE HUNTSVILLE PUBLIC LIBRARY FOUNDATION AGREES TO THE FOLLOWING:

1. It will prepare a written financial and administrative report at the end of each fiscal year, such report to be presented to the Huntsville Public Library Board.

2. The Foundation Board of Trustees shall include among its membership the member designated by the Huntsville Public Library Board, and the Executive Director of the Library, the latter of whom shall be an ex-officio (non-voting) Trustee of the Foundation.

3. The Foundation exists solely to solicit, receive, and administer gifts of money, stocks and other real and valuable property from various and all non-government sources.

4. The Foundation shall, no less often than annually, disburse to the Library Board all available funds, except:

    a.   funds restricted as to disbursement by way of their gift

    b.   corpus to support endowment

    c.   corporate stocks, bonds or other financial instruments where the Foundation and Library Board are agreed that it is in the best long term interest of the Library to retain them in the Foundation.

5. The Foundation shall receive the funding requests of the Library Board from time-to-time (as agreed below) and shall advise the Board of its apparent ability and plans to fulfill said requests. In the event of an unplanned or unexpected gift, the Foundation shall consult with the Board as to the most advantageous use of the gift.

6. The Foundation and Board shall have the same fiscal year and shall meet at least once annually in joint session.

THE HUNTSVILLE PUBLIC LIBRARY BOARD AGREES TO THE FOLLOWING:

1. The Library Board shall submit its funding requests to the Foundation annually in advance of the beginning of the Foundation's fiscal year, or otherwise as requested by the Foundation.

2. Library Board members currently serving as members, officers or Trustees of the Foundation shall resign from the Foundation except that the Trustee appointed and designated by the Library Board and the Executive Director of the Library shall continue as Trustee and ex-officio Trustee, respectively, of the Foundation.

3. The Board shall have the same fiscal year as the Foundation.

ALL PARTIES TO THIS AGREEMENT, resolve to work in close harmony for their common interest in the library including working with other groups supportive of this activity such as but not limited to groups like the Friends of the Library. Finally, in witness and recognition of these actions the By-Laws and other authorizing instruments of both parties is attached and made a part of this Resolution and Agreement.

Jane G. Roberts, Chairman, HUNTSVILLE PUBLIC LIBRARY BOARD

Richard E. Reeves, Chairman, HUNTSVILLE PUBLIC LIBRARY FOUNDATION"[31]

Library Director Donna Schremser attended the City Council meeting on Thursday, or Wednesday work session, 17-18, 1988 to ask council members to reconsider their $1.92 million appropriation. She had asked for $2 million. Seems as if the heating and cooling system in the new building cost more than was expected. There was also a parking problem at the library as folks were flocking to the new facility. Councilman Jimmy Wall recommended removal of a fence behind the library and a parking lot on Davis Circle, which contained 25 unused parking spaces.[32]

Marelle Pruitt was honored by the City Council on Tuesday, November 24, 1987 with a resolution commending her 40 years of work with the library. She began as an office manager in 1947, became head cataloguer in 1955 and served in a number of voluntary library-related capacities.[33]

There were and are continuing problems with unattended children being left at the library. The library "orphans" are not a new problem, but the new facility seems to have attracted more such children. Apparently parents who both work find it convenient to dump their kids in the library. It becomes more of a problem when the library closes at 5 or 6 P.M. and then the library supervisors have to stay with them until the parents pick them up. If wage-and-hour workers work overtime, then they have to get compensatory time some other time during the normal workweek. Some teenagers made "improper" use of the sitting rooms, but that was curtailed by installing light switches that do not turn off.[34]

Regina Cooper, director of the collection department, was elected vice president-president elect of the Alabama Library Association (ALLA) in April 1988. She then served as president of the ALLA during the year April 1989-April 1990.

You can't please everybody! In 1989, two years after the new library opened, an unhappy potential reader wrote a letter to the editor of *The Huntsville Times*. The reader, a man, said the facility was fine, but there was a definite lack of literature for anyone over the age of 10. The library had hundreds of thousands of dollars tied up in computers, copiers, microfilm machines, children's books, and recliners, but had one of the worst selections of books in the country. [Wish he had named some of the several hundred libraries that he must have visited.] He ranted and raved several more paragraphs before he ended with, "The way it is being run now, our money is being wasted." The *Times* artist led the article with a drawing of a man slouched in a chair, reading a book while smoking. As of the 2004 telephone book, he no longer resides in Huntsville. Hopefully he moved to a city with a better library, does not smoke up our books, and we should be grateful he is no longer in town. His name shall not enter this history.[35]

April 19, 1989 – The lease for the Madison Mall Branch was up for renewal. The current lease was for $7,600 per year, but the new lease called for a five-year fixed rate of $10,000 per year. In addition, the library would be required to purchase six advertisements in the Mall publications each year for about $4,000 per year. The Mall manager agreed for the library to pay a fee, but not place ads, so the savings to the library would be about $2,800 per year.

A sample bookmobile schedule for June 1989 is below:

"-Monday- Bruno's, Bailey Cove/Weatherly   2:30-4:00

Sandhurst Park/Green Cove Rd.	4:30-6:00
-Tuesday- Madison Cross Rds.	2:30-4:00
Boy's Club-Girls Club/Mason CT.	4:30-5:00
-Wednesday- Locust Grove Day Care	1:30-3:00
New Market Post Office	3:30-4:00
-Thursday- Research Park/Alternating 188	
Sparkman and 6000-C Technology	11:30-1:00
Hazel Green Methodist Church	2:00-4:00
Meridianville Post Office	4:30-5:00
-Friday- Triana Town Hall	10:30-12:00
Discount Food Mart/Monrovia & Jeff Rds	12:30-1 :00
Harvest Fire Station	1:30-3:00
The following stops will begin the week of June 19th:	
-Monday- Colonial Hills Summer School	11:00-11:45
Girl's Club/Meridian St.	12:00-1:00
Boy's Club/Abingdon	1:15-1:45
-Tuesday- Calvary Friendship Cen./Northwoods	1:30-2:00
-Wednesday- Terry Heights Summer School	10:00-11:00"[36]

Faxing service was available in 1989 at the main library and the Eleanor Murphy Branch on Charlotte Drive. Customers could have library material faxed to their home of business, but with some restrictions. The maximum number of pages to be faxed was six, it could only be faxed for local calls, and the service was only for library materials, not the customers' papers.

The library had a wealth of market research data available in 1989. Some examples follow: Abstracts of significant information appearing in thousands of newspapers, business magazines, government reports, trade journal, bank letters, and special reports. Industry data sources included bibliographic financial and marketing data for 65 major industries in the United States and abroad. FINDEX provided abstracts summarizing all industry and market research reports, studies, and surveys commercially available from U.S. and international publishers. ECONBASE provided econometric time series covering subject areas such as economics, business conditions, finance, manufacturing, household income distribution and demographics. CENDATA provided statistical data, press releases, and product information from the Bureau of the Census.

In 1989 the City of Madison Branch Library moved from the Recreation Center to a storefront location in Hughes Plaza, 151 Hughes Road, directly across the street from the Madison City Hall. The branch now housed 12,000 volumes and the staff grew to 2 full-time and 2 part-time employees.

The Information and Periodicals Department had a Telecommunications Device for the Deaf (TDD) in 1989. A TDD was a special typewriter along with an acoustic coupler, which allowed deaf persons to communicate by telephone. (OPTIONS, Volume 1, Issue 4, October 1989, Huntsville Public Library.) According to David Lilly, head of the reference department, the TDD became non-operational in the late 1990's and was not repaired. During almost a decade, the TDD was used less than twenty times. The TDD needed comparable devices at both ends, so words could be typed and sent over the normal telephone line. The continuing requirement for such a device is probably doubtful in today's age of the computer and email.[37]

October 18, 1989 – The Director, Donna Schremser, reviewed for the Board a Staff Development Day program the San Antonio Public Library had presented. She would like to institute such a program here, which would involve closing the library for one day. The Board agreed that the idea should be planned and implemented.

The Decade of the 1980's ends with comments that library patrons put in the suggestion box at the circulation desk in late 1989.

"-The hours the library are open are the best of any city I've lived in. More trouble needs to be taken re-shelving the books. Movie collection is great.

-You don't let the library stay open long enough on Sunday.

-Books are returned overdue, fines paid and still the computer says the fine was unpaid at next checkout. Too many people behind desk who will not check out customers. What are they doing? (I'm here 25 times each year.)

-There are more Danielle Steele books in large print needed and also Jackie and Joan Collins. When you look for them, they can't be found. They are your three best authors.

-I recently became a member of your library. I am very impressed with your facilities and selection, but I noticed that your Science Fiction selection is rather old. Do you have the newer titles at another branch? If not I would like to suggest some check into new titles. With the science field in this area I feel there to be a great demand for this field. Thank you!

-Need more books-New books should be 7 days only--No renewal

-Think about getting three small children from the car to the door on a busy night. Walking in the roadway is a real nervous-maker. Walking in the plantings teaches the wrong lesson about respect for public property. Sidewalks aren't that expensive and they're more civilized than walking in the road.

-MORE PARKING MORE PARKING CLOSER PARKING MORE PARKING LIGHTED PARKING. Great Library!

-Your parking lot was full! Great!

-The parking area appears to always be filled to near capacity. Is this being used by library patrons or others??? Is there a means of having this checked out since there could be some hardship placed on the patrons. What about more parking spaces----

-BIGGER PARKING LOT

-The Public Library is a very clean and nice place to be. The people who work here are very helpful and extremely friendly. I enjoy coming to the library and hope to visit you again soon.

-I THINK THAT THIS LIBRARY IS VERY NICE AND CAN HELP WITH ANYTHING!

-I have been doing a lot of library work for my college course Children's Literature and the ladies working in the children's section have been more than helpful. Many, many thanks to them!

-I think you should have teen magazines in the library. I really do love your library. Do you know what I said? "I said it looks like a castle and I'd love to live there;" Do you need any weekend or summer volunteers if so I'd love to help out!

-Ms. Sara McDaris is truly a Child Development professional who's(sic) love for her job and children shines through. She does a great job of handling the children in that she establishes rules, even explains and enforces these rules making clear what she expects and will tolerate with expectation increasing and tolerance diminishing as the children get older. All the children seem to "test" her far less often and for the most part are cooperative and orderly. I would like to see our "Miss Sara" get some sort of commendation. People like her make Huntsville a fantastic place to raise children.

-We are very pleased with this library and usually are here twice a week. The book selection is good and we also enjoy the video tapes and software (would love a more extensive software collection). You have a nice, friendly staff. Keep up the good work!

-Have a TV room for the video movie section. Assign the room time and movie. This would be nice for classrooms or family outings.
-Please--the Japanese sculpture is the only one I can imagine being chosen! The others would embarrass a 2nd grader! (RE Books -- Do get more LARGE PRINT for nursing home patients - Please!)
-More Parking
-Bring back the other light pen at check-out. It is faster for everyone and easier for the workers.
-A change machine on the 2nd floor that dispenses nickels only. More parking.
-Stay open longer on Saturday. I work during the week, the only time I can come here is Saturday. I will be writing you further on this matter.
-More Parking
-If you can't provide sufficient parking then parking tickets should not be issued.
-More parking. 2 more computers in children section.
-The parking places are not real good and on Sundays it's a nightmare.
-I am very disappointed in the small number of popular CD in relation to the classical CD. It would be immensely appreciated if you could purchase more in the way of "easy listening" CD's.
-I know several people (including myself) who would like you to carry MORE CLASSICAL COMPACT DISCS.
-The public library should have two disk drives on the computer at the first floor. Thank You And let people about 14 of age check out videos.
-Please have a wider selection of audio cassettes and some of them don't work!!
-I was disappointed to find that the movie discs in audio-visual are the RCA 10-15 year old selectavision type, which practically nobody uses anymore. No stores sell these machines and no store sells these discs. With the growth of CD popularity are the new Laserdiscs which at present are expensive and new; your patrons would probably welcome this new format, especially for the sound clarity in operas and musicals and ballets. I certainly would! If you need volunteers in future fundraising, I would be happy to donate some time.
-This place needs a place where you can lison (sic) to English tapes.
-I would like a Thursday morning reading program for children.
-I would like to suggest that the library have each school's Reading books. The students aren't allowed to take their "Reading" books home with them. It would be helpful if the student can get the book outside the classroom. For example; Heath "Rare Hen's Teeth" is used for the 5th grade in the City Schools.
-Wish you could have good movies like the Baseball movies. How to play baseball, and football etc.
-Your restroom smells nice.
-The public library should let 11-year olders go up stairs."[38]

      That was a nice mixture of comments. Of course, you can't please everyone all the time, but maybe some of the complainers just could not find a parking place.

Chapter 11

Fort Book

"The opening of a free, public library, then, is a most important
event in the history of any town."

James Russell Lowell
Books and Libraries, December 22, 1885
Writers on Writing

In June 1984, Library Director Donna Schremser told the finance committee of the Huntsville City Council that a bigger library was needed. The current library on Fountain Circle had about 34,000 square feet, but 80,000 square feet will be needed during the next twenty years. Such a new building might cost $7.8 million.

Mrs. Schremser asked the committee for money to employ local architect Billy Herrin of Jones and Herrin for building analyses, schematic design documents, energy studies and other preliminary work. That phase might take 6-8 months.

The finance committee recommended to the full council that $85,000 first be spent on design alternatives. There were several ideas about the form of the expansion. Two options were to build a four-story addition and renovation of the existing building or a two-story addition and the purchase of the Huntsville-Madison County Chamber of Commerce building immediately behind the library. The Chamber had not begun the construction of its new building, so no definite plans could be made.

The library officials wanted to have specific design plans to show the community and hope that industries and groups will want to donate to the effort so the city won't have to finance the entire project. Most City Council members agreed that the city would not be able to pay for an $8 million expansion.[1]

By putting forth an estimate of $7.8 million, it was obvious Mrs. Schremser had been investigating the idea for some time. Robert Rohlf was the director of the Hennepin County Library in Minnetonka, Minnesota, a western suburb of Minneapolis. He was a former director of administration at the Library of Congress and had served as a library consultant for more than 100 libraries in 25 states.

The library board, Mrs. Schremser and Mr. Rohlf had devised a program for an expansion into the adjacent Huntsville-Madison County Chamber of Commerce property that detailed needs down to the square foot. Mr. Rohlf had worked with library officials for about a year, as of September 1984, to help define the library's needs. He said all you have to do is walk in and look around the Fountain Circle library to be convinced it was inadequate.

Rohlf offered the glass half-empty or half-full argument. He said the council looks at the library and said we have so much now, why do we need this much. The other side is, we have so little now compared to what we should have. The expected need in twenty years was the proper goal. Probably the most telling statement by Rohlf was, "One of the experiences that I've had over the last 20 years is that I've never seen a library that was overbuilt. They all get too small too soon." The statistics provided in other chapters showed that Huntsville was well below equivalent Southeastern cities in everything except circulation per capita.

Huntsville had a very high education level and the city was growing. Its residents were highly motivated. Rohlf said highly educated and highly motivated cities are typical heavy library users. "You've got those types in Huntsville. I think those of us in the library business profession have been able to analyze pretty well what makes a community a library user."

Even though the city has several libraries, Rohlf said those tend to cater to the faculty needs. "In fact, in some university libraries you wonder if the students aren't just there as a necessary evil."[2] A public library tries to make its collection as available to suit the general user, which definitely includes wider variety of children's books. Those are not found in university libraries. Public libraries have little in common with university libraries. In 2004, a one-year library card in order to check out books at the University of Alabama in Huntsville Library was $50. At Alabama A&M it cost $15 and at Oakwood College it was free.

Circulation in 1984 was 585,437, 18 percent higher than 1983. The library was forced to reduce the loan period from 3 to 2 weeks. Another pressing need was for more parking spaces. The parking lot across Fountain Circle was inadequate and was metered as well, which does not encourage people to stay long at the library. But the city fathers (and mothers) are always looking for additional revenue. The new library would include a public lounge with tables, chairs and vending machines, a subregional library for the blind and physically handicapped and a permanent Friends of the Library bookstore.[3] The Friends of the Library are a crucial support system to provide additional funds for the library and enhanced the circulation of books throughout the supported area. Guntersville, Decatur and even the small Arab library had an internal Friends bookstore.

In May 1985 the plans for the new library were unveiled to the public. The building will be on the northeast corner of Monroe and St. Clair Streets. The site was an earlier garbage dump and was prone to flooding, but project officials do not see it as a problem. There will have to be considerable drainage preparation work done.

The outside architecture was rather cumbersome to describe. Billy Herrin, the project architect from Herrin and Jones, provided this philosophical concept to guide his approach: traditional characteristics of Huntsville with the "new, forward-thinking part." The hip-roof traditional atrium atop the building was repeated on a smaller scale along the arcade at the main entrance. The arcade, or covered walkway, continued the familiar Southern front porch concept to give the building more traditional ties, and "ties the past to the present." The predominantly brick material to be used would have the same effect.

Herrin's words and thoughts do not describe the outside, and I shall not try. My 1,000 words will be saved, you have to look at the picture or go there. The internal features will be simply described below to grasp the details of the new library's features. But the word descriptions just fail to give the perspective of this wonderful building, outside and inside. A visit is necessary to gain the full impact.

- Building is three times larger.
- Seating capacity will be 940, versus 118.
- A three-story atrium as a focal point.
- Adult services area will be larger that the entire ground floor in old current building.
- Audio-visual will four times as large.
- Natural light.
- Large parking area for up to 200 cars.
- Snack shop.
- Much larger genealogical area.

- A public auditorium.
- Several small quiet rooms.

The third floor was designed for future growth. It will contain a 20,000-square-foot "shell" of unfinished space that can be used if needed or for storage. It's cheaper to build it now and fill it later.

Herrin acknowledged that some people may criticize the open atrium space on all three floors. He said, "The cheapest thing would be a big metal building, but this will be a magnet for the city." Donna Schremser noted that more people used the library than any other building in town.[4] They were both exactly right. Why are churches and banks much larger than they need to be functionally? It is because they want to give the impression of grandeur, quality, and power. So it should be with libraries. Where else in our world is there such richness and variety of ideas and freedom of thought? What is more powerful than an idea?

The groundbreaking ceremony for the new Huntsville-Madison County Public Library was held at 11: A.M., Wednesday, October 9, 1985. Local dignitaries wielding the silver shovels included Mayor Joe Davis, City Council President Ernest Kauffman, County Commissioned Jerry Craig, Library Board chairman Jane G. Roberts, Library Board vice-chairman Frank Morring and Library Development Council chairman Guy J. Spencer Jr.

The new facility will cost $9.9 million. The city issued bonds for $8 million, $1.9 million was expected to come through fund raising from corporate and individual donations. The fund drive would continue through February 3, 1987. Gifts were tax deductible.[5]

The Library Development Council consisted of business executives from throughout the City. Guy J. Spencer Jr., president of the Spencer Companies, Inc., served as chairman. The vice-chairman was Harry M. Rhett Jr. and Richard Holloway, director of Huntsville Support Systems of the Boeing military Airplane Company worked as chairman of the development fund. Richard E. Reeves, co-founder and chairman of General Digital Industries, was the development vice-chairman.

M. Louis Salmon, attorney and partner in the firm of Watts, Salmon, Roberts, Manning and Noojin, served as chairman of the Pattern Gifts Division for contributions of $10,000 or more. John M. Cockerham, president of John M. Cockerham and Associates, served as chairman of the Advanced Gifts Division for donations between $5,000 and $10,000. William D. Gilchrist, regional executive officer of Central Bank of the South, was chairman of the Special Gifts Division for donations of $5,000 and less. Carol Madry served as public relations chairman.

Eugene Monroe Jr., president of Monroe Business Equipment, chaired the Advance Gifts Division. Mrs. J.R. Brooks, an active leader of several Huntsville volunteer groups, was chairman of the Special Gifts Division. The credit for the enlistment of the development committee leadership goes to Mrs. Jane Roberts, Chairman of the Library Board. A professional fund-raiser was also hired.[6]

On February 20, 1986, the Huntsville City Council announced that Universal Construction Company of Decatur, Alabama won the library construction contract with a bid of $4.48 million. There were eight bids, with Watkins Construction Company the only one from Huntsville. As of this date, Donna Schremser, library director, announced that the fund raising had reached $830,000.[7]

The fund raising had reached $1,058,324 by the end of March 1986. The campaign had some 200 volunteers calling on area corporations and individuals for pledges. The largest single contribution so far was $150,000 by an unnamed donor. The Junior League donated $15,000 for furnishing the "story hour alcove." The $1.9 million was for furnishing the library, not for the building construction.[8] The Junior League donation makes this an appropriate place to provide a breakout of the $1.9 million. The discussion about the different ways to give a gift was the following paragraph.

"Should you desire, your gift may be identified through a suitably inscribed and mounted plaque. It may be named in honor of a family, organization or event, or it may serve as a memorial to a deceased friend or loved one. The named opportunities listed at right (below) are for your convenience in selecting an appropriate gift commensurate with your desire and ability to give, and they are not based on actual costs. The costs shown have been set based on visibility and importance to the overall project.

ENTRY COLONADE	$150,00
ENTRY ATRIUM	250,000
MAIN CIRCULATION CENTER	25,000
Adult Reading Room	25,000
Fiction Reading Room	10,000
Computerized Card Catalog Area	15,000
Current Periodicals Reading Room	10,000
INFORMATION AND PERIODICALS	
DEPARTMENT	100,000
Study Rooms (5)	2,500 each
Group Study Room, Computer	
Equipped	15,000
Business Information Center	25,000
Periodicals and Microfiche/Reading Area	25,000
Study Rooms, Computer Equipped (4)	10,000 each
Foreign Language Center	25,000
Business Area Meeting Room	7,500
CHILDRENS AND YOUNG ADULT SERVICES	100,000
Circulation Center	10,000
Leisure Reading Area	25,000
Pre-School Area	25,000
Young Readers' Computer Center	10,000
Story Hour Alcove	15,000
Media Center	10,000
Young Readers' Exhibit Center	5,000
Young Adult Area	15,000
AUDIO VISUAL DEPARTMENT	100,000
Media Center	10,000
Public Service Desk	10,000
Recording Booth	5,000
Dark Room	5,000
HUNTSVILLE HERITAGE ROOM	100,000
Archives	30,000
Rare Books (Environmental and Security	
Controlled)	20,000
Historical Exhibit Area	10,000
ADMINISTRATIVE SERVICE SUITE	50,000
Reception Area	20,000
Director's Office	10,000

Board Room	25,000
BLIND AND PHYSICALLY HANDICAPPED DEPARTMENT	50,000
COMPUTER ROOM-LIBRARY MANAGEMENT NETWORK	50,000
COMMUNITY ROOM	100,000
Lobby	25,000
Main Room (Capacity: 200)	75,000
Small Room (Capacity: 30)	25,000
PUBLIC LOUNGE	75,000
BOOK & GIFT STORE	100,000
ALCOVE READING ROOM	10,000
FLAG POLE AND MOUNTING BASE	10,000
GARDENS	25,000
Large Garden	10,000
Small Gardens (2)	5,000 each
ENDOWED BOOK FUNDS	20,000
Named Endowment for General Use	5,000
Named Endowment for Special Collections	10,000"[9]

On May 23, 1986 *The Huntsville Times* carried a full page on the library, featuring an artist's conception of the library and a letter from the two principal fund-raising leaders, Richard Holloway and Jane Roberts. It was soliciting support for finishing the library and provided a form by which to send in your contribution, which could be by credit card. The publicist did well by this ad.[10]

By August 10, 1986 the fund raising had reached $1,180,000, which was not much of an increase from March. Perhaps the momentum was flagging.[11]

"'Fort Book' Massive, But Donations Aren't" was the story title of *The Huntsville Times* story on December 7, 1986. The partially finished exterior of the new library was in a photograph, and the building looked massive. Donna Schremser, director, said the distinctive structure might look intimidating, but promises when visitors eventually enter "they will feel at home here." She was right! Billy Herrin, architect, said it will be a "series of excitements." He was right!

The parking fee for the 50 spaces across from the Fountain Circle library was raised to 50 cents per hour. City officials have promised not to charge parking fees for the 196 spaces at the new building.

The donation campaign was intended to last five years. So far the large gifts have totaled $880,000. Major corporate contributors include Morton Thiokol, $50,000; *The Huntsville Times*, $40,000; Teledyne Brown, $25,000; First Alabama Bank, $25,000; AmSouth Bank, $25,000; and Raytheon, $20,000.[12]

The Library Board was provided a tentative schedule for the move into the new building at the Board meeting, January 27, 1987.

"February 1   Begin Publicity campaign to make public aware of closing dates.

March 8   Monroe to complete installation of 3rd floor furnishings

March 16-20   Move Archives, rare books and HHR overflow from basement. Also Heritage Room workroom material which will not be needed.

March 18   Monroe's to complete installation of 2nd floor

March 19-23   Technical Services Reference workroom

March 24-28	Subregional Library for B & PH, International Media Center
March 28-	Encourage patrons to check out extra books during April 5 this week. Books will be circulated for 30 days, to be due back after we reopen at the new building
March 30- April 3	Alabama Library Association Convention: No moving to be done this week.
April 6-24	COMPUTER DOWN
April 6-10	Computer Room Extension Department
April 10	Administration Department except for Shirley's material for payroll and daily cash requirements
April 15-25	LIBRARY CLOSED
April 15-17	Boxing books in Circulation, Reference, Young Readers, HHR, Audio Visual material, and Friends Bookstore
April 17-21	Moving company to move boxed books and shelving which we will disassemble
April 18	Use Student Assistants all day if needed to complete packing
April 20-24	Unpack, shelve and clean-up
April 25	R E S T
April 26	Dedication and reopen

We plan for a Monday-Friday, 8:00 a.m. to 5:00 p.m. work schedule for all library employees. However, overtime may be required if necessary during the move. Any overtime will be compensated with time and a half as required by the wage and hour law and may be taken during the month of May."[13]

The target opening date for Fort Book was Sunday, April 26, 1987. The staff would be moving the reference material, periodicals and historical holdings. The burning issue was how to move over 200,000 volumes to the new building in the shortest disruption time to the patrons. One group of patrons volunteered to form a human chain for the .6-mile trip, but what if it rained? There were some other ideas. The library staff finally decided to encourage the 60,000 cardholders to check out as many books as they wanted by April 15, and return them on April 26th.

The staff packed the boxes and the library hired professional movers for the remaining volumes starting April 14. The process closed the library down for nine days. In 1985, Birmingham closed for a month to move.[14] Bravo to Donna Schremser and her staff!

Earlier in this chapter there was a non-description of the outside of Fort Book. I still like to call it the Citadel of Knowledge. Let us now hear what the architect, Billy Herrin, had to say about his creation, because he was the man with the vision and expertise to put it all together. His thoughts are important, because you need to think his thoughts when you visit in order to appreciate what he created, and to see if his ideas are worthy of our city.

"Anyone can design a building, but it's the play on emotion that makes the difference between a good building and an ordinary building.

I didn't want it to be a 'cute' building. I didn't want it to be a 'fad' building."

Herrin believed that if a building is "to make a statement," it should have a distinctive shape. It sure does. It has fourteen sides.

"You may not like it, but you can't miss it. It's changed the skyline. It's evoked emotion simply by its sheer size."

To some, the building seems foreign to its surroundings. Too massive. Its bulk is squeezed onto a too-small, inappropriate site. Shapeless and formless, seamed together by overpowering brick wall resembling some medieval fort. Decorated with diverting pyramids.

Dominating, But relating to nothing. To my readers who have not seen the building, can you now visualize it? It is not as bad as you envisioned.

Herrin welcomed the criticism, because he thinks it adds to the structure's mystique.

"There's an unknown about it. People don't understand why it looks the way it does. They don't understand why it doesn't look like the old, typical Carnegie library. They don't like it because there is not stone, no Corithian (sic) columns, because it doesn't say Ex Libris on top."

Herrin described it as "a bridge building," a bridge between historic Huntsville and high-tech Huntsville.

"We used traditional forms, shapes, colors, textures and materials, but put them together in a modern, 1987 way."

He wanted brick that reflected the heritage of Huntsville: a brown range rather than red. Like the Episcopal Church of the Nativity. Or the color of brick you can find under the First Methodist Church's white stucco skin.

He wanted the pyramid form. You see it all over Huntsville. On the Stockton House on Franklin Street. On the old Dallas Mill. He wanted a distinctive roof shape. He wanted high ceilings – a regional Southern tradition.

"Everywhere you turn there's a surprise."

Now let us go inside and look for those surprises. Go through the sliding glass doors and a skylight provides natural sunlight. Now proceed under a lower ceiling and the circulation desk is in the atrium to draw your eyes upward to the third floor.

Herrin calls his atrium "a participator space. Not just something to look at. It asks you, 'Come into me. Be a part of me.' It dares you to enter and not look up."

Direct sunlight is bad for books, so the windows are recessed to maximize sunlight, but not directly. The windows are at different angles. There is a minimum of windows on the south side because of the sun angle.

The side rooms are angled for partial separation of departments, but allow for staff visibility for security.

There are many more subtle architectural features, so, please, on your next visit, walk slowly around the facility to think and take in the atmosphere.[15]

In September the library officials were able to get the City Council to approve an additional $140,000 for the new library, primarily for utilities and maintenance costs associated with a structure four times as large as the previous one.[16]

When the library opened in April 1987, the fund raising had collected $1.35 million. In November 1987, Donna Schremser reported that the amount was now $1.73 million, or 91 percent of the goal. The library recently received a $50,000 gift from the *New York Times* Foundation through the local CBS affiliate here, WHNT-TV.

The library board brought in $21,500; staff and employees, $37,677; large corporations (gifts of #10,000 and up), $1.17 million; small business and individuals (gifts of $5,000 to $10,000), $223,891); individuals, $166,123; other categories, $107,914.[17]

Madison County contributed $50,000. Since the county cannot raise funds, its budget is limited. But the residents of the county continue to receive full benefits of the library.

The final note in this chapter about the creation of Fort Book, circulation was up twenty percent in the first year of operation. This proves the adage that I just made up, if you build a better library, the people will come to check out more materials.

Chapter 12

Library Activists In New Hope

*"Perhaps no place in any community is so totally democratic as the town library.
The only entrance requirement is interest."*

Lady Bird Johnson, 1912-
The Quotable Book Lover

The Town of New Hope was located in southeastern Madison County, Alabama. The town's center was about two miles east of U.S. Highway 431, which ran between Huntsville and Guntersville. You cannot accidentally pass through New Hope, you have to make a concerted effort to get there. But that does not bother the 2,300 folks who populated the town. New Hope might typify a small town in North Alabama. Some things are old and kept that way. Other things are replaced by something new and modern. The history of New Hope was quoted below from the standard metal historical plaque erected through the auspices of the Alabama Historical Association. New Hope's plaque was put up in 2001 about 30 yards immediately to the south (left) of the Library.

"VIENNA (NEW HOPE)

Originally known as Cloud's Town, this community was incorporated in 1832 as Vienna. It prospered as a market town before the Civil War. On May 29, 1864, the 12th Indiana Cavalry, commanded by Lt. Col. Alfred Reed, seized the town. They built a stockade and named it for General Peter J. Osterhaus. The hit-and-run tactics of Confederate Col. Lemuel Mead and Lt. Col. Milus E. (Bushwacker) Johnston caused Union Officers to retaliate by burning Vienna to the ground on December 15, 1864. Only the Masonic Lodge and the Post Office/Tavern remained. By 1883, Vienna was back to its pre-war size and was reincorporated as New Hope."

This is the story of the New Hope Library. The secretaries of the Friends of the New Hope Library kept exceptionally good records, so detailed information was available to show the effort by the Friends' organization to start a library and almost all information in this chapter came from the notes and minutes. It will concentrate on the early formative years of the branch and provide a lessons-learned of how to start a library in a small community.

New Hope was serviced by a bookmobile from Huntsville as far back as 1947. The service had stops and starts for some years. In the 1980s the bookmobile was regular, but there was a slight problem. The books returned could not be checked out the same day because the manual check-in could not be accomplished immediately and the books returned to the proper shelf. Those who got in first maybe got what they wanted, but the late ones usually were disappointed.

In October 1987 Louise Mathews decided to do something about the library service. She mobilized some of her friends and they went around the town and surrounding area to get signatures on a petition to create a branch library. One of those friends was Mayme Claire Maples, who was the contact person for the bookmobile visits to New Hope.

Mrs. Maples was interviewed by telephone on August 17, 2004. She was one month shy of her 90th birthday, and despite having a stroke in 1993, her mind immediately started to relate the library's early events from 1987-8. She was born in Nashville, but moved as an infant to

Farley, Alabama, now subsumed into Huntsville at the intersection of U.S. Route 231 and Green Cove Road. Farley Elementary School at that intersection carries on the name. Her original given name was Maime, but a teacher said it was more sophisticated to spell in Mayme, and so it was adopted. Mayme always loved to read books, so she was obviously very sophisticated. Her middle name started out as Clair, but an "e" was added for the same reason. What is in a name? Apparently a lot.[1]

Four months later, on Tuesday, February 23, 1988, Donna Schremser & Susan Markham from the main library in Huntsville met with a group of 62 interested people at the New Hope High School to determine the amount of interest and to specify the requirements to establish a branch.

On March 4, 1988, Louise Mathews and Priscilla Scott went to the New Hope City Council meeting to seek physical and financial help. There was another meeting with the council on May 31, 1988, at which the council made a promise of necessary support.

With promises floating in the air, it was time for action. The first official meeting of the Friends of the New Hope Library was held on Thursday, June 16, 1988. It was held in the basement of the New Hope United Methodist Church. Louise Mathews thanked all the attendees and introduced Susan Markham, the Huntsville-Madison County Public Library Outreach Coordinator. Susan Markham outlined the events leading up to this meeting. The new Hope City Council agreed on June 2, 1988 to support the branch library with $500 per month starting October 1, 1988. An agreement had been reached with Horace Barnett to rent from him the old Church of God building on Route 431. A two-year lease, with an option for one year was signed. The building was about a half mile north of the Main Drive and Route 431 intersection, which was abandoned and a pale green color in 2004.

Susan Markham identified other monies being available for the branch as follows:
- $1200-Annually from the New Hope City Council for new books, etc.
- $500-Donation from Mr. Merritt Robbins
- $2500-State grant received from Jerry Craig, District 3 County Commissioner
- $9000-Huntsville-Madison County Public Library
- $2000-Friends of the Library, Huntsville-Madison County Public Library

Susan Markham mentioned several possible responsibilities of the Friends of the Library, including fund raising activities, a tea for open house, a summer reading program, a Christmas program, and providing volunteer staff for the branch.

Susan Markham then presented a proposed slate of officers for the Friends organization.
-President: Louise Mathews
-Vice President: Mayme Claire Maples
-Secretary: Priscilla Scott
-Treasurer: Imogene Butler
-Volunteer Coordinator: Aileen Moon

The slate of officers was unanimously elected. The officers would then appoint an Advisory Council of representatives from the New Hope community. It was decided that the Friends would meet the third Thursday of every month. Two training sessions were to be set up for volunteer librarians, although the sessions would be the same.

Plans were made to begin fixing up the building and making shelves, with the goal of opening September 18 or 25.

Library hours were discussed, to include story hours for pre-school children, evening hours for student research and browsing, afternoon hours for people not going to school, and Saturday and Sunday hours for working folks. Ms. Markham was to draw up a tentative schedule to see how many people volunteered and then to adjust the hours to the volunteers' response.

It was decided that the $500 from Merritt Robbins would be used for the children's department furnishings. Susan Markham would order the furnishings through the main library since it receives a 30 percent discount on excellent quality furniture.

Money makers suggested were: bake sale; quilt raffles; yard sales; book fair; and the membership drive. Susan Markham mentioned that memorial funds were also a good source, and that the person donating the money could then select the category of book to memorialize the deceased. A book would be purchased by the Library and a book plate would be in the front of the book as a memorial. Books "In Honor Of" can also be purchased for special occasions or special persons.

The membership drive was set up for June 25 at the Piggly Wiggly store on Route 431 and a later one at the Band Parents dinner at the school. The Friends organization was off and running, less than eight months after Louise Mathews started her petition effort. Bravo, Louise.

The Executive Committee of the Friends met June 21, 1988, at 10:00 AM, with Susan Markham at the prospective library building. Two ideas for an outdoor sign submitted by Henry Phillips were discussed. Phillips would construct and paint the chosen design. A post office box was rented for $28 per year. The phone would not be hooked up until the computer was installed so compatibility can be checked. Susan Markham suggested that maybe only the executive committee be trained to make entries into the computer once a day rather than train all the volunteers.

The contract with the building owner, a Mr. Bennett, almost did not come about. There were two restrooms in the back of the building. Susan Markham told Mr. Bennett that the smaller of the two rooms would be used as a storeroom and the commode should be closed off. Mr. Bennett closed the hole by stuffing an empty corn-can into the hole. Susan Markham told him that was entirely unsatisfactory. Mr. Bennett drove off in a huff, spewing foul language and spinning stones from his tires. The Mayor of New Hope had to get involved to arrive at a satisfactory solution for the women who had to work in that ill-kept building.[2]

Susan Markham presented a possible letter to all businesses in the new Hope-Owens Crossroads area. It was decided to also send a letter to all churches in the area. Louise Mathews turned over several checks and membership applications to Imogene Butler for deposit. So far, 17 members had signed up, for a total of $180. Total deposits were now at $680.

Louise Mathews mentioned that Merritt Robbins had offered to acquire a Pepsi wagon and furnish hot dogs and buns any time the Friends would like to use it as part of fundraisers. The Executive committee agreed to ask Edna Hamer to be the Chairman of the Membership Committee.

Susan Markham agreed to make up a list of physical things the library might need, in order to have suggestions if persons or businesses would like to donate a certain item rather than just a monetary contribution.

The Executive Committee of the Friends met at the new building on July 18, 1988. The treasurer reported a present balance of $1,064 and almost 80 people had signed up to be members.

Susan Markham reported that she asked the person who worked on the Huntsville Library to plan the decorating ideas also. She advised that it would be better to purchase less expensive children's furnishings for now, and then make a major purchase when the library was in a permanent place. Louise Mathews would contact someone about donating blinds for the windows.

Susan Markham presented a proposed Library Hours Schedule of 24 hours per week. The officers discussed the schedule and decided to add an additional 2 hours on Sunday. The open hours were

-Monday   2:00 – 8:00
-Tuesday   2:00 – 6:00
-Wednesday closed
-Thursday   10:00 – 6:00
Story Hour   10:30
-Friday   10:00 – 1:00
-Saturday   10:00 – 1:00
-Sunday   2:00 – 4:00

Sixteen years later in 2004, the hours were the same, as the Library was not opened on Sunday because the Executive Committee dropped the idea on September 12, 1988 before the Library opened.

Twenty-four volunteers were needed to give 2 hours each week with the above schedule, plus some substitutes and on-call volunteers.

The Executive Committee of the Friends of the New Hope Library met at 6:15 P.M., July 21, 1988, prior to the general meeting. Copies of the Constitution and By-laws were passed out to each officer. They were read, discussed and approved unanimously. It was decided that the secretary would also act as the Historian for the group, to keep records of events and other special memorabilia. It was also agreed that it would not be necessary to name the persons making motions and seconding them. [I wonder if the Secretary, Priscilla Scott, made that recommendation? When this author went to the New Hope Library for the first time, Priscilla Scott was on volunteer duty and she provided many details and knew where all the papers were. Lucky me.]

The volunteer hours chart was discussed and it was agreed to leave the open hours at 26 until it became evident that there would not be enough volunteers to fill the hours faithfully.

The Friends of the New Hope Library met July 21, 1988 in the basement of the New Hope United Methodist Church. There were 26 persons attending. Mayme Claire Maples read the Constitution and By-laws, which the officers had approved. She explained some details to the group to clarify membership and use of the Library. A person was not required to be a Friend of the Library in order to get a library card or use the books there. The library card would be free to any Madison County resident. Anyone living outside Madison County would be required to pay $10 per person, or $25 per family.

Susan Markham introduced the proposed library hours. She stated that the hours were only desirable hours and not necessary above 20 hours. It would depend on the response of the volunteers whether the library could stay open 26 hours per week. Aileen Moon showed the schedule chart and asked for volunteers to sign up after the meeting for 2-hour shifts using the "Buddy System." There was discussion as to the hours to be open and what the volunteer would be expected to do. All volunteers will not be required to use the computer, only those who feel comfortable using it will enter information necessary at the end of each business day.

Louise Mathews presented a calendar of work to inform the members of the progress so far and to come. She asked for volunteers to clean up the inside of the building now that the other furnishings had been removed. Help was also needed to clean after the shelving and painting were completed by the county workers, and for moving books in early September.

The Executive Committee of the Friends met again on August 1, 1988. Discussion was held concerning possible discounts on the telephone installation. It was decided that the secretary would compose and submit a letter to the Telephone Cooperative to be presented at their regular meeting on the 2nd Tuesday. The original installation fee was $60.15. It was decided to wait until heating was necessary to do any further inquiring about gas heaters. The air conditioning seemed to be working fine.

Possible names were considered for the Advisory Board. The issue was tabled because some of the candidates had not yet joined the Friends organization. It was agreed that nametags should be purchased to be worn by those soliciting memberships, as well as regular volunteers when the library opened.

It was decided to take action on Merritt Robbins' offer to get a Coke (an earlier meeting minutes cited Pepsi) wagon and sell hotdogs at the Piggly Wiggly on August 20. The Executive Committee will visit the Gurley Branch Library on Friday, August 5. The Gurley Branch had opened several months earlier in a similar-sized renovated building. Louise Mathews showed a drawing of the future circulation desk.

The Executive Committee of the Friends of the New Hope Library met August 15, 1988. Louise Mathews announced that G & G Lumber would donate poles for the outside sign, the blinds were ordered from Wal-Mart and Mae Rose Vann agreed to cover the benches and make a rocking chair pad. The material for the covers was on display. It was decided to go ahead and purchase a rocking chair if one was not donated. [It was unclear for whom the rocking chair was intended, since such furniture is not part of most libraries. I will allow the reader's imagination come up with the answer.]

The date for having the Pepsi wagon at the Piggly Wiggly was changed to September 2-3. Piggly Wiggly would donate the hotdogs and buns and Pepsi would donate the drinks and ice. It was decided to try to get groups or persons to have booths of crafts, etc. The Library would get $10 per booth.

Susan Markham prepared a flyer to put in the area newspapers announcing the next Friends meeting on August 18 in the church basement. The group discussed the Opening Day: who to send the printed invitations; who would speak; and information to put in the program, etc.

Training sessions for the volunteers would be Tuesday, September 20, 9:30 AM and 2:00 PM. A third session for working volunteers would be Thursday night, September 22, at 7:00 PM. All session were held in the Library. Susan Markham mentioned work still to be done by the county and repairs and improvements were discussed.

The Friends met on August 18, 1988, in the Methodist Church basement. The Treasurer reported a balance of $1,621.39, with a bill from James Jones outstanding. She also reported that over 150 members officially signed up at present. Aileen Moon, Volunteer Chairman, reported on the schedule set up. There were a number of openings left, but plenty of volunteers to be assigned wherever needed.

Louise Mathews reported that the days at Piggly Wiggly were changed to one day on October 1, from 8 AM to 5 PM. The majority of the members present agreed to charge $5.00 per booth for crafters, etc. with them furnishing their own tables. The spaces would be marked off for them. It was also decided that this would be a good time to have a raffle, and a book fair included in the day's activities. Nolan Hill volunteered to get all the help needed to man the Pepsi wagon for the day.

Susan Markham gave a progress report of the work on the building. The county was painting, building shelves, repairing the restroom and roof. They would also build a new circulation desk. She had the fabric on display for covering the benches and rocking chair, and the descriptions of the furniture being ordered. County Commissioner Jerry Craig provided $2,500 from the District account.

The Friends Executive Committee met on September 12, 1988. Lorraine Butler and Helen Carpenter reported on the progress of plans for the Opening Day Tea. They had plans to serve 300-400 people with Russian tea and punch, sausage balls, sand tarts, brownies, cheese straws, open-faced sandwiches, cookies and nuts. It was agreed that the committee could go ahead and purchase the paper supplies needed and be reimbursed. Barbara Smith agreed to keep the guest book.

The Executive Committee decided not to open the Library on Sundays, unless a greater demand for it was known. Susan Markham reminded the group that volunteers must be trained before they can serve.

The telephone line was installed and the number at the Library was 723-2995, and still is in 2004. The New Hope Telephone Cooperative generously waived the installation and deposit fee.

The afghan for the raffle was on display. It was made and assembled by Mayme Claire Maples, Mable Floyd, Aileen Moon and Louise Mathews. Tickets would sell for $1.00.

The Friends of the New Hope Library met at the Library on September 15, 1998, with 27 members present. Imogene Butler reported that the membership was over 200. Aileen Moon reported that there were 75 volunteers. Susan Markham reported that New Hope's was the sixth branch of the Huntsville-Madison County Public Library. She mentioned that a book was donated in memory of James William Richard, and a memorial fund would be started for anyone wishing to donate.

Everything was ready for the Fund Fest on October 1 at the Piggly Wiggly. The rain date was October 8. [I like to type Piggly Wiggly because my spell-check software puts a red line under Piggly, but not Wiggly.]

Justine Jones agreed to head up the incoming books at the Senior Center and the booth that day. Charlotte Mann and Kathy Guthrie will work the Library Craft table, Georgia Mae Adair will see about the dunking booth, Mayme Claire Maples will be in charge of the raffle, which will include a crocheted afghan and a VCR cleaning and lubrication, donated by Lunar Electronics.

Louise Mathews thanked Billy G. Jones for furnishing the extra chairs for the meeting. She also mentioned that Loy McGreuder at the bank donated $200.

The New Hope Library Branch was officially opened on Sunday, September 25, 1988. A crowd of about 70 people attended and enjoyed the food and the work of the many volunteers to get the building ready. The library was staffed by 30 volunteers.

A month after the opening of the New Hope Library, the Friends of the New Hope Library met on October 20, 1988, with 11 members present. The Treasurer reported expenditures of $933.19 to the Huntsville Public Library for purchases of furniture and other supplies; $35.66 for concrete and sign supplies; and $7.83 to the bank for checks. Receipts for memorials were $150. The Friends had 261 members on that date.

Louise Mathews reported from Susan Markham that as of October 18, 792 books had been checked out of the New Hope Branch, and 89 new library cards were issued. Remember, all computer statistics were recorded only at the main library, and then fed back to each branch.

The Fund Fest brought in $704. The friends would have a float in the Homecoming parade. The title will be "Story Hour" and will also show the day and hour. Priscilla Scott will be in the rocking chair with children in the small red chairs, with the periodical rack and someone reading there. [Aha, the rocking chair mystery was solved. It was still in use in the children's department in 2004]

It was decided to have a Harvest Book Fair on November 19, from 8 to 4 at the Library. Priscilla Scott described a Book Reading contest for November to include putting a feather on a turkey for each book read. The group decided to check with Huntsville about a good number of books to expect a child to read for a certificate. The same approach would be taken in December with a Christmas theme.

Louise Mathews brought up some proposed plans for erecting a Veterans' Memorial in the front yard of the Library with a flag and plagues for each veteran. It was decided to table the idea since it should only be done on city property and they did not have enough knowledge on the subject.

Louise Mathews acknowledged Mrs. Nolan Hill as being the new mayor's wife and thanked her for representing him at the Friends' meetings. Imogene Butler read an invitation from the Gurley Friends to a Tea welcoming their incoming mayor and town council.

The Friends met November 17, 1988, with only nine members present. Attendance dropped from 17 to 11 to 9 in the last 3 meetings. Has the enthusiasm waned? There was no treasurer's report, but there was much discussion about the $95 telephone bill and the $150 gas bill. It was discovered that there was a leak from the tank outside as well as a leak near the pilot light in the heater. The gas company would replace the estimated gas loss at no charge. [The minutes did not address the problem with the telephone bill. Most of the calls should have been local. Maybe the Telephone Cooperative was recouping from their no-charge installation service?]

Library maintenance was the main topic of discussion. The ladies had been using their own equipment and doing it as needed. Louise Mathews would check into getting a sweeper to keep at the Library. [If there were men volunteers, we could have overlooked the dust and dirt for several years before a sweeper was needed.]

Kathy Guthrie stated that Mrs. Glover of Dixie Pest Control had agreed to donate the $30 First Call charge and then it would run $12 per month. It was decide to see if the weather change would make any difference in the amount of bugs. [Bugs in Northern Alabama?]

There was a discussion about some more physical improvements: floodlight at the back corners of the building; weather stripping around the door, and the need for a small electric heater behind the circulation desk. It was agreed to purchase a small heater and Charlotte Mann agreed to check and buy a heater. Another training session for volunteers was set for November 29, with a computer-training session the same day.

The Friends meeting for December was a Christmas Pajama Party on the 15th. Apparently the secretary, Priscilla Scott, did not have pockets in her pajamas because no notes were taken.

The Friends Executive Committee met on January 6, 1989. Susan Markham reported that they had checked on a sweeper at Service Merchandise and she would pick it up that afternoon. It was also decided to have Susan pick up a filing cabinet. Dear readers, please remember the professionalism and dedication of Susan Markham whenever and wherever branch libraries are mentioned. Bravo, Susan!

More volunteer training sessions were discussed and it was decided that volunteers could come and observe, but would still have to go through training. They must also be a member of the Friends of the Library, and have paid their membership fee, or it could be paid by someone else in their name.

A book sale was discussed and it was decided to wait until spring and have just two per year. Imogene Butler gave the treasurer's report:

-Expenses: $28.48   Christmas supplies
            $19.97   Electric heater
            $39.72   Fire extinguisher
            $30.96   Halloween supplies
-Income $77.86   Book sale and memberships
-Balance $2,303.40

Louise Mathews asked if the group wanted to make a flower fund ruling for families of volunteers. It was decided not to do that. It was decided to bring up the possible donation of $200 from the Friends to purchase more children's books at the next regular meeting.

Susan Markham reported that the Summer Reading Program would be READ ALABAMA READ. The group looked forward to getting some student volunteers for the summer. Susan also stated that magazines should only remain on the rack for two months and then be removed and stored or disposed of.

The Friends of the New Hope Library met on January 10, 1989, with ten members attending. It was agreed to donate $200 toward the purchase of new tape books for the children's department. There was further agreement to donate $200 to purchase more of the books on Mrs. Wall's reading list, as well as junior biographies. The need was recognized to obtain more books in the Easy Reader section as many of the children have read all the books.

Aileen Moon reported that there were 266 members of the Friends of the Library, and there were 44 volunteers. She would like to increase the volunteer staff to 48. Kathy Guthrie reported 29 participants in the children's reading program in December.

The branch also needed to pick up some Interlibrary Loan forms for persons who make requests that are not available in any of the Huntsville Public Library branches. The forms would have to be filled out and then the books picked up at the main Huntsville Library.

The Friends Executive Committee met on February 11. Susan Markham reported that National Library Week would be April 10-14. There will be a Volunteer Tea on Sunday, April 9, in the auditorium of the Huntsville Public Library from 2 to 4, and all volunteers were invited. Susan Markham would like to see each branch act together with the school library to promote reading, especially focusing on the award winning authors, age level divisions and well known illustrators. Mrs. Linda Hill will check on the possibility of getting a P.T.A. program in March. Karen Butler and Neta Grooms will work to coordinate with the school libraries. Louise Mathews will try to coordinate with Mrs. Presley at the Owens Cross Roads library. For readers unfamiliar with the geography, Owens Cross Roads is a community of 700, one-third the population of New Hope, and was to the immediate northwest of New Hope. They were close neighbors.

Susan Markham will check into getting the Dixie Pest Control to begin serving the library in March. Yes, readers, apparently there were bugs in North Alabama.

Governor Guy Hunt declared that this would be the "Year of the Young Reader," along with National campaign of the same title.

There was discussion that more care was needed on re-shelving books in the proper place. Refresher training?

The Friends met on February 16. No attendance noted. Linda Hill and Karen Butler reported that the March P.T.A. was always the Bonnets and Bows parade by the elementary children. Possibilities would include having the Middle School students dress up in their favorite book character as well as having Susan Markham speak for a few minutes, and maybe make a public presentation of the February top readers.

The secretary read a notice about a "Friends" workshop at the Huntsville Public Library on Wednesday, March 1, from 9 AM to 12 PM.

Priscilla Scott moved, and it was agreed, that the Friends just meet on the 3rd Thursday night and not have an Executive Committee meeting on the Monday before unless one needs to be called to make emergency decisions.

Kathy Guthrie reported that Dixie Pest Control was donating the initial $30 cleanout and that the monthly charge would be $12 instead of the regular $15. Huntsville will be paying for this and plans to pay for the full year ahead and so a 5 percent discount will be made, total $136.80.

The Friends met on March 16, 1989. The handwritten record shows eight attendees. Louise Mathews announced a new training session for April 11. The February reading program was a success with 18 readers of 93 books.

Susan Markham reported that the New Hope Library would receive grant money of $6,500 from the "Pork Barrel Legislation," thanks to Albert Hall and Lowell Barron. The group voted to purchase a new book drop for $1200 and a light pen for the computer when the money becomes available.

There will be a poster contest during National Library Week, with the theme "The Best Book I Ever Read." A book sale will be held on April 8 and Louise Mathews will round up the volunteers.

The Friends met on April 20. The treasurer reported a balance of $2,222.10. Aileen Moon reported that 12 new volunteers received training.

Sixteen people from New Hope attended the Volunteer Tea at the Huntsville Public Library on April 16. Aileen Moon received a Volunteer Coordinator of the Year Award. All volunteers received a certificate for their work.

Louise Mathews suggested the group make a community quilt for the next membership drive. She appointed Mayme Claire Maples to chair the planning committee. Barb Smith will assist. There will be an open house at the new Madison Branch on May 7, and all were invited to attend.

Bernice Dilworth and Edna Hamer will create a membership renewal letter to be approved at the next meeting. Kathy Guthrie reported on the March reading program. There were 20 readers, with 135 books read. Lisa Butler received a certificate for the most books read with 32.

The poster contest had 3 entries, 1 in each category: 5-year, 1st grade and 3rd grade. Each contestant received a book. [Not much competition.]

The Friends met on May 18. Mayme Claire Maples brought up the discussion of the quilt for the raffle. It was decided to meet at Priscilla Scott's house to select fabrics and start cutting the pieces to be given to the members to sew. No date was set yet.

Susan Markham reported the circulation for April was 1,123 books checked out. It was approved to buy an outdoor book drop to benefit customers who bring books back but find the building closed. Susan Markham will order it in Sand Beige and speak to Jerry Craig, the county commissioner, about pouring a concrete platform for it.

The Summer Reading Program will begin June 20 and end July 28. The theme was "Read, Alabama, Read." The schedule was Thursday, 10:30 – 11:30 for pre-school and Tuesday, 2:30 – 3:30 for school age. The cut-off date for the reading contest was August 1. There will be a

Mardi Gras party celebration at the Huntsville Library on August 5 to cap off the summer reading program. Susan Markham suggested each branch might prefer to host its own party.

It was agreed to have a Popcorn and Movie Family Night on July 31. Susan Markham will furnish to movie and projector and the Friends will provide refreshments. Louise Mathews, Priscilla Scott and Charlotte Mann were appointed to the planning committee.

There will be a training session on the Summer Reading Program in Huntsville. The six themes were: 1. Beaches; 2. Green Growing Things; 3. Family Roots; 4. Who's Hat; 5. Farms; and 6. Celebrate Reading.

The Friends met on June 15 and the treasurer reported a balance of $1,973.25. Aileen Moon reported that four volunteers had dropped out for the summer, but some extras have asked to help in the summer.

Susan Markham had a sample membership renewal letter and will draft one with New Hope's accomplishments and requests to be mailed to the community.

Tony Pitts was introduced from the Mount Zion Church. He wanted to find a location to hold a Revelation Seminar. Susan Markham stated that it would be against the library system's policies to hold that type of meeting in the library.

Mayme Claire Maples reported on the quilt plans for membership drive. She had samples of "Martha Star" and "Broken Dishes." The group voted on "Broken Dishes" and will meet Monday morning at Priscilla Scott's to cut the pieces.

It was approved to buy a chalk and flannel board and some bookmarks for the Young Readers.

The Friends of the New Hope Library met on July 20. There was a discussion on computer use problems and it was decided to have a special meeting to meet those problems.

Susan Markham from Huntsville presented a proposed membership letter to be mailed shortly after August 1. Some changes were approved. She also brought flyers to distribute for the Family Night Movie and some T-shirt information. It was decided to table the ordering of any T-shirts.

The quilt was ready to put in the frames and the Senior Center agreed to let the Library quilt there. The membership tea was discussed

Joe Hill was present to discuss the possibility of historic discussions and possibly a booklet on New Hope's history. Possible lead speakers would be Charles Rice and Elizabeth Carpenter. Possible names for the occasion were mentioned. "New Hope Remembers" seemed to be preferred. The Library Fund Fest was scheduled for October 7 at the Piggly Wiggly.

The Friends met on August 17, with sixteen members present. The treasurer's balance was down to $824.82, after expenses of $28 for a post office box, $896.39 for the book-return box, $100 for an advertisement in the football schedule and $17.56 for quilting supplies.

Barb Foster reported on the Summer Reading Program. There were 83 children participating with 10 having perfect attendance. There were 62 of school age and 19 pre-schoolers. Susan Markham reported she had ordered two each of Mrs. Wall's Reading List books (for extra credit).

The First Anniversary Tea will be September 24 from 2-4 PM. Joe Hill had talked to Charles Rice and Tressy Maples had agreed to speak. Elizabeth Carpenter will also speak. The planning committee included: Joe Hill, Chairman, Susan Markham, Publicity, Jerry Craig, Aileen Moon, Imogene Butler and Carolyn Mann, Food. The theme will be "New Hope Remembers – Then and Now." Ranee' Pruitt, Huntsville's Archivist, will prepare a brochure of New Hope's history. Huntsville will absorb the cost of the brochure and New Hope will receive $1.00 for each brochure sold.

The Friends met on September 11, 1989. Aileen Moon reported that 25 new volunteers were seeking to be trained, if Susan Markham could set up a day.

Plans for the Membership tea were in progress. Jerry Craig will provide the public address system and the main library will print the programs for the day. Mayme Claire Maples will keep the registration table, Carolyn Mann will be chairman of the punch bowl and Aileen Moon will sell the New Hope Remembers booklets. Priscilla Scott will bring extra chairs from the Owens Cross Roads Methodist Church. Mrs. Merritt Robbins will provide the flowers for the punch table and Mrs. Williams will bring flowers for the registration table.

The slate of officers from the first year of the New Hope Library were returned for another year. The question was asked why Huntsville Public Library employees did not have to pay fines and New Hope does. It was explained that it was one of the benefits of employment over volunteers. Barbara McMillan mentioned that the Madison Branch sold book bags for $0.35 each, and that it might be a good idea for New Hope.

The friends met on October 19. There were now 112 new members. Aileen Moon reported there would be another training session on November 2. Earnest Guthrie and Carolyn Mann were appointed as Publicity Co-Chairmen. It was voted to purchase 20 chairs and 2 tables.

It was agreed that treats would be available at the Library from 4-6 on Halloween, October 31, so kids could come by and pick up their pumpkin for the reading program and a treat. Several members volunteered to come in costume to help out.

Charlotte Mann mentioned that for a renewal to be made for sure on the computers, you need to enter it twice. Renewals can be made over the phone, but each book can only be renewed one time by the same patron. A note should be made on the Date Due card if it is a renewal.

Louise Mathews introduced Beverly McCrain to the group. She is the daughter of James L. Brewer, the author of *Mules, Missiles and Men*. He had donated three books to the Library and the books were on sale also. Ms. McCrain spoke to the group about her father's present bedfast condition and then shared a little of his life that was in his autobiographical book.

The Friends met on December 7. Apparently for the first time in 15 months of operation, both the president and treasurer were missing at the same time, but no matter, business goes on. There were 26 readers and 137 books read during the October reading program. The top reader was Evan Giles with 18 books. In November, 21 readers read 96 books. The top two readers were Heather Phillips with 11 and Misty Lyon with 10. It was suggested that a poster might be made to publicize the top readers of the months.

It was voted to hold the Christmas party on December 21 from 6-7 PM, and that it would continue to be held on the regular 3rd Thursday in the future years.

Susan Markham mentioned that the Summer Reading program is already underway and will be called "Splash Down With Allie Alligator." There will be a meeting in February to plan the kit contents, etc. In December the libraries will accept a can of food per overdue book instead of a fine, so it's a good time to clean the slate on overdue books. Susan also reported that the county commissioners had given $129,000 for a new van for the bookmobile. The new budget for the New Hope Branch is $1,800 for books.

The Friends met on January 18, 1990, with 11 members present. There was $2,339.73 in the library's account. It was agreed to change the meeting time from 7 to 6 PM.

Imogene Butler suggested that New Hope needed to have more input into which magazines were subscribed for the branch. They might need to keep *Newsweek, Sports Illustrated* and *Time* for students doing research. There was also discussion about needing to recycle the outdated magazines.

The total reading for 1989, excluding summer, was 516 books by 97 readers.

The Friends met on February 15 with 11 in attendance of the 120 paid members. Kathie Guthrie reported that Barbara Foster, Charlotte Mann, Leslie Phillips, Barb Smith and herself attended the Summer Story Hour planning meeting in Huntsville. The New Hope group will be responsible for planning one of the sessions and it will be on weather. Linda Hill and Barbara Foster will act as liaison to announce the Summer Reading Program at the schools.

It was agreed to have a $10-booth at the annual PTA Spring Fling. This would be a 10' x 10' area to sell plant starts and used books. In the 1980's in Huntsville there was a bookstore called Books As Seeds, so the combination is quite appropriate.

There was much discussion with Susan Markham about subjects New Hope still needed on the shelves.

Mayme Claire Maples read a resolution to honor a former friend of the library, Mary Jane Mattich, who passed on February 3, 1990. The resolution was approved and will be placed in the file and a book, chosen by the family, will be purchased in her memory.

The Friends met on March 15 with nine members in attendance. The membership total was now at 150. The numbers above are generally consistent with other volunteer organizations. The core of activists was usually less than ten percent of the total numbers. These people were enthusiastic and dedicated to creating a better organization. They continued to work because they were motivated by the opportunity to create ideas and plans, and then execute the plans. There were probably many who would help if asked to do certain jobs, but it's the creative and imaginative folks who make things happen.

There was discussion about volunteers. It was decided to ask Susan Markham to include on the list of volunteer memos that: "Volunteers not on duty, but in the library, should not be behind the desk unless asked by the volunteers on duty." In this case, the close-knit community of people who know each other made it difficult to enforce a work discipline because all were volunteers. An outside authority was needed to establish written rules that would be self-enforcing, hopefully.

Louise Mathews announced that student volunteers would be utilized through the summer months. They must be 12 or older and under the supervision of an adult volunteer.

Barbara Foster read a letter that will be given to all teachers and faculty at the New Hope and Owens Cross Roads schools. It pertained to the summer library program, which will be from June 4 to August 18. It was also requested they work with the library to have materials ready for specific assignments. The Owens Cross Roads faculty had already asked for a presentation on March 21. Kathy Guthrie and Barbara Mann will attend and speak for the Library.

Charlotte Mann reported that County Commissioner Jerry Craig donated $300 for books for the summer program.

The Friends met April 19, 1990 with 11 attendees, and the treasury stood at $2,493.82. Nolan Hill, Mayor of New Hope, was present and spoke to the group about future plans for development of downtown New Hope and especially the new library location. The City Council has $6,000 in a certificate of deposit that was obtained by State Representative Albert Hall for the purpose of a new library building. State Senator Lowell Barron had also promised $5,000 that would be earmarked for the library. The city plans to renovate the Butler Building on Main Street and the surrounding five-plus acreage. The building would house the library, the administrative offices, as well as historical memorabilia.

There was much discussion following the Mayor's presentation and the general consensus was that the library would stay in the current building for another year if Mr. Bennett would agreed to renew the lease for another year.

Louise Mathews reported that Jim Wilkerson had agreed to keep the grounds mowed and will bill the library monthly. It was agreed that the Friends would subscribe to *Southern Living* with the discount that Imogene Butler received.

The Friends met on May 17, with 24 members and guests present. Louise Mathews introduced the special guests and the speaker, Mr. Jesse Culp. Mr. Culp shared a few yarns from his book, *The Good Ole Days.* His book was a collection of columns he wrote for *The Birmingham News.*

Susan Markham reported on the Summer Reading Program and furnished a schedule of nine weeks from June 5 through August 16, excluding Fourth of July week. There would be a kick-off meeting at the Huntsville Library on May 31.

Susan also reported that the lease on the building was being renewed for one year and another air conditioner would be requested for the children's department.

The Friends met on June 21 with only six ladies in attendance. The main news was the upcoming marriage of Kathy Guthrie and this was her last meeting with the Friends. Presumably she will not have time to volunteer for the Friends.

The following were named to the nominating committee: Leslie Phillips, Aileen Moon and Linda Hill. Only Aileen was present, so the other two still needed to be asked. This proved the old adage, if you were not at the meeting, you cannot say no.

And once more the Library Fund Fest will be held at the Piggly Wiggly on October 6.

The Friends met on July 19 with nine members in attendance. Just think, it could have been a nice round number of ten if Kathy Guthrie had been there.

Leslie Phillips reported for the nominating committee and presented names for the four offices: President, Priscilla Scott; Vice-President, Arlene Duncan; Secretary, JoDella Powers; and Treasurer, Charlotte Mann. The nominating committee still had not found a candidate for Coordinator of Volunteers.

Louise Mathews mentioned that the Merchants of New Hope were trying to get together a Founder's Day Festival for October 13-14. Since that would be a week after the planned Fund Fest, perhaps the library should just have a booth at the Founder's Day festival. A wait-and-see approach was agreed upon.

The friends met on August for the election of officers, and there were some changes from the original nominations. The electees are as follows: President, Priscilla Scott; Vice-President, Arlene Duncan; Secretary, Irmgarde Erskin; Treasurer, Charlotte Mann; Membership, Jennie Smith; and Volunteer Coordinator, JoDella Powers. The group gave a vote of acclaim to Leslie Phillips for her undaunted work in getting the slate completed. [Wonder how many folks were avoiding Leslie during the search period?]

Louise Mathews reported that four books were donated to the library by Anne Marie Brianaid in memory of Ralph Brainaid, Jr. Nancy Harris was present to share plans on the Founder's Day Festival, to be held in downtown New Hope, October 12-14. The Friends voted to have a booth and make a $15 donation to the Festival Committee.

A special meeting of the Friends was held on August 30, 1990 for the election of new officers. This event marked the end of the library's first two years of operation. The new team now faced different challenges and can build on the accomplishments of the original group. This also marks a reduction in this author's coverage of the important events in all the minutes to this date.

Some the activities by the Friends were now oriented toward the new location in the Butler Building. Mayme Claire Maples will write a letter to the Mayor and City Council to request the new library be named Elizabeth Carpenter library of New Hope. (19 Jan 91)

Mayor Nolan Hill addressed the progress of the new library at the Friends meeting on February 20, 1991 The county men were building shelves and the building should be ready for occupancy by spring break week, the last week of March. Volunteers will be needed to pack the supplies in the circulation desk and the storeroom.

The group agreed to spend $350 toward an "American Library of Classics," a 60-volume set.

The year-long planning and preparation of the new library facility was finally ended on May 25, 1992, when the Elizabeth Carpenter Library was officially opened at 5496 Main Street, which was still the location in 2004.

Libraries cost money, just like other city and county services. That money must come from somewhere. Less than a year after the new library was opened, a financial crisis came to a head.

On July 16, 1992, Donna Schremser, Director, Huntsville Madison County Public Library, sent a letter to the mayor of New Hope, Nolan Hill, requesting an appropriation of $9,270 for the fiscal year to begin on October 1, 1992. This letter apparently elicited less money than expected.[3]

On February 4, 1993, Susan Markham, Head of Branch Operations, and you've read her name dozens of time in this chapter as she helped the people of New Hope get a branch library, wrote a letter to Mayor Billy G. Jones, Town of New Hope. It is quoted below:

"Dear Mayor Jones,

Attached is the budget request for the Elizabeth Carpenter Library of New Hope for Fiscal Year 92/93. [Not attached by this author.]

The Elizabeth Carpenter Library of New Hope is thriving in the new location. In FY 91/92, we checked out a total of 9,834 items. At present, we are circulating 31% more items than at this time last year. We project that we will circulate at least 13,000 items during FY 92/93. The weekly programming for children is generating 7-10 attendees during the winter months and 50 attendees during the summer months. Adult functions sponsored by the Friends of the Library are also well attended. In all, the entire community is very supportive of the Elizabeth Carpenter Library of New Hope and is especially proud of the beautiful facility.

One of the reasons for the success of the library is that the library, opened 24 hours per week, is staffed using approximately 30 volunteers from the New Hope area who are committed to serving their community. However, the same core group had been volunteering their time since the library opened in September 1988 and may soon tire of the responsibility. In addition, we are at the point of growth that a part-time salaried employee is needed to be "in charge"; to manage the day-to-day operations, the programming offered for adults and children, and make decisions regarding the types of materials needed for the library so that we meet the needs of the community. Please understand that the employee would in no way uproot the efforts of the volunteers, but would facilitate the smooth operation of the library. Realistically, we understand that you may be unable to fund a part-time employee at this time. However, we wanted you to be aware that the need exists and give you an idea of the funding level required to hire a qualified person. We are optimistic that this position can be added in FY 93/94.

Another major reason for the success of the library is that until recently, we have always been able to offer current materials for both children and adults. This includes best sellers and materials needed to support the school curriculum and general reading for pleasure and informational needs. However, due to lack of funding, we have purchased no new materials for the New Hope location since September of 1992. To date, we have received no income from the Madison County Commission, nor from the Town of New Hope.

Now that you and the new council are aware of the needs of the library, I am hopeful that we can receive monies immediately so book purchases can resume. Rather than the $9,270 amount listed on the budget submitted in July, 1992, we are asking for $5,500. This amount includes $3,000 for books and other materials and $2,500 for New Hope's automated circulation system. $3,000 for books is not a large amount of money when you consider the average price of an adult book is $25.00 and the average price of a children's book is $13.50. In addition, you will notice that the Friends of the Library have agreed to contribute $1,500. $1,000 of this amount will be used for books and other materials. They contributed over $3,000 towards the new facility by purchasing 4 lounge chairs, lounging table, 2 sets of children's tables with 4 chairs each, bookends, and many other small items needed for the library.

I look forward to working with you, other officials of your town, and the Friends of the Library in continuing to meet the needs of your community. We are very appreciative of your past support and your proven interest in the library by providing the community with such an outstanding facility.

Please feel free to contact me at 532-5961 if you need additional information."[4]

That letter seemed clear enough, however, the capability of small communities to provide adequate funding lags behind their desire to do so. Apparently the above letter of February 4 did not produce the desired results, but it did start some action. On June 11, 1993, Lowell Barron, State Senator for the 8th District, wrote the following letter to the New Hope Library.

"I have placed $1,000 in a special appropriation for your library. These funds will be available in the 1993-94 fiscal year (After October 1, 1993).

These funds are what the folks from South Alabama call "pork" however, I think you'all can put this to good use for our constituents."[5]

That folksy letter was the way things go in Alabama. He took a dig at the South Alabamians, because we North Alabamians like to feel superior to them, although over the past 150 years the southerners had maintained more political clout than the northerners. My word processing dictionary made a big red line under "you'all." It just did it again.

The New Hope library sent Senator Barron a hand-written, appreciative thank-you letter, which invited him to visit New Hope during the Frontier day celebration on October 8-10.

In business, when the first communication does not achieve the desired results, the follow-on effort goes by the name, "Strong message follows!" Well, here it is. The following letter from Donna Schremser to Mayor Jones of New Hope, with information copies to the council members and the Friends of the Library, is quoted.

"The Huntsville Public Library has made repeated requests for funding for the Elizabeth Carpenter Library of New Hope during the past 12 months. None of our requests have resulted in the much needed funding for the operation of your public library, with the exception of a small portion of the costs relating to the computer terminal.

We have worked with the citizens of New Hope to provide good library service. When the citizens of New Hope wanted a permanent library, they undertook the responsibility to provide funding for this library. We cannot continue to subsidize library service to the Town of New Hope at the expense of other municipalities in Madison County.

The following expenses will have been incurred for the New Hope Library for the fiscal year ending September 30, 1993:

- Books — $3,000
- Periodicals — 310
- Salaries for Outreach Staff — 1,128
- Branch Run Courier — 616
- Payroll Taxes — 150
- Insurance on Collection — 300
- Postage for New Hope Overdues — 300
- Office Supplies — 300
- Cataloging Supplies — 400
- Computer System — 2,500

The total operating expense of the Elizabeth Carpenter Library of New Hope is $9,195 for the fiscal year ending September 30, 1993.

To date we have applied the following revenue sources to those expenses:

- Friends of the Library — $2,000
- Overdue Fines — 200
- Madison County — 1,600
- State of Alabama — 2,800
- Town of New Hope — 1,050 (Includes Aug. & Sep. 1993)

Total revenue to offset expenses is $7,650. This leaves the Huntsville Madison County Public Library with a projected deficit of $1,545 for this fiscal year. We would have been faced with a deficit of $3,545 had we not discontinued purchasing books for the Town of New Hope with the exception of funding provided by the Friends and our initial outlay of $1,000 at the beginning of the fiscal year.

The deficit of $1,545 must be paid in full by September 30, 1993, or we will sever our relationship with the Elizabeth Carpenter Library of New Hope.

On October 1, 1993, the Huntsville Madison County Public Library will remove all books and equipment purchased by the Library System. This will result in the loss of some 60% of the book collection and the computer terminal and light pen. Current library cards will be honored at the Main Library and other branch libraries within the system.

Should the Town of New Hope desire reinstatement of services from the Huntsville Madison County Public Library after October 1, 1993, the Town must pay the sum of $1,545 and guarantee an annual appropriation of sufficient amount to cover the operating expenses of the Elizabeth Carpenter Library of New Hope. The Town of New Hope must also provide timely and regular payment to the Huntsville Madison County Public Library."[6]

That letter seemed clear enough to be understood. Apparently the bill was paid.

Albert Hall, State Representative for District 22, which includes part of Madison and Jackson Counties, send a signed (Albert) MEMO to the Elizabeth Carpenter Public Library of New Hope.

"You should have already received a letter from the state Finance Department regarding library funds. Please respond to the Department's request promptly. If approved, the funds you receive are to be used for library building purposes.

Hopefully you will be receiving some funds in ¼ payments this school year. I certainly hope you'll put them to good use."[7]

Representative Hall sure does a lot of hoping about New Hope. Handwritten on a copy of the memo in the library's files was the following:

- "Unhappy-
- Wrote letter today-
- 250 @ 4 payments.
- Not a grant.
- We are in budget – High School"[8]

The letter in bullet # 2 above was written to the director of the New Hope Library on November 8, 1993 and is quoted below:

"You recently received a memo, dated November 2, regarding library funds. The memo indicated that the library funds are in the approval process and this is certainly incorrect. The designated money is in the approved 1993-94 budget, as I requested, and will be issued to you in four quarterly payments of $250 each.

By the time you receive this, you should have received a letter from the Finance Department along with a contract for you to sign and return in order for the money to be disbursed. I understand that the first quarterly check should be cut in late December, however, I suggest that you do not make a purchase until you have the money in the event there is a delay. I urge you to return the paperwork to the Finance Department as soon as possible.

The incorrect memo you previously received was sent upon my instruction from the Madison County Legislative Office; however, I did not compose the memo and was unaware of the wording until I received a copy today. I apologize for the misunderstanding and hope it has not caused you any concern or inconvenience.

It is an honor to be able to work for you and to assist you in getting additional funds for your library. Improved schools and better education for our children are very important issues, and you can be assured that I will continue to work for you.

Please let me know if you have any questions or if I may assist you further.

Sincerely, Albert Hall"[9]

In May 1995, as more branch libraries were being planned by the library director in Huntsville, it was decided that a paid position in New Hope was appropriate. Priscilla Scott, mentioned above, was hired for 20 hours per week.

In April 1988, 9 of the original volunteers and 16 additional volunteers were working 2-4 hours per week, or more if needed. For security purposes, at least two people will be on duty at all times.

In 2000 Mary Lou Glass became the paid head of the library, but Priscilla Scott remained a very active volunteer. Staffing a branch library for 24 hours per week, with at least two persons, adds up to 48 hours. The paid librarian was paid for only 20 hours, leaving 28 to be filled by volunteers. The volunteers needed training, and the library system must maintain procedures that meet professional standards. New Hope and the other branches with volunteers must have a notebook of rules and procedures to maintain high standards of patron service and professional standards. Some excerpts from the 30-page Volunteer Handbook follow:

"Elizabeth Carpenter Public Library of New Hope Volunteer Job Description
Qualifications:
• Mature-18 years or older
• Responsible
• Level-headed
• Dedicated

- Friendly and helpful

Responsibilities and Duties: (Discussed in detail on the following pages)

- Be familiar with general policies, rules and regulations of the Huntsville-Madison County Public Library System
- Be familiar with the opening and closing procedures of the library.
- Be familiar with the Dewey Decimal System.
- Be familiar with Branch Run Operations.
- Know who to call for assistance.
- Know how to help a patron find material.
- Be familiar with the operation of the automated circulation system.

A Note to Our Patrons about the Huntsville Public Library's Retrieval of Long Overdue Items

Library patrons receive the following notices through first class mail:

First Notice -10 Days late

Second Notice - 20 Days late

Third Notice - 35 Days late

Patrons whose materials are 50 days overdue receive a letter mailed regular first class and certified mail advising that she/he has 10 days to return materials or the City Of Huntsville will prosecute through Municipal Court. They may prosecute anyone who has failed to return any item(s) valued at more than $25, which are borrowed from any public library facility within the City of Huntsville.

If the patron does not return materials before that deadline, their names are turned over to the Municipal Court. Once their names have been forwarded to Municipal Court, they will be issued subpoenas and assigned a court date.

Some patrons believe that if they return materials after their names have been sent to court, this excuses them from appearing at their assigned cant date. THIS DOES NOT EXCUSE THEM OR CLEAR THEIR CHARGES WITH THE CITY OF HUNTSVILLE.

Any citizen who receives a subpoena must appear in court or an arrest warrant is issued. PATRONS ARE NOT ARRESTED FOR OVERDUE LIBRARY MATERIALS BUT FOR FAILURE TO APPEAR IN COURT.

Damages

Books:

List price charged for books damaged beyond repair. Partial damage prorated.

Cassettes:

List price charged for album and cassettes damaged.

Video Tapes:

List price, or prorated against extent of damage.

Compact Discs:

List price, or prorated against extent of damage.

DVDs:

List price, or prorated against extent of damage.

Lost items

In the event a book or audio visual item is lost, patron will be charged the price of the item when purchased by the Library.

Computer Use
Public Access Computer Procedures

-All public access computers in the Huntsville Madison County Public Library System may be used by adults and children ages 10 and older. The Youth Services Department of the Main Library and some Branches have computers that are specifically for children, and have no age limits. To use all other public access computers, children ages 9 and under need to be supervised by a responsible person who is at least 14 years old-

-Copies made on computer printers are $.15/page, with the exception that there are no charges for print-outs made of searches in our online catalog.

-Usage time limitations are specific to each location. Generally, patrons are limited to 1 hour at a time. Exceptions in the Main Library include the Training Center where the limit is 2 hours; and the Youth Services Department, where it is 1/2 hour, with the option for students to request longer sessions for homework, school assignments, or presentations.

-Patrons are required to use only the software available on the library computers, and are not allowed to load software on a computer's hard drive, or use their own software on a floppy disk.

-Disks may be purchased for $1.00; headsets for $2.00.

-Patrons may access personal e-mail accounts that are web-based like Hotmail, Yahoo and America Online.

-Individual departments or Branches may have additional procedures that are specific to each location and based on their users' needs.

Internet Safety Policy
Internet Access

The Library collection is supplemented by the wide variety of resources available through the Alabama Virtual Library and the Internet. Computers are provided for our users to access these online resources in the Library, and free classes are available in the Regional Computer Training Center for those who wish to improve their computer and Internet skills.

The content of the Internet is unregulated, and the Library has no control over the resources available there. Information found on the Internet may be reliable and current, or it may be inaccurate, out of date, illegal, obscene or sexually explicit. Because the Library cannot monitor or control the information available through the Internet, users access the Internet at their own discretion.

In order to provide equal access for users to its computers and the Internet, the Library sets time limits for computer usage and requires user sign-up or reservations.

Users are expected to utilize the Library computers in a responsible manner and to respect the rights of other users. Any actions that will cause damage to computer software or equipment, or will result in the invasion of privacy or harassment of others will not be allowed.

The Library will have no liability for direct, indirect or consequential damages related to the use of information accessed through the Library's Internet service. Since software and information downloaded from any sources, including the Internet, may contain computer viruses, users are advised to utilize virus-checking software on their home computers. The Library is not responsible for damage to users' disks or computers or for any loss of data, damage or liability that may occur from the use of the Library's computers.

Responsibilities of Parents/Guardians of Minors

Parents/guardians are responsible for their minor (under the age of 17) children's use of the Library's resources and facilities. This includes using the Internet at any of the Library locations.

Parents who believe that their children cannot responsibly use the Library's Internet access are requested to monitor their children's Internet use.

The Library will assist parents/guardians and children in the use of the use of the Internet, and suggest specific web sites that are age and content appropriate for children.

Unacceptable Uses of Computers

The following general uses of the Internet and Library computers are not permitted:
-Viewing graphic sexual materials
-Downloading and installing software on Library computers
-Hacking the Library network, including unauthorized use of network logins
-Using the Internet for unlawful purposes
-Using chat sites

The following types of Internet and Library computer usage are prohibited for minors as specified in the Neighborhood Children's Internet Protection Act (NCIPA):
-Access by minors to inappropriate matter on the Internet and World Wide Web
-Uses that compromise the safety and security of minors when using electronic mail, chat rooms and other forms of direct electronic communications
-Unauthorized access, including hacking, and other unlawful activities by minors online
-Unauthorized disclosure, use and dissemination of personal identification information regarding minor Access by minors to materials harmful to minors

Penalty for Violation of Policy

Any user who fails to comply with this policy will receive a warning and will forfeit the remainder of his computer time. After the first warning, users continuing to violate this policy will be issued a six-month trespass warning and will be barred from using any Library facilities for this period of time.

Adoption

This Internet Safety Policy was adopted by the Board of Trustees of the Huntsville Madison County Public Library at a public meeting, following normal public notice, on June 26, 2002.

Headsets

Due to Public Health concerns, the Huntsville-Madison County Public Library no longer loan Shared Computer Headsets for Public Use.

Patrons are welcome to bring in personal headsets suitable for computer stereo use, or to purchase a reusable quality stereo headset at a service desk for $2.00 each. Any headset purchased becomes property of the patron, and must be taken with the patron upon exit from the Library.

The Huntsville-Madison County Public Library is not responsible for purchased or personal headsets left on the premises, or damaged due to patron misuse.

Behavior Within the Library

The following are general policies governing behavior within the Library as adopted by the Board of Directors:
1. No smoking
2. Shirts and shoes must be worn at all times
3. Food and drink are limited to Public Lounge only
4. Children should not be left in the Library unsupervised by parents or adults for extended periods of time

5. Consideration for patrons' needs for quiet in study areas is appreciated

6. Library patrons are prohibited from carrying guns or other weapons into the Main Library or any branch Library. Patrons who have permits for guns will be asked to lock their guns in their cars. If they refuse they will be asked to leave the library.

Parents will be notified of incidents involving minor children that occur in the Library or Library parking lot. Parents will be provided with a copy of the security report. Minors who are repeat offenders may be denied access to the Library.

Gifts and Memorials

The Library Board is grateful for all donations and gifts. It is through the generosity of individuals and groups that areas of library service have been developed and the library collection enriched to an extent that would not otherwise have been possible.

The Library, as a non-profit organization, may issue receipts for donations that may be used for Internal Revenue Service tax deduction purposes. The Library cannot set a value on gifts, this is the responsibility of the donor.

OPENING AND CLOSING PROCEDURES

Opening:

1 . Switch "Open" sign and turn on lights.

2. Sign in on Volunteer sign-up sheet, recording your hours and read the Volunteer Notebook to check for any new instructions.

3. Bring up computer. (Instructions given on page.)

4. Stamp date due cards with a date 2 weeks from present date.

5. Count money in the tray in the far left cabinet and record on Cash Receipts chart with your initials.

6. Empty bookdrop and set computer to backdate discharge date to the last day the library was open. (Instructions on page 16.)

7. Shelve books on cart, watching for due date cards that have been removed and to make sure the book is ours.

Closing:

1. Fifteen minutes before closing, announce that the library will close in 15 minutes.

2. Count the money in the cash tray and record the amount on the Cash Receipts chart along with your initials.

3. Make sure all "loose ends" of the day are taken care of and the circulation desk is free of unnecessary clutter.

4. Sign off the computer.

5. Try not to leave a large number of unshelved books, and make sure tables and chairs are cleared.

6. Turn off the lights and change the door sign to "Closed".

7. Make sure the front and back doors are locked before leaving.

BRANCH RUN OPERATIONS

Being a branch of the Huntsville-Madison County Public Library system gives us the opportunity to share material with other branches. Patrons may return materials to the New Hope Library that were checked out at another branch, and may return our items at another branch. We also may borrow or lend items from other branches as requested by patrons. A courier comes from Huntsville twice a week to deliver these materials. When the items come in, they will be discharged before reshelving.

When requesting material from another branch, fill out the Branch Request form (large green form shown on the following page.) Place the form in the routing envelope always kept in the left corner of the circulation desk.

When a request comes to us from another library, locate the book and using the Intransit form (small green form shown on the following page}, find out which branch is making the request and the patron's name and phone number. Write the name of the book on the form. After checking out the book to the appropriate branch, put the green slip in the pocket of the book and place it in the large box under the desk. This is where we keep all items to be sent out. To check an item out to a branch use the branch check-out codes kept in the corner behind the circulation computer monitor. These are used instead of ID numbers. For example, our code is NEW LOAN. This will be explained later in the handbook under Computer Circulation Functions.

Each Tuesday and Thursday after "Branch Run" patrons who have received requested material will be called: After contacting the patron the book will be kept at the desk for 1 week. If the item has not been picked up by then, it will be discharged and sent back to its home library.

HELPING A PATRON FIND MATERIAL

Assisting patrons in finding material is a very important part of our work. The more we can help patrons learn their way around in the library, the more comfortable they will be in using it. Card Catalogs are no longer a part of modern libraries. All library holdings are listed in computer databases. The database that is used by the Huntsville-Madison County Library is called iBistro. All of the public computers are set to come up on the library homepage when you enter the Internet Explorer. Under the catalog tab click guest login and enter. On this screen you will see that you may search by words or phrases, author, title, subject, series, or periodical title. You may also choose all branches to search or individual branches.

It is a good idea to become familiar with the Huntsville-Madison County Library website. This is what patrons often visit at home, and it is much easier to help them find their way around the library if you are familiar with what they have been looking at.

Give yourself time to become proficient in assisting patrons in finding material. But, remember, the more you practice, the better you will get!

On the following pages you will be given some frequently used symbols in the library. It will be very helpful to you to familiarize yourself with them. Also a physical map of the New Hope Library will help you learn where everything is."[10]

The Volunteer handbook also included six pages of computer screen instructions for the Automated Circulation System.

This chapter on the Elizabeth Carpenter Public Library of New Hope ends with the death of its originator and driving force, Sarah Louise Mathews, who died on April 25, 2002 at the age of 77. She worked at Redstone Arsenal during World War II and was a volunteer at the library from its beginning in 1987 until 2001. Her papers left with the library included this handwritten memory:

"Christmas Thinkings From 1988

At first, working for our Library didn't seem to be much to do. I didn't know it would turn into one of the most enjoyable and full-filling time in my life. Its work, yes, but also fun. The time doesn't seem quite as long since the first idea was mentioned to me.

Ms Susie Hill, our very able and lovely, helpful, Bookmobile Librarian, ask me if I thought New Hope & Owens Cross Roads areas were ready for a Branch Library.

In our first conversation she didn't tell me the Outreach Dept. was discontinuing our Bookmobile. My first question. How could we get a branch started here. Then first idea, try to see how many interested persons would be able to help doing so.

She suggested a petition with names of such would surely go a long was with Huntsville. So with, Yellow Pad, in hand off I go!!

Every where I go, so goes the pad. I'd ask – explain and a name was signed. I can honestly say I was only turned down once for the Petition, and believe it or not, the same local man wasn't interested in joining the Friends of the Library. His answer was, when asked to join, 'Louise, are you still running around with that long yellow pad trying to get somebody to sign something or give you $5.00 for something that you'll never see? And instead of my being mad or embarrassed, I just laughed at his answer and said, 'Well, ole school buddy, just watch our speed – we may fool you!' And believe me, he was at our Grand Opening. I said, 'Hi, ____ ____, told you so didn't I?' He didn't have an answer. And I have yet to see him in the Library. But we really haven't missed him – but could have used him.

I hope that in the near future, with the help of our able-bodied Miss Priscilla, we could get the first papers and petitions, all other pictures, etc. – put them in a scrapbook or some such that will be a lasting memory for each and everyone that has worked so hard for our Library, and all the love and respect of our Elizabeth Carpenter namesake.

I can't stop here. I'm not able to give each and everyone that has worked so tirelessly for the library. They all know their worth.

But I can give a couple "pat on the back" to those from Huntsville Public Library. We certainly could never have done our City proud without their help. Mrs. Susan Markham, Mrs. Donna Schremser and Mrs. Donna Noojin, Geoffrey Jolly and all their lovely helpers - then I think – how many out here that should be thanked before we even were ready for the Huntsville Crowd. Mr. Nolan Hill, Mr. Jerry Craig, the County workers, the private citizens who gave their time; sign workers; brick layers & 75 bricks; flowers; plants; business managers, (those who gave $500 to $10); materials and someone to deliver them; flowers and food for our Grand Opening day; food and presents for Christmas parties. There is just no way I can remember them all and say a "thank you" to each one.

I know they would not want to be singled out. One family moved out of the area and gave a $100 bill, didn't want to be named! And that did more for me - to pour on more coal! Get the Show on the Road.

Get us a Library."[11]   **Thank you, Louise!**

Chapter 13

Outreach And More Outreach

"Books are not men, and yet they are alive.
They are man's memory and his aspiration
The link between his present and past,
The tools he builds with..."

Stephen Vincent Benet, 1898-1943
American poet

The 1990's started with an editorial in the *Huntsville News* about the need for county archives. Seems as if the rain was coming through the 4th floor roof of the Elbert Parsons Law Library on Eastside Square. The county records were all wet, literally. In December 1999 the law library's bound volumes of newspaper files were transferred into the hands of the archivists at the Huntsville Public Library's Heritage Room. The law library used to have an archivist-librarian, but no one was caring for the material in recent years, so materials started to disappear.

"We believe that the library is also the best place for the county's public records, although it seems logical to ask the county to bankroll the cost of archival and conservation work needed to make these materials safe and accessible for public use."[1]

The conservation of the county's records finally came to fruition eleven years later when a new probate judge was elected and took positive action. But, that story will be told in the chapter on the events of the third millennium. The moral of this story is that the public library is more than a book depository and lending institution, it has the qualified personnel trained in preserving materials and the techniques needed to properly conserve our public heritage.

The Huntsville-Madison County Public Library system conducted an annual staff development day in recent years, normally in the late winter-early spring. The 1990 staff development program on February 28 will be used as an example of the activities held during such an event.

"8:00-8:30   Continental Breakfast
8:30-9:15   Keynote Address: Judith Drescher, Director, Memphis Public Library and Information Center
9:15-9:30   Orientation to the Day
9:30-10:15   Discussion of Long Range Plan
10:15-10:30   Coffee Break (At the conclusion of Coffee break, employee paychecks will be distributed) [This significantly increases attendance at such events]
10:30-12:00   Department Presentations. Employees will be divided into groups for tour of Library.
12:00-1:00   Lunch On Your Own
1:00-3:00   Employees are free to choose from among the following mini workshops
1:00-1:30   Effective Customer relations. Presented by Parisians Youth Services Reference Area

209

CLSI Refresher Training. Presented by Sue Royer: Circulation Desk, First Floor (CLSI is the name of the company that provided the automated cataloguing and control system)

1:30-2:00   Public Speaking without Fear. Presented by Jack Robertson, U.S.B.I. Meeting Rooms A & B

Basic Reference Skills Using New Technology: Presented by Information & Periodicals Department.

Effective Customer Relations. Presented by Parisians Youth Services Reference Area

Stress Management (Includes Assertiveness Training and Exercise Programs). Presented by Jim Pierce and Ken Hendrix, Counseling Associates. Auditorium (NOTE: THIS PROGRAM IS ONE HOUR)

2:00-2:30   Do I Want to Pursue the M.L.S? (Master of Library Science) Presented by Philip Turner, Dean, School of Library and Information Science, University of Alabama. Staff Meeting Room

Managing Your Personal Finances. Presented by Larry Newberry and Ken Griffin, First Alabama Bank. Meeting Rooms A & B

Windmill… Working with the Handicapped Patron. Presented by Melissa Musgrove, Huntsville Rehabilitation center. Information and Periodicals Meeting Room

2:30-3;00   Managing Your Personal Finances. Presented by Larry Newberry and Ken Griffin, First Alabama Bank. Meeting Rooms A & B

CLSI Refresher Training. Presented by Sue Royer: Circulation Desk, First Floor

3:00-3:15   Break and reassemble in Auditorium at 3:15

3:15-4:15   February Meeting of Library Board. Jane Roberts, Chairman, Presiding.

4:15-4:30   Recognition of Employees with 10 or more years of service to the Library.

4:30-   Reception Honoring Employees Hosted by Board of Directors.

DON'T FORGET TO TURN IN YOUR EVALUATION BEFORE YOU LEAVE"[2]

Behind the program was a spreadsheet showing the year-to-year 4th quarter circulation (Oct 88-Dec 89 & Oct 89-Dec 90) in empirical numbers and percentage increase or decrease. Madison had the most dramatic increase, with 94 percent, reflecting the area's population growth. New Hope led the decreases with 20 percent. The entire system had a 12 percent growth in circulated items, from 370,509 to 416,729.

The employee's packet for the day included seven pages of information about people with disabilities: language, interviewing and attitudes. There were also 27 True-False questions about handicapped persons, Myths, Misconceptions and Realities of Disability. The answer sheets for the questions provided five and a half pages of explanations for the answers.

The Library's Long Range Plan, 1990-1995, was provided. The plan established 13 goals, as each goal contained several objectives. This vintage 1990 plan will be compared later to the Long Range Plan prepared in 2003.

The featured item in the employees' packet was a 34-page document containing almost everything one might want to know about the Huntsville-Madison County Library. The first item described the authority and responsibilities of the Library Board and provided the names of the current board. The next items were one page for each of the departments, which provided the names of the employees, functions, responsibilities, equipment, and holdings. The first floor departments were: Audio Visual; Circulation; Maintenance; and Youth Services. The second floor departments were: Adult services; Blind and Physically Handicapped; Information and

Periodicals; International Media Center; and Technical Services. The third floor departments were: Administration; Acquisitions; Archives; and Heritage Room.

The Extension and Outreach Services included: Outreach Services; Bookmobile; Bessie K. Russell Branch Library; Eleanor E. Murphy Branch Library; Madison Public Library; Madison Square Mall Branch Library; Gurley Public Library; New Hope Public Library; Madison County Law Library; Alabama Library Exchange; and Library Management Network, Inc.

The Technical Services Fact Sheet contained some statistics on the monthly average of material processed.

- Items Processed   3,500
- Items Discarded   1,200
- Books Transferred   50
- Books repaired   300
- Items Entered into CLSI   3,500
- Items Discarded from CLSI 1,200

A Book Processing Flowchart was provided for the processing of one truck load of books.

- Gathering books (1 hour)
- Property stamping (2-3 hours)
- Searching in CLSI (1-2 days)
- Cataloging on Bibliofile (1-5 days)
- Loading MARC** records (1-2 hours)
- Editing MARC records (2-3 hours)
- Printing Catalog cards (1-2 hours)
- Printing Labels (1-2 hours)
- Technical Processing (Pasting, labeling, covering, striping) (1-3 days)
- Checking and revising (1-2 hours)
- Entering into computer (1-2 days)
- Distributing (immediately)
- Filing catalog cards (1-2 hours)
- Filing shelflist cards (2-3 hours)

Average processing time for a truckload of books is 2-3 weeks.

MARC is a Library of Congress **Machine-**R**eadable Cataloging record.[3] [This is the end of the staff development day section.]

Inflation is with us. The Information and Periodicals Department information sheet in 1990 cited the cost of a printer copy at $.05 and in 2004 it was $.20.

Susan Hill, the Bookmobile Librarian, was chosen as the outstanding Youth Services Librarian for 1990 for Alabama. Ms. Hill was the first Huntsville librarian to receive this award. The Alabama Library Association cited two important factors that contributed to the award.

First, Ms. Hill formed the Polar Trekker's Club in November on the Bookmobile to follow the 1990 International Trans-Antarctica Expedition and to stimulate interest in Antarctica, polar life, penguins, past explorations of this fragile continent and the spirit of international cooperation. The children received information and nutrition packets about the expedition, samples of the high-energy bars used by the trekkers and a certificate of participation. The American Library Association recognized Ms. Hill's efforts, and she was asked to write an article about the program for national publication in its magazine *American Libraries.*

Second, Ms. Hill wrote a grant proposal, with her supervisor, to the Library Service and Construction Act based on a trial program Ms. Hill had been doing at Mason Court. For the past two years she had made Mason Court one of the Bookmobile stops, and she believed she was reaching many people who might not visit a library otherwise. She said the children look at the Bookmobile as a non-threatening, fun place. Parents also have started coming with their children.[4]

April 18, 1990 – A patron submitted a written complaint about a book in the library, which contained inaccuracies about Wernher von Braun and Arthur Rudolph, two of Huntsville's famous German rocket scientists. The board directed Mrs. Schremser to write a letter to the patron, explaining that the library strives to present all sides of an issue, and the library cannot purge all inaccuracies on its shelves.

The Bookmobile continued to be a success at Mason Court, and in August 1996 the Oscar Mason Center became a full-service Branch Library. Bravo to Susan Markham!

August 28, 1990 – A patron wrote that he was highly offended by *The Haunting of Cassie Palmer*, because he judged it unacceptable reading for young people and it was irresponsible for it to be in the library. The book was about the occult and conjuring up spirits. The patron admitted to only reading the introduction and back cover summary. The library board voted to have the director write a letter to the patron thanking him for his concern, but the book would remain in the library. {I wonder if he and his children (grandchildren) are now reading *Harry Potter*?]

In October 1990, the Comprehensive Early Intervention Services Council (CEISC) presented materials for and about children with disabilities to Donna Schremser. The CEISC, which includes representatives of community agencies that provide services to young handicapped children, had received a $6,200 grant to establish a resource center at the library. A photograph and caption were in *The Huntsville Times,* October 21, 1990.[5]

December 19, 1990 - Donna Schremser, Director, was elected Vice-president/President Elect of the Public Library Section of the Southeastern Library Association at its recent convention.

December 19, 1990 – The base appropriation from Madison County would be $129,000. The county will match the Detention Home Grant with new money. An additional $12,000 for the branch in Hazel Green will be matched. The total from Madison County would be about $145,000.

When was a week not seven days? In 1991 National Library Week was nine days long, April 12-20. The Madison County Commission sponsored Madison County Library Day on Friday 12, by hosting a Book Fair, with free ice cream and a visit by a county commissioner from 3-5 P.M. A highlight was the nearly completed branch to be opened in Hazel Green in mid-June. Commissioner Tillman Hill prepared barbecued chicken plates, which sold for $5 to raise money for the new branch.[6]

The eighth branch of the Huntsville-Madison County Public Library system opened Monday, June 24, 1991 in Hazel Green. It was in the Taylor Shopping Center on the west side of Route 431, on the north side of MacDonald's. For the past two years Hazel Green was the most heavily used bookmobile stop.[7]

The Marshall Space Flight Center, part of the National Aeronautics and Space Administration (NASA), and the Huntsville Public Library cooperated in Project LASER (Learning About Science, Engineering and Research) in 1991. Project LASER was a broad program whose volunteers worked with area schools to provide speakers on a variety of subjects, supply consultants, tutors and science fair judges. A Discovery Club was the process by which LASER programs were provided to children at the library. Some of the programs presented include: Magnets and Magnetism; Aerodynamics and Paper Airplanes; Microbes and the Space Station; Our Sensational Sun; Spacelab, Marshall's Involvement; The Earth: Our Own Space Station; Mission to Planet Earth; Mission to Mars; and How to do a Science Fair Project.[8]

In 1991 the Huntsville-Madison County Public Library installed the Online Public Access Catalog (OPAC), which was a computerized card catalog that enabled a patron to search for a particular book by title, author, subject or keyword. It contained the holdings of 12 libraries in 25 locations in North Alabama. This system was just one of many improved search systems that continued to expand the reach of library patrons across the state.[9] This was just one more step toward the standardization of data among libraries.

A special city council meeting was held on Thursday night, August 29, 1991, to discuss Mayor Steve Hettinger's ten-year capital improvements plan. Library director Donna Schremser had requested $5.4 million over the next ten years, to include four new branches and renovation of two existing ones. The capital plan called for deleting the four new branches, a savings of $3.4 million. The renovations needed to existing branches were a new roof, addition of a meeting room, and a children's area and interior renovation of the Eleanor Murphy Branch ($194,0000) on Charlotte Drive and the addition of a meeting room and replacement of a wooden porch with a permanent entry porch at the Bessie Russell Branch ($65,000) on Sparkman Drive.

The top priority on the library's development plan was an 11,000-square foot branch in the Bailey Cove/Mountain Gap area, which would serve about 25,000 residents within a three-mile radius. The branch was to eventually have 50,000 volumes. It would cost $1.5 million to acquire land and build, with a first year operating budget of $250,000.[10] Mrs. Schremser said the demand for a branch from Southeast Huntsville residents was tremendous. She also said the branch would eventually see annual circulation of over 300,000 items. The branch was eventually established in an existing building in 1997 and the circulation for the first fiscal year, 1997/1998, was 193,344. Growth was steady in the following years: 214,403; 241,569; 251,299; 271,324; and 277,292 in 2002/2003.[11] The annual rate of growth had slowed for two main reasons: the total population of the served area had a slight decrease; and the population was aging as children were the biggest driver in circulation statistics. The above trend pointed to several more years before circulation would reach the projected estimate, but in retrospect 13 years later, it was quite accurate insofar as the state of estimating goes. There were many things that can happen that make such long-term estimates go awry, and this situation had no historical baseline from which to start, except demographic analysis by the library staff.

The two other proposed library branch locations: Northeast Huntsville Research Park near UAH and Madison Mall; and Big Cove/Dug Hill area, did not come to fruition as of this date.

City Council held another budget hearing on Thursday night, September 19, 1991. Donna Schremser, Library Director, presented statistical data showing that the library system was chronically under-funded in recent years. The library's fulltime-equivalent employees had an average salary of $17,440, despite the fact that more than half of them have bachelors or masters degrees in library science.

Comparative statistics from Huntsville and eight other similar sized cities in the Southeast were provided. Huntsville's per capita library expenditures were $13.40, behind Lexington, Kentucky ($32.70), Greenville, South Carolina ($18.11), Winston-Salem, North Carolina ($17.70), and the five other cities. Huntsville also ranked the lowest among the nine cities in the number of books, which ranged from 880,564 for Norfolk, Virginia to 353,000 for Huntsville. Huntsville was third in utilization per capita at 6.4, only behind Prince William, Virginia (7.1) and Winston-Salem (6.5).

The City of Huntsville provided 72.6 percent of the library funding, followed by the State of Alabama at 8.6 percent and Madison County at 4.3 percent.[12] Huntsville has about 62 percent of the county's population. The remainder of Madison had about 38 percent of the population, but pays only 4.3 percent of the fare. Is that fair? Maybe it was fair if the Madison County residents do not use the library as much as the city folks do.

September 18, 1991 – The library board voted to withdraw all support and supervision of the law library as of September 30, 1991. There had been many months of meetings and non-meetings about issues concerning the law library.

On Tuesday noon, October 15, 1991, best-selling author John Grisham spoke to a crowd of over 150 people at a sold-out box lunch at the Huntsville-Madison County Library. At this time he had written two successful novels, *A Time to Kill* and *The Firm*. He had been receiving up to three requests to speak and had stopped making appearances. He did have a soft spot for Huntsville and he had three requests from three different groups in Huntsville. It was the combined efforts by the library, the Huntsville Bar Association and the Huntsville Literary Association that brought him to Huntsville. People have an attraction to libraries because they are seen as free to all, equal to all, and the heart of the American culture. Grisham talked about how he came to write his first two books, as his career turned from an attorney to an author. Huntsville was fortunate to have him speak, as his home state is Mississippi.[13]

In December 1991, Comcast Cablevision donated videotapes of the proceedings of the Huntsville City Council. Comcast had only begun broadcasting the council live in May 1991. The tapes were stored in the archives room of the library's and can only be viewed in the library.[14]

A patron wrote a letter to the library board in January 1992 asking that *Secret Agenda*, by Linda Hunt, be removed from circulation because of inaccuracies and distortions about the German rocket scientists, particularly Wernher von Braun and Arthur Rudolph who put Huntsville on the map. The patron identified and labeled the items in three categories: 1. Lack of integrity; 2. Inaccurate; and 3. Intent to incite hatred. The writer, one of the German scientists, was the same one who complained in April 1990, cited earlier, about a different book. The board again did not remove the book.

May 20, 1992 - The board and the director had to deal with many issues other than books. A dog owned by a homeless man, tied up at the entrance to the main library, bit a child. The parents sued the library, naturally, because the homeless man had no money. The library's insurance company told the parents that it would pay up to $5,000 in medical expenses and told the director not to worry about the lawsuit.

During National Library Week in April 1992, a three-judge panel of the U.S. Court of Appeals for the Third Circuit ruled unanimously that public libraries are for intellectual, professional or entertainment purposes only. In May 1991 a federal district judge in New Jersey ruled that the Town of Morristown could not enforce a rule limiting its library to patrons "reading, studying or using library materials." Nor could it enforce a rule that said patrons must not "harass or annoy" others by intimidating stares, loud noise, etc. Nor could it enforce a rule requiring that patron hygiene not be "so offensive as to constitute a nuisance."

The Morristown adapted such rules because a homeless man who was a constant "patron" did all those things. He sued and won initially. The Appeals Court reversed the decision.[15] The next time my readers go into the library, particularly in the winter, check out those several obviously homeless persons in the magazine area on the first floor. For the male readers, check out the restrooms. Should you report them? Are they harming anyone? Perhaps he was reading an interesting story in a magazine and just fell asleep. It would not be the first time it happened in a library.

During National Library Week in 1992, the *Huntsville News* wrote an editorial about using a friendly library. This editorial will be quoted, because the newspapers reach a wide audience and usually are attuned to the sentiments of the area's citizens. We must remember that freedom of the press really refers to those that own the press or write for it. The rest of us have a limited freedom of the press because our efforts are subject to the approval of the editorial page editors. We Huntsvillians should be appreciative that our press speaks forcefully about supporting our library system, because it is the heart of our culture. The library personnel cannot tell us how great it is, they just deliver performance for us to enjoy. David Bowman, the editorial page editor, should receive credit for this editorial, but most importantly for the profound thought he buried in the editorial, which will be highlighted.

"On the occasion of April 5-11 being National Library Week it seems like a good opportunity to remind several groups, some large and some small, about the remarkable institution known as the Huntsville Public Library.

One group – those Huntsville library patrons who checked out 1.5 million books and other materials, a ratio of 6.2 per capita in 1991 – need to be reminded that a library that has continued to rise steadily in its circulation figures should be getting corresponding increases in appropriations from city, county, state, federal funds.

If you're one of the cast of thousands who are in the library on a typical weeknight, or weekend, please urge your public officials to be more generous with operating and acquisitions funds for it.

Equally important, join up as a member of the Friends of the Library. Individual and corporate support for the library is the competitive edge that will help make our really good library a much better library.

The library is not just books. It has a good collection of periodicals of all kinds, sound recordings, newspapers from all over the place, and an international media center for foreign-language holdings.

The most remarkable change this past year has been the computerization of all its catalog of holdings. Card-catalog entries continue to be maintained as well for offering a user-friendly option for library patrons.

A third group, of uncertain but significant size, includes a large number of corporate-sector users who need first-rate business and technical information and don't have to buy the materials themselves.

These folks, from top executives on down, should be active lobbyists for passing the hat for additional materials that presumably can be earmarked for the business and technical (second floor) department of the library. That department gets tremendous usage daily, as any librarian will tell you, and your own eyesight can confirm, every single day of the week.

The next time, for example, you feel tempted to give to some 'political action committee' (PAC) money to get your favorite politician re-elected, think about a worthy cause that needs the money far more urgently. That's your local public library. [Author's bold]

Fiscal Year 1991 saw the Huntsville Public Library getting about 72.6 percent of its income from the City of Huntsville.

Fiscal Year 1992 saw the city's portion shrink to 69.3 percent and a hold-steady special appropriation of $2.2 million proposed. Fortunately, a bit more was shaken loose to keep things from taking backward steps in the face of steadily rising costs of library materials like new books and periodical subscriptions.

The next year for the library is being planned for now. Give a contribution and a word of encouragement for that library you have come to know and love...."[16]

"The Huntsville/Madison County Public Library has come up with a new program for developing library research skills and has coined some new words to describe the events associated with it.

'Adventurmation,' 'Fact Findomania,' 'Jungle Exploration,' and 'Research to Succeed' are among the activities planned for students in grades four through 11 during the six sessions of Library Camp set for July [1992]

Library Camp's goal is to make doing book reports fun and term papers fun. [Mission Impossible?] The skills learned will be helpful in retaining vocabulary, research and learning skills obtained during the school year. The summer months provide the time needed for uninterrupted, focused study.

Camp participants will learn how to use a dictionary, thesaurus, almanac, various indexes, the library's on-line catalog, research tools from both the Youth Services and Reference Departments, Infotrac and Newsbank, and how to organize research papers."

The sessions were held from 9 a.m. until noon. All sessions were $48 per student. The fee included a Liberty Camp T-shirt, a 1992 World Almanac, syllabus and refreshments.[17]

June 10, 1992 - Mrs. Donna Schremser, Director, was elected to the board of directors of the Public Library Association. The friends of the library donated $9,000 to purchase six public access computer terminals and to build a table for the terminals.

July 15, 1992 - Joyce Smith, Subregional Library for the Blind and Physically Handicapped, was nominated by the board for the Spain Rehabilitation Center's Lotus Award. She received a certificate as the first runner-up for the award. Joyce Smith also received the Alabama Rehabilitation Association's Homer L. Jacobs Award. Bravo, Joyce.

July 15 1992 – The library was awarded three Library Services and Construction Act grants for 1993:

- $40,000 for a new bookmobile. It would cost about $85,000. The library requested $20,00 from the city capital fund and would ask for a $40,000 special appropriation from Madison County.
- $10,000 for a new branch library in northwest Madison County. County commissioner Grady Abernathy would need to match this with $25,000.
- $25,000 in Major Urban Resource Library funding for materials.

The Bookmobile continued to roll during the summer of 1992. The Bookmobile schedule for the summer is below, as an example of the services provided to keep the children's reading interest at a high level.

"Bookmobile Schedule, Summer 1992

Monday

First Baptist Church	Blue Springs Road	10:00-11:00
Monrovia Elementary	Monrovia Road	1:00-1:45
Harvest	Harvest Fire Station	2:00-3:00
Madison Cross Roads	YMCA, Opp Reynolds Road	3:30-4:30

Tuesday

Northwoods Housing Community	Yukon Street	2:30-3:00
Mason Court Housing Community	Holmes Avenue	3:15-3:45
Butler Terrace Housing Community	Seminole Drive	3:50-4:15

Wednesday

Triana	Triana City Hall	10:00-11:00
J.E. Williams School	Barren Fork Road	11:15-12:00
Searcy Housing Community	Dallas Avenue	2:30-3:00
Boys and Girls Club	Abingdon Avenue	3:15-3:45
Valley Bend Apartments	Valley Bend Apartments	4:00-4:30

Thursday

Colonial Hills Elementary	Meridian Street	10:30-11:00
Research Park	USBI Parking Lot	11:30-1:00
Brunos	Weatherly and Bailey Cove	2:00-3:00
Challenger Middle School	Chaney Thompson Road	3:15-4:15

Friday

Riverton Food Value	Winchester Road	1:15-2:15
Locust Grove Day Care	County Lake Road	2:30-3:30
New Market Brady's Super Value	Winchester Road	3:45-4:30

The bookmobile will not run in inclement weather.
If a stop is missed for any reason, overdues are not charged."[18]

David Bowman of the *Huntsville News* followed the library budget issues with great diligence. His article on September 28, 1992 reported that the library's budget will be level-funding, which is the same $2.2 million that it received the last three years. The library had asked for $2.4 million. The library board will now have to make some decisions on how to make up the approximately $250,000 shortfall. The tentative plan would close the Eleanor Murphy Branch on Charlotte Drive two nights a week and Sundays, close the Madison Square Mall Branch two nights a week and Sundays, and close the Main Library on Sundays. He went on ask whether we will have The Incredible Shrinking Library? In the same editorial he said the City Council approved by a vote of 3-2 a total of $200,000 worth of property tax breaks for 23 local companies.[19]

The planned closings would save about $68,000 a year in staffing, utilities and security. Other cuts would be $145,000 in the book budget, $3,000 for microfilm and $15,000 for audiovisual materials. The Main Library had an estimated 4,000 patrons on Sundays.[20]

Let us now turn our attention to one of the reasons the library needs to have increased funding support. It is the problem of unreturned materials, which has been a problem for at least two thousand years. In 1982 the Huntsville City Council passed Ordinance No. 82-367, which made it unlawful to fail or to refuse to return books or materials checked out of the library. Improvements to the library's automation system made it possible to streamline the process for getting back the material. The library employees now get a printout of patrons with overdue materials by dates and can print out a bill or collection notice.

In September 1992 a Huntsville family with about $500 in overdue borrowed books had to answer to a city judge. Donna Schremser, Library Director, said that at any given time, about $10,000 worth of library books, recording or periodicals are up to one year overdue. There is a backlog of $25,000 worth of materials that the library will probably never see again. Some people move and the library cannot find them.

The library policy follows:

- A notice is sent out when a book is 10 days overdue;
- A second notice is sent after 20 days;
- After 35 days a bill is mailed with a letter of intent to call the patron to appear before the city magistrate;
- Ten days after the letter of intent is sent out, names are turned over to the magistrate, starting with those whose materials have the largest assessments or overdue charges;
- Anyone with overdue materials valued at $25 or more will be subject to appear before the magistrate.[21]

Is that system fair? The library director has the responsibility to properly account for public monies. If the director did not take such action, then she is not doing her job. Is it all right for a citizen to steal public property without be called to account and give restitution? An out-of-print text usually costs more money to replace than it cost originally. It becomes a constant drain on the library's budget.

"A Huntsville woman was startled last Thursday [September 22, 1992] to find a notice posted to her door informing her that a warrant had been issued for her arrest. Her crime? Failure to return overdue library materials.

She said she had checked out some books and videotapes that were due on Sept. 28 – less than a month before the warrant was issued. She turned herself in on Friday and was fingerprinted, mug-shot and locked in a cell for about half an hour.

The cost of getting out of jail was $145. (A look at city jail records showed a person arrested for trespassing was bonded out for $70.) On Monday morning, she had to miss work to appear in Municipal Court, where she entered a *guilty* [author's italics] plea and was fined $90.

The 38-year-old woman said she is outraged that local law enforcer are spending time and money tracking down people with overdue library books rather than people who have committed violent crimes. The police who booked her into the jail apparently felt the same way, she said, and were making jokes like, 'Get out the shackles! We have a dangerous criminal here!'

After the experience of being locked up with prostitutes and repeat DUI offenders, she said she will never check another book out of the Huntsville Public Library.

A 26-year-old New Market woman was also arrested last weekend for failure to return library materials. She was released from jail after more than an hour's incarceration and paid a $200 bond. This woman pleaded not guilty and will go to trial on the charge next month."[22]

The public library has been part of the broad American cultural fabric for less than 100 years, starting with Andrew Carnegie's philanthropy. The first tax-payer-supported true public library was in Boston in 1854. It is now widely accepted as a right of all citizens, and non-citizens, to visit a free library and check out materials.

Does that right also give the patrons the right to deprive others of the right to read the same materials? The United States is a country of laws, although some people do not always like them if they are applied to themselves. Obeying the law is inherent to preserving our culture.

The woman cited above complained about the perceived pettiness of her crime, but it was a crime. Several years ago, the police chief of New York City decided that one of the tools to fight crime was to crack down on petty crimes, such as graffiti, littering, etc. This produced results on bigger crimes, because the people realized that failure to enforce petty crimes led to more crimes being committed because enforcement was lax on all crimes. The library is not in the enforcement business directly, but it has a responsibility to report crimes to the proper authorities, as do responsible citizens. Mrs. Jane G. Roberts, Chairman, Huntsville Public Library Board, wrote, "We feel that we are being good stewards of the taxpayers' monies which purchase these materials. Library patrons who do not return material are not just stealing from the library, they are stealing from every citizen who has purchased, and who may want to use, these materials."[23]

The paragraph above was taken from the *Huntsville News*, to include the quotation by Jane Roberts. Now for the rest of the story. Jane Roberts was a fierce defender of the library during her long tenure as chairman of the library board. The quotation was just the last two sentences of a letter she sent to the *Huntsville News*. Her full letter is quoted below and you be the judge.

"September 23, 1992

Letters to the Editor, The Huntsville News, P.O. Box 1007, Huntsville, AL 35807

Dear Sir:

On behalf of the Library Board, I feel I must respond to the article in The Huntsville News which made reference to a recent arrest of a local citizen who was charged with failure to return materials to this "hallowed" institution. The Board resents the manner in which the reporter treats this as a frivolous charge.

The fact is that thousands of individuals borrow books and audiovisual materials with no intention of returning them. At any given time some $10,000 worth of library materials are at least three months and up to one year overdue. Library patrons receive two overdue notices, a bill, and a final letter which states the patron has 10 days to return materials, or he or she will be called to appear before the City magistrate.

The Huntsville City Council in 1982 felt this matter was serious enough to enact an ordinance and provide for "up to $100 fine and/or up to 30 days in jail" for what we consider theft of library materials. Printed on the back of some 144,000 library cards issued by the Huntsville Madison County Public Library are the words "Huntsville City Ordinance No. 82-367 makes it unlawful for any person who has been issued a membership card by the Huntsville Public Library to fail or refuse to return any material borrowed from the Huntsville Public Library, with all overdue assessments or late charges."

We feel that we are being good stewards of the taxpayers' monies which purchase these materials. Library patrons who do not return materials are not just stealing from the library, they are stealing from every citizen who has purchased, and who may want to use, these materials.

Sincerely,

Jane G. Roberts, Chairman Library Board"[24] Bravo, Jane!

What prompted Mrs. Roberts letter? How many of my readers remember the good old days when the morning delivery of the *Huntsville News* brought good reading to the breakfast table with the section called, "Police Beat." It gave names, ages, addresses and charges. The police beat item in the above case was, "A patron of the Huntsville Library found himself behind bars Monday morning after he failed to return items borrowed from that hallowed institution. Arrested on a charge of failure to return library materials was Kenneth Lockhart, 34, of Old Railroad Bed Road. Specifics of the charge were unavailable."[25]

The library director released a press statement on October 29, 1992 to explain the policy, which caused the publicity cited above.

"The library, funded by your tax dollars, has taken many years and millions of dollars to build the current inventory of 375,000 volumes. This collection serves some 240,000 people. Last year nearly 1.7 million items were checked out. In the state of Alabama, Huntsville's circulation ranks second only to Birmingham (which has over a million volumes and serves more than 800,000 population). Currently there are approximately 11,000 items, valued at $252,000 overdue from January to August 30, 1992, alone. Many patrons are on a waiting list to borrow these books, but cannot because individuals will not return these materials. The Library Board faced this problem squarely 10 years ago, when in 1982 unreturned library materials exceeded 25,000 volumes, a loss to taxpayers of $375,000. The Library Board requested the Huntsville City Council adapt an ordinance which would make it *unlawful to refuse to return materials.* [italics original] The council enacted the ordinance in September 1982."[26]

Have the director and the library board been overacting or under reacting to the problem of over due materials? Are they being good stewards of the public's books, videos, etc? During 1992 the library sent out 29,259 1st Notices for overdue materials. It sent out 11,708 2nd Notices, which equates to 40% of the patrons did not bring back the materials. Do you think that it should be lower in our so-called law-abiding society? During January through July the library sent out a 3rd Notice before sending a bill for the amount of the book (replacement price). During those 7 months, 22% of the original delinquent people received the 3rd Notice, meaning they had ignored the first 2 notices. Most of them probably preferred to say that they did not receive the first two notices. A bill was sent to 77% of the folks who received the 3rd Notice, which was 17% of the original number who received the 1st Notice. That 17% represents the number of citizens of our city and county that had blatantly refused to accept the fact that they had stolen public property until they were presented with a bill. Should they be allowed to disregard the law? Perhaps 17% of my readers will answer yes.

Starting in August, the 3rd Notice was dropped and the bill for the materials became the third notification. A letter of intent to turn the matter over to the City Magistrate if the book or the fine was not received within ten days was made the fourth (last) notification. During the five months of the revised notification system, approximately the same percentage of people received second and third notices. But now the fourth notice was a serious ultimatum. Three hundred forty-nine people, 3% of the original total for those 5 months, now received the strong message from the library. Of course, during the entire period, the library was expending more resources of time and money to send out the notifications. Let me restate the two questions posed above. Have the director and the library board been overacting or under reacting to the problem of over-due materials? Are they being good stewards of the public's books, videos, etc?

The saga of the library users who do not return materials continued into April 1993. From August 1992 to April 8, 1993, the Municipal Court had issued 178 summonses to appear in court or arrest warrants. Of those, 70 resulted in either a dismissal or a guilty or not-guilty plea. The rest remain active cases. Donna Schremser said the library selected five people who have current books out that people need or want, or who have as many as ten books out on one subject. The number five is what the court wants to work with. The library agreed that was a manageable number every week.[27]

Various items in this history discussed some of the sources of income to the library.
"HUNTSVILLE-PUBLIC LIBRARY BUDGET FY 1992 -1993 PROPOSED
SOURCES OF INCOME

City of Huntsville	$2,440,955
State of Alabama	$275,600
Madison County	$200,000

City of Madison	$74,175
Hazel Green (Comm. Hill)	$37,400
Commissioner Craig	$7,000
Town of Gurley	$4,000
Town of New Hope	$9,270
Friends	$67,000
Gifts	$13,000
Foundation	$40,000
Fines	$157,000
Photocopies	$75,000
LMN	$4,000
Interest/Dividends	$11,000
LSCA MURLS	$25,000
LSCA Foreign Language	$20,000
LSCA Title I	$10,000
Miscellaneous	$3,000
Hawthorne Trust	$7,800
Building Fund Proceeds	$42,000
TASC Rent	$2,400
Computer Charges	$8,000
TOTAL INCOME	$3,533,600"[28]

News Flash, October 21, 1992, Huntsville Public Library plays a key role in murder mystery. Let's hear a cheer for our library. A library book was a communications device between Betty Wilson, later convicted of murdering her husband, Jack, and the man who actually did the killing. The library was subpoenaed for its records about the book.[29]

November 18, 1992 – The library board approved Donna Schremser's recommendation that the card catalog be removed from the public area in January 1993. The technical services department stopped maintaining the catalog about a year ago. Computer terminals were being added, and the tables to support the terminals, courtesy of the friends of the library donations. Will the library patrons accept these new-fangled machines after decades of looking at 3 x 5 cards for their desires? Will there be numerous complaints?

February 17, 1993 – Tom Dyer, Certified Public Accountant, met with the board to review the library financial audit. Dyer said he had been working with Shirley, the library's financial manager, auditing the library's books (financial) for several years and everything is in good order. He said he had not written a management letter because he did not feel it was necessary. He reviewed several items in the audit for the board. The board discussed the investment of the Pruitt Funds (a donation). The board discussed the growing need for investment policy and outside advice. [There will be more about Tom Dyer later in this decade.]

The Huntsville-Madison County Public Library celebrated its 175th birthday during the month of April 1993. It was started in 1818, although it did not really become a free public library until the Carnegie Library in 1916.

May 24, 1993 – The board reviewed a seven-page investment policy for the first time. The times are changing, as I can imagine the folks back in the 1930's, 1940's and 1950's wished they had to worry about investment policies. Libraries are now big business and need to devote considerable effort to the fiscal responsibilities of the day.

June 23, 1993 – The library would receive four grants from the Library Services and Construction Act (LSCA) in Fiscal Year 1994: $25,000 MURLS; $10,000 Collection development in the area of economics; $10,000 Service to Triana; and $10,000 Service to youth at risk at the Northwest YMCA. The director presented some statistics to the board covering fiscal years 1989 through 1993. The base year was 1989 and increases were presented year-by-year in empirical and percentage numbers. During the 4 years, the budget increased 26 percent; volumes owned increased 25 percent; circulation increased 45 percent (late 1993 projection); employees increased 11 percent; and circulation per employee increased 30 percent. The bottom line was that circulation and circulation per employee increased faster that the budget and employees. Bravo to Donna Schremser and her staff! Keep this in your mind for an item later in the decade.

Another item discussed was the fine for a lost book or audiovisual item. The patron would be charged the price of the book when purchased by the library, plus an additional $7.25 itemized as follows:

- Book jacket: $1.25
- Barcode label: $ .25
- Book pocket: $ .25
- Date due card: $ .50
- Processing fee $5.00 [Looks reasonable to this author.]

"COLLECTION EVALUATION - June 1993

The purpose of this evaluation is to identify weaknesses in our non-fiction book collection and areas where more titles need to be added. The first section covers the collection in the main library. Special collections were done separately. Special collections include: Information & Periodicals, Youth Services, and Branches (Bessie K. Russell, Madison Library, and Hazel Green/Meridianville Library).

Prices for the books were based on average book prices quoted in the 1993 Bowker Annual.

This evaluation was completed by Collection Development Committee members Regina Cooper, Barbara Liaw, David Lilly, Sue Mitchell, AnneWhite Fuller, Linda Putnam, Judy Purinton, along with Donna Noojin, Linda Luttrell and Sally Barnett."[30]

The evaluation results were listed on seven pages. Each 3-digit numbered category was listed, followed by the number of titles **needed**, the average price for that category and the total cost in that category. Two simplified examples are shown:

- 150-Psychology, 35 titles, $42.67 average price, $1,493.45 total.
- 560-Paleontology, 10 titles, $79.72, $797.20.

As you can see, books were not cheap in 1993 and cost even more in 2004. Folks, it costs money to stock a library and you can use it for free.

In July 1993, the library received a set of historical document audiotapes. The documents recorded were the United States Constitution, the Bill of Rights and the Declaration of Independence. A local businessman, Mike Kelly, who formed International Associated Marketing in April 1993, provided the tapes. He hoped to market the tapes to stores and libraries and our library received one of the earliest copies of the tapes.

In August 1993, the library had a new and much bigger bookmobile at the cost of $80,000.[31]

One of the major issues the director and staff of the Huntsville-Madison County Public Library had to deal with constantly were the different funding sources in the county. An example of the multifarious sources and amounts is below:

"HUNTSVILLE MADISON COUNTY PUBLIC LIBRARY
County Match for $100,000 City Capital Plan Book Funds

County's 13th Check	$14,227
Commissioner Rob Colson	$8,000

Carryover	$1,500
Commissioner Faye Dyer	$8,000
Commissioner Tillman Hill	$18,000
Commissioner Glen Nunley	$15,000
Commissioner Mike Gillespie	$8,000
Commissioner Jerry Craig	
Town of New Hope	$5,000
City of Madison	$7,250
Town of Gurley	$2,000
Commissioner Prince Preyer	$5,000
Increase in County General Fund	
Total:	$89,947"[32]

In December 1993 the library tried a novel approach during the Christmas season for persons who owed fines for late return of materials. The patrons could pay their fines when they returned the books by substituting cans of food for money. The food was given to the Salvation Army and the library got their books back.[33]

The next library saga covered will be the attempt to raise property taxes to support the library. In early April 1993, library officials wanted a countywide vote on a proposed 2-mill property tax to build new library locations and improve the existing main library and branches. This tax would mean an extra $12 per year for residents with property with a $100,000 home, which is less than the price of one book. The officials drafted a local bill, which was expected to be introduced into the 1993 Alabama legislative session and would allow for the vote in the county in 1994. The estimated revenue for the first year was about $3 million.[34]

On April 5, a *Huntsville Times* editorial supported the proposal.

"...libraries are nothing without their collections. So a portion of the tax proceeds would be used to expand the library's collection of books and other materials.

The demand is undeniable. The number of local citizens using the main library and its branches continues to climb. The downtown library, constructed six years ago amid the criticism that it was too large, is already bursting at the seams. At the same time, the size of the library's collection is not on a par with libraries in cities of similar size in the Southeast.

Over the years, the library has become an essential adjunct of the public school system. School libraries are not open at night; the public library is. Students of every age group use the library for required reading materials and research projects.

As the taxpayers consider this proposal, they should bear in mind that the library cannot deliver the necessary services by cutting in other areas. Its sole function is that of a library, and to carry out that function is dependent on local government. Salaries of library employees are generally lower that the earnings of other local government workers. Indeed, were it not for the Friends of the Library and a host of volunteers, the library could not operate at its present level.

Americans live in an age when information is their most important tool. The library has tried to meet that need but has no self-funding mechanism. The 2-mill property tax would fill in the gaps – and at a cost of $12 a year to each family owning a $100,000 home.

It doesn't seem fair that the library, as an essential government service, should have to come up with ways to finance itself when the same burden is not placed on other essential services. That question, however, should not obscure the obvious reality that the library needs help and needs it soon. If the voters of Madison County are not willing to provide that help, they and their children will be the ones to suffer."[35]

A public hearing on the subject was held Tuesday night, April 6, in the main library auditorium. Only 38 percent of the county residents owned their own home according to one citizen, therefore, the tax would be unfair to those 38 percent. Many of the homeowners were also retired, thereby putting an extra burden on those retirees. Mrs. Jane Roberts, chairman of the library board, pointed out that the tax would also apply to commercial property. Donna Schremser, library director, said that Huntsville and Shreveport, Louisiana are the only two cities among nine in the Southeast between 225,000 and 300,000 that do not collect property taxes as part of their funding for libraries.[36]

The proposed projects for the tax money in the next ten years were:
- Bailey Cove-Mountain Gap area branch - $1.5 million; 1996, 1997.
- City of Madison branch - $1.1 million; 1997, 1998.
- Gurley branch - $250,000; 1997, 1998.
- Hazel Green branch - $600,000; 1996, 1997, 1998.
- Northeast Huntsville branch - $173,000; 1998-2005.
- Research Park branch - $1.3 million; 1999, 2000, 2001.
- Each of those projects would also receive operating money from 1996 through 2005.
- New Hope and Triana would receive operating money for the 10-year period beginning in 1996.
- An extra $650,000 for books.[37]

The effort came to naught in 1993, but was revived in the 1994 session of the legislature. Representative Howard Sanderford of Huntsville continued to push for the 2-mill levy vote. Representative Albert Hall of Gurley continued his opposition to the bill from last year. He said that rural residents were outnumbered by Huntsville citizens and could face a tax increase regardless whether they opposed the tax. That is the way the vote works. The majority get their way and the minority lose. But Albert Hall did a good job protecting his constituents from tax increases and from getting better informed. Mayor Steve Hettinger of Huntsville said, "It's a little disappointing they don't let the people vote their support or displeasure." Representative Dewayne Freeman from Huntsville expressed his concerns that the library tax could hamper efforts to win local support for education reform, which could also call for new taxes. Mrs. Schremser replied that the library improvements would play into that concept. *"If the public library is not an educational resource, what is it?"*[38] [author's italics]

The library was always fighting the image that it was just a place to go for a person to borrow a book. The modern library was so much more, as shown below.

"HUNTSVILLE PUBLIC LIBRARY

TOP TEN WAYS WE IMPROVE THE QUALITY OF LIFE

1. 179,344 citizens have library cards, 70% of our population, while the national average is 40%. On an average day, 3,500 citizens visit the Main Library or branch libraries.

2. The Library is the preschooler's door to learning, helping children get ready to start school at age 5. Elementary children keep their reading skills active as thousands participate in our summer reading program each year.

3. The Library is the homework center and resource after school, evenings and weekends, for public and private school students in Huntsville. The Online Catalog is available for searching from all schools with modem access, and titles can be held for students at the Main Library or branches.

4. Reference Librarians have helped local citizens answer 200,000+ reference questions, that's one question every 1.5 minutes. Citizens can get reference assistance in person or by telephone.

5. The Huntsville Heritage Room is the official archive for the history of Huntsville, providing local scholars, newspapers, television stations, genealogists, Alabama history students, and many others with a rich treasure of books, microfilm, historic documents, and photographs.

6. The Subregional Library for the Blind and Physically Handicapped provides free talking books by mail, along with machines, to 335 citizens, who borrowed 13,446 talking books this year. This department also provides Braille transcribing service.

7. The American Library Association honored our International Media Center for its outstanding service. The IMC assists residents who do not read English as their native language. The IMC is also a valuable resource for students studying foreign languages and citizens who need to learn a foreign language for work or travel abroad. This department has an outstanding collection of foreign films, and represents nearly 50 languages. This is the only collection of its type in Alabama and one of the finest in the Southeast.

8. Citizens dial into the Library's online catalog from home or office to search the holdings of the Huntsville Public Library and 16 other libraries in North Alabama. With reciprocal borrowing agreements in place, local residents have access to nearly 1,000,000 titles in North Alabama. For titles not available in our region, the Library will borrow the book from another library in the United States through interlibrary loan.

9. The Library provides limited Internet access free of charge to local residents at the Main Library. Library staff are available to provide orientation and assistance in searching this information superhighway.

10. Outreach Services to inner city housing communities, nursing and retirement homes, day care centers, and other institutions, ensure access to library service to all segments of our community. We are particularly proud of our outreach services to economically disadvantaged children to help them succeed in school and give them a lifelong love for reading."[39]

The library tax measure has been introduced but has not been debated by the local legislative committee. The committee's approval is needed to move the issue to the floor of the house. The previous two sentences demand further explanation! The committee cited was not in Montgomery, but was the committee made up of the legislators whose district has part of Madison County. There is a euphemism called "legislative courtesy," which means not to interfere with a fellow legislator's bill. In so many words, obstructionist legislators like Albert Hall from Gurley are able to hold the county, and particularly Huntsville, hostage to his views by not letting the bill leave Madison County. The other local legislators follow suit for fear of reprisal. That is the way the Alabama legislators keep their power over local issues, instead of acting like statesmen to deal with the larger problems of Alabama!

Many Madison County residents support the proposed tax. Sixty three percent of county residents have a library card, which were nearly 170,000 citizens. That was one and one half times the national average of 40 percent. There was a 40 percent increase in usage during the last 4 years, but with virtual level funding.[40]

Huntsville City Councilman Jim Putnam said he would try to kill the proposed citywide referendum because city leaders refuse to use their influence to stop the Huntsville Housing Authority plans to buy and renovate a University Drive apartment complex for low-and-moderate-income housing. Putnam further said that the money did not include any new or expanded facilities in his District 5 neighborhoods. Putnam cast the lone dissenting vote as the city council passed a resolution asking the state lawmakers to vote themselves a tax increase.[41]

In April 1994 the Alabama Legislature approved the referendum to be held in Madison County for a 2-mill tax levy. The bill contained the following provisions, which apparently helped some recalcitrant legislators vote for it.

225

- The tax would be in effect for eight years after which it would come up for another vote.
- At least 30 percent of the proceeds must be used to fund rural operations.
- The tax would automatically be repealed if the county or city reduced its library appropriations from present levels.
- Rural residents would be excluded from the tax in rural precincts that vote it down but the countywide vote passes.
- Three additional members would be appointed to the present five-member city-dominated board as follows: one each from County Commission Districts 1, 2, and 4, provided that none of the new appointees reside in the Huntsville city limits.[42]

The Citizens for Better Libraries, chaired by Ernest C. Kaufmann II, joined forces with the Public Library's Board of Directors, the Huntsville Library Foundation and the Friends of the Library to explain how that money will provide needed long-term funding to meet the growing demands place on the local library system.

In *The Huntsville Times* Sunday paper of May 29, 1994, Donna Schremser, Director, Huntsville Public Library, wrote a lengthy column asking for support in the upcoming 2-mill tax vote for the library. The case was well made again, as it had been done before.[43]

The property tax referendum for the library was held on Tuesday, June 7, 1994. The results? **Defeat!** *The Huntsville Times* editorial of June 12, 1994 will provide the after-action perspective.

"The library: voter anger

The talk on the street and several recent letters to the editor all make the same argument as to why voters here rejected a 2-mill property tax for the library: the people were protesting recent actions by the City of Huntsville, namely the changed (and still changing) garbage and trash policies and the City Council's decision to help a private developer build a new downtown hotel.

More than 23,000 people countywide voted against the library tax. Certainly, not every one of those was casting a protest vote against the hotel or the garbage changes. Neither issue, for example, affects voters outside the Huntsville city limits.

In Madison, voters had only recently imposed an 11.5-mill property tax for county schools. Many of them apparently believed they were paying enough. Out in rural Madison County, there persists an anti-Huntsville sentiment. If the library is seen as a city-dominated program, then the tax issue could have inflamed that sentiment.

Actually, library usage by non-city residents is proportionally greater than the money contributed to the library by Madison County and the other incorporated municipalities. Why should county residents pay more when they're already getting a bargain?

As for Huntsvillians, taking their frustration out on the library wasn't exactly fair. The library board isn't involved in either garbage or hotels. Indeed, the library was forced to ask the voters for a special tax because other city priorities has resulted in level funding over the past several years.

Note the library has been doubly penalized – once by the city, again by the voters angry at the city. A member of people who voted against the millage have gone out of their way to emphasize that they don't have a problem with the library itself. A few even sent flowers to the library director.

So if this anger is real, what other means did the voters have to register their objections? Neither the hotel nor the garbage changes were submitted to referendum, and under the law, such referendum would not be legal without a special act of the Legislature. What were disenchanted citizens to do?

A direct opportunity

One thing they could have done – and still can do – is register their views at the ballot box later in the summer. Three City Council seats are up for election, and incumbents are running in two of the districts.

District elections should mean that voters can address in their neighborhoods without seeing their wishes subjugated to other views elsewhere in town. At least that's how the system is supposed to work – but it only works if people vote. And in Huntsville, off-year elections often draw only a quarter of the registered voters.

They won't like hearing this, but Huntsvillians (some of them, anyway) who voted against the library tax didn't have a good reason to do so. But the law doesn't require a good reason; the majority of those who vote make the decision.

Let's hope that as the library struggles to meet demands, some of those who voted against the tax will find a way to help the library. Remember, voluntary contributions are just as useful as taxes."[44]

There were 85 voting precincts in the 1994 election in Madison County. Approximately 50 of those were in the City of Huntsville, which comprised 67 percent of the population. Only 14 precincts voted yes on the referendum, a clear **no** vote from within the city. None of the county precincts voted yes. Refer back to the last four provisions in the referendum cited previously. The county voters would receive fair consideration if the city voters approved, which did not happen.

The voters have spoken. They have the lowest taxes and are willing to pay any price to keep them that way, even to ensure their children are less prepared to become well-informed responsible citizens of the future. The ultimate test of parents is what kind of adults they raised.

If you think education is expensive, try ignorance. A study found that someone at age 50 with little education had the disease pattern of an educated person ten years older. " In 1960, mortality rates for white American men with the highest levels of education were roughly 10% lower than those of white men with the least education. By 1990-97, the difference has increased to 70%. A similar, though much less pronounced, trend was observed in the mortality rates of white women."[45]

In August 1994 the library board held a luncheon for John Ehinger, editorial editor for *The Huntsville Times*, to present him the board's Distinguished Service Award. Bravo, John, your handiwork was frequently cited (without name) in this history. You have influenced many Huntsvillians and county residents,

In October 1994 a library branch was opened in Triana, a small community of about 400 folks in the isolated southwest corner of Madison County. It was housed in the north end of the Triana Youth Center at 280 Zierdt Road. The population was probably not big enough to support much library traffic, but the town's isolation made it deserving of the branch anyway. The selection was limited, but the branch served as an opportunity for the area residents to select books, audio, and video materials that can be ordered and delivered to the branch. The branch, in 2004, had two Internet computers. The library was open 16 hours per week, and had one paid staff member who covered all 16 hours. If she did not come to work, the library did not open. It had a large-screen television, the donor of which could not be determined. There were no volunteers nor was there a Friends of the Library group. There were 1,300-1,500 volumes, including reference materials, fiction and non-fiction for children, picture books, and paperbacks. It was not an impressive library operation, neither inside nor outside. Ten local children attended the Storytime End of Summer Party hosted by the librarian, Myrtle Binford, on July 22, 2004.

In December 1994, the Huntsville Public Library announced there would be a $50 fee to use the auditorium in the main library and $25 for use of the smaller conference room and the rooms in the Eleanor Murphy Branch on Charlotte Drive and the Bessie Russell branch on Sparkman Drive. Donna Schremser, library director, said the rooms needed refurbishing and estimated the cost at $20,000. "We're asking the people who use and abuse the rooms to pay for them." She added that the library does not have enough money to replace the carpeting, the wallpaper, broken equipment and items stolen from the rooms over the past seven years.

Many of the over 100 groups that use the rooms during the course of a year said that they had not budgeted for such an expense. They said the library should have budgeted for wear and tear, and provided better security to prevent vandalism and theft. In so many words, if its free, I'll use it, and let somebody else (the library) worry about it. Three groups offered to hold fund-raisers for the library. Mrs. Schremser said the fees might not be needed in 1996.[46])

"November 22, 1994

Donna B. Schremser, Director Huntsville-Madison County Public Library

P.O. Box 443, 915 Monroe Street Huntsville AL 35804

Dear Ms. Schremser:

Your letter (11/1/94) proclaiming The Library Board's intention to levy fees for patron's use of meeting rooms was read with disbelief and dismay.

In addition to the thought that the action subverts the necessary egalitarian nature of such a fundamental institution as the public library, it is sickening to think that such an economically fortunate city and county can not provide proper library facilities for its citizens. Our well-heeled city and county governments stand as in a flush watershed in the flow of money from federal programs and associated commercial enterprises. For these governments to decline to fully support our public library is simply unthinkable. For The Library Board to attempt to reconcile and salve the apparent bad judgments of our local officials by taxing non-profit groups is disconcerting and disappointing.

These comments are submitted on behalf of the Nighttime Great Books Discussion Group.

Yours truly,

Townsend L. Walker. Sr.

Copies to:

Board: c/o Mrs. Roscoe 0. Roberts, Jr., Chairman

Steve Hettinger, Mayor

City Council: c/o Mr. James P. Putnam, President

County Commissioners: c/o Mike Gillespie, Chairman"[47]

That was a beautiful letter, one that I would have liked to have written had I been involved in the issue. The writer made sure that the appropriate governing officials received the letter to reinforce their responsibilities in this matter. Bravo, Townsend Walker!

It takes all kinds of people to make the world go around, but why do they seem to associate with our Huntsville-Madison County Public Library?

"February 9, 1995

Mr. Stephen Baker, 1506 Owens Drive, Huntsville, AL 35801

Dear Mr. Baker:

We regret to inform you that your Interlibrary Loan privileges are suspended until further notice. This is a result of the loss by you of "Mercury Poisoning from Dental Amalgam", which you reported lost on January 4, 1995, when, in fact, the book was not lost, but was given/mailed by you to the White House with an accompanying letter from you.

The book was returned by the White House to the loaning library along with a letter of explanation as to how and from whom they had received the book.

Again, the acquiring of materials from other libraries through our Interlibrary Loan service is a privilege and you have abused this privilege.

Sincerely,

Patti Nicolaysen Interlibrary Loan

cc: D. Schremser

    D. Lilly"[48]

On March 15, 1995, the Library Board passed a resolution naming the Hazel Green's new library building after Tillman Hill. Hill was the District #1 Commissioner of Madison County from 1976 to 1996. He funded the new building and used county workers for the site preparation and much of the construction. The land was donated by the Lowe Family, represented by the grandson, Carlton O'Neill. This new building is set back from Route 431 a hundred yards and is a hundred yards north of the MacDonald's Restaurant.

When you walk around the inside, you will be struck by the emptiness of one third of the bookshelves. The building was provided enough shelving to provide adequate capacity for 20 years. Patrons can go to the iBistro Library Catalog for the Huntsville Library's system to look up books throughout the county and have them delivered to the Hill Branch. The "iBistro" library electronic catalog was set up by Sirsi, a Huntsville founded company that has world-wide customers for the service. The Madison County Commissioner for District #1, Roger Jones, contributed $17,500 in 2003 as a typical per year amount to the Huntsville-Madison County Main Library. Each district commissioner contributes in a similar manner, but the county district funds are not earmarked for the neighborhood libraries.

The library has three computers for Internet access. The librarian's desk is not in a position to monitor the contents of the computers continuously, so the employees must wander around to perform that task. Their familiarity with the local people makes this task easier, compared to the main library where total strangers are using the computers.

The library was staffed by 3 part-time employees and 12-15 volunteers. The area also had a strong friends of the library group with 8-10 folks on the steering committee to support the library. In succeeding years the friends group held numerous fund-raising activities, such as 1500 chicken dinners cooked and delivered throughout the library branch service area. In 2000 they held a comic "Womanless Wedding" at the Hazel green High School auditorium. A mock wedding was staged by men (town fathers?) all dressed as women, and there were sure some ugly "women."

The librarians keep in touch with the librarians at Hazel Green High School across the highway from the branch. Brochures are available at the school library, publicizing Tillman Hill Branch special events such as a program for teens on the second Tuesday of each month. The program provided "cool" music, a movie, sodas and snacks. Maybe the teens might be enticed to borrow a book. The teens those days were over programmed with so many other activities that reading a book (for fun?) might be far down the list. But the program has a cost, because the library had to pay $250 per year to a company to show old movies.

There were numerous problems and issues raised about the use of the library rooms by outside groups for decades. After one recent situation, the director and library board established a lengthy policy in 1995:

"Rules For Use of Auditorium and Conference Rooms

The Meeting Rooms of the Huntsville-Madison County Public Library are primarily available to the following types of groups:

1. Educational.
2. Civic.
3. Cultural.
4. Governmental (Meaning a group sponsored by a city, county, state or federal agency.)
5. Employee groups of commercial firms provided that the meeting room is not used for any sales, promotional, or profit-making type meeting.
6. Profit-making organizations sponsoring an educational type of program of a non-profit nature, provided the meetings are opened freely to the general public.
7. Any meeting of the Friends of the Library or Library Foundation.
8. Denominational groups, organizations, or associations affiliated with more than one church, will be allowed the use of the meeting rooms when no religious services are to be conducted. The rooms may not be used in order to provide a forum to organize or build membership for one particular church, congregation or equivalent thereof.
9. All groups may be required to provide written documentation of the above (which may include charter, bylaws, or articles of incorporation or such other documentation as may be requested) to the Library Administration 72 hours prior to the use of the meeting room.
10. Individuals are not eligible to use the library meeting rooms unless they officially represent one of the groups that meet the requirements listed above.

The Library will enter a letter of agreement with groups using meeting rooms on the following basis:

1. Any group which charges an admission fee except where the admission charge is nominal and for a nonprofit educational purpose.
2. Groups seeking reservations for a series of meetings, which would designate the library meeting room as the regular meeting place for that organization for any substantial period of time.

Library meeting rooms cannot be used for the following:

1. Dance or musical recitals.
2. Graduation ceremonies.
3. Gaming clubs.

The Director may deny use of the auditorium or other meeting rooms to qualified groups for the reasons listed below:

1. A qualified group whose program contemplates political action as opposed to temperate discussion. The distinction drawn by the Board is not the distinction between controversial and non-controversial discussions. The discussion of controversial subjects in the library meeting rooms is neither forbidden or discouraged. The test, however, is one of action as opposed to discussion.
2. A qualified group using it for an initial introductory or explanatory meeting to be followed by other meetings in another location where fees will be charged.
3. The group has violated a rule or has misrepresented the purpose of the organization or the meeting to be held at the library.

All meetings must abide by the following general rules:

1. The distribution and/or consumption of alcohol is prohibited.
2. All meetings must be open to the general public.
3. Groups using the meeting room will be expected to conform to all library rules as required of other patrons.

4. All fees, $50.00 for the use of the Auditorium, $25.00 for the use of the A/B Meeting Room must be paid in advance.

5. The meeting room must be left in a neat and orderly condition upon completion of the meeting.

6. Groups which are not considerate of library policies will be denied further use of the meeting rooms.

7. Groups which have been approved to use the meeting rooms will receive a copy of these policies and must have a responsible party sign the accompanying form that they will abide by these policies."[49]

The library system, including a city and a county, made it more difficult to manage funds when they came from multiple sources. There was one city source, but as many as 12-14 county sources. The following memorandum was just one example of the multiplicity of funding sources.

"TO: Larry Conwell
   City Finance Department
FROM: Donna Schremser, Library Director
RE: County Match for City Capital Plan Funds DATE:
March 7, 1995
Funds from the County, above FY 1993 funding, to match the City of Huntsville Capital Plan funds for books in the current fiscal year are verified as follows:
Madison County Commission has provided $5,846 above FY 1993 funding to date.
The Robert Neaves Center directly purchased $2,500 in books for the Library in October, 1994.
Commissioner Rob Colson provided $5,000 from his district on February 23, 1994.
Commissioner Tillman Hill has appropriated $16,000 from his district budget, and the Hazel Green Friends of the Library have funded $4,000. All $20,000 of those funds have been received.
To date the Town of New Hope has provided $2,400 and the Friends of the New Hope Library has provided $600 for books, a total of $3,000.
The City of Madison has provided $5,148 of their total increase over FY 1993 appropriation of $10,297 for books above the previous fiscal year.
The Town of Triana has provided $684 to date for books.
Total matching funds for books from the County received to date to match the City of Huntsville Capital Plan monies for books is $42,178.
Total request for release of funds from City of Huntsville Capital Plan is $42,178."[50]

The Library raised the per-day fine by 5 cents in April 1995. Most of the people interviewed at the library did not protest the increase, particularly since the county voters failed to pass the 2-mill levy to benefit the library. One patron, who shall remain unnamed, paid a 90-cent fine at the old rate, said, "I think it's enough, people pay enough."[51]

The Huntsville Times, as usual, was ready with an editorial,

"The library: necessary steps

Society never seems to run out of angry people. [this author's italics] So some testy taxpayer will probably rush to the Huntsville City Council to complain about the higher fees for overdue books at the public library.

What the public must understand is that the library here is one of the community's most popular government services. And public use and expectation are growing all the time. Some seven out of every 10 Madison Countians have library cards; nationally, the figure is three out of 10.

Come April 1, the new fine for overdue books will be 15 cents per day, an increase of five cents. Some skinflint is sure to howl, but other public libraries charge more. In Mobile, the fine is 50 cents a day.

After several years of level appropriations, the library managed to get an additional $50,000 out of the City Council this year, which was remarkable because the council was cutting other agencies. Still, both the library and the community would have gained enormously if local voters had approved the 2-mill property tax that was defeated in a public referendum last year.

In an information age, libraries are more important than frills. They are essential services. They offer not only books, magazines and newspapers but also videotapes, computers and software, compact discs and even works of art. House Speaker Newt Gingrich, who wants to cut off federal money for public radio broadcasting, is a big fan of the nation's libraries.

But just because libraries are free to the users, they're not free to operate or to staff. If local residents want the present library system maintained and improved, they're going to have to pay for it. People who keep materials past their due date are denying others the chance to use those materials. That abuse costs money, too.

And for those who just can't stand the thought of an extra nickel a day, there's an easy and obvious alternative: *Return the books on time.*"[52] [this author's italics]

"Once upon a time..." are those wonderful words that we've all heard with pleasure, because we children knew that we were going to be read a story from a book. How many of you have read a story to your own children or grandchildren that began with those magical words?

Less than one hundred years ago children did not go to school, but started to work before ages 8-10. Fast forward to the modern era. Now we cannot do enough for our children. They go to school for at least 12 years, with a few exceptions. We drive them to the library. They search the Internet for information. Children's books are a lucrative and fast growing industry. They come in all shapes, sizes, materials and colors. The books open a wider universe to all children, regardless of age.

Libraries are more than books. Libraries are gathering points for story telling. The Huntsville Library's International Media Center has a strong collection of foreign films. The Computer Center on the second floor is usually being used to capacity. The Heritage Room on the third floor contains an ever-increasing amount of genealogical material. In 1996 the library offered many features for learning about our world, and especially in Huntsville, learning about things beyond our earth. But this has been true for many years, and will continue in the future. *The Huntsville Times* continues to be a constant supporter of the public library, because the library was the fountain of our culture. And when you go to the library, you can drink from a fire hose of knowledge and reading fun.

Well, readers, it is time to have another episode of the city versus county funding issue. A letter follows:

"**Huntsville**, A Future on the Horizon
Jim Putnam, Huntsville City Council, Representing District Five
P.O. BOX 308 HUNTSVILLE, ALABAMA 35804 (205) 532-7375
November 7, 1995
Mrs. Roscoe O. Roberts, Jr.,
Chairperson Huntsville Public Library Board...
Dear Mrs. Roberts,

The City Council recently learned that the Madison County Commission has, in some cases, reduced or eliminated funding to agencies and organizations supported by the City of Huntsville. It has come to the Council's attention that this reduction in funding, again in some cases, has resulted in reduction of services to citizens of the City of Huntsville.

This is a serious concern to the City Council and the Council is disturbed that county funding reductions are being passed on as reductions in services to city residents. By resolution (copy enclosed) [not available], the City Council has adopted the position that if it is determined that any agency or organization supported by city funding reduces services to city residents as a result of reduced funding by the Madison County Commission, then those agencies will be subject to review to consider reductions in City Council funding for the remainder of the year, and subject to reductions in future years. The City of Huntsville simply cannot afford to continue to pickup additional costs to provide services for those who live outside of Huntsville and do not pay a fair share.

We appreciate the service the Library provides to our citizens and look forward to a continued cordial relationship.

Sincerely,

Jim Putnam, President of the City Council

JP/hf Enclosure CC: Mrs. Donna Schremser, Director"[53]

Bravo, Jim!

On December 1, 1995 the library initiated the Quick Pick program. These were hot titles that rent for $2 for one week, but you cannot reserve them or check them out more than once. Patrons want the hot titles immediately, and the fee system helped defray book costs and kept the books moving through the system to reach more people in a shorter time.[54]

The library staff does more than ladle out books. They use their creativity to raise money to improve library services. The library needed money to replace a Bookmobile with a broken air conditioner. They gave local leaders a tour in the Bookmobile. When the ride was over, the workers handed out paper towels to wipe the perspiration off. And got their money. When a promised donation from a county commissioner was slow in coming, Susan Markham, the library's director of extension and outreach, stopped by with an empty satchel and told him she wouldn't leave until he filled it up. She got her money. Bravo, Susan!

September 25, 1996 – The board discussed how the names for branch libraries were chosen, and that a branch could either be given a name in honor of a particular person, or a name that has a geographical designation indicating the community in which the branch was located. For the library's new branches, the board prefers to have names which are indicative of location. If an individual had been influential in the establishment of the branch, then the board may honor that person by naming the branch meeting room after him/her, and placing a portrait of the person in the branch.

Four branches were opened in 1997, each of which took varying lengths of time to bring to fruition. The library officials applied for federal grants, which required endless hours of grant-writing, money–seeking and budget-juggling. Donna Schremser, library director, credited enthusiasm, imagination and hard-work thinking from the staff to allow the library to expand so dramatically in one year.

The largest library branch was the City of Madison Branch, which opened in June 1997. The City of Madison underwent tremendous growth from 1989 onward. In 1980 the population was just over 4,000. In 1990 it was almost 15,000 and in 2000 it was 29,300. In 2004 the population was estimated at 34,000 and still growing. The average age of a Madison resident was 42 years, which meant loads of children. Those demographics went in the general plan for the library's internal arrangement. The building's outside architecture was meant to be contemporary, not traditional. Jeanelle Moritz, head librarian, said that 75 percent of the Madison residents had library cards compared to the national average of 40 percent.

The Madison library building was funded by a tax levy voted by the residents of Madison City. The building cost was almost $1.5 million. The architect was Larrel Hughes and the contractor was Woodward Construction. The branch was placed in an open area several hundred yards from the intersection of Hughes Road and Old Madison Pike, less than a half mile from the city's municipal complex. It was in a convenient location and can be accessed from the aforementioned roads.

The building was sited with two sides close to a wooded area. The green roof blended with the tree foliage. The building front and right sides were open and visible from the main roads. Parking lots were on three sides, with a roomy covered drive-through area available in case of inclement weather and handicapped persons.

The entrance foyer was designed with specific community needs in mind. All but the smallest library buildings had a community meeting room, which can be used for story hours, special library events and as a non-library community meeting place. The Madison building, therefore, had the restrooms immediately to the left and the meeting room immediately to the right. Both can be easily accessed if the room was used for a community meeting without going into the library proper. There was a second set of doors that can be closed to the library for non-library events if needed.

The Frank Morris Meeting Room had a fire-code limit of one hundred persons and had small kitchen facilities hidden behind folding doors at the left front. There was also a concealed chair storage space. The plaque for Frank Morris outside the meeting room also included Braille words.

Larrell Hughes did a wonderful job meeting the general requirements of the library's program document and satisfying the library committee's desires as the items surfaced. Beyond the foyer the library opened up into one large room that allows the eyes to rove at will to take in all aspects of the multifunctional space. Upon entering the large room, take time to look up to the ceiling and the large skylight in the center. It illuminates the central area and was a focal point. The skylight was heavily tinted, but there was radiant heat which warms up the circulation desk when the sun angle was just right. But look around more closely so you do not overlook the supporting metal supports and the air ducts that were painted a matching green so they were almost oblivious to the casual observer.

The entire library administrative and checkout area were centered in the middle of the area. Everything was placed around that area. The library staffing was to be minimal, so the employees needed to be able to observe the maximum area with ease. Behind the checkout and information semicircle, the workroom was to the right and the friends of the library bookstore was to the left. This building was thoughtfully designed to separate the children (Noise) and the adults (Quiet). The children's area was to the right and consisted of several sections. To the far right was the children's story area, which was partially into the eastern bay window area.

In the right rear was the teenage area, separated from the children's area by a semi-opaque glass-block wall and another glass-block wall on the other side. But the teenage area was easily observable from the central desk. Observation was always of importance in libraries. Around the back of the central area was the reference deck and reading tables. This area required an employee to be at the reference desk if observation was needed.

The left side of the building was the adult area, divided as usual by category of reading material. On the west side of the building, at the outer edge of the adult book area was a bay window area with lounge chairs for comfortable reading. Try it and you'll like it. To the immediate left was an adult reading room separated by a glass-block wall. It had a normal width door, which made it very quiet inside for serious reading. Walking through the door was just like turning off the noise switch. Some of the frequent visitors to this room refer to it as the sleeping room because it was just so, so quiet and out of the mainstream of the hustle and bustle of the remainder of the library. The Sleeping Room was 21 x 39 feet in dimension. Try it and you'll really, really like it.

Outside the right rear of the building, connected through the children's area, was an 18 x 30 feet patio. Around the area was a see-through brick wall and gate. The patio had one tree and a rubberized metal table with four benches around it. The tabletop had the alphabet and the numbers in holes on the top for the kiddies.

There was a 33 x 48 feet patio with 2 picnic tables and 4 other benches outside the left rear of the building, connected through the adult area. Beyond this patio was a wooded area was a 58-yard long nature trail, which led to the end of the Cottonwood Trail cul-de-sac. The parking lot on the west side also had a covered walkway leading to the entrance.

The Madison friends of the library raised over $135,000 to equip and furnish the inside of the library. The children's area was smartly furnished for the children of the 21st Century. It always seemed like a beehive of activity whenever I visited the building. As was done for the main library in Huntsville, donations were sought associated with specific internal features and furnishings. The meeting room went for $25,000, the Internet Center for $5,000 and the display case for $1,000.

There were 6 Internet computers, 2 play-station computers and 4 iBistro catalog computers. The capacity was 124,000 books and 9,400 video and audio tapes.

The Richard Showers Branch Library was opened in June 1997. It was located in the Dr. Richard Showers, Sr. Recreational Center at 4600 Blue Spring Road. The Center also housed the YMCA and Girls Inc. after-school programs, so there were children coming and going to different activities. It had seven computers in its two rooms. It was designed for patrons from eighteen months to eighteen years old. It had no friends of the library organization. A memorial to Dulcina DeBerry, the first Negro librarian in Huntsville, was on the wall with her picture and story.

The Oscar Mason Branch opened in August 1997. It was located in the Oscar Mason Community Center on Holmes Avenue. It had six computers and provided computer classes to adults. It had two rooms. It conducted many children's programs. The toddler time story hour was observed. The librarian read and showed pictures from the books and elicited responses. They demonstrated plenty of enthusiasm. This was a crucial age for children to become interested in books. Reading to children even before eight months old was important for their long-term development.

Madison County had an insatiable thirst for books and other library materials. Huntsville's circulation per capita was 7.46 in 1996, second highest in the nation behind Denver's 12.29. Madison County has 75 percent of its inhabitants holding library cards, almost twice as high as the national average of 40 percent. Compare some statistics with our neighbor to the south, Birmingham. Birmingham had 19 branches, 300 employees, a $12 million budget and made 1.5 million loans. Huntsville had 12 branches, 130 employees, a $4 million budget and made 1.9 million loans. Another way to look at the numbers is: in Birmingham it cost $8 per loan; while in Huntsville it cost $2.10 per loan. Another comparison was that Birmingham made

5,000 loans per employee, while Huntsville made 14,615 loans per employee. Perhaps "insatiable thirst for books" was an understatement.[55]

On Thursday, October 2, 1997, the Huntsville Subregional Library for the Blind and Physically Handicapped celebrated its 30th anniversary. It is the oldest such library in the country. It provided recorded books and magazines to people who were blind or otherwise disabled, those disabled who can't hold a book or turn pages and people with reading disabilities because of such health problems as strokes.

Joyce Smith, the original director who retired in 2001, remembered "we had an empty room" and lots of dreams. Gradually the room filled up. It grew from 22 clients in 1997 to 435 in 1997, 30 years later. The youngest client was 2 years old, and the oldest was 102.[56] The department was called subregional because it was subordinate, and still is, to the regional blind library in Montgomery, Alabama. All materials were provided by the National Library Service, which was an element of the Library of Congress. All materials were free. The Huntsville library paid only for office supplies and salaries.[57]

Gabrielle Liddon, coordinator of the International Media Center, said the library division boasted 60-70 foreign language magazines, more foreign language films than anywhere in Huntsville, English-as-a-second language tapes and foreign language newspapers. The Center was honored by the American Library Association for its substantial efforts in bringing foreign-language material to hundreds of patrons in the city. Do you think you are smart and know everything? Stop in some time and go through the stacks, shelves and containers of foreign material. See how much you understand. Do you know what they call a person that speaks two languages? Answer: bilingual. Do you know what they call a person who speaks three languages? Answer: trilingual. Do you know what they call a person who speaks only one language? Answer: American! Ask Gabrielle Liddon, who was born in the Alsace region of France, but the territory has bounced between Germany and France. She speaks English, French, German, Spanish and Italian. How about you?

Ms. Liddon said there were 17 languages represented in the International Media Center. In each of those languages she tried to have available fiction and nonfiction adult books, fiction and nonfiction children's books, movies on tape, dictionaries, and encyclopedias, and magazines. The largest checked-out language was Chinese. Her old-time patrons were the ones who ask for more when they have read everything. The largest percentage of patrons were English speakers born in the United States, who want to brush up on language and culture before they visit a foreign country.

The library on Fountain Circle did not have an International Media Center. The one in Fort Book was the brainchild of Bob Schremser, the husband of library director, Donna Schremser. He was a librarian and had seen such centers in other locations. The International Media Center was well placed by the elevator and front stairs for easy access.[58]

The time was now April 1997, and it was National Library Week, but it was also the 10th anniversary of Fort Book. As usual, *The Huntsville Times* provided in-depth coverage of the library's facilities. An article about the International Media Center, written by Anne Marie Martin, started with, "A Turkish man browses through the shelved books. A young Korean woman sits at a table reading a magazine. A Chinese man picks out a couple of videos labeled with Chinese characters. An American woman checks out a taped refresher course on French to prepare for a trip to Paris." What a great country of immigrants and what a great city of immigrants. Huntsville was all of that, and more.

The Huntsville Times laid out some library statistics for the year 1997.

- 203,775 library card holders

- 4,000 daily visitors (all branches)
- 8,500 children in the summer program
- 450,000 books
- 19,935 videos
- 10,650 compact discs
- 1,864,048 books, tapes and discs checked out in a year.

The circulation in 1987 was 937,667, so it almost doubled in the last ten years to 1,864,048. The number of library cardholders increased from 106,554 in 1988 to 203,775 in 1997. The moral to this story: Build a great edifice like Fort Book; staff it with professional and energetic personnel; have good financial support from government officials; and the patrons will flock to use it.

In the chapter about the 1980s I used the term, Golden Decade. That decade (11 years) ran from 1987 through 1997. Fort Book opened in April 1987. The Gurley Branch opened in May 1988 and New Hope in September 1988. The Madison Branch moved to a new home in May 1989. In October 1994 the Triana Branch opened. In 1995 the Hazel Green/Tillman Hill Branch opened in March. The Oscar Mason Branch opened in August 1996. The grand finale of that decade was 1997, and it was enough to take your breath away. A bigger and better Madison Branch opened in June, quickly followed by Richard Showers Branch in June, Monrovia Branch in July and Bailey Cove Branch in August. The driving forces behind that library tree of many branches were Donna Schremser, Director, and Susan Markham, Head of Outreach. **Magnificent, Ladies!**

The last several paragraphs were about our wonderful library. But now we must regress to the topic of Money, Money and more Money. Our public library was almost totally supported by public monies, yours and mine. We citizens collectively have the responsibility to pay attention to where our money was going. Our City Council representatives made the strategic decisions about the library, and the library director made the tactical decisions about the specific disposition. In between was the Library Board, which oversees the director. The four components of the system, citizens, council, board and director each had different roles to play with varying degrees of responsibility and authority. Each participant needs to be a player in this equation. The newspaper allowed the players to find the information about the library's finances. The citizens must then play their part to show their approval, disapproval or neutrality through one of several means of communication to any of the other participants. Americans were free to write letters and make telephone calls to the three-elected/appointed groups/officials. Make use of this opportunity if you feel the urge.

In 2004 a joke was going around in Moscow: In America there is democracy and the people have freedom to criticize President Bush. We have democracy in Russia, we can also criticize President Bush [but not President Putin.] Let's get back to the money.

"Library asks city for extra $255,000

Opening two branches, upgrading its computer system and accepting a grant from the Gates Library Foundation have helped strain the Huntsville-Madison Public Library's budget.

Library officials turned to the Huntsville City Council for help. Officials outlined at a work session Thursday night their reasons for wanting an additional $255,000 from the city this budget year.

"We really find ourselves in a bind," said Jane Roberts, chairman of the library board. Donna Schremser, director of the library, told council members that the request would be "about like a one-timer."

"If we get over the hump this year, its not like we're going to be back every year asking for more money at midyear," Schremser said.

Council members said they would consider the request at the midyear budget review at their April 16 (1998) work session.

City law requires the city to keep 10 percent of its budgeted appropriations in reserve. Now, the reserve has about $400,000 more than the 10 percent level.

Councilman Mark Hall, who is chairman of the finance committee, said the city has consistently given the library more money every year, including one year when it cut appropriations for other agencies. He said after the meeting that other agencies would have pressing demands for more money at midyear, too.

The city this year gave the library $2.7 million from the operating budget and $100,000 from the capital budget. The council increased the library appropriation $100,000 while keeping the money level for other outside agencies.

The city's additional money went to secure the Gates Foundation grant. The money was used for hiring a computer trainer and equipment. The value of the Gates grant was about $300,000 in computer hardware and software. The foundation, started by Microsoft founder Bill Gates and his wife, gives the grants to provide computers and software to public libraries to train library workers and residents to use the Internet. The Regional Computer Training center opened in February 1998. [The Gates Foundation Library Program Grants were given first to the states that needed them the most. Guess what folks? Alabama was number 1 on that list. The Alabama Public Library Service received $248,400 from that grant, of which Huntsville received just over $129,000 and we were the very first in the country to receive our personal computers as part of that grant.[59]

After the work session, Schremser said the library is spending about $99,000 this year for trainers' salaries, telephone lines (which are costing about $1,800 a month) and other items connected to the Internet training center. It will cost the library about $50,000 a year after this year to run the training center, she said. At that rate, in five years it will cost the library as much to run the center as it got from the Gates grant.

Asked after the meeting if receiving the grant was worth it, Schremser said, "The option was, don't have any computers and don't teach the public anything." [How would readers of this history vote?]

Library officials also told the council that opening the Bailey Cove and Blue Springs Road Recreation Center library branches cost about $220,000 and $42,200, respectively. Asked after the meeting if those branches may have to close, Schremser said that would be a board decision."

The library also spent about $180,000 this year to improve its eight-year-old computer system separate from the Gates Foundation program. The library board had to borrow $180,000 from a line of credit at a bank since the fiscal year began Oct. 1, Schremser said. She said it will take about two years to repay the loan.

The library's operating budget has also been hit this year with increased costs of vandalism and increased security ($48,000) and maintenance and upkeep ($68,000.) Here's how the library board said it would use the additional $255,000:

- Restore book budget cuts, $98,000
- Restore audiovisual budget cuts, $12,000
- Supports for Russell branch floor, $5,100
- Bailey Cove branch roof repairs, $2,000
- Refurbish six study rooms, $8,400

- Refurbish eight public rest rooms, $30,000
- Replace six microfilm readers in the Heritage Room, $14,000
- Recover columns on first and second floors, $5,000
- Replace wall covers and molding at four windows and entrance, $2,000
- Replace three water fountains, $1,800
- Replace automatic doors at main library entrance, $8,900
- Salary increase for employees, $48,000
- Part-time computer center trainer, $15,000
- Blue Spring branch tutor/librarian."[60]

You now have all the information that the City Council, Library Board, and the Director had to make the decisions. What are your choices? Did you make those selections based on your usage preferences? Did you make those choices based on the general needs of over 203,000 library cardholders? Well, what was your vote?

Mayor Loretta Spencer told the City Council the city did not have the money. The council voted the midyear appropriation package down, 3-2. Councilmen Bill Kling, Mark Hall and Richard Showers voted against, while Ken Arnold and Glenn Watson for it. The Library Board then voted the following action to cover the shortages.

- Shortened the library open hours from 72 to 65, closing at 5 p.m. on Thursday instead of 9 p.m. and closing at 5 p.m. on Friday, Saturday and Sunday instead of 6 p.m.
- Fines for overdue books would be 25 cents per day, cassette tapes and compact discs increased to 25 cents a day, with the maximum fine changed from $7 to $10.
- Fines for overdue videotapes remains at $1 per day, but the maximum goes from $12 to $15.
- The charge for residents outside Madison County was raised from $10 to $15.
- Some high-priced magazines and newspapers will be dropped.

The council did vote to approve the repairs to the falling floor at the Russell Branch, the roof at the Bailey Cove Branch and the replacement of the damaged wall coverings and molding in the main library.

Earlier in this chapter some statistics were given comparing Birmingham and Huntsville. The *Times* article that discussed the 3-2 council vote also gave more statistics. Eight southeastern cities with similar populations between 225,000 and 286,000 (Huntsville's at 268,700 in the library area) were compared. Huntsville was 7 of 8 in total budget, having only 39 percent of Birmingham's. Huntsville was 7th in volumes owned. Huntsville 75 percent of the population holding library cards was 12 points higher that the next city. Huntsville was second in total loans and by far the lowest in cost per loan (budget divided by circulation). Now, all we have to do is get our city "mothers and fathers" to read those statistics.[61]

Mayor Loretta Spencer asked the city auditor's office to review the finances of the many agencies that get city tax dollars. The results were nothing new.

- A heavily used system that is weakly supported.
- Huntsville is 1st in Alabama in total circulation, but only 5th in per capita dollars.
- Huntsville is below the national average in city library spending per person, at $16 versus the national average of $22.
- Salaries are not too high.
- Spending on books is low.[62]

Well, readers, it is time for our periodic quote of a *Huntsville Times* editorial.

"Meet the library's needs

The library is an essential service. We must find a way to give it the resources it needs to do the job we expect it to do.

It's a good idea, this plan by Mayor Loretta Spencer to conduct independent audits of boards and agencies that receive city money every year. It substitutes facts and figures for arguments and counter-arguments.

But there's always the reality of unintended – though perhaps not unforeseen or unwelcome – consequences.

The city's audit of the library's finances is in. It shows, first and foremost, that all the things the library board has been saying are true – things about the library being used more than other libraries while getting much less in local tax support. A library serving a community the size of this one should have 844,000 items on its shelves. This library has 480,000.

That, of itself, puts Spencer and the City Council in the difficult position of trying to explain why they can't allocate more money to the library. Last spring, the library sought an additional $255,000 from the city. The council said no but later relented – a little. It gave the library $87,000 above what it had originally budgeted. At that time, Spencer, stung by criticism from the library's supporters, outlined all the money the city had provided the library over the past few years. Indeed, that dust devil of a controversy may well have been one factor in Spencer's decision to conduct the audit.

So does the library need more money? Yes. Should the city provide it? Yes – some of it. The library serves not just Huntsville but all of Madison County. The figures suggest that county government isn't paying its fair share when library usage by non-city residents is taken into account.

But there's a problem. The County Commission, which lacks the authority to impose taxes for most services, says it has no money, and it's telling the truth. It can't afford a new jail, which it desperately needs. It's struggling with parking needs around the courthouse. And it's under increasing pressure for more services for the county's growing population.

Still, the commission should do more if it can find a way. But it's clear that demands placed on the library by the community will require even greater assistance.

Several years ago, the library went before the voters seeking a tiny property tax increase to help out. The voters, angry with the city over other issues, said no. Perhaps it's time to go back to the voters.

In City Hall, at the courthouse and in every living room in Madison County, the public must acknowledge the fact that the library is a basic and essential service. Whatever the mechanism, the community must find a way to give the library the resources it needs to do the job we expect it to do.

The mayor's audit has cleared the air. Now let's find a solution."[63]

The paper stated the case, but have you ever wondered how many residents do not take the paper or read it? Those people don't get the word, and do not want to be informed! I wonder how many of the non-readers voted no to the tax proposal?

Keeping in mind the above information about the library's request for additional money, in *The Huntsville Times* of October 20, 1998 was this item. District 2 County Commissioner Faye Dyer had received $18,109 in discretionary money during the last fiscal year to give to the library. In July, during the time the library audit was being conducted, Mrs. Dyer apparently asked Mrs. Schremser, library director, to provide the salaries of the five highest-paid employees. The request apparently was not answered, so Dyer sent Schremser a terse, two-

240

paragraph letter in early October repeating her original request, after the city's audit was complete and released.

Dyer said, "We've already written the check out; it's sitting in the county safe. It's not that I think they're bad or don't deserve the money, but I've just heard a few rumblings that they're not as efficient as they need to be." Dyer also said that her husband's past employment with the library also weighed heavily in her decision not to turn over the money. Tom Dyer was a certified public accountant who performed audits for the library from 1986 until 1997/8, when he asked to be released from his contract. Mrs. Dyer said the Alabama Ethics Commission told her she should not give discretionary money to any agency where her husband had worked in the same budget year. Doing so could be construed as a conflict of interest, the ethics board said. It is obvious that either Mrs. or Mr. Dyer was in the wrong business if public money is tied up because of one family's ethics situation.

Mrs. Dyer further said "four or five" constituents asked her about the library's budget after the library voted in April to reduce operating hours and to increase fines on overdue books. Did those four or five folks believe that less money did not have consequences?

Donna Schremser declined to release the salary information to the *Times*, but she would provide it to Faye Dyer. The audit found that salaries in Huntsville were below the national average. As for inefficiency, as perceived by some of Mrs. Dyer's constituents, Huntsville has 106 full-time employees, whereas, Columbia, South Carolina, with roughly the same size served area, has 218 employees. The efficiency issue should rest on such facts.[64]

"The pot is calling the kettle black" is an old saying which brings us to the point, have there really been any impartial studies that tried to study the "efficiency" of government institutions. Efficiency is normally an oxymoron when it comes to government. I've been inside the government, and I've observed it from the outside. Wonder if Mrs. Dyer's work force is ready to stand the test for efficiency? Could they stand the test for friendliness? Do they have over 4,000 customers at their doors every day? If I had to bet a large sum of money on efficiency, the library or a county office, it would be an easy choice!

The check is in the mail according to *The Huntsville Times* of October 30, 1998. Madison County Commissioner Faye Dyer, who had been withholding $18,000 in tax money for the public library, released it. Dyer got the list of the five highest paid employees, as did the *Times*.

- Donna Schremser, library director, received an annual salary of $75,000. She worked at the library since 1977 and has been director since 1981.
- Emma Miller, head of the main library services, received $49,254.
- Susan Markham, head of extension and outreach services, is at $46,916.
- Regina Cooper, head of acquisitions and collection development, $44,004.
- Susan Royer, assistant library director, $34,412.[65]

The library profession has never been the profession to be in if your goal was to make good money. Let us look at some comments by the library's managers.
"MEMORANDUM
DATE: April 29, 1998
TO: Library Board
FROM: Director
SUBJECT: Report from Library Managers' Meeting
I wanted to report to the Board on our discussions at our quarterly Managers' Meeting, which we held on Monday. Of course, we had extensive discussion on our funding situation and how the Library services would be affected. The Managers know this is a tough year, but they

emphasized how much they like working at the Library. I am proud to share their comments with you.

We get to see new books.

The Director looks out for us.

Our families are important here, and the Library lets our family come first.

Flexibility! Flexible work hours and schedule.

There is an emphasis on training and funds available for conferences.

We get daily feedback, right on the job, from patrons.

Every day we're learning something.

The staff is a family and supports the personal times that occur in our lives.

We get to meet diverse people.

We have a good relationship with the community.

We like being "do-gooders." We like making a contribution to society.

Technology is exciting.

The Library looks at skills we have- not just degrees we have.

We look to staff first in hiring.

Staff development is important.

We get and like positive feedback from patrons.

There is a openness to knowledge here, and we are instrumental in getting and giving knowledge.

We have family activities for the whole staff- like the LSO barbecue.

Training.

We are empowered to speak for the Library in the community.

Consistent raises.

Being remembered.

We empower people.

We have a pleasant workplace, and it is clean.

Our benefits are good- pension plan, personal days, health insurance.

The Library forces us to be extroverts and work with people.

Makes us willing to try new things.

We have camaraderie within the staff.

There is a lack of competitiveness between departments, branches- we work together. This is a well used library.

We work in a place that is wildly successful.

The Library is important in the community and to newcomers.

The Library is a safe place for children.

Most of us love our jobs and our areas/branches.

We can be honest here, and we are able to say negative things."[66]

[Well, readers, how many of you are prepared to say that about your workplace?]

The wide spectrum of comments from happy and satisfied employees is reflected through several prisms. But the most important one is the library's leadership. Employees in the most attractive physical environments will be unhappy if the leadership has a style that grinds on the employees. Donna Schremser described her role as director as "Earth Mother." The employees are treated as a family, and they can come into her office any time to discuss problems and receive immediate feedback. This open door policy facilitates the flow of information and heads off problems that might not otherwise surface in a formal hierarchical structure. She had long working relationships with many of the staff. They know they will be supported when they develop ideas to make the library better. She expects great things, not mediocrity.[67]

Library officials decided to start the year 1999 with a return to the old open hours on Thursday and Sunday. Friday and Saturday hours will remain the same.[68]

Below is an example of the type of information provided by the technical services department.

"Technical Services Monthly Statistical Report, March 1999

I. Library Holdings	Total-Feb	Added Mar '99	Total Mar '99
Book Volumes	494,808	2,441	497,24
Book Titles	218,333	891	219,224
Audio Cassettes	15,141	35	15,178
Video Cassettes	20,951	202	21,153
Compact Discs	13,871	187	14,038
Books on CD	25	9	38
II. Miscellaneous Statistics			
Book Vol. Repaired		361	
Book Vol. Transferred		18	
III. Branch Statistics			
Books for Madison	23,699	599	24,298
Books for Gurley	5,304	41	5,345
Books for New Hope	7,378	125	7,521
Books for Hazel Green	14,138	253	4,438
Books for Monrovia	4,007	52	4,119
Books for D-home	1,498	58	1,558
Books for Triana	2,854	58	2,912
Books for Blue Spring	2,554	40	2,594
Books for Mason Court	3,952	75	4,027
Books for Bailey Cove	18,115	584	18,679"[69]

Earlier in this chapter a tax measure was surfaced in 1993 for new library buildings. The issue went nowhere. In that initiative was $250,000 for a new Gurley Branch building. The library's friends in Gurley were unhappy with the current building as it was falling apart. The library had a collection of 10,000 books and about 1,000 people in the Gurley area had library cards. The book lending business was doing well in Gurley. Those persistent volunteers had increased the building fund up to $30,000, but that was far short of the $300,000 need for a new building. The Huntsville-Madison Public Library developed the architectural plans for a new building, but money was not forthcoming. Throughout the late 1990s those persistent folks kept leaning on the city fathers, local legislators and county officials.

Persistence pays. In 2000 a new building designed for a library was opened in Gurley. The money and the labor came from many sources: the Huntsville management team; the state legislators; the county officials; other volunteers; and more fund-raisers. It happened because it was a true team effort by many folks to provide the current beautiful library at 225 Walker Street, just a short distance from the previous decrepit building. Below is an October 1999 document which demonstrated the planning and coordination necessary to ensure the project would be completed.

"Gurley Public Library Building Project 10/99

The Madison County Construction Crew will build the facility under the direction of Don Sanders, Foreman. They will be working under the supervision of Jerry Craig, Madison

County Commissioner, District 3. Other County employees will do all electrical and plumbing work. Five subcontractors will be required: roof, sheet rock, brick, carpet and tile.

Estimated supply costs for the new building are approximately $83,000, with no labor costs being charged. For comparison, the total project with labor costs is estimated at $143,500, for a savings of $60,500. Larrell Hughes confirms these projected costs are in line for the project.

Combined current revenue held by the City of Gurley and the Friends of the Gurley Library is $75,095. Commissioner Craig is aware of available State allocations that will finalize the amount needed for completion. In addition, several pledges are outstanding from earlier fund-raising efforts.

The Construction crew, using Madison County contracts and bidding out all items not under contract, will purchase building supplies. The City Clerk for Gurley will be responsible for paying all outstanding receipts, upon approval of the Gurley City Council. The Library will have no fiscal responsibility.

The building process will begin in late February or early March, dependent upon the weather: Completion date is slated for mid-August. The Construction crew will build the shelving and circulation desks during the winter months. Community help has been approved for assistance in sanding the shelving materials.

Susan Stokes, Interior Designer for L. Hughes and Associates is donating her assistance in providing interior layouts and color/materials selections."[70]

The new building contained a meeting room with a capacity of 50 persons named after Jerry L. Smith, a dedicated volunteer who died in 1998. There were four Internet computers and one iBistro library catalog computer. The friends of the library bought two free-standing carousels, just inside the front door to the left, which held the donated paperbacks for sale to raise money. The locally made shelves were not completely filled yet. The top shelves were almost nine feet high and empty because they were unreachable without a ladder, but they did provide excess capacity for the future. Several of the older branch buildings had been stuffed to capacity for many years. The friends of the library had 30-40 people participating, who had a goal of collecting and contributing $1800 per year for books and other materials. The Huntsville main library paid the utility bills. The fifteen volunteers kept the library open 25 hours per week in 2004. It is closed on Sunday. The library contained over 13,000 volumes.

In two of the earlier chapters there were items about the cleanliness of the library building. Since that time, scientists and housewives have proven that dirt does not go away by itself, so the folks in 1999 were still fighting the problem, witness the following internal memo:
"WAR ON DIRT [main library]
June Issue [1999]
The following has been accomplished since the last Board meeting:
We have a contract with a temporary service to provide a fill in janitor when one of our full time janitors is sick or on vacation. That is an additional expense, but helps keep everyone on schedule.
Polished all brass rails
Stripped and waxed back hallway
Dead shrubs pulled up
Extensive work on grounds
Let bids for meeting room carpet 5/17/99
    Cost will be approximately $5,000 for auditorium, A & B Meeting Rooms & Entry
    Recommend approval of bid with Carpet Systems
Larrell Hughes preparing recommendations for wall coverings and bathroom partitions

Exploring options for improving Youth Services, but we will need to wait until summer reading is over before actual work is done. We are looking at...

Options for kid chairs- new rubber covers or paint

Organize all AV together

New banners- primary colors would free up some banners for additional signage elsewhere

Options for preschool area- beanbag chairs, rugs

Working with Rock-Tenn Recycling to provide bins for office recycling, recycling of newspapers and magazines, and cardboard boxes. That will help eliminate clutter in workroom areas and offices and will generate some income for the library. We should be able to start that within the next two weeks."[71]

Money has always been important to a library's founding, maintenance and growth. The building, collection and services of the Huntsville Library in the 1950s were modest by today's standards. There is little value trying to compare 1950 with 2000 in approximate comparative economic or financial terms. The two situations were worlds apart. Today's sources of revenue are many compared to fifty years ago. The Huntsville Library had worked hard over the years to serve its patrons. The library personnel use the term patron to signify the people who borrow materials, because in a loose sense the citizens of the city and county pay taxes, which support the library. But the primary meaning of patron is one who is wealthy or influential, and used that position to help another person, or in this case, support the library. The Huntsville Library's patrons in 1999 were identified below:

"POLICY GOVERNERING RESTRICTED AND ENDOWMENT FUNDS

The following are designated funds managed by the Library Board of the City of Huntsville:

Restricted Reserve Funds

The Library has four $25,000 certificates of deposit, which are invested annually and mature each quarter of each fiscal year. These funds are set aside for emergency use only upon the approval of the Library Board. Interest income is deposited into the Library General Fund operating budget.

Total Restricted Reserve Funds $100,000

Thomas M. Moore Endowment Fund

Thomas Moore, Jr. bequeathed $600,000 to the Huntsville Public Library with the stipulation that the principal be invested and the return on that investment be utilized for the Library book fund specifically for the purchase of nonfiction and reference materials. This fund is invested in a mixture of treasury notes and government backed securities, and income from the fund is received monthly into the Library's General Fund operating budget. Anticipated yearly income is $36,000.

Total Thomas M. Moore Endowment Fund $600,000

Ephraim Camp Endowment Fund

The estate of Dr. Ephraim Camp provided a bequest of $100,000 to the Huntsville Public Library with the stipulation that the principal be invested and the return on the investment be utilized for the Library to purchase business reference materials for the Main Library Information and Periodicals Department. The fund is invested in a mixture of treasury notes and government backed securities, and income from the fund is received monthly into the Library's General Fund operating budget. Anticipated annual yearly income is $6,000.

Total Ephraim Camp Endowment Fund $100,000

Donald and Robbie Schnepf Endowment Fund

Established by a $100,000 gift from Robbie Schnepf, with the stipulation that the principal be invested and the return on the investment be utilized for the Eleanor E. Murphy

Branch Library to purchase fiction, best sellers, history, biographies, and mysteries. The fund is invested in a mixture of treasury notes and government backed securities, and income from the fund is received monthly into the Library's General Fund operating budget. Anticipated annual yearly income is $6,000.

Total Donald and Robbie Schnepf Endowment Fund $100,000

Friends of the Library Marelle Pruitt Endowment Fund

This fund began with a $10,000 bequest from the estate of Marelle Pruitt, former member of the Library Board and member of the Friends of the Library Board of Directors. The Friends of the Library have contributed to the fund each year, and the general membership of the friends can designate additional gifts to this special endowment. The fund has grown to $78,000 and is invested in government backed securities. Proceeds and additional contributions are reinvested in the fund, and once it reaches $100,000 the proceeds will be used to enhance the Library's book fund. Anticipated annual yearly income is $6,000.

Total Friends of the Library Marelle Pruitt Endowment Fund $78,000

Marie Eigenbrod Endowment Fund

Mrs. Eigenbrod made a $10,000 gift to the Library in appreciation of the many years of enjoyment she has received from using the Library. The fund is to be invested in a certificate of deposit, renewing annually, and the proceeds are to be used to enhance the Library's book fund. Estimated annual income from this fund is $500.

Total Marie Eigenbrod Endowment Fund $10,000

Susan Strong Grosser Endowment Fund

Established by a $10,000 gift from the estate of Susan Strong Grosser, the fund is to be invested in a certificate of deposit, renewing annually, and the proceeds are to be used to enhance the Library's collection of classic and enduring children's fiction and nonfiction books. Estimated annual income from this fund is $500.

Total Susan Strong Grosser Endowment Fund $10,000

Cecil and Margaret Ashburn Endowment Fund

Mr. and Mrs. Ashburn have established a permanent endowment fund with two gifts totaling $50,000. Mr. Ashburn requested that $10,000 is used to upgrade microfilm reader printers in the Huntsville Heritage Room, and the balance of $40,000 is invested and the proceeds are used to benefit the Archives and special historical collections of Huntsville Public Library. The fund is invested in a certificate of deposit, renewing annually. Estimated annual income from this fund is $2,200.

Total Cecil and Margaret Ashburn Endowment Fund $40,000

TOTAL ENDOWMENT FUNDS $938,000

Huntsville Public Library: Other Restricted Income

In addition to the restricted and endowment funds managed by the Library Board, the Library also receives income from the following sources, which place restrictions on the expenditures of those funds:

Marguerite C. Hawthorne Trust

This fund provides income to the Library that must be spent on music or books about music specifically for the Huntsville Public Library. The total fund is managed by U.S. Trust in New York City, and the Library receives 4% of the annual income of the trust payable quarterly. Total anticipated income annually is $10,000.

Caroline Powell Barrett Memorial Endowment Fund

This fund was established with memorial donations to the Huntsville Library Foundation. The Foundation manages the fund, which totals $9,800. The proceeds will be used to purchase children's books as well as adult books in the areas of marine biology, American history, and art. Total anticipated income annually is $500.

Jane Knight Lowe Endowment Fund

This fund was established with a grant from the Jane K. Lowe Charitable Foundation to the Huntsville Library Foundation. The Foundation manages the fund, which totals $10,480, and the proceeds will be used to purchase contemporary and classic fiction and children's books. Total anticipated income annually is $500."[72]

September 29, 1999 – Melissa Shepherd, head of Information and Technology Services, designed a Staff *Intranet* page. It included a staff directory, library policies, personnel policies, and activity calendar and forms that can be e-mailed to the proper person. The library received $60,000 from the foundation. Homer Hickham, a Huntsville resident, received $1,000 as an honorarium for being the speaker at the Vive le Livre in 1999. This was very modest compared to the usual fees asked by other nationally known speakers.

"Ready Rollers are aiming high!

By Dr. Kevin L. DeLaine, SON staff writer

On October 6, 1999 at 9:00 a.m., the Huntsville-Madison County Public Library unveiled the Ready Readers Van at the Meridian Street Head Start Center at Colonial Hills Elementary School where the principal is John Humphrey. Susan Markham, Associate Director of Branch and Outreach Services at Huntsville- Madison County Public Library, quoted that 'The program is fully funded by a $67,000 grant from the Library Services and Technology Act and targets a population traditionally under-served by the library. We hope to set a good example for the rest of the nation's libraries to follow.'

The project will include: "Ready Reader" van for on-site visits, thematic unit kits, parents/teacher resource collections and training, make-and-take learning activity materials, and deposit collections, which will include picture books, board books, books on tape, videos, music cassettes/cds, puppets and manipulatives. The project will work with 2 outreach librarians, each will visit a site and give 'demonstration' storytimes. Free services will be scheduled during regular hours. Caregivers will select programming kits and deposit collections for use. The service will place emphasis on childcare facilities, which will help eliminate the ongoing state-defined academic problems with the Huntsville City Schools. 'I think this program is very outstanding; it helps the child to develop social skills that he or she can learn on a daily basis, and it benefits children with diverse ethnic, backgrounds' said Barney L, Humphrey, a Child Development Specialist.

Mayor Loretta Spencer, who has taken a personal interest in children's literacy issues, was also present when the van was unveiled. Mayor Spencer and Mrs. Carol Townsend, Headstart Center Manager at Meridian Street Head Start demonstrated the variety of creative learning activities it has to offer to the Headstart students. The Reader Van will begin making rounds to eight daycare and Headstart centers in October, and will expand its route gradually to include stops throughout the city of Huntsville and the Madison County area.

Reporters note: (When young children begin kindergarten, they should be ready and able to learn how to read. If not, these children will lose out on a great opportunity to get a job, or either go to college. We need to support our teachers and volunteers with our time and skills. Reading Readiness is empowerment to our children so they can be ready to tackle any obstacle in today's world. With dedicated, supportive volunteers, we can make a big difference in our child's life today by the empowerment of reading."[73]

October 19, 1999 – The Huntsville-Madison County Public Library is one of the few public libraries in the country to have a copy of the book *Fortunate Son* because the book has been withdrawn from distribution and publication. The Board decided that since the book is no longer available, the Library's copy should be placed in the Archives collection. [There were two other books with the same title, but the one above was written by J.H. Hatfield, published in 1999 and was about George W. Bush, before he was elected President of the United States.] The library actually had 4 copies of that book, and in 2004 there were 2 copies in the main library and 1 in Eleanor Murphy branch. Hardback copies over the Internet in 2004 could be bought for $75 to $150.

The employees in the Huntsville-Madison County Public Library faced over 4,000 daily patrons every day, and they treated them with courtesy. The circulation counter was the focus of the patron-friendly atmosphere. They were quick to say, "May I help you," and then actually doing it until your needs were satisfied. The staff development days held in the spring featured speakers from local companies that were similar to the library, such as grocery stores and other companies that have face-to-face encounters with the public that want to sell something to the public. Those encounters were always friendlier and more effective than going to a government office to ask for something. Government offices are usually friendly, but they are not always dedicated to meeting the customers' needs, after all, they have important (?) work to do. The important work at the Huntsville-Madison County Public Library was to satisfy the patron's needs, and they did that with professionalism, knowledge and courtesy.

Chapter 14

And The Beat Goes On

*"Everything you need for a better future and success has already been written.
And guess what? All you have to do is go to the library."*

Jim Rohn
www.cyber-nation.com/victory/quotations

Fort Book was a popular place as there was a constant flow of people in and out of the building at most hours. On Tuesday, July 21, 2004 there were fifteen folks patiently waiting in the outside covered area for the doors to open at 9:00 A.M. The library was truly a community building in most locations, and Fort Book was no exception. Three of the waiting people were obviously homeless men ready to use the restrooms and then settle into a nice soft and deep lounge chair. The other twelve folks were probably searching for a variety on information and materials. Maybe some headed for the Heritage Room to chase down a long-lost ancestor. Probably most people just wanted to check out books or audio-visual material.

The chapter will focus more on the internal operations of the library operations in the 21st Century. The operations were more extensive with a larger main library and eleven branches than they were in the 1960's with only two branches and a smaller main building. The size of the budget over the decades has also grown dramatically. The information age of the last two decades made the 1940's and 1950's look like the Dark Ages in comparison. There was a lot of behind-the-scenes work going on that needed explanation so readers can appreciate the library personnel better. One does not just push a button and books, videos, and music CD's magically appear from nowhere into the patrons' hands. The library's website was www.hpl.lib.al.us and it contained a multitude of information about the main library, the major departments, and the eleven branches.

How do books and other materials find their way into the library and onto the shelves? The Acquisition Department subscribed to numerous periodical publications that provided information about new material being published and distributed. Probably the leading source was the monthly *Library Journal*, which provided lead-time of 3-4 months before the materials would be available. The acquisition personnel provided a copy of the magazine to each branch and circulated one copy in the main building to the adult, children's and reference departments. The *Library Journal* provided synopses of the most logical candidates for public libraries to buy for their patrons. The books desired were marked in the copies and returned to the acquisition personnel for consolidation. Decisions then were made on the total number of copies that will be purchased, after consulting the demographic data of the patrons, the budgets of the branches and other constraints.

Another accession method was more automatic, based on judgments of the most popular authors that the patrons will clamor for. The library maintains a standing list of automatic distribution of a certain number of copies of, for example, Stephen King, Tom Clancy, Scott Turow and John Grisham. President Bill Clinton's book, *My Life*, came out in the summer of 2004, but its release date was known in advance. The library placed its order and the book was received within a week of the release in the desired number of copies, because the book's popularity was anticipated by the library personnel.

A third method was even more automatic. McNaughton Books were pre-selected books that are rented to libraries for a certain period, for example two years. This service provides the library with a wide-range of mostly fiction books that readers might like. At the end of the period the books were sent back and disposed of through other channels. This system kept the library supplied with current bestsellers at a minimum cost without having to keep the books on the shelves indefinitely before disposing of them.

Endowments, memoriam and other gifts are also sources of books. Each item was entered into the computer to control the life cycle of the material from entrance to glorious, or maybe inglorious, final exit from the Huntsville-Madison County Public Library system

The Accession Department controls all incoming material. Personnel prepare a card for each item, which designates the source, destination location, library's Dewey Decimal System designation and any special instructions. The materials were loaded onto a cart and delivered to the Technical Services Department.

The head of the Technical Services Department sorts the materials to be distributed to the four cataloguers, who specialized in categories of material, such as adult books; children's books and audio-visual. The cataloguers entered the information on the card into the library's database. They then print out, in groups of 24 for books because there are 24 labels on a page, the library number for the item. The material and the page of labels were returned to a cart and moved to the cataloguing assistants.

The five assistant catalogers conducted several operations on the materials. The hard cover books were placed spine up in a device to hold it temporarily. The assistant placed a piece of cardboard even with the bottom of the spine. The label was placed above the cardboard and centered on the spine. Thus, each processed label was in the exact same space on all books in the library system.

Some books, such as McNaughton, came with a plastic cover to protect the dust cover. The assistant taped a plastic cover on those that needed one.

Soft back books required additional preparation to ensure a longer life. The cover from the first sheet was flattened using a stick while the book was held in a form. A piece of stringy plastic tape was stretched down the crease to bind the cover and front page into place, and the top of the tape was guillotined by an embedded knife. The procedure was repeated at the back cover. The tape helped prolong the bond between the covers of the pages. The book was placed spine up again in the form and a four-inch clear tape was pulled from the top to the bottom and then guillotined. The tape was centered over the spine and was smoothed out by a stick, first on the front, then the spine and then the back. The result was a clear scotch taped spine that extends to an inch and a half on each cover.

Both hard and soft cover books now received a card envelope, which has the security device stuck on the back. A bar code was prepared and attached. A small sticker indicating main or the branch designation was added, and finally an ink stamp of the Huntsville-Madison County Public Library was added. The finished products were placed on the cart and routed back to the department head for quality control. When satisfied, the department head had the cart taken to the storage room where the items were segregated by destination.

The materials were boxed by designation and a truck delivered the materials daily to the biggest and busiest branches (Bessie K. Russell, Madison, Eleanor Murphy and Bailey Cove), while others received only one or two visits per week. At each location materials were picked up and returned to the main building. Some materials may be routed to the branch of origin, for example, and item might be checked out at Madison, but is returned via the bookmobile at the person's work location. Other materials may be headed for repair or the dustbin of history.

Floyd Turner was the driver for the branch delivery route for ten years as of 2004. There was a room in the back of the first floor main library that was the focal point of branch distribution. Each branch had a vertical, four-shelf identified space. The circulation and technical services personnel placed the outgoing materials in the correct place. Every weekday morning Floyd Turner started to load the individual materials into plastic crates and label them. At five minutes before 9 A.M. he drove to the Clinton Street post office and backed up to the dock. He pressed the buzzer and in a few minutes he was faced with a large cloth bag on four wheels, which contains 12-14 small hand-carried plastic baskets. He loaded the baskets into his truck and was off to the library. Everything was put on a hand dolly and taken to the third floor mailroom. On the Monday morning I observed, there were five baskets of little green audio-cassette boxes. He sorted out the green boxes, left the remaining mail on the floor in baskets, and took the green boxes to the blind and handicapped office on the second floor.

Floyd Turner then returned to finish loading up books for his morning run to the Bessie Russell branch on Sparkman Drive, Monrovia branch on Jeff Road and the Madison branch off Hughes Road and Browns Ferry Road. Many of the materials had a 4 x 4 inch paper taped to the outside. When the main circulation desk checked in the materials, the computer automatically spits out the paper to indicate that the material was wanted at another location, so it was then routed to the proper shelves in the stocking room. He collected out going baskets at each place, with Madison contributing 5 large and 4 small crates. The large crates weigh 90 pounds, so they were not an easy task to manhandle them at least four times in and out of his truck just one way.

The goal of the library was to process incoming material and get them on the shelves in 24 hours, or maybe in two days at the latest. The system was under constant pressure to meet that goal. Each morning before the library opened, shelvers were at work sorting through the material, which was returned yesterday after they were checked back into the library. The shelvers attended workshops on evaluating the condition of books. The personnel inspected the book for damage, and if there was none, the book was re-shelved and made ready for loan again, along with the new acquisitions placed on carts from the Technical Services Department. High priority items like Bill Clinton's book go to the top of the stack. Books like Clinton's could be received in the morning, be pushed through the processing cycle and be on the shelves by 9:00 A.M. the next day, in less than 24 hours. The process described was finely tuned to keep the books on the shelves for the patrons and minimize the time the books were not available. In the late 1990's the magazines were automated to maintain better control of them.[1]

Bill Clinton's book was released on June 22, 2004. The Huntsville-Madison County Public Library received 14 copies of the hardback book, 6 books on compact disk (CD) and 2 on audio tape. I checked the status of the material on the library's Internet site on July 22, 2004.There were only 4 books not checked out, while there were no copies of the CD available with an estimated wait of 6 days and no copies of the audio tape available with an estimated wait of 15 days. The library's services were popular and in demand.

An earlier chapter briefly discussed memorial books. There are several variations of gift books. Diane Metrick, Administrative Secretary to the director, handled the initial control of such donations. A form was completed with the donor's name and address. An acknowledgement section ensured that a response was sent to the appropriate address. Two basic categories were identified: "In Memory of" and "In Honor of." There were two additional categories: "Gift of" and "Endowment Fund of." In each of the four situations, in 2004 Teresa

Thrower, a cataloguing assistant, was responsible for implementing the action by preparing the appropriate book plate, inserting in the front of the book and maintaining computer control of the complete process. Sometimes the donor specified the book and in other cases the library had discretionary control of the selection.[2]

De-accession was the opposite of accession and is a fine word for describing the removal of material from the library. De-accession does not show up in the dictionary, so de-selection is used. Actually, if the truth were known, the librarians called it "weeding out." Well, whatever we call it, those items are not longer available to be loaned to the library's patrons. Judy Purinton, head of adult services, explained some of the processes involved in the removal of material. If the book was damaged in some way: cover or pages torn, water or other fluids; or others ways folks manage to damage the public property, the shelver collected the damaged materials and provided them to the responsible department for further evaluation. Some books will be repaired by the technical services department. Other books might be so badly damaged that they end up in the waste dumpster. Some books might be in the middle ground and find their way to the Friends of the Library used bookstore.

Each respective department head then evaluated the impact of the contents of the book. Perhaps the contents contained outdated material, so the loss was not significant. The book might be discarded if outdated and a newer book with up-to-date information can be obtained. Perhaps the computer records show that the book was only borrowed twice in 15 years. The department head may remove the book for lack of usage to make room for more heavily utilized books. But an out-of-print book might not be able to be replaced, so it is maintained. The department head must also consider the balance of subject materials within the department. Summer time was the period of the greatest evaluation and weeding out of books as a matter of routine to keep the shelves supplied with the books that were current and most used. Another consideration was the amount of money available in each department for the purchase of new books. The point is that the department head uses a broad spectrum of considerations to determine the fate of each item reviewed.[3]

Barbara Liaw, director of technical services, estimated that repairing a book costs about a third as much as replacing the book. A decision on each damaged book was made by Technical Services whether to repair or replace. During 1988 about 30,000 new volumes came into the Huntsville/Madison County Library system, while 10,000 were discarded. About 4,000 were paperbacks that cost less than $2, so that was an easy decision to discard. The other 6,000 received a repair or replace decision. Most of those decisions were made by Eydie Scott, a repairer par excellence. Mrs. Scott saves the local taxpayers thousands of dollars each year with her skillful use of special library glues and tapes, wax paper, scissors, razor blades, saddleback stapler, covering pad, and cutting boards.

If one or several pages were missing, Ms. Scott will order the same book on an interlibrary loan from another library with that book and make double-sided copies of the necessary pages. Then it was back to the tried and true glue, wax paper and rubber band process. If the book was worth salvaging, Ms. Scott can do it. She always has a backlog of books for repair. If a patron asked for the book while in was in repair, the computer would indicate the status and then she could fix that item quickly to meet the patron's request. The library staff continually worked hard to help the public get what it wants.

Some books were of little value, such as a 20-year old medical book, which would be replaced by a newer edition. Others fall into similar categories and might be passed to the Friends of the Library for sale. Others may be trashed. Ms. Scott also handled this task with professional thoroughness. The barcode, pocket and security device were removed and the action noted in the computer inventory.

There was certainly much wear and tear on books, and they will eventually have to be discarded or given to the Friends of the Library for sale. But how about those careless and unthinking folks who leave gum, underline in ink, spill Kool-Aid, tear out pages, make crayon marks, insert their own artwork, or otherwise just don't give a thought about defacing the public's property and being inconsiderate about the next reader. Don't you just wish you could grab those people and shake them until they give a reason for their actions?[4]

The Madison Square Mall Branch, which opened on August 1, 1983, was closed in September 2000 due to declining circulation.[5]

The Alabama Virtual Library (AVL) started to operate for library customers on December 1, 2000. Users could go to any Huntsville Library branch and receive their own Personal Identification Number (PIN). The PIN would allow the patron to log into the Library's computer system (known as WebCat) from their home or office computer and help themselves to a variety of Library services. The WebCat was previously only available for library personnel.

The Alabama Virtual Library provided a world of quality library information licensed for Alabama library users. Materials included magazine articles, newspapers, encyclopedias and other reference sources. Access was granted to all Alabama citizens at Alabama public libraries and at libraries of public education facilities. The AVL was supported by the Alabama Commission on Higher Education, Alabama Department of Postsecondary Education, Alabama Public Library Service, Alabama State Department of Education and the Alabama Supercomputer Authority. The AVL was funded by the Governor and the Alabama Legislature. The website was www.avl.lib.al.us.

The AVL allowed users to:
- Renew material online.
- Check user status, such as number of items checked out, when they are due and
- Any fines outstanding.

The instructions said that the unique password would expire after one year and a message would notify patrons 30 days in advance to renew. That finally happened to this author after three years. In November 2004 I renewed my password, now for a year. If the account was not used in a year, it will likely be dropped.

The first AVL page allowed the patron to search by age groups, using school level selections, or ten different topics such as business, education, government, literature, news, reference, etc. There was also a dazzling array of 57 databases available, half of which are not easily identifiable as to what they contain. Then, after you had selected the database, the screen provided blanks to be filled in with key words and other search criteria. As the old cliché goes, "Do not try this at home," because the array of choices was confusing unless you know exactly what you are hunting for. But, it was designed to operate from the convenience of your home or office. The modern age of the Internet was wonderful and a thousand times better than thirty years ago when trying to do research. The AVL was accessible from school and library computers without a remote access card or the use of a password. An information sheet on the AVL was available near the front desk of the main library and most branches. David Lilley, head of the reference department, reported in April 2001 that 15,599 persons had signed up for the AVL. In October 2004 the number was about 28,000.

In February 2001 Joyce Smith, the head of the Blind and Physically Handicapped Department, retired and was succeeded by Joyce Welch, who worked in the department for over two decades. The room on the second floor now has a full Bible in Braille, which occupied approximately five linear feet of space. The blind library contained catalogues for families or individuals to look for items, which might be helpful to blind and physically handicapped persons. The number of items in Braille seems to be declining, but still available were unexpected items such as the three-volume 2000-2004 National Basketball Association Schedule. Talking books have become more popular, and if you visit the library, you will see shelf upon shelf of talking books ready to be mailed free of charge to a requesting patron for thirty days. There are over 16,000 talking books in the national system, which included current best sellers.

Persons can be eligible if: they have vision of 20-200 or less with correcting lenses or if they have "tunnel vision" no greater than 20 degrees; if they have a visual disability that prevents reading standard printed material; if they have physical limitations that prevent using standard printed materials; or if they have a reading disability resulting from an organic dysfunction. The disability must be certified by a physician or other competent authority.

Joyce Welch said the Blind library had about 400 patrons. She also said she has the best job because she gets to talk with such wonderfully positive people, despite their handicap. There was now a capability to access daily newspapers from throughout the nation by computer and hear them read aloud. This was a free service, it only required registration. You just enter your special identification number and security code and you can get many newspapers with a few keystrokes on the computer.[6]

Al Bellingrath, a volunteer in 2004 in the blind department Monday, Wednesday and Friday for two hours each day, opened each green box containing tapes, checked that the tapes were there, rewound (if not, he did it), damaged, and then restocked them in the proper numbered order. His log showed that about 300-350 tapes were returned each week.

Joyce Welch and her assistant, after the tapes are logged in and ready for restocking, looked into the computer for each individual listening preferences. The computer automatically selected tapes not heard by that patron before in that category and printed out a list of tapes for the next shipment. All material expenses, including postage, were courtesy of the Federal government. Joyce estimated about 100 tapes are sent out each week.

Joyce Welch, head of the Subregional Library for the Blind and Physically Handicapped said that in 2008 digital talking books were expected to be available. In addition, Braille books will be available to be downloaded on personal computers with special software. The information age had made more material available, and the digital age promised even more. What a wonderful world in which we live.[7]

"Due to Public Health concerns, the Huntsville-Madison County Public Library will no longer loan Shared Computer Headsets for Public Use. Patrons are welcome to bring in personal headsets suitable for computer stereo use, or to purchase a quality stereo headset at a service desk for $1.75 apiece. Any headset purchased becomes property of the patron, and must be taken with the patron upon exit from the Library. The Huntsville-Madison County Public Library is not responsible for purchased or personal headsets left on the premises, or damaged due to patron misuse."[8]

"From Cradle to Grave" is an oft-repeated slogan for some products or company services. The Huntsville-Madison County Public Library just put the final touches on its program, which might be termed, "Before the Cradle to Beyond the Grave." Endowments were identified late in the last chapter, which allowed people to contribute to the library long after they were dead. Now Susan Markham, head of outreach services, developed the *Raise a Reader* program. Before they get to their first cradle, babies born at Huntsville Hospital and Crestwood Hospital will receive a packet of information, including an application for a library card and a certificate for a free board book. {I am uncertain if they had to provide a thumbprint or a picture for identification.] Don't laugh, because this was serious business.

A new baby becomes familiar with his mother's voice more than any other voice. His mother feeds him and changes his diaper. She is in constant contact with the child as she fulfills the baby's needs for air, food, water, and sleep. She talks and sings to the baby in soft tones. She is providing the baby's physiological needs.

Abraham Maslow, 1908-70, American psychologist, established a hierarchy of human needs, writing that human beings are motivated by unsatisfied needs, and that certain lower needs need to be satisfied before higher needs can be satisfied. At the bottom of the need's pyramid are the physiological needs cited above. The little baby becomes a crying tyrant, and stays that way until his physiological needs are satisfied by his mother. She is touching and talking to the baby and he starts to recognize the second need, that of safety. Her touch and voice becomes a safety cocoon. The baby falls and experiences pain, which many times is banished immediately because she is in her mother's arms and close to her body.

The little tyrant has been fed, changed and feels safe touching his mother. Now, to distract the child's attention, she holds a book or magazine in front of them both and reads aloud. The book captures the baby's eyes, while feeling comfort and safety. She turns the page and the baby tries also. The baby feels a new texture, the paper, and tries to eat it.

At this point, the mother introduces the baby to Sir Francis Bacon, 1561-1626, English essayist, philosopher and statesman, who said, "Some books are to be tasted, others swallowed, and some few to be chewed and digested." The baby will try to chew books for some months, but gradually Mommy's guidance will teach the child that books do not go in the mouth. The child has learned to respect books and enjoy the pictures, while Mom reads the words. The child is still in the safety of mother's arms and body touch.

The child learns to turn the pages while Mom points out pictures and names the objects. Now Mommy points and the child can say the names of the objects. The child has now entered the third need, love. The little tyrant is no more, with a few exceptions, and loves to be on his mother's lap, listening to words, looking at pictures and saying names. Mommy reads to the little tyke before bed each night so he associates reading with going to sleep. That further reinforces the reading function.

A picture of my daughter-in-law and my grandson told the whole story. Mommy was sitting in a chair wearing shorts. The child sat on Mommy's lap with his back against her. Their bare legs were touching, providing security and bonding. Mom held a magazine in her hands and the little boy's hands were on Mom's, as he reinforced the holding of the magazine upright. She was reading over his shoulder close to his ear so her voice was soft and loving. His eyes were intently focused on the page, as he was totally enthralled by the experience. He and his Mommy were as one reader, each receiving maximum satisfaction from the experience.

But he has already entered the next higher need, esteem. He now has developed self-esteem, because he has mastered words and pictures, and is praised for that accomplishment. He gets attention and recognition because he continues to master new skills. The reading process becomes self-reinforcing if started early. But starting that process at age 4-5 years is a more difficult task because there are many more new sensory experiences available to the child.

The child has achieved and satisfied the four basic needs described by Maslow; physiological, safety, love and esteem. Eventually the child will become an adult, and hopefully satisfy Maslow's fifth need, self-actualization, which is the desire to become more and more what one is, to become everything that one is capable of becoming. Some examples are seeking knowledge, peace, esthetic experiences, self-fulfillment, oneness with God, etc. Perhaps he or she will write a book, as I have.

The Huntsville library's Ready Readers Van program was developed by a grant from the Library Services and Technology Act in 2000. It contained literacy kits and other resources to aid day care providers in teaching young children the fundamentals of reading. Two outreach librarians, Julia Aquila and Patricia Kuhn, who each worked 20 hours per week, visit a site and give a demonstration story time using the site's own children. The caregivers come to the van to select programming and deposit collections for use by children at the site. The free service was scheduled during regular hours. The materials used in the demonstration were available for checkout from the van. The Ready Reader van serviced all of Huntsville and the Madison County area, with service area emphasis on childcare facilities which feed into schools with ongoing state-defined academic problems within the Huntsville city schools.[9]

The Ready Readers Van also served the Headstart program, part of the Federal No Child Left Behind Program. Reading kits were provided to teachers, which included tri-fold pamphlets named Feed Me A Story and Enjoy the Fun of Reading to Your Kids. The Feed Me A Story document said, "Your child will develop half of his or her ability to read by age 4. To make the most of those years, you must expose your child early and consistently to reading. Otherwise, your child runs the risk of being behind classmates when he or she enters school." It provided guidance on reading aloud to your child and learning to listen. "Remember, you don't have to teach your child to read, just to want to read." The brochure provided a suggested reading list of many titles in the following categories: All ages; Infants & toddlers; Preschoolers; Spanish all ages; Spanish preschoolers; and Spanish infants & toddlers (ex. Me Gusto Como Soy!)."

The Enjoy the Fun of Reading to Your Kids brochure gave guidance under the following paragraph headings: 'Start young and stay with it; Motivate your children to read; Knowledge is power; Home is where the heart is; Talking about stories; The more the merrier; One more time; and It is part of life." Since my readers have been reading and learning, it is time for a pop quiz. Who is credited with the phrase, **"Knowledge is power?"** The answer: Roger Bacon, 1561-1626, English essayist, philosopher, and statesman. He was also credited with, "Necessity is the mother of invention." He believed in the scientific approach: Do not assume principles and deduce conclusions, but start from the particular and go to the general (experiment and observe).

In 2001 Tommy Ragland, Madison County probate judge, started to organize and put on shelves county records that had been on the floor in a storage room on the third floor of the library. Some of the heritage room records were also in the same room. Under the leadership of Rhonda Larkin, county archivist, and her crew of volunteers, the Madison County Records Center made great strides in identifying old probate documents and putting them on the Internet. Stop by the door immediately to the right at the top of the third floor stairwell and visit Rhonda and her volunteers. It was a nice place to find records and the operations are constantly being improved. You can also search its website: www.co.madison.al.us/mcrc.

There is an old saying that a little nepotism never hurt anybody, or maybe that a little nepotism goes a long way. Whatever, but the Huntsville library decided it needed a nepotism policy in 2002, which is below:
"Employment of Relatives
A relative shall include the following degrees of kinship:
1. Parent, step-parent, or parent-in-law
2. Spouse

3. Child or stepchild; daughter-in-law, son-in-law
4. Brother, brother-in-law, step-brother
5. Sister, sister-in-law, step-sister
6. Grandparent, grandparent-in-law, step-grandparent
7. Grandchild, grandchild-in-law, step-grandchild
8. Aunt or uncle
9. Niece or nephew

No two or more "relatives" shall be permitted to work in any same department or branch of the Library.

No two or more "relatives" shall be permitted to work in any department or branch if the relatives would be in any positions within two levels of supervising and being supervised by one another. In the event that two employees of the Library elect to be married, then to avoid any conflict with this policy, one or both employees may transfer to a non-conflicting vacant position which is advertised to be filled."[10]

March 21, 2002 – Mrs. Schremser reported that patron Mr. Wayne Haygood, who was concerned about funding for the library, had asked his church to put the Library funding problem on its prayer list.

The Alabama Library Association (ALLA) published annual statistics about the public libraries in the state. Each city and county system was in a different demographic and economic situation, so statistics were not always meaningful by exact comparison. For the year 2002, some of those statistics are presented below in comparison with libraries serving populations over 50,000 people.

- Huntsville was third in population served at 276,902, behind Birmingham and Mobile, and ahead of Montgomery.
- Huntsville was fourth in funding from local sources with $3,527,200, but was only seventh in local income per capita. That was a sign of under-funding by the Huntsville City Council and the Madison County Commissioners.
- Huntsville was third in total income with $4,569,996, but still seventh in total income per capita.
- Huntsville ranked sixth in books per capita, but second in borrowers per capita.
- Huntsville ranked third in visits per capita, but was sixth in visits per hour.
- Huntsville ranked third with 74.88 items circulated per hour of open time.
- Huntsville ranked third in personnel expenditures per capita.

Grants from the federal and state levels were important to enhance library support beyond that from the appropriate local governments. The Alabama Public Library Services' website, www.apls.state.al.us provided a list of 54 Funding/Grant Opportunities/Free Materials that were available. The Huntsville Madison County Public Library management team took advantage of those opportunities and was awarded several grants. Some examples follow:

- 2003
  - Children at Risk-General-$19,792
  - Library Techology-$59,152
  - SOLINET Initial Membership Grant-$20,000
- 2002
  - Children at Risk-General-$20,000
  - Library Technology-General-$59,744
- 2001

- Digital High-Speed Data Transmission-$54,400
- Library Technology-General-$42,704
- 2000
  - Children at Risk-General-$26,800
  - Collection Development-General-$10,000
  - Library Automation-General-$47,025

The grants listed above came from the Library Services and Technology Act (LSTA). LSTA was part of the Federal Museum and Library Services Act, last authorized in 1996. This act originated as the Library Services Act in 1956 and acted as a stimulus to a wide variety of library activities. Libraries received public support because it was not reasonable to expect any one person to purchase or possess all the information sources necessary for personal growth, education and research and work and community responsibilities. The public good, which emerged from the provision and use of library resources, flowed freely beyond the boundaries of an institution, community or state which provides them. Further, access to the aggregate system of U.S. libraries, which librarians created with federal encouragement and support, increased the public good beyond what one library could ever supply, and made support and improvement of library services a goal in the national interest.[11]

The selection process for appointment to the Library Board was explained by Mrs. Gail Phillips, Secretary to the City Council. Persons desiring to serve on the board were advised to forward a letter to the City Council stating their interest in why they would like to serve on the board. Those letters are the basis for selecting an individual to fill a vacancy when one occurs. The letters were kept on file for only one year. The terms of the five members were staggered, so it was likely that a vacancy will occur during any given year, but the historical record shows that most serve multiple terms. For example, in March 2004 the five current members had the following term-expiration dates: Cutter Hughes, February 2005; Charles Kettle, February 2006; Carol Casey, February 2007; Teresa Noble, February 2008; and Lady Shivers Tucker, February 2008. The selection was done by the city council, based on the political horse-trading that goes on in any such body of elected officials. Mrs. Phillips said there were no quotas for minorities, lawyers, or financial expertise in the selection, which probably boiled down to who you know on the city council.

The five-person Library Board served four-year terms, for which they can be reappointed. They received no compensation. One of board members in 2004 was Cutter Hughes. He was first appointed in 1995 as a replacement in the middle of a four-year term. He was a lawyer, which was frequently helpful to explain to other board members possible ramifications in certain situations. He was a legal advisor to the board previously. His heroes were Benjamin Franklin and Thomas Jefferson. One could not have two more noble heroes who loved books. Benjamin Franklin started the first lending library in America in 1731, in Philadelphia, with fifty subscribers. It was not public, but only for those who paid. Hughes went to law school at the University of Virginia, which was founded by Thomas Jefferson in 1819. In August 1814 the British burned Washington, D.C., to include the Library of Congress, which contained books originally ordered from England and other valuable acquisitions. In September 1814 Thomas Jefferson offered to sell his personal library of an estimated 9,000-10,000 volumes to the United States Government. President James Madison signed into law on January 30, 1815 a bill authorizing the purchase of Jefferson's 6,487 volumes for the sum of $23,950. Those volumes became the basis for the current Library of Congress, now the largest library in the world.

The library's Long Range Plan 1990-1995 will now be compared with the Strategic Plan 2003 To 2008. There was hardly any comparison. The 1990 plan had 13 pages written in size 14 font, double spaced, with loads of white space. It contained 13 goals, 49 objectives below those goals and 26 sub-objectives. The majority of the objectives had no sub-objectives. The document apparently served the library staff well during that era, but it certainly did not provide a detailed and comprehensive approach to planning the library's future.

The 2003 plan had 45 pages in the basic document written in size 12 font, single-spaced, with the minimum of white space. There was an Appendix A, Information Technology Plan, consisting of 32 pages, including computer connection diagrams. Appendix B, Bailey Cove Branch Plan, had 20 pages. Appendix C, Madison Public Library, had 16 pages. The total of 113 pages compares most favorably with the 13 pages of 13 years earlier. There was, also, far more substance to the 2003 plan.

There were 2 & ½ pages of planning assumptions/factors focused on demographics and employment in Madison County. The body of the plan was divided into services, facilities and administration. The services section had seven goals, which were further divided into 39 objectives. Each objective had a means of measuring achievement. Each objective had a list of strategies to achieve that objective. Most importantly, a person(s)'s name was assigned to each objective and strategy. This clarified responsibility for achievement of the objectives and strategies. In a similar manner the facilities had 1 goal, 5 objectives, and strategies below that. Administration had 1 goal, 6 objectives and subordinate strategies. The 2003 To 2008 plan was an excellent document to help the library staff work toward improvements in the future and represented a high degree of sophistication. Much of the credit for the plan's style goes to Arthur G. Lange, Jr., a consultant, who was a retired Army colonel and was well known and respected as an instructor of management. The execution of the plan does rest completely on the management skills of the library's leadership. Donna Schremser deserves strong kudos for recognizing the need for an improved strategic plan and following through to involve the staff to write the plan.[12]

Melissa Shepherd was head of Internet and Technology Services since 1999 and was the key staff member behind the continuing upgrade of computer and Internet services. Technology upgrades were a moving target, so the following excerpt from the Strategic Plan 2003 to 2008 is only a snapshot synopsis of the current technologies in 2003:

"230 PCs in our network, 121 of which are for use by the public. 32 of the public access PCs are for library catalog/AVL use, with SIRSI's iBistro. The remainder are full-use systems, for Web access, as well as access to productivity and educational software. Seven of 11 branches are equipped with NT Domain servers.

A Regional Training Center was established in January 1998, through a grant from the Gates Library Foundation, and with the stipulation that all public training be free of charge. The center offers technology courses for Library staff, North Alabama regional library staff, and the general public. The current facility includes twelve Gateway PCs (200 MHz), an HP network printer, and a destination teaching monitor. An additional adaptive workstation is available, with software to assist patrons with low vision in accessing the Internet, taking classes, or using Microsoft Office. All thirteen PCs are available for public use during public lab hours.

All PCs running SIRSI WorkFlows are connected to the LAN, and the Windows NT server, and operate under Windows 9x, NT, 2000 Professional, or XP Professional. An html-based SIRSI product called iBistro allows patron access to the library catalog and to view their accounts, both in-house and on the Library website.

The main server is located in the computer room, and workstations are located on all three floors of the Main Library. On each floor the workstations connected to area hubs, and the hubs are cabled to the computer room. An NT 4 server running MS Proxy server 2.0 and Smartfilter blocks chat sites for all public computers with full Internet access. A test server running AIX 4.1 is available to staff for testing automation upgrades prior to "going live".

The automation server is an IBM RISC 6000 running UNIX AIX 4.2 and hosting the SIRSI Unicorn library automation software and databases. A CISCO 4500M router, a CISCO 3800 router, a CISCO PIX firewall connect to 5 branches through fractional T-1 lines, and the remaining 6 branches through 56K dedicated frame relay lines. The network bandwidth is 10BaseT, and the protocol is TCP/IP. A 24-port CISCO Catalyst 1900 switches network traffic in the Main building. We are connected to the Internet by a fiber connection running at 10baseT provided through the City of Huntsville's internal network. This connection is maintained by AREN, formerly the Alabama Supercomputer, who provide our Internet access, DNS hosting, and maintenance of our network equipment.

The Library system has 121 public access computers, none below a Pentium 166Mhz CPU, 89 access the full WWW. There are 105 staff computers, of which 105 are connected to the Internet. FY 98-99; 90 PACs, 72 staff; YTD increase of 26Y6, 33% resp.

Branch Libraries:

At each branch, PCs connect to a hub and router communicating with the server in the Main Library through either a 56K frame relay line, or a fractional T-1 line.

Bookmobile:

The Library has one Bookmobile, using Cellular service and a PIII laptop to connect to the Main Automation Server. "[13]

Cover to Cover, the Newsletter of the Friends of the Huntsville-Madison County Public Library, March/April 2002 issue, featured "Get Caught Reading, What Would Happen if Everyone Read the Same Book at the Same Time?"

"Have you ever wondered what would happen if everyone read the same book at the same time? The Library, *The Huntsville Times*, and area bookstores are working together to start a community-wide book club. We want you to "Get Caught Reading" during the months of April, May, and June. We plan to announce the book selection April 14. 2002. Readers will have until the week of June 10 to complete their reading and attend one or more of a series of programs and book discussions at various locations throughout Huntsville and Madison County. Our primary goals for our first, and we hope ongoing, reading club are to promote a shared sense of community, stimulate discussions and ideas, and to advocate the joy of lifelong reading.

Huntsville/Madison County is not the first community to start a community-wide book club. Chicago started its book club with To Kill a Mockingbird by Harper Lee [an Alabamian]. Rochester, N.Y. read A Lesson before Dying by Ernest Gaines, and Seattle selected The Sweet Hereafter by Russell Banks. What will Huntsville and Madison County Read? We have assembled a panel of community readers and considered all of the suggestions submitted to us through our Web page and survey card campaign. We will announce the selection in *The Huntsville Times* on Sunday, April 14 as we kickoff National Library Week. [It was *All the King's Men*, by Robert Penn Warren.]

Our potential for success for "Get Caught Reading" is high. As the busiest Library system in the State of Alabama with over 2.1 million loans last year alone, we know this is a community of voracious readers. We want to provide our readers with the opportunity to discover new authors, new points of view, and new opportunities to join with other readers in a common and shared spirit of community. We look forward to reading with you!"[14]

The same issue quoted above also provided the following coming attractions:

"Monday, March 4, Madison Public Library Noon - 1:30 p.m.

Brown Bag Book Discussion features Amsterdam by Ian McEwan

-Tuesday, March 5, Monrovia Public Library 7-8 p.m.

Can We Talk? Book Club (Call 837-6153 for book selection)

-Wednesday, March 13, Main Library Auditorium Noon - 1 p.m.

Brown Bag Luncheon Series

Gardening in North Alabama, presented by Jean Lee, Master Gardener

-Saturday, March 23, Main Library Auditorium 10 a.m. - 2:30 p.m.

-Dale Short Writer's Workshop $30 (includes lunch and book) Call 532-5950 by March 15 to make your reservation.

-Sunday, March 24, Main Library Auditorium 2 p.m.

Hertha Heller Sunday Forum Series

Harvey Cotton of the Huntsville Botanical Gardens

-"Take a Break" @ your library

During Spring Break week, the Bailey Cove Branch has many exciting activities for preschool and grade school kids. Highlights include...

Tuesday, March 26, Bailey Cove Branch 9 am-8 p.m.

Game Day for grades 2-5

Come by any time on Tuesday to join in games of cards, chess, checkers, puzzles, and board games. No registration required.

-Wednesday, March 27, -Bailey Cove 2 p.m.

"Yoga for Kids" (grades 1-5)

Guest instructor, Kym Strathum, will teach basic yoga positions for kids.

-Thursday, March 29, Eleanor E. Murphy Branch 3:30 p.m.

Children's Easter Party for ages 3-7

-Friday, March 29, Bailey Cove Branch 9 a.m. - 5 p.m.

Spring Craft Day for grades 2-5

Come by any time Friday to make and take Easter and spring crafts. No registration required.

-Wednesday and Thursday, April 3 & 4, Bailey Cove - 9 a.m. - 12 noon

Discovery Toys Fair to benefit the Bailey Cove Branch Library

-Wednesday, April 10, Main Library Auditorium Noon - 1 p.m.

Brown Bag Luncheon Series

Local author Doris Gilbreath shares her story of Huntsville's most famous four-footed citizen, Lily Flagg. [that was a cow, for non-Huntsvillians]

-Wednesday & Thursday, April 17 & 18, Bailey Cove 10 a.m.

National Library Week @ your library "Don't Eat the Books" a Fred & Alfie puppet show by Mary Jones and Betty Pate for toddlers and preschoolers

-National Library Week is April 14 – 20

Check with your favorite branch for special activities.

At the bottom of the page was the statement, " A city with a great library is a great city."[15] [Yes readers, that's Huntsville.]

Cover to Cover, November/December 2002, featured:

"eBooks @ your library! THOUSANDS OF TITLES ARE AT YOUR FINGERTIPS
EBooks have arrived at the Huntsville Madison County Public Library! We have over 11,000 electronic books that have been digitized for reading on a computer screen. They can be viewed on a PC or Macintosh computer that has a connection to the Internet. Most of the eBooks are nonfiction, with plenty of "Dummies' Guides", small business materials, test study guides, legal and medical guides, and other great titles for quick reference.

The eBooks are located at the website of www.netlibrary, the company that supplies the titles. The website is www.netlibrary.com. To read eBooks, each user must have a personal account with a login name and password. A user may sign up for a free eBook account at any of our library locations. The only requirement is that a user must also have a current Huntsville Madison County Public Library card.

The eBooks are included in the library's online catalog. An eBook listing has a call number beginning with EBOOK and is described as an ELECTRONIC BOOK with INTERNET as its location. The record has an electronic access link that takes the user to the netLibrary website where the eBook is stored.

Users can also browse the library's collection of eBooks by going directly to the netLibrary website at www.netlibrary.com. Users may login there and search our entire eBook collection. A bonus with eBooks is the capability to perform full-text searches of a single eBook, or thousands of titles simultaneously. It is also possible to browse topic categories.

Just as with a traditional print book, only one user may read an eBook at a time. An eBook may be viewed for 15 minutes, or it may be checked out for 4 hours. It is automatically checked back in after 4 hours. It may be checked out again if it is still needed.

To start the eBook collection, the library received a $10,000 federal Library Services and Technology Act grant that was awarded by the Alabama Public Library Service.
Sue Royer, Deputy Director"[16]

Ebooks were initiated at the Huntsville library in July 2002. By October 2004, 2,411 people, but not necessarily different ones, had used an ebook. The total number of accesses during that period was 14,711, but the number of actual users was only 4,533, or 30.8 percent. [This author is unsure about ebooks, because I do not think they will catch on and replace paper that you can carry many places that you cannot carry a computer.]

Also in the same issue was an item that the "library had recently received a $20,000 federal grant through the Alabama Public Library Service for the purchase of materials in Spanish and bilingual formats and made available at the Bailey Cove, Madison, and Hazel Green branch libraries and on the bookmobile. The grant was in response to the growing Hispanic population in Madison County. According to census data, this population has doubled in size since 1990 and is predicted to grow by an additional 54% by 2008. Additionally, many families have expressed an interest in giving their children an opportunity to learn a second language at an early age. Materials are primarily geared for children and include books, books on tape, videos, and interactive "take-home" backpacks with activities for parents and children to share together. Bilingual programming for story hours will be implemented after the holidays."[17]

The library staff continued to be innovative in developing community programs sponsored by the library. One such program is quoted below:
"A CELEBRATION OF HEROES

Summary December 11, 2002

'A Celebration of Heroes' originated as a way to get the Public Service Department at the Main Library working together on a project. Due to the nation's renewed interest in patriotism and American heroes since 9/11/01 and Madison County's large military population (over 32,000 veterans and over 2000 WWII veterans), a series of related programs were planned that dealt with veterans of America's wars. The staff worked with various organizations in the community including the Veterans' History Museum, the Veterans Coalition and the 8th Air Force Association to put on 15 programs running from September 17 to December 7, 2002. Our programs reached a pivotal point the weekend of November 1-3, when we hosted a WWII USO Canteen Dance on Friday complete with swing band, dancers and storytellers, and hosted best-selling author and Vietnam veteran, Homer Hickam on Sunday evening. We were able to launch our Library of Congress Veterans History Project during this weekend and to reach many of the people targeted for the project. As part of the weekend events, we also premiered a five-minute video, developed by local media specialist Dick Curtis, publicizing the library's role in the Veterans History Project. A small plane flew over the city flying a banner advertising our program. Military paraphernalia and related library materials were on display throughout the Library from September to December.

A total of 1100 people attended the programs during 'A Celebration of Heroes'. These events served a dual purpose of increasing the programming at the Library and making the Library more visible in the community. The programs honored the veterans living in Madison County and educated the public about the experiences and sacrifices made by our veterans during WWII, the Korean War, the Vietnam War and the Persian Gulf Conflict. A special effort was made to attract students from local schools with several high school social studies departments offering extra credit for attendance. In fact, each of the sessions was taped and are available for educational purposes at the city schools. Veterans around the area expressed appreciation to the Library for remembering their service and for educating the public, especially the younger generations, about these crucial events in the fight for America's freedom

'A Celebration of Heroes' far exceeded my expectations for a series of library programs. All of the Public Service Departments (as well as, a few other staff members) were very excited about this project and worked hard to make it successful. They were able to present an impressive array of programs on a shoestring budget. (See the attached brochure for a detailed listing of the events.) [Not shown] Not only did it foster teamwork among the staff but it provided the Library with lots of good public relations and generated very positive feelings about the Library and its services among the Madison County veterans' population.
Regina Greer Cooper, Associate Director Main Library Public Services."[18] Kudos to Regina Cooper.

The Huntsville Times featured a "Partners for Charity" full-page advertisement for the various charitable organizations in the area. Each page had a commercial sponsor. We will now take a commercial break to tell you that the sponsor of the library advertisement on Wednesday, March 31, 2004, was Mattress King, "Alabama Largest Sealy Dealer" We will now go back to regular programming. At the top of the page was the library's mission statement. It is the heart of our library system and deserves repeating.

"THIS IS THE PUBLIC'S LIBRARY

Our mission is to enrich the educational, recreational, and cultural life
 of our community. Our knowledgeable and courteous staff will serve as
the gateway to library materials, information, and programs."

The Huntsville-Madison County Public Library has fulfilled that mission statement throughout its history. The library increased its services to keep up with rapid growth of the area during the 1950s and 1960s. The high technology and information age found fertile ground in Huntsville, and our library modernized and expanded to provide even more services to the public. Our dedicated and proactive library staff have led the way for all Madison County residents to have available the most modern services. The library has reached out to those folks who, for some reason, do not go to the library. The remainder of the full-page cited above follows:

"Did You Know!!!!

- We are the busiest library in the state and one of the busiest in the South. We have over 4,000 patrons visit each day. That's over 1.4 million visitors each year!!
- We have over 200,000 cardholders. 75% of Madison County residents are Library card holders. The national average is 40%.
- We are open 26,764 hours a year – more than any other non-profit business in Huntsville.
- Over 40,489 children and adults attended programs presented by the Library last year.
- We have free access to the Internet available on every computer.
- We have a regional computer training center free to the public offering classes in basic and advanced computer skills, a wide range of popular programs, and basic and advanced Internet skills.
- The Subregional Library for the Blind and Physically Handicapped is on the 2nd floor of the Main Library. We have taped recordings of books, magazines, and newspapers as well as playback equipment available free of charge to Library Patrons with disabilities.
- Check out books – The Library has 11,000 titles that you can read from your home or work computer. Register at any branch – it's free!"[19]

The "Get Caught Reading" selection for 2003 was *Seabiscuit*, by Laura Hillenbrand. Available in the library locations was a Reader's Guide to *Seabiscuit*. It was on a tri-fold of an 8 & 1/2 x 11-inch colored paper. Inside was a description of the book's contents and ten questions to consider during the discussion.

The *Cover to Cover* newsletter was an 8 & 1/2 x 11-inch tri-fold on 11 x 25 & 1/2-inch sturdy stock. Each of the bimonthly issues contained a feature story on page 1, a Friends' Forward on page 2 written by a member of the organization, page 3 featured an item about one of the branches, page 4 reviewed several books, page 5 listed the coming attractions, and page 6 contained another special item and the mailing address. It was highly informative about books and activities, and had an attractive layout. Bravo to the Friends of the Library and the library staff!

"I have what I consider to be the greatest volunteer job in our Friends of the Library Book Store effort. My task is to research and price the books which may be considered rare and/or otherwise valuable.

It's been a rewarding learning experience. I've been a "casual" book collector for much of my life, thanks to my maternal grandmother Annie Elise Hopkins Certain. She was an avid collector, and had passed on some of her "prizes" to me.

I've discovered several web sites which display prices that thousands of dealers are asking for the titles which they have in stock. I usually price our donated books at only a small proportional fraction of the prices which the dealers ask.

Occasionally, a donated book seems valuable enough to be auctioned on the internet site eBay.com. I've had several auctions which have netted $200.00+ (each) for our Book Store. But, the eBay stuff is only a trifle compared to our total operation.

The everyday contributions of our many volunteers are what really count. They're the ones who are responsible for the more than $100,000.00 that we've given to our Main Library each of the past several years, for the sole purpose of buying new books." Childs Berry[20]

Why does Huntsville and Madison County have such a popular library? There are many answers to that question. One of the answers was the quality of employees that worked in the library system. The top-level employees were the professionals, defined as personnel with a Master in Library Science (MLS) from an accredited university. Their education provided them with a broad base of knowledge about all facets of library operations, defined as program-oriented to perform planning, administrative and supervisory roles. In 2004 there were 28 MLS professionals and 15 in librarian positions with equivalent experience employed with the system. The library had 106.7 full-time equivalent (FTE) employees in 2004.

Paraprofessionals were the next level below the professionals. They are task oriented, for example, acquisition, cataloguing, repair, circulation and interlibrary loans. According to Jack Fitzpatrick, Cataloging Department, Auburn University Libraries, and Chairman of the Alabama Library Association's Paraprofessional Roundtable, the American Library Association tends to use "library support staff," which is used interchangeably with the Alabama Library Association's "paraprofessional." Paraprofessionals, however, are clearly distinguishable because they perform distinctive library-unique tasks, compared to information specialists or custodian staff.[21] Paraprofessional was a more descriptive word toward increasing the professionalism within library associations. Two members of the Huntsville-Madison County Public Library in 1997, and still there in 2004, were quoted in *The Alabama Librarian*:

"One year ago I became an Audiovisual Acquisitions Librarian. I had experience in selections and a library computer course on the Internet. I also had an MLS. I had no practical experience acquiring AV materials using a computer. Our department had one professional and three paraprofessionals. When my job started a fourth paraprofessional was added who would work with me in AV Acquisitions. The three paraprofessionals who ordered books taught me and the 4th paraprofessional how to order, receive, and invoice on the computer. This involved teaching us great detail in a short amount of time with no break from their own work. Their patience was endless and the moral support unflagging. In addition to what they had been specifically asked to teach us, they often made suggestions which made our work easier and more efficient. The 4th paraprofessional had previously worked in the Audiovisual Department and was very helpful with sources of AV materials and with preparing the materials for the technical services department. Six months after my job began, we changed our server and had to start all over again with a new computer program. The paraprofessionals asked pertinent questions about the new program and made many suggestions on how to improve it. They also were vital in helping me make the transition from the old program to the new one. I believe I have learned more in this one year than ever before and I have the paraprofessionals to thank for most of that knowledge. I am very grateful to them and think they are invaluable to our library." Patsy Gray, M.L.S.

"Our paraprofessionals are vital to the success of our library. With a Main Library, 12 branch libraries, and our bookmobile, paraprofessionals staff key positions in our library system. In the community libraries of Hazel Green, New Hope, Gurley, and Triana our branch heads are paraprofessionals. Two of our City of Huntsville branches are headed by paraprofessionals, both of whom have worked more than 30 years for the library. Our Subregional Library for the Blind and Physically Handicapped is headed by a very dedicated and knowledgeable paraprofessional.

Paraprofessionals also head some specialized departments in our Main Library. These individuals have undergraduate degrees in areas that strengthen our services, especially social work, early childhood education, and history among others." Donna Schremser, Director.[22]

The full-page advertisement announced "The Great Big Book Bash" on Saturday, April 10, 2004. The Bash had children's book illustrator, Michael White, demonstrate his drawing techniques to children. White, who illustrated the popular children's book, *The Library Dragon*, held interactive drawing sessions with students in a thousand schools across the nation. There were three program times of 90 minutes each, starting at 9 a.m., 12 p.m., and 3 p.m. The tickets were $10 person, but children must be accompanied by a ticket-holding adult. The proceeds will benefit the Library Book Fund and was organized by the Library Foundation. Governmental agencies do not provide adequate funding to keep enough library books coming into the facility, so the library has to hold fund-raising events. The Library's website is www.hpl.lib.al.us.[23]

Library service to nursing homes and assisted living facilities was another outreach program. Sarah Bradford selected books, 95% large-print, for distribution to the target locations. Books on tape, CDs and videos were also provided. The materials were checked out to the facility in the main library building. Sarah and Floyd Turner visited the locations every 3-4 months and rotated the books. Each facility controlled the 50-75 books at its location. In 2004 service was provided at 26 locations. The books at Atria Assisted Living on Bailey Cove Road were shelved in a reading and quiet room with comfortable furniture. Kate McLemore, activity director, said that some folks read in that room, while others took the books to their rooms to read.[24]

On April 5, 2004, two young boys sat on the floor with their backs leaning against the back bookshelf in the back left corner of the Monrovia Branch Library. Aged 10 and 7, they worked on their home-schooled assignment with books strewn about them. They were almost oblivious to the 50 adults talking just 15 feet away. They obviously were not going to let those noisy adults spoil their quest for knowledge. The head librarian, Mary Lacey, said there are many home-schoolers in the Monrovia area.

Fifty feet away, at the other side of this small building, a four-year girl sat on a padded chair at a computer. Her feet dangled six inches off the floor. She was wearing earphones as she played children's games on the computer. This is called pre-home schooling, as she was the sister of the two boys. She was definitely oblivious to those noisy adults just four feet away, as I was one of them.

Now, about those noisy adults. It was money that brought them together, a normal occurrence for centuries. We had gathered around a check for $100,000, which was 4 by 1 ½ feet, setting on an A-frame for everyone to admire. The featured attraction, other than the money, was U.S. Representative Robert "Bud" Cramer, Fifth Alabama Congressional District. He brought the check for a new library building.

The location of this event was the Monrovia Public Library Branch, located on Jeff Road in northwest Madison County. The building in 2004 was a double-wide mobile home donated to the library by the Tennessee Valley Authority in 1997. The branch library had outside return boxes for books and videos. Inside were three computers and an iBistro library catalog. The entire unit was 25 by 60 feet, so it was tight inside. As a sign of the information age, the table for pre-reader tykes held three keyboards and one telephone – without cords, the toys of the Information Age. But that does not bother those make-believers.

Dale Strong, District 4 Commissioner, Madison County, said the new 5,000 square foot library would be named after Woody Anderson, the local Ford dealer and community activist. Anderson died recently and was represented by his wife, Cathy. The library will be part of a new community center, which was scheduled for completion in 2005. The Monrovia Library's 60,000 checkouts was the largest number of checkouts of any rural library within Madison County. That number equated to 230 for each day the library was open, but one has to visit the facility to better appreciate the situation. The library also had an active Friends of the Library organization.

A reader of *The Huntsville Times* wrote a question to the paper in May 2004 about the deteriorating condition of the lounge chairs in the magazine and newspaper reading room. The answer:

Donna Schremser, director of the Huntsville-Madison County Library, said the library does not have money to replace or reupholster the large, maroon, vinyl-covered chairs. There are currently about 200 of the chairs in service on all three floors of the library and about 700 are in storage. They have been in service at the library for 17 years. Those chairs were all reupholstered several years ago at the cost of $500 each. The library is planning to include a coffee shop with tables and less expensive chairs and the library board intends to start accepting bids from vendors in late June.[25]

The Eleanor E. Murphy Branch on Charlotte Drive was a full service library in 2004. Carolyn Courtenay, head librarian, had been at the branch for 25 years. There was a meeting room (small fee) with a seating capacity of 40 persons. That was the only unstuffed place in the building. The kindergarten through eight grade school population decreased 8-10 percent from 1997 to 2002, as the adjacent serviced neighborhoods were aging. In general, Huntsville was spreading out, with the greater propensity of younger parents to move outward. The library's children's story hours were held in the meeting room, as most of the other branches had a nice multi-colored carpet to attract the children.

The branch had 4 Internet computers and 1 iBistro catalog computer for the patrons. All shelves are stuffed like sausages. Space and breathing room were at a premium. But the branch continued to be busy. The friends of the library were active, as the friends store in the back right corner was also stuffed. It was open when the library was open as payment was made at the circulation desk. I bought one of the friends book bags for $5, which was a bargain for the heavy-duty canvas bag with the outline of the building and the branch name on the side. The branch was open Monday-Thursday, 9a.m.-8p.m.; Friday and Saturday, 9a.m.-5p.m.; and closed on Sunday for a total of 64 hours per week.

The Bailey Cove Branch Library at 1409 Weatherly Plaza was a busy place in 2004. The building was originally a hardware store, but was completely remodeled to current library standards when the city bought the building in 1997 and started the first branch in that area. It had 11 computers for the patrons: 8 for Internet access; 1 play station; and 2 iBistro catalog research stations. There was a large children's area with a multicolored design carpet for the children to sit on during story hours. There was also a 50-person capacity room for meetings (small fee) and book sales. On the circulation counter was a copy of the 3rd Edition of *Cooking by the Book*, a collection of cooking recipes by library employees from many locations. It was a fund raising effort by the library. The branch was open Monday-Thursday, 9a.m.-8p.m.; Friday and Saturday, 9a.m.-5p.m.; and Sunday 1-5p.m. for a total of 64 hours per week. The branch head was Mary Wallace. There were 4 children's play stations.

During April, May and June 2004 the Huntsville-Madison County Public Library, *The Huntsville Times* and the area bookstores worked together again for "Get Caught Reading," a program to encourage residents to read the same book and participate in discussion groups and other activities. The 2004 selection was *The Hornet's Nest: A Novel of the Revolutionary War*, by former President Jimmy Carter. It was touted as the first work of fiction ever written by a president of the United States. That selection was correlated with the event described in the next paragraph.

The Huntsville Museum of Art, during the period May 22-July 18, 2004, was one of only eight museums nationwide to host *Becoming a Nation: Americana from the Diplomatic Reception Rooms, U. S. Department of State.* The exhibition featured decorative and fine arts, and documented the beginnings of the Department of State and the original of American foreign policy.

The library was a proud partner of the exhibit, along with many other agencies in Huntsville. The library was a natural focal point for hosting lectures on the subject and holding children's activities to support the event. The library's activities are below:

"-Thursday, May 27, 7:00 pm, Main Library Auditorium

"Carry me Back to Ole...Searching the Bottom of the Barrel for Your Migrating Ancestor's Previous Residence in the Old South." Robert S. Davis, History Instructor at Wallace State College will lead this discussion co-sponsored with the Tennessee Valley Genealogical Society.

-Sunday, June 6, 2:00-4:00 pm, Main Library

Inventing the Cotton Gin: Machine and Myth in Antebellum Alabama, The cotton gin was developed in ancient Asia but has acquired an almost mythological status in America. Join Auburn History Professor Dr. Angela Lakwete as she explores the myth and the machine in its Old and New World forms and its impact on Alabama and culture and economics.

-Monday, June 7, 7:00 pm, *Get Caught Reading* discussion of *The Hornet's Nest* in the Main Library Auditorium.

-Tuesday, June 8, 10:00 am, *Get Caught Reading* Discussion –Bailey Cove Library-*The Hornet's Nest.*

-Wednesday, June 9, noon, Brown Bag Lunch-Main Auditorium. Discussion of *The Hornet's Nest.*

-Thursday, June 10, 7:00 pm, Huntsville Heritage Room-Main Library. *Locating your American Revolutionary War Ancestor* with James Maples. James is Vice President of the Alabama Society Sons of the American Revolution and vice President of the Alabama Cemetery Preservation Alliance. He will present a program of finding aides for American Revolutionary soldiers using sources located in the Huntsville Heritage Room.

-Friday, June 11, 10:00 am, Movie and Book Discussion-*Johnny Tremain* at the Bailey Cove Library- (for grades 4-7) This story of a tragically injured young silversmith who ends up hip-deep in the American Revolution is inspiring, exciting, and sad. Winner of the prestigious Newberry Award in 1944, Esther Forbes' story has lasted these 60 years by including adventure, loss, courage, and history in a wonderfully written, very dramatic package.

-Thursday, June 17, 7:00 pm, Main Library Auditorium, *Early American Samplers: Presentation and Exhibit,* Linda Worley has owned and operated "Patches and Stitches" a needlework shop located on Humes Avenue for over 26 years. She is a collector of fine early American needlework, her most prized possessions are her antique American samplers dating back to 1736.

-Monday, June 21, 4:00 pm, Family Movie Night-Madison Public Library-*Johnny Tremain*. In colonial Boston, a young silversmith's apprentice injures his hand and finds himself befriended by the Sons of Liberty and caught up in events of the American Revolution. Join us for this special showing the Walt Disney depiction of Esther Forbes' Revolutionary War novel *Johnny Tremain*. Bring your friends and some snacks!

-Monday, June 28, 6:30 pm, *Get Caught Reading* Book Discussion at Madison Public Library-*The Hornet's Nest* by Jimmy Carter.

-Monday, July 12, 6:00 pm, Monday Night at the Movies at Madison Public Library-*The Patriot*.

-Wednesday, July 14, noon, Brown Bag Lunch-Main Library Auditorium. Christopher Lang, Alabama Humanities Speaker presents "Classical Furniture of the Tennessee Valley: Discovering Antique Alabama Furniture.

-Tuesday, July 20, 4:00-5:00 pm, "Becoming a Nation" Art Show. View interpretations of the theme "Becoming a Nation," by youth patrons of the Bailey Cove Library. Meet the artists and enjoy light refreshments.

-Friday, July 23, 10:00 am, "Becoming a Nation: Felicity's Story" an American Girls Party at the Bailey Cove Library. Experience 1774 through the eyes of Felicity, an American girl. Come in period costume and enjoy a skit, crafts, and period food."[26]

The bookmobile operations in the summer of 2004 were a valuable contribution to the outreach efforts of the Huntsville-Madison County Public Library. These operations will be described in detail to provide perspective to the overall mission of the library. The summer was a much busier time than the winter for the bookmobile. Six Huntsville elementary schools were on academic alert by the state regulating agency, so a *Camp Success* was conducted at those schools during the summer. The children met at the schools under teacher supervision, and the bookmobile visited to keep books flowing through the children's hands and mind. Each grade level, starting with the lowest, was released to visit the bookmobile in turn. It only takes about ten kids to overrun the bookmobile at any one time. It was a joy to watch the process. They filed in and deposited the books from last week into baskets by the door. The children were gently reminded by the librarian, Geoffrey Jolly, who was the consummate jolly professional. The children then scrambled around in their designated-age shelves to discover new books to take home for a week. Jolly nicely advised one boy whether he had really wanted a Spanish-language book, which he did not. The bookmobile had six linear feet of Spanish-language material, which was considerable since the limited shelving had to serve adults at corporations, folks at retirement homes, as well as the total spectrum of youth ages. Within each customer grouping were "best sellers," new fiction, DVD's, Videos, CD's (music and books), large print fiction, large print mystery, and adult and junior biographies. The variety in such a small area was a credit to Geoffrey Jolly. He smoothly steered all children to the appropriate shelf, while trying to answer my questions and check out books at the same time.

Geoffrey Jolly was the bookmobile librarian for 14 years, as of 2004, and the current bookmobile is also 14 years old. The bookmobile route in the summer of 2004 was on a two-week cycle. Some stops were on each week, while others were only visited once in two weeks. The Week 1 schedule follows:

Monday
-9:00-10:00   Lakewood Elementary *Camp Success*
-10:15-11:15   Rolling Hills Elementary *Camp Success*

-11:30-12:15	Adtran
-2:00-2:30	Locust Grove Baptist Church
-3:00-4:00	Martin Luther King Elementary *Camp Success*
Tuesday	
-9:30-10:00	Mayfair Towers
-10:15-10:45	Johnson Tower
-11:00-11:30	Summitt Apartments
-1:45-2:45	West Huntsville Elementary *Camp Success*
-3:00-4:00	Lincoln Elementary *Camp Success*
Wednesday	
-9:00-10:00	Blossomwood
-10:15-11:15	Whitesburg
-1:45-2:45	Montview Elementary *Camp Success*
-3:00-3:30	University Park
-3:45-4:15	Squaw Valley
Thursday	
-9:00-10:00	Challenger Elementary
-10:15-10:30	Opportunity Center
-10:45-11:30	Hunter Chase/Madison
-11:45-12:15	Teledyne Brown
-2:00-3:00	Lockheed Martin
-3:15-3:45	Valley Garden
Friday	
-10:00-11:00	Wyle Laboratories
-11:15-12:15	First Baptist Church

Adults can check out 5 music CD's, 2 audio books on CD, and 5 audio books on tape per visit. Young readers can check out 10 books, 3 videos, 5 audio book tapes, 2 audio books on CD, and 5 music CD's at a time. Long gone were the days when only books were available at the library. If you think that only books are available, you are quite ancient. Of course, for the ancient, there are large print books available. The elderly can have books for one month instead of the usual two weeks.

The adult fiction was kept current in the bookmobile because of limited space. Best sellers were weeded out when they were three years old because the readers want only the "hottest" books. Patrons were allowed only one renewal. Many patrons used the bookmobile as a convenient way to return books, regardless of which location the books were signed out.

Three Springs was a commercial home for troubled male teenagers and was located in the extreme western section of Madison County on Browns Ferry Road. In the summer of 2004 it was a biweekly stop on the bookmobile's Thursday route. It was also a special case for the library. There was security so the occupants would not run away. The prospective patrons were escorted to the bookmobile in groups of three, each group accompanied by a staff member. Three patrons were allowed on the vehicle to find books, while the escort stood in the door. The next three patrons, with their escort, sat on the steps outside in the sun, waiting their turn inside.

The patrons were not allowed adult books which might have sex and violence in them. Geoffery Jolly guided them to the appropriate shelves. One young man brought a book to check out that had the word Murder in the title. Jolly gently told the person that he could not check it out. The patron found another book. The contents could not be immediately discerned from the cover or title. Jolly carefully read the synopsis on the inside of the front and back dustcover to deem it acceptable as far as could be determined, and checked it out.

"Altruism and Teens - Not an Oxymoron!

Stephenie Walker, Youth Services, Madison Public Library

It's pleasantly shocking when we live in a community where young adults between the ages of 13-18 compete to be chosen for volunteer work at the library. Students these days, at worst are viewed as idle, unreliable, and more interested in the next new video game or what Jennifer Lopez is wearing. At best, they are just too busy. Between soccer practice, church choir, summer jobs, and camp, most have trouble finding enough time to spend with their family and friends over the summer holiday.

A remarkable thing is happening at the Madison Library, as well as other branches across the county. Shortly after Spring Break, first a trickle, and then a barrage of teens were in desperate need of volunteer positions. It seems more than ever in the cut-throat world of college applications and scholarships, volunteerism is held in high regard. Ambitious students have a better chance of being accepted in their first choice colleges if they have an impressive community volunteer record.

This summer the Madison Public Library accepted 38 student volunteers to assist with summer programs and library functions. 'Having to rely on teen volunteers can be tricky; during the summer there is always the lure of something more exciting to do...shopping, swimming, or just hanging out with friends,' says library manager Helen Lee. "Not only are these young adults consistent and reliable, they are also meticulous and exacting in their work. They are wonderful role models for our youngest patrons as well!"

Over 50 applications were submitted, and 30 were chosen to supplement the 8 regular year-round student volunteers already in place. The teen volunteers then attended a mandatory orientation and training session offered by library staff. To complete their summer program, teens must volunteer at least 15 hours and help facilitate two children's programs. Several students are back for their second and even third summers in the volunteer program:

'This summer Madison Public Library is busier than ever but our wonderful teen volunteers have made a significant difference and enabled staff to continue to provide top-notch service to our patrons.' Lee concluded.

So the next time you return your books, videos, CDs and DVDs, remember that the backbone of any non-profit organization is its volunteers. You might ask yourself, how can I give back to my community? The answer is no further than the closest branch of the public library." The six paragraphs quoted above were from *Cover to Cover*, July/August 2004, the bimonthly publication of the Friends of the Huntsville-Madison County Public Library.

Seventy-five memorials and honorariums were given to the library during April-June 2004, and were listed in the Friends' newsletter.[27]

"Dear Friends,

The library needs your help this month. I am sure you are aware that the library has the highest per capita circulation rate of any library in Alabama, while its budget is one of the lowest for a library of its size. You may not be aware that the library has been level-funded by the city for the last seven years. This high facility usage and no increases in funding have led to a number of maintenance problems, some of them very costly. There are major problems at the library entrance with leaking windows with a need for a re-design. After 17 years of wear and tear it is vital that the library replace carpet on the second and third floor. There are also structural problems with the ceramic tile throughout the library. There are other problems with such things as wallpaper and plumbing, many caused by vandalism.

We need you to help us by contacting the mayor and your representative on the city council and telling them you support the library and an increase in funding to help solve some of these problems. At the bottom of this page I have included a list of these decision-makers and their e-mail addresses. Please tell them you are a member of the Friends of the Library and that you want a facility we can be proud of! Thank you!

Sincerely, Sally A. Howard, President, Friends of the Library" The above also included the names and e-mail address of the mayor and city council members.[28]

The summer of 2004 was also the time for The Brown Bag Book Club series, which featured a variety of noon book reviews and discussions at several of the larger locations. For example, Dr. Paul Gray discussed "Poison and Poisoners of Ancient Rome" at noon on Wednesday, August 11, at the main library's meeting room. Attendees brought their own lunch, while drinks and desert were provided for the 29 attendees. The Roman emperors, their wives and relatives were a distrustful group.

The modern day library was not just a place to find books, but was a general-purpose location for learning. Computer skills are necessary for jobs and entertainment. The library provided computer training for free, just sign up. Below are the computer offerings in the late summer of 2004.

"Huntsville-Madison County Public Library

Regional Computer Training Center

Public Class Schedule Signup for this schedule begins Monday, August 9 at 9:00 a.m.

EBOOKS AT YOUR LIBRARY

(learn how to search for electronic books and work with your account; requires Basic Internet)

Tuesday, August 24 9:30 a. m. - 11:30 a. m.

ALABAMA VIRTUAL LIBRARY

(a description of each AVL resource and how to use it; requires Basic Internet)

Wednesday, August 25 9:30 a.m. - 11:30 a.m.

KEYBOARDING FOR BEGINNERS (CLASS 3 OF 3) {using Letter Chase Typing Tutor; requires Keyboarding Part 2}

Wednesday, August 25 1:30 p.m. - 3:30 p.m.

BASIC PC SKILLS

(for those just starting to use computers)

Tuesday, August 31 9:30 a.m. -11:30 a.m.

KEYBOARDING FOR BEGINNERS (CLASS 1 OF 3)

 (using letter Chase Typing Tutor to introduce you to basic keyboarding skills)

Wednesday, September 1 9:30 a.m. - 11:30 a.m.

BASIC PC SKILLS

 (for those just starting to use computers)

Wednesday, September 1   1:30 p.m. - 3:30 p.m.

WINDOWS

(getting around in Windows; requires Basic PC Skills)

Wednesday, September 8   9:30 a.m. - 11:30 a.m.

KEYBOARDING FOR BEGINNERS (CLASS 2 OF 3)

 (using Letter Chase Typing Tutor; requires Keyboarding Part 1)

Wednesday, September 8   1:30 p.m. - 3:30 p.m.

BASIC WORD

(word processing; requires Basic PC Skills)

Friday, September 10   9:30 a.m. -11:30 a.m.

LEARNING EXPRESS
(sponsored by the Alabama Public Library Service, this database contains more than 300 interactive online practice tests for school and career goals)
Monday, September 13   9:30 a.m. -11:30 a.m.
BASIC INTERNET
(for those just starting on the Web; requires Basic PC Skills)
Tuesday, September 14   9:30 a.m. - 11:30 a.m.
SPYWARE, PLUGINS, & POPUPS
(an introduction to the software you need to survive on the web)
Wednesday, September 15   9:30 a.m. -11:30 a.m.
KEYBOARDING FOR BEGINNERS (CLASS 3 OF 3)
(using Letter Chase Typing Tutor; requires Keyboarding Part 2)
Wednesday, September 15   1:30 p.m. - 3:30 p.m."[29]

Since the Regional Computer Training Center opened on February 17, 1998, through October 21, 2004, the following numbers of people have received training: 1988-2232; 1999-1766; 2000-1965; 2001-2402; 2002-2001; 2003-1401; and 2004-1113. The coordinator and instructor was Stormy Dovers.[30] The number of people receiving training has perhaps dropped the last two years because computers are more widely proliferated and there are more skilled people, especially children, who can teach relatives and friends. There are also other organizations that provide computer training, such as the Academy for Lifetime Learning at The University of Alabama in Huntsville for seniors. A reminder, back in 1997 this training center was funded by a grant from the Bill & Melinda Gates Foundation. At that time only 28 percent of the public libraries offered public Internet access. In 2004 that number was 95 percent and our main library Internet computers frequently had waiting lists. In 1997 the library received computers as part of that grant. Anyone very familiar with computers realized that a 1997 version was ancient, so those computers were being replaced as budget constraints allow. (Royer)

Raising money for the library was big business. For example, Donna Schremser, the director, reported to the board on April 18, 2004 that every author that had been asked for the Vive le Livre had either turned the library down or wanted $100,000. Retired General Tommy Franks, Commander, United States Central Command, and commander of forces in the Iraqi War of 2003, was one of those who wanted $100,000. The library finally secured the services of Christopher Buckley for a fee of $20,000.

The Library Foundation's principal function was to raise money for books through the annual Vive le Livre famous-person, dinner speaker program each autumn. The foundation board consisted of 19 people in 2004, including the library director, a library board member and a library staff member. Each year there was a separate committee to organize the Vive le Livre, with some people from the prior year and some newcomers. A list of the speakers, by year, speaker fee and foundation profit is below:

Year	Speaker	Fee-$000	Profit-$000
• 1988	Mark Russell	7.5	25
• 1989	Art Buchwald	10	13
• 1990	Mark Russell	15	15
• 1991	Robert Inman	7	12
• 1992	Molly Ivins	9.5	23
• 1993	Dave Barry	15	24
• 1994	Terry Anderson	15.5	11
• 1995	Scott Turow	15	24

• 1996	Pat Conroy	18	45
• 1997	Tom Wolfe	20	31
• 1998	John Berendt	15	54
• 1999	Homer Hickam	1	66
• 2000	Al Franken	25	34
• 2001	Doris Kearns Goodwin	30	50
• 2002	David McCullough	30	56
• 2003	Bob Woodward	30	85
• 2004	Christopher Buckley	20	91[31]

You can derive certain advantages from being an after dinner speaker. Mark Russell's fee doubled in two years. The trend of upward fees is partially due to inflation, but most of it is the demand by the hot names, and their agents, to make a bundle while they're hot. We all should thank our hometown boy, Homer Hickam, for his token fee. Bravo, Homer!

In mid-August 2004 my invitation arrived to participate in the Huntsville-Madison County Public Library's annual Vive le Livre (Long Live the Book) fund-raising event. The outside of the invitation card featured an open book in light blue color with light blue and blue-outlined white stars of various sizes floating out of the book. Above the book were the words, "Vive le Livre 2004" and "Long Live the Book."

Inside the card was printed in blue the following:

"The Huntsville Library Foundation

Invites you

To spend an evening with

Christopher Buckley

"The quintessential political novelist of his time"

Fortune magazine

Author of *No Way To Treat A Lady, Florence of Arabia* and others

Thursday, September 16, 2004

Cocktails at six o'clock

Dinner at seven o'clock

Von Braun Center, North Hall

R.S.V.P.

Reply card enclosed

Benefits the Huntsville-Madison County Public Library Book Fund"

The enclosed Reservation Card contained seven boxes that could be checked.

- AUTHOR'S CIRCLE, $5000 – 8 Reservations for Dinner and Speaker Reception with Mr. Buckley, 6 p.m.
- PATRON, $2500 – 4 Reservations for Dinner and Speaker Reception with Mr. Buckley, 6 p.m.
- SPONSOR, $1000 – 4 Reservations for Dinner and Speaker Reception with Mr. Buckley, 6 p.m.
- BENEFACTOR, $500 – 2 Reservations for Dinner and Speaker Reception with Mr. Buckley, 6 p.m.
- SCHOLAR, $125 – 1 Reservation for Dinner and Speaker Reception with Mr. Buckley, 6 p.m.
- BIBLIOPHILE, $50 – 1 Reservation for Dinner and Speaker, 6 p.m.
- REGRETS WITH DONATION FOR LIBRARY BOOK FUND $____

Your participation is greatly appreciated[32]

There was also an insert, which indicated that Barnes & Noble Booksellers was a partner with the library and would donate a percentage of the money spent on books at its store to the Library Book Fund.

A User Guide for Learning Express Library .com was found on the table to the right of the entrance to the main library. The table usually contains a variety of handouts, to include some from outside groups which wish to advertise. The Alabama Public Library Service purchased Learning Express Library database for all public libraries in the state. The database contained more than 300 interactive online practice tests for school and career goals. This resource was available on the public access computers in the Huntsville-Madison County Public Library system. The tests ranged from advanced placement English literature and composition to U.S. citizenship. The peach-colored handout provided easy instructions in words and computer screens. Those instructions were provided below without the computer screens.

"Registration through a public access computer within the Huntsville Madison County Library System is required. Once you have registered you will be able to access Learning Express Library from home, work or school on any Internet-capable computer.

To begin, on any public access computer in the Library System click the Desktop Shortcut or point your Web Browser to the following url: http://www.learningexpresslibrary.com/

1. Once you have opened the Learning Express site, you will need to create a user account. A Staff Member will be more than happy to assist you if necessary. Click on the 'New User Button' to open the registration page.
2. Enter your Library card number into the first field marked 'User Name.' Choose a Password and enter it into the second field marked 'Password.' Enter it again in the field marked 'Verify Password.' You may be prompted to use another User name if the one you've requested is already taken. **Please note: The Library is not responsible for maintaining or keeping a record of your password.**
3. Click on any one of the subjects you are interested in learning about.
4. While on this page you may want to add an email address so that the site may contact you if you need your password, or review the courses you've already taken. To begin the course, click on the 'Start' button.
5. Review the page to see the Course and then click the 'Start Course' button to begin.
6. Click on 'Next' or 'previous' to navigate through the course.
7. Practice tests are available after a series of lessons. Click on the 'Radio Buttons' to answer each question of the test.
8. Check your answers and review. You are welcome to retake the test in order to better your scores. **Please feel free to contact a Staff Member with any questions you may have about Learning Express Library."**[33]

The Bailey Cove Branch Library parking lot was full and overflowing into the next business area on Wednesday morning, September 15, 2004. A passerby on Bailey Cove would be tempted to stop in to see if $50 bills were being handed out. But there was a better deal than that underway. It was preschool story time. There were at least 30 children inside, which included several in mommy-slings as those mothers had other children participating. The children listened to about 15-20 minutes of stories, then swarmed around the counter to pick up paper, crayons and stick glue to continue the encounter with words, pictures, and paper.

Two adults were reading in the adult area, shielded from the children's din by glass-block walls on three sides. I was afraid to ask them if the noise bothered them because I thought they might tell me the truth. In another section of the library, but contiguous to the children's area, were five home-schooled children industriously working on their studies beside their mothers. They were dedicated to their effort. The five computer terminals were occupied. What a wonderful atmosphere of learning and enjoyment.

The Bailey Cove Branch was the scene of another typical library service activity on the night of September 23, 2004. Mary Wallace, head librarian, organized a book discussion group. The topic of this day was *Mauve, How One Man Invented a Color that Changed the World*, by Simon Garfield, 2001. There were 4 participants, in addition to Mary Wallace, when I entered the room a little late at 5 minutes past 6 p.m. One of the participants had prepared five questions, which were used as a basis for discussion. It was a spirited discussion. The group size of six people, despite the small number, represented the typical percentage of personalities: 1 person dominated 50 % of the time by rambling off the subject, but her comments on the book were appropriate; another person took 20% of the time by talking slow; 3 others divided the remaining time with concise thoughts; and the 6th person barely spoke. But overall it was a good discussion. Mary Wallace asked me at the end of the session if I would like to be added to the email notification list. I declined by explaining that I was really a spy working on this history, which drew mixed reactions, but I think they were in favor of such a library history.

The Huntsville Times lead story for the Arts in Brief page on September 19, 2004 was headlined by:

"Library honors freedom with banned books. The Madison Public Library, 130 Plaza Blvd., will 'Celebrate the First Amendment…Read a Banned Book!' during Banned Books Week Saturday through Oct 2.

Suggested books include the Harry Potter series by J.K. Rowling, 'Frankenstein' by Mary Shelly, the Bible, the Koran, 'Uncle Tom's Cabin' by Harriet Beecher Stowe 'The Handmaid's Tale by Margaret Atwood, 'Of Mice and Men' by John Steinbeck, 'Annie On My Mind' by Nancy Garden, 'The Catcher in the Rye' by J.D. Salinger and 'Fallen Angels' by Walter Dean Myers. For more information, call 461-0046."[34]

The Huntsville Times featured a "Partners for Charity" full-page advertisement for the various charitable organizations in the area. Each page had a commercial sponsor. We will now take a commercial break to tell you that the sponsor of the library advertisement on October 2, 2004 was Ashley Furniture Homestore, You're Gonna Love This Place. We now go back to regular programming. The advertisement was for the Friends of the Library, founded in 1958. Its mission statement is "To promote the interests of the Huntsville-Madison County Public Library system and its patrons, providing volunteer services and assisting the Library Board, the Huntsville City Council and the Madison County Commission in attaining the Library's stated goals of progress and improvement of the Library.

DONATIONS TO THE LIBRARY

In 2003, the Friends of the Library donated $130,000 to the Library for the purchase of books. The bulk of this amount was earned through the sale of books, magazines and audiovisual materials in the Friends' Bookstore, which is staffed and managed completely by volunteers. Donations from the community include materials in a wide range of topics, from Engineering and Math to Religion and Philosophy, from Foreign Language and English Literature to Sports and Games, and many more. These are all sold at very reasonable prices. Our sales and profits have increased each year, so the Friends have been able to help the Library more and more.

HERTHA HELLER FORUMS

Originally organized by Hertha Heller, a founding member of the Friends, these three Sunday afternoon programs in January, February and March, are diverse, interesting and well-attended programs provided to the community, free of charge. Details for 2005 are on this page under "Upcoming Events."

STUDENT AWARDS PROGRAM

The Friends of the Library honors student volunteers for their service to school libraries each year. The students receive certificates, and their names appear on walnut plaques provided by the Friends and on display in each school's library. This continuous recognition at school is augmented by a display in the Main Library's Youth Services area, where winners' names and photographs are displayed throughout the Summer Reading Program."

Also on the full page advertisement was a membership form, which prompted people to join the organization at various amounts of money, and to give a donation for a memorial or an honorarium book[35]

The cartoon, Family Circus, by Bil Keane, in *The Huntsville Times* on October 3, 2004, had a wonderful library theme. The mother was departing the library carrying three books. Her four children were in line behind her, each carrying books. One also has a knapsack full of books. Coming out the double doors also were the contents of the children's books: Cow jumping over the moon; Three men in a tub; Cupid; Mother Goose; football player; King Arthur; a scientist; a tiger; etc.[36] The cartoon represented well the library's contribution to the early stages of learning. Yes, many parents can afford to buy many of the nursery rhyme books, but others cannot. But very few parents can afford to buy all the books necessary to expose children to the variety of stories, animals, and people in history that pique a child's interest in reading and learning about our world.

Donna Schremser and her management team made their 2004-05 budget presentation to the city council work session on Monday, October 4, 2004. The submission was previously submitted on-line to the city and was in the council members' notebooks. The library director was given eight minutes to highlight items as she desired, and then five seconds to ask the question, "Are there any questions?"[37]

Since 2003 the main library had a self-checkout scanner on the right side going in and left side going out. Touch the screen to start the prompts. Wave your library's barcode card across the reader. Next pass the book's barcode across the scanner. Voila! A thermal receipt comes out of the slot, which is put in the book's packet. The security alarm will go off without the receipt.

The two branch libraries instituted in the 1960's were a result of Huntsville's population explosion in the 1950's. The Golden Decade of library expansion, 1987-1997, was a lagging result of Huntsville's and Madison County population explosion in the 1960's from 117,000 to 186,000. Population growth from 1970 through 2004 continued its upward spiral, albeit at a slower pace, although the 1980's increased more with 42,000 compared with an increase of 10,000 the previous decade. The Department of Defense and NASA facilities continued expanding, which brought more employment and a need for more housing. The increasingly affluent population demanded better education, which increased the need for more libraries. Money and education were natural partners, which increased the demands for more of each. Eventually, governments try to catch up with the major trends and support infrastructure improvements, to include libraries.

A national survey in 2002 of the number of public library branches per main library was divided into population groups. Madison County, the area served, had a population of 272,000, which placed it in the bottom 10% of the 250,000-499,000 group. That category had an average of 10.9 branches, and the Huntsville library had 11 branches. The category smaller, 100,000-249,000 averaged 5.8 branches. Interpolating those numbers, Huntsville had three more branches than the average for its size.

The Huntsville-Madison County Public Library's Strategic Plan 2003 To 2008 had facilities goals of investigating the need and feasibility of establishing branch libraries in two fast growing communities; Hampton Cove, in southeast Huntsville separated from the city center by Huntsville Mountain; and the Riverton/New Market area of northeast Madison County out Winchester Road. The probability of branches in those two areas in the near future is medium, considering the availability of money.

I'd previously run across a book, *The Happy Bookers, A Playful History of Librarians and Their World from the Stone Age to the Distant Future,* by Richard Armour, 1976. I looked on the library's website and discovered two copies in the system. One copy was at the Eleanor E. Murphy Branch on Charlotte Drive and the other at the main library. I first went to the Charlotte location, but could not find it on the shelf. The librarian looked it up in the computer inventory and discovered it was last checked out in 1987 and not returned. That was suspicious, and just think of the 17-year late fine for that book. I immediately went to the main library, found it on the shelf and self-checked it out. Then I went, book in hand, to ask Julie Blackwell, manning the desk in the adult section, to look it up on her screen. The screen now indicated that the Charlotte copy was "not returned" and that someone had checked out the main copy on October 7, 2004, which was me. The screen also indicated that main's copy was previously last checked out in 1991. The not-returned book from 1987 illustrated the problem the library has of trying to keep tabs on its inventory. Before computers it was difficult to keep track of books not returned, because it took a new request for the library to discover that it was missing, but it was much easier in the age of computers. The book had 132 pages, with lots of white space and wonderfully illustrated cartoons, and was a quick read. The author provided facts about the subject and added brilliant satire and humor throughout. Librarians should read it because they will smile knowingly throughout the entire book. Other patrons will gain knowledge of book and library history, and be entertained. I found a copy on the Internet and bought it for my library.

The library's public relations effort was divided into three major categories: national programs; locally generated programs; and the library foundation. The national programs included library week, banned books week, and library card signup month. The American Library Association provided themes and materials, usually through the Alabama Library Association.

The locally generated programs included children's reading hours, summer reading programs and Huntsville-unique programs such as space activities, get caught reading and coordination with the art museum's special exhibits. The main library personnel took the lead to develop materials and handouts. Each branch had different capabilities to implement such programs. Each of the branches also had different capabilities to contact local newspapers to publicize their events.

The library foundation's mission was to raise money, so events as the Vive Le Livre received significant publicity because they have the potential to raise the most money. Kathryn Dilworth, the library's publicist in 2004, as did her predecessors, maintained close contact with *The Huntsville Times* with weekly or special items of interest so the paper could send reporters to cover the stories. The publicist was also the editor of *Cover to Cover.*[38]

The digitization of seemingly everything was sweeping the country in the early years of the 21st century. Libraries had to react to the digitization rage because much of their materials were old, some really old. The challenge was great for the Huntsville Library, so their plan is quoted below:

"Huntsville Madison County Public Library Digital Collection Plan
2004-2009

Vision

The online digital repository will be established and maintained by HMCPL in recognition of the increasing importance of electronic access to unique materials of value to students, creators, scholars, researchers, and educators. The digital repository shall continue to grow and reflect the needs of the user in the spirit of co-operative research and scholarship with other like-minded institutions.

Mission

The mission of the HMCPL Archives is to serve as a repository for rare and unique materials pertaining to the history and development of the city, county, state, and region. This project serves to facilitate the mission of the HMCPL Archives by providing for improved access and preservation of the collection while actively encouraging a greater level of scholarly research than is possible through the physical facility.

Purpose

The purpose of HMCPL's digital collection project is to make more accessible the valuable materials housed in the Archives Department and to participate in regional and statewide initiatives such as the Cornerstone Project. Currently these materials are not available for everyday handling by the general public. Through the digitization of selected photographs, and in the future, manuscripts and other materials, the citizens and students of Alabama will be able to access images of great historical significance heretofore unknown to them.

Audience

The primary audience of the digital collection is middle school, high school and college students who are doing research for history papers and projects. As a participant in the Cornerstone Project, HMCPL's digitization efforts will support topics detailed in Alabama Moments in American History: Supplemental Teaching Materials for High School Teachers. Other patrons may use the collection for genealogical studies or for research in writing books or articles. Digitization of these materials will help these users draw on images and manuscripts previously available to only a select few. Our audience will expand from local (Huntsville) to one that is worldwide.

Collection Description

The HMCPL Archives was created in 1973 to house the rare, fragile and unique material that has been part of the collection since the Library was established in 1818. The Archives contains primary source materials on the history of Huntsville, Madison County and the early years of our State, including the following:

• **Manuscripts** include records of churches, local organizations (DAR, Historical Society, Genealogical Society, etc.) and early businesses (cotton mills, general stores, etc.); diaries; journals and scrapbooks. Three special collections are:

The Clay Family Papers, covering the period from 1812 - 1877: These include Alabama statehood correspondence from Clement Comer Clay (Alabama Governor), Civil War correspondence from his three sons: Clement Claiborne Clay, John Withers Clay and Hugh Lawson Clay.

The Marie Howard Weeden Collection (Huntsville artist and author, 1886 - 1972): The collection is composed of correspondence, biographical and genealogical sketches, magazine works of poetry and paintings.

Huntsville's Textile Mill Village Oral and Photographic History Project: A collection of fifty-five audio taped interviews of workers from the three major cotton mills in Huntsville: Lincoln Mill, Dallas Mill and Huntsville Manufacturing Company. Especially interesting are the stories that relate to the village housing.

Photographs include over 25,000 positive photographic prints from the Huntsville and Madison County area. The prints date from the 1850's. They depict street scenes, schools, churches, cotton mills, portraits, public buildings and historic homes from the Twickenham District and Olde Towne. A recent addition to the collection is the Monroe Collection of over 15,000 photographs, which contains images dating from 1875-1950.

• **Rare Books** include the private library of Henry B. Zeitler of Mooresville, Alabama. A special strength of the Zeitler collection is its more than 10,000 volumes on the Civil War. With the Archives' added holdings, this is one of the most valuable Civil War collections in the Southeast.

Goals and Objectives

Goal I. Collection Policy and Development - HMCPL will create and maintain a digital collection policy which will be included in the Library's broader Collection Development Policy, and will adhere to the standards detailed in the main policy.

    Objective: Write a digital collection policy for the creation of a new electronic resource that draws from existing photograph and manuscript collections owned by the Archives Department. (2004)

Goal II. Preservation/Access - HMCPL will promote the preservation of and access to the archival materials through digitization.

    Objective: The materials to be digitized will be drawn from existing photograph and manuscript collections owned by the HMCPL Archives Department. (2004 - ongoing)

Goal III. Institutional Support - HMCPL will support ongoing efforts to digitize the archival collection by providing staff and exploring funding/support options.

    Objective 1: Provide staffing for project. (2004 - ongoing)

    Objective 2: Investigate equipment needs of the project. (2004 - ongoing)

    Objective 3: Explore options for financial support of the project. (2004 - ongoing)

Goal IV. Ownership, Intellectual Property Rights, Copyright - HMCPL will make a good faith effort to establish the ownership, intellectual property rights and copyright standing of the archival collection so that the Library violates no laws in the digitization, display, reproduction and distribution of photographs, manuscripts and other materials.

    Objective: Establish that HMCPL has ownership and digitize/display rights to the photograph and manuscript collections and other archival materials as possible. (2004 - ongoing)

Goal V. Interoperability - HMCPL will make every attempt to conform to established standards to ensure interoperability between HMCPL and other repositories.

    Objective: Create a collection that is accessible to search and retrieval from multiple types of systems. (2004 - ongoing)

Goal VI. Access to Digital Content - HMCPL is Z39.50 compliant and will utilize the hardware and software provided by the Cornerstone Project to create and manage collections of images and metadata for search and retrieval.

    Objective 1: Obtain assistance with scanning at the Cornerstone Project's scanning center at Auburn University Library. (2004 - ongoing)

    Objective 2: Use Endeavor's Encompass system to aid in creating collections of digitized images, creation of metadata, and search and retrieval. (2004 - ongoing)

Objective 3: : Provide the Cornerstone Project a high-profile space for linked access through the Library's existing website and Unicorn catalog to spotlight HMCPL's digital collection on the HMCPL website. (2004 -2005)

Goal VII. Metadata Standards - HMCPL will follow established standards for creating metadata records of digital resources.

Objective: Create and enter metadata for each image following the Cornerstone Project's established standards. (2004 - ongoing)

Goal VIII. Digital Formats - HMCPL will provide digital images to be accessed on the Cornerstone Project's and HMCPL's websites.

Objective: Provide JPEG images for access on the Cornerstone Project's and HMCPL's websites, and store TIFF files as archival copies. (2004 - ongoing)

Goal IX. Preservation of Physical Items - The digitization project will promote preservation of archival materials by preventing damage from frequent handling.

Objective: Minimize need for handling of original materials during the digitization process and afterwards through online access and copying of images to DVDs or CDs. (2004 - ongoing)

Goal X. Sustainability - The digital resources collection will be an ongoing part of the library's collection.

Objective: HMCPL will begin the digitization project by participating in the Cornerstone Project for the State of Alabama, and will continue to build a collection that will be relevant to the city, county, state, and region. (2004 - ongoing)

Goal XI. Marketing and Promotion - HMCPL staff will publicize and promote usage of the digital collection and will actively encourage scholarly research.

Objective: Publicize the digital collection through HMCPL and local media. (2004 - ongoing)

Goal XII. Reaching the Alabama K-12 Audience - HMCPL staff will actively promote the use of the digital collection to city and county school students.

Objective: HMCPL will communicate with teachers and students throughout Huntsville and Madison County schools to let them know the importance of the digitization project, and specifically the Cornerstone Project. (2005 - ongoing)

Goal XIII. Staffing and Training - HMCPL staff will support the digitization project and provide in-house training to promote staff awareness of the digital collection.

Objective: Training sessions will be held system-wide to familiarize staff with the project so that they may explain and promote the digital collection to patrons. (2004 - ongoing)"[39]

Huntsville has been a hotbed of technology ever since the German rocket scientists arrived. Donna Schremser reported that Sirsi Corporation has requested that the library beta test their new software product Mindleaders. The library would receive free use of the software through December 2004. Mindleaders offers test and certificate training. A beta software product is the last (hopefully) test by the preparing company, which is done by the eventual purchasers/users. Sirsi is a Huntsville-based library software company with worldwide customers, so this was a wonderful opportunity to test drive before we buy.[40]

In 2004 the Library paid an annual fee of $9,900 to Sirsi for the iBistro card catalog software. That money pales in comparison to the amount of personnel resources that the library would have to devote to produce a similar capability. Melissa Shepherd estimates it could take five personnel to collect and maintain the date about each book that flashes onto the screen when the title is entered. The Huntsville library was looking at wireless computer capabilities in 2004, but standards have to be established by the wider community, as well as security issues.

Improvements such as wireless were heavily dependent on grants, which the library staff diligently pursues on a continuous basis.[41]

The Madison Branch Library was a veritable beehive of activity in 2004. Helen Lee, the branch head, generated many program ideas to make the branch even more attractive. For example, she created the following flyer:

Shop

The Madison Public Library
Your one-stop source for all your information needs...

Business, Academic and Recreational

- Alabama Virtual Library (AVL)
- E-books
- Reference USA
- Value Line
- Morningstar
- 150 magazines and 19 national newspapers
- Videos, DVDs, music CDs, book tapes and book CDs
- 7 computers with internet access and word processing
- 2 computers "just for kids"
- Adult Reading Room with the latest fiction and non-fiction
- Wonderful year round programs for kids and teens
- Literary Giants Book Discussion for adults and young adults
- Monday Night at the Movies
- Recommended reads or "What do I read next?"

The Madison Public Library
Is
Family Friendly
We offer programs and materials for any age and interest!
We welcome and encourage your input.
Do you want something we don't have?
How can we provide better service?
We aim to please; this is your library!

Sign up for your library card today!"

Another example was the three Get Reading programs in the fall of 2004. Helen Lee led the Literary Giants group, which discussed *A Prayer for Owen Meany*, by John Irving in October and *Crossing the Safety*, by Wallace Stegner. Stephenie Walker led the The Eclectic Readers group with *Mountain Beyond Mountains*, by Tracy Kidder in October and *Bel Canto*, by Ann Pachett in November. Lance Young led Metamorphosis (Book to Film Group) with *Girl with a Pearl Earring*, by Tracy Chevalier (book) in October and the same title in a movie starring Colin Firth and Scarlett Johansson in November.

Helen Lee's father was in the Army and her husband was in the Army, so she was well schooled in the military culture. The Madison area's population was thick with people whose jobs were connected to military support and some of them were in Iraq. Susan personally generated the flyer below because of her knowledge of the military:

"Conflict in Iraq
Links to resources on the war in Iraq

These websites include history, current events and statistics on Iraq.

Country Profile: Iraq Profile of Iraq including the latest news, demographic and economic facts, historical overview, timeline of key events, and information about Iraqi leaders and media. Site also includes key stories, news analysis, links, audio features, and a video for the most recent live coverage. From the British Broadcasting Corporation (BBC).

http/news.bbc.co.uk/1/hi/world/middle east/country profiles/791014.stm

Timeline: Iraq

A brief chronology of key events covering 1922 to the present about Iraqi government and politics. Includes topics such as political history, foreign relations, Iran-Iraq War, oil, chemical weapons, Kuwait, Kurds, Oil-for-Food, weapons inspectors, United Nations resolutions, and the United States. Also from the British Broadcasting Corporation.

http://news.bbc.co.uk/1/hilworld/middle east/737483.stm

CIA World Factbook - A brisk and easy to use compendium of facts on Iraq's history, society, politics, economy, communications, transportation, and military.
http://www.cia.gov/cia/publications/factbook/

Hot Spot: Iraq Informative website by National Geographic that includes maps, articles, and lesson plans for K-12.

http://www.nationalgeographic.com/iraq/

International Data Base

Demographic statistics by the US Census Bureau, including past, present and projected future data, plus population pyramids.

http://blue.census.gov/cgi-bin/ipc/idbsum?cty=IZ

US Department of Energy

Energy profile of Iraq.

http://www.eia.doe.gov/emeu/cabs/iraq.html

Library of Congress Foreign Area Handbook

Authoritative discussions of Iraq's history, society, culture, economy, security. Also summaries of the historical setting of the Persian Gulf, the role of Islam, Gulf wars, and much more.

http://lcweb2.loc.gov/frd/cs/igtoc.html

U.N. Oil-for-Food Program The Program that covered 24 sectors of need in Iraq, in addition to providing food to 60% of Iraq's 22 million people before the war. On 3/28/03 the U.N. Security Council voted to resume the program to enable the UN to continue to provide humanitarian assistance to the people of Iraq.

http://www.un.org/Depts/oip/

U.S. Central Command Operation Iraqi Freedom briefings, news, links, photos and video of the war.

http://www.centcom.mil

Operation Telic UK Ministry of Defense information about the UK part in the war in Iraq.

http://www.operations.mod.uk/telic

ICRC The International Committee of the Red Cross is the only humanitarian relief organization at work in the combat zones of Iraq as of 3/25/03. An important source of information on the condition of civilians and prisoners of war.

http://www.icrc.org/eng

USAID The United States Agency for International Development: Assistance for Iraq fact sheet. USAID has the primary responsibility along with the Defense Dept. to provide humanitarian and reconstruction assistance to the people of Iraq during and after the war.

http://www.usaid.gov/iraq/

U.S. White House Text of President Bush's statements, news and links to the White House information on National & Homeland Security.
http://www.whitehouse.gov
UK Online United Kingdom government information on the war in Iraq and other topics.
http://www.ukonline.gov.uk
DefenseLINK An extensive list of links to U.S. military organizations, news, fact sheets and information for military families.
http://www.defenselink.mil
Deployed Military Family Support U.S Defense Dept. "Deployment can be a difficult time for both members and their families." A list of Web sites to find resources for coping during times of separation, as well as providing vital information on support and policies for military families.
http://www.dtra.mil/deployedsupport/
Compiled by Helen Lee 4/16/03" Bravo, Helen!

Readers always want the latest popular books, whether they are biography or fiction. The Madison branch in October 2002 started to put colored stars on the books' spines. Books acquired during 2002 had gold stars, books in 2003 had red stars, etc. The first three months after acquisition the books were placed in the sleep room, otherwise known as adult reading. Then the books were moved to the regular stacks. The staff and patrons could move quickly along the stacks and identify the recent years of acquisition.[42]

Nearly all patrons at the main library visit the circulation desk – on the way out. The folks who visit the circulation desk on the way in just drop off materials and move on, although some people ask questions. A contrasting hotbed of interaction was at the circular reference desk on the second floor. David Lilly told me the time to catch the action was on a Sunday afternoon when lots of folks, including students, visited the desk. On October 31, 2004, I observed the operations for one hour from the inside of the desk, 1:20 to 2:20 p.m. Pam Payne and Silvia Elsner were kept hopping all the time. The following is a journal of the activities:

- All 10 Internet computer stations were occupied, with 4 persons on the waiting list. Each person can sign up for 30 or 60 minutes. During the next hour 17 people came by to sign up, but some did not want to wait. Meanwhile, the two stand-up computers were fully occupied as they had a 15-minute limit. Some folks were sent up to the computer training center on the third floor where there were 11 computers continually occupied.
- Two people signed up to get their Alabama Virtual Library (AVL) cards.
- One person signed out for the day's Sunday paper, and a second applicant was disappointed because the first one still had it.
- One patron needed an extra pen.
- A lady wanted an article in the October 21, 1991 issue of *TIME* magazine. She was first sent to the magazine paper's shelves on the second floor rear. It was not there, so the next place would be the microfilm drawers in the same area, but one of the library employees tried the Alabama Virtual Library because that would be easier, and the magazine was found but the lady did not know the exact title of the article. Eventually she went back to the microfilm and searched. The result was not observed.
- Another patron wanted poetry essays by Stephen White and a search was done on AVL.

284

- A young man wanted information on Hugh Hefner, the founder of *Playboy* magazine.
- There were three study rooms in use, as they were controlled from the reference desk. Three others were not occupied.
- The next patron wanted *Valueline,* the mutual fund rating group.
- The next man wanted manuals about automobiles, repair I think. He was later seen at the copy machine, so he was apparently successful.
- I received a religious solicitation while I was standing inside the reference desk.
- A man wanted to watch television while his young son did research. The library does not have a TV watching area, but that's a thought for progress. [Should the library employee have suggested that he read a book?]
- The man at the copy machine needed singles for a $5 bill and was accommodated by Pam Payne.
- The Huntsville-Madison County Public Library was clearly dedicated to serving. A University of Alabama in Birmingham student wanted old history books so she could determine how historians changed history. That was a tough question to answer, and she was on the computer searching when I left the area. Incidentally, historians are continually revising history, as strange as that might seem to the average person. Some years ago, Paul Johnson, a noted historian, was asked to predict the future and he replied that he couldn't, because he had difficulty predicting the past.
- Two women were looking for artists in California, so they were guided to Who's Who in the Art World database.

This history of the Huntsville-Madison County Public Library has provided only a sampling of the library's activities over the years. The evidence demonstrated the dedication and professionalism of the library's employees, library board members and library supporters toward providing the reading, and non-reading, citizens with the best opportunities for educational, recreational and cultural enhancement. **They have accomplished the mission!**

"THIS IS THE PUBLIC'S LIBRARY

Our mission is to enrich the educational, recreational, and cultural life of our community. Our knowledgeable and courteous staff will serve as the gateway to library materials, information, and programs."

NOTES

Chapter 1 – The First Century

1. Asheim, Lester, *Persistent Issues in American Librarianship*, p. 2.
2. Ibid., p. 9.
3. Ibid., p. 29.
4. www.cr.nps.gov/nr/twhp/wwwlps/lessons/50carnegie/50settin...
5. McMillan, Malcolm C., *The Land Called Alabama*, p. 169.
6. *Alabama Republican*, June 20, 1818.
7. Constitution Village Script, May, 2004.
8. Pruitt, Ranee, interview, October 13, 2004.
9. www.ushistory.org.
10. *Alabama Republican*, October 26, 1818.
11. Ibid., October 31, 1818.
12. Ibid., November 21, 1818.
13. *Sesquicentennial Commemorative Album*, 1955, Contributors: Mrs. C. H. Russell and Mrs. Claude Herrin.
14. Constitution Village Script, May, 2004.
15. Ibid.
16. *Alabama Republican*, October 29, 1819.
17. Ibid.
18. Constitution Village Script, May 2004.
19. *Huntsville Historical Review, The*, Summer-Fall 1995, Volume 22, No. 2, p. 14.
20. www.abebooks.com.
21. Ibid.
22. *Sesquicentennial Commemorative Album*, 1955, Contributors: Mrs. C. H. Russell and Mrs. Claude Herrin.
23. *Alabama Republican*, January 22, 1820.
24. *Old Huntsville*, Volume 52.
25. *The Huntsville Times*, June 18, 1972
26. *Old Huntsville*, No. 137.
27. *Alabama Republican*, December 7, 1821.
28. Ibid., February 15, 1822.
29. Ibid., March 1, 1822.
30. Alabama Legislative Act, December 29, 1823.
31. *Alabama Republican*, June 18, 1824.
32. Constitution Village Script, May 2004.
33. *Alabama Republican*, April 29, 1825.
34. Unidentified newspaper, Huntsville Library vertical files.
35. *Southern Advocate*, March 7, 1837.
36. Shera, Jesse H., *Foundations of the Public Library*, p. 78.
37. *Sesquicentennial Commemorative Album, 1955*, Contributors: Mrs. C. H. Russell and Mrs. Claude Herrin.
38. Ibid.
39. www.etc.princeton.edu/CampusWWWCompanion/whig_cliosophic.
40. McMillan, Malcolm C., *The Land Called Alabama*, p. 152.
41. Pruitt, Ranee, interview, October 13, 2004.
42. McMillan, Malcolm C., *The Land Called Alabama*, p. 216.
43. Pruitt, Ranee, interview, October 13, 2004.

44. Shera, Jesse H., *Foundations of the Public Library*, p. 44.

45. Ibid., 222.

46. Ibid, 196.

47. McMillan, Malcolm C., *The Land Called Alabama*, pgs. 155-6.

48. American Library Association Yearbook, 1976, p. 2.

49. McMillan, Malcolm C., *The Land Called Alabama*, p. 240.

50. Ibid., p. 257.

51. American Library Association Yearbook, 1976, p. 2.

52. Ibid., pgs. 3-4.

53. *Sesquicentennial Commemorative Album, 1955*, Contributors: Mrs. C. H. Russell and Mrs. Claude Herrin.

54. *The Weekly Mercury*, August 26, 1891.

55. Chapman, Elizabeth Humes, *Changing Huntsville, 1890-1899*.

56. Ibid.

57. Unidentified newspaper, Huntsville Library vertical files.

58. *Sesquicentennial Commemorative Album, 1955*, Contributors: Mrs. C. H. Russell and Mrs. Claude Herrin.

59. Proceedings of the First Meeting of the Alabama Library Association, November 21, 1904.

60. http://www.anes.uab.edu/alachron.htm.

Chapter 2 – Carnegie Was Here
The Library Board minutes are identified by the date and a hyphen, for example, "August 4, 1936 – " when the date is at the beginning of a sentence or paragraph.

1. www.cr.nps.gov/nr/twhp/wwwlps/lessons/50carnegie/50facts1…

2. Bobinski, George S., *Carnegie Libraries*, Appendix B, p. 222.

3. Ibid., pgs 18-21.

4. Ibid., Appendix B.

5. Ibid., pgs. 24-27.

6. www.cr.nps.gov/nr/twhp/wwwlps/lessons/50carnegie/50visual.

7. Bobinski, George S., *Carnegie Libraries*, p. 57.

8. Ibid., p. 62.

9. Ibid., p. 67.

10. Ibid., p. 68.

11. Ibid., p. 62.

12. Ibid., pgs. 150-1.

13. Huntsville Library Board, November 7, 1913.

14. Ibid., November 11, 1913.

15. Proceedings of the City Council of the City of Huntsville, Alabama at its Regular Meeting held Thursday evening, February 24, 1914.

16. Ibid., November 3, 1914.

17. Library Board, February 14, 1914.

18. Proceedings of the City Commissioners of the City of Huntsville, Alabama, February 9, 1915.

19. Ibid., April 27, 1915.

20. *Huntsville Mercury-Banner*, Tuesday, April 15, 1915.

21. Proceedings of the City Commissioners of the City of Huntsville, Alabama, May 25, 1915).

22. Ibid., October 11, 1915.

23. *Sesquicentennial Commemorative Album, 1955*, Contributors: Mrs. C. H. Russell and Mrs. Claude Herrin.

24. Proceedings of the City Commissioners of the City of Huntsville, Alabama, December 7, 1915.

25. Ibid., December 14, 1915.

26. Library Board, March 21, 1916.

27. Library Board, February 29, 1916.

28. Proceedings of the City Commissioners of the City of Huntsville, Alabama, March 7, 1916

29. Ibid., April 4, 1916.

30. Ibid., April 11, 1916.

31. Ibid., April 18, 1916.

32. *Sesquicentennial Commemorative Album, 1955*, Contributors: Mrs. C. H. Russell and Mrs. Claude Herrin.

33. *Old Huntsville*, #132. February, 2004.

34. Proceedings of the City Commissioners of the City of Huntsville, Alabama, August 29, 1916.

35. Ibid., March 20, 1917.

36. Ibid., April 17, 1917.

37. Ibid., January 22, 1918.

38. Ibid., February 12, 1918.

39. www.anes.uab.edu/alachron.htm.

40. Bobinski, George S., *Carnegie Libraries*, pgs. 162-3.

41. Ibid., pgs. 183-93.

42. Library Board, November 11, 1926.

43. Winger, Howard, *Seven Questions about the Profession of Librarianship*.

Chapter 3 – Regional Library
The Library Board minutes are identified by the date and a hyphen, for example, "August 4, 1936 – " when the date is at the beginning of a sentence or paragraph.

1. *Sesquicentennial Commemorative Album, 1955*, Contributors: Mrs. C. H. Russell and Mrs. Claude Herrin.

2. Snyder, Sarah, typed manuscript.

3. McMillan, Malcolm C., *The Land Called Alabama*, pgs. 368-9.

4. Huntsville Library Archives, March 16, 1937.

5. Ibid., undated.

6. Ibid., undated.

7. *The Huntsville Times*, June 5, 1938.

8. Huntsville Library Heritage Room vertical files.

9. *The Huntsville Times*, October 20, 1938.

10. Ibid., July 6, 1938.

11. Record, James, *A Dream Come True*.

12. Ibid.

13. *The Library Journal*, September 1, 1937.

Chapter 4 – World War II Comes to Huntsville
The Library Board minutes are identified by the date and a hyphen, for example, "August 4, 1936 – " when the date is at the beginning of a sentence or paragraph.

1. Proceedings of the City Council of the City of Huntsville, Alabama at its Regular Meeting held Thursday evening, February 8, 1940.

2. Huntsville Library Archives.

3. www.newdeal.feri.org/eleanor/er4b.htm.

4. Huntsville Library Board archives.

5. Ibid.

6. Ibid.

7. Ibid.

8. Ibid.

9. Maulsby, Ann Geiger, The Dulcina DeBerry Library, *Huntsville Historical Review,* Volume 22, #2.

10. Galvin, Hoyt R. *Planning a Public Library, iii.*

11. Huntsville Library Board Archives.

12. Ibid.

13. Work Projects Administration, May 7,1941.

14. Ibid., July 7,1941.

15. Huntsville Library Board Archives.

16. Ibid.

17. Ibid.

18. *The Huntsville Times,* March 3, 1943.

19. Huntsville Library Board Archives.

20. Cook, Mrs. Robert, correspondence, December 1, 2004.

21. Huntsville Library Board Archives.

22. Ibid.

23. Ibid.

24. *The Huntsville Times,* January 7, 1945.

25. Huntsville Library Board Archives.

26. Ibid.

27. Ibid.

28. Galvin, Hoyt R., *Planning a Public Library,* 58.

29. Huntsville Library Board Archives.

30. Ibid.

31. Ibid.

32. Sisk, Alice, interview, November 3, 2004,

33. *The Huntsville Times,* Jul-Dec, 1945.

34. (Snyder, Sarah, typed manuscript, D.O. Class of 1947, Heritage Room vertical files.)

35. www.ala.org.

36. American Library Association Yearbook 1976.

37. Huntsville Library Board Archives.

38. Ibid.

39. Ibid.

40. Ibid.

Chapter 5 – Space Comes to Huntsville
The Library Board minutes are identified by the date and a hyphen, for example, "August 4, 1936 – " when the date is at the beginning of a sentence or paragraph.

1. The Huntsville Times, August 9 1950.

2. *Sentinel,* Scottsboro, March 6, 1951.

3. *The Huntsville Times,* March 27, 1951.

4. Torrence, Missouri L., *Dulcina DeBerry: Door Opener.*

5. Huntsville Library archives.

6. Huntsville Library Newsletter, circa late 1951.

7. Stieg, Margaret F., *Public Libraries in Nazi Germany,* p. 150.

8. Piszkiewicz, Dennis. *Wernher von Braun,* pgs. 65-6.

9. Huntsville Library archives.

10. Huntsville Library Newsletter, circa late 1951.

11. Huntsville Library archives.

12. Ibid.

13. Ibid.

14. Huntsville Library Board.

15. Huntsville Library archives.

16. Ibid.

17. *The Huntsville Times*, May 29, 1952.

18. Huntsville Library Board.

19. *The Huntsville Times*, September 26, 1952.

20. Ibid., August 1952.

21. Huntsville Library Board archives.

22. Ibid.

23. *The Huntsville Times*, November 25, 1952.

24. Huntsville Library Board archives.

25. Ibid.

26. *The Huntsville Times*, April 30, 1953.

27. Ibid., May 1, 1953.

28. Ibid., April 26, 1953.

29. Ibid., May 3, 1953.

30. *Redstone Rocket*, June 25, 1969.

31. Gingerich, Owen, *The Book Nobody Read*, p. 130.

32. *The Huntsville Times*, March 1, 1955.

33. Huntsville Library archives.

34. *The Huntsville Times*, July 23, 2003.

35. Ibid., March 17, 1955.

36. Ibid., April 30, 1957 & June 13, 1973.

37. Purinton, Judy, interview, May 17, 2004.

38. Huntsville Library archives.

39. American Association of University Women. *A Half Century of AAUW in Alabama, 1927-1977.*

40. *The Huntsville Times*, January 24, 1958.

41. Library Board, March 18, 1958.

42. Library Board, April 15, 1958.

43. *The Huntsville Times*, June 1, 1958.

44. Huntsville Library Archives.

45. *The Huntsville Times*, September 3, 1958.

46. Ibid., January 1, 1959.

47. Ibid., November 5, 1958.

Chapter 6 – Finally, A Bigger Building

1. Shera, Jesse H., *Foundations of the Public Library*, p. 248.

2. *The Huntsville Times*, May 3, 1960.

3. Ibid., June 24, 1960.

4. Ibid., October 2, 1960.

5. Ibid., November 3, 1960.

6. Ibid., February 19, 1961.

7. Ibid., September 29, 1961.

8. Ibid., September 1961.

9. *American Library Association Yearbook, 1976.*

10. *The Huntsville Times*, April 9, 1963.

11. Huntsville Library archives.

12. *The Huntsville Times*, December 5, 1963.

13. Ibid., December 28, 1969.

14. *Huntsville News*, 15 January 1966.

15. *The Huntsville Times*, October 10, 1965.
16. Library Board Minutes, October 19, 1965.
17. *Huntsville News,* January 15, 1966.
18. *The Huntsville Times*, March 13, 1966.
19. Ibid, March 27, 1966
20. Ibid., March 20, 1966.
21. Bell Telephone News, May 1966.
22. *The Huntsville Times*, May 15, 1966.
23. Ibid., August 14, 1966.
24. Huntsville Library Board files.
25. *The Huntsville Times*, November 27, 1966.
26. *Huntsville News,* May 12, 1967.
27. *The Huntsville Times*, September 3, 1967.
28. Ibid., March 26, 1968.
29. Ibid., February 28, 1968.
30. *Huntsville News,* March 11, 1968.
31. *The Huntsville Times*, March 3, 1968.
32. Ibid., March 19, 1967.
33. Ibid., July 23, 1967.
34. Ibid., October 7, 1967.
35. Ibid., October 1, 1967.
36. Wiley, Peter Booth, *A Free Library in this City*, p 176.
37. Torrence, Missouri L., *Dulcina DeBerry: Door Opener.*
38. *The Huntsville Times*, May 25, 1968.
39. Ibid., June 2, 1968.
40. Ibid., August 4, 1968.
41. Ibid., October 14, 1967.
42. Ibid., March 3, 1968.
43. Ibid., March 24, 1968
44. *Huntsville News,* May 29, 1968.
45. *The Huntsville Times*, June 18, 1972.
46. *Huntsville News,* May 29, 1968.
47. Pruitt, Ranee, interview, October 13, 2004.
48. *The Huntsville Times*, April 21, 24, 25, 1968.
49. Ibid., May 5, 1968.
50. Ibid., May 19, 1968.
51. Ibid., December 8, 1968.
52. Ibid., December 15, 1968.
53. Ibid., November 26, 1968.
54. Ibid., April 13, 1969.
55. Ibid., May 6, 1969
56. Ibid., June 22, 1969.
57. Ibid., August 17, 1969.
58. Ibid., December 21, 1969.
59. Ibid., November 30, 1969.
60. Ibid., August 31, 1969.
61. Huntsville Library Heritage Room vertical files, undated paper.
62. *The Huntsville Times*, November 5, 1969.

Chapter 7 – Cooperized?
1. *The Huntsville Times*, December 1, 1967.
2. Ibid., December 2, 1967.
3. Ibid., December 3, 1967.
4. Ibid., December 3, 1967.
5. Ibid., December 4, 1967.
6. Ibid., December 5, 1967.
7. Shirer, William L. *The Rise and Fall of the Third Reich*, pgs. 333-4.
8. *The Huntsville Times*, December 6, 1967.
9. Ibid., December 8, 1967.
10. Ibid., December 10, 1967.
11. Ibid., December 10, 1967.

Chapter 8 – Outreach and Controversy
The Library Board minutes are identified by the date and a hyphen, for example, "August 4, 1936 – " when the date is at the beginning of a sentence or paragraph.
1. Huntsville Library Board files.
2. Ibid.
3. *The Huntsville Times*, May 10, 1970.
4. Ibid., August 9, 1970.
5. Ibid., June 7, 1970.
6. Ibid., June 21, 1970.
7. *Venture*, Volume 1, Number 9, November 1970.
8. *The Huntsville Times*, January 6, 1971.
9. Ibid., January 10, 1971.
10. Ibid., March 11, 1971.
11. Ibid., March 16, 1971.
12. *Huntsville News*, August 22, 1971.
13. *Impact, Model Cities*, Vol.2, No. 15, May 1971.
14. *The Huntsville Times*, November 21, 1971.
15. Ibid., January 14, 1972.
16. *Huntsville News*, January 28, 1972.
17. Paine, Thomas, *The Rights of Man*, p. 357.
18. *Huntsville News*, March 25, 1972.
19. McMillan, Malcolm C., *The Land Called Alabama*, pgs. 306-7.
20. *The Huntsville Times*, March 6, 1972.
21. *Huntsville News*, April 15, 1972.
22. *The Huntsville Times*, May 15, 1972.
23. *Huntsville News*, August 22, 1972.
24. *The Huntsville Times*, April 24, 1973.
25. Ibid., August 20, 1972.
26. McMillan, Malcolm C., *The Land Called Alabama*, pgs 110-1.
27. *The Huntsville Times*, August 20, 1972.
28. *Library Notes*, June-September 1972.
29. *Huntsville News*, January 29, 1973.
30. *The Huntsville Times*, April 19-20, 1973.
31. Press release, Huntsville Library archives, May 1, 1974.
32. *The Huntsville Times*, May 18, 1978.
33. American Library Association Yearbook, 1976.
34. Huntsville Library Annual Report, Fiscal Year 1975-76.

35. American Library Association Yearbook, 1976.
36. *The Huntsville Times*, February 16, 1975.
37. American Library Association Yearbook, 1976.
38. Ibid.
39. Huntsville Library Heritage Room, vertical file, March 28, 1976.
40. Huntsville Library Annual Report, Fiscal Year 1975-76.
41. *The Huntsville Times*, May 5, 1977.
42. Ibid., August 15, 1976.
43. Ibid., September 10, 1976.
44. American Library Association Yearbook, 1976.
45. *The Huntsville Times*, November 15, 17, & 18, 1977.
46. Roberts, Mrs. Roscoe (Jane), telephone conversation, March 20, 2004.
47. Huntsville Library Board files.
48. Grand Jury Report, Circuit Court, County of Madison, State of Alabama, January, 1978.
49. *The Huntsville Times*, Jan 27, 1978.
50. Library Board, February 15, 1978.
51. *The Huntsville Times*, May 19, 1978.
52. Towery, Martin, interview, October 7, 2004.
53. *The Huntsville Times*, November 12, 1978.
54. Huntsville Library Board files.
55. Ibid.

Chapter 9 – Public Radio
1. *Huntsville News*, November 1, 1972 and *The Huntsville Times*, November 1, 1972.
2. *The Huntsville Times*, January 20, 1974.
3. Huntsville Library Heritage Room vertical files.
4. *The Huntsville Times*, February 9, 2004.
5. Ibid., July 2, 1975.
6. Huntsville Library Heritage Room vertical files, August 26, 1975.
7. *Huntsville News*, November 9, 1975.
8. *The Huntsville Times*, January 16, 1976.
9. Ibid., April 20, 1976.
10. WLRH Public Radio News, October 13, 1976; *The Huntsville Times*, October 12, 1976 and October 14, 1976.
11. Huntsville Library Heritage Room vertical files.
12. *The Huntsville Times*, April 1, 1977.
13. Augustine, Norman. *Augustine's Laws*, p. 73.
14. *The Huntsville Times*, April 1, 1977.
15. Ibid., May 6, 1977.
16. Ibid., July 14, 1977.
17. Ibid., July 14,1977.

Chapter 10 – The Golden Decade Begins
The Library Board minutes are identified by the date and a hyphen, for example, "August 4, 1936 – " when the date is at the beginning of a sentence or paragraph.
1. Huntsville Library Heritage Room vertical file, July 1980.
2. Hamilton, John Maxwell, *Casanova Was a Book Lover,* p. 179.
3. Basbanes, Nicholas A. *A Gentle Madness*, p. 467.
4. *The Huntsville Times,* January 7, 1981.

5. Huntsville Library Board archives.

6. Towery, Martin, interview, October 7, 2004.

7. Huntsville Library Board archives.

8. *The Huntsville Times*, February 24, 1982.

9. Ibid., April 29, 1982.

10. www.server2.walkerweb.net/carlelliott/.

11. Huntsville Library Board archives.

12. Ibid.

13. *The Huntsville Times*, September 3, 1982.

14. Ibid., April 18, 1982.

15. Ibid., September 3, 1982.

16. Huntsville Library Heritage Room archives.

17. *The Huntsville Times*, March 4 & 17, 1983.

18. Huntsville Library Board archives.

19. Ibid.

20. *The Huntsville Times*, Aug 12, 1984.

21. Ibid., March 27, 1984.

22. Roberts, Mrs. Roscoe (Jane), telephone conversation, September 28, 2004.

23. *Huntsville News*, September 9, 1985.

24. *The Huntsville Times*, June 6, 1986.

25. *The Alabama Librarian*, April/May 1987.

26. Huntsville Library Board archives.

27. *The Huntsville Times*, August 12, 1987.

28. Huntsville Library Board archives.

29. *Huntsville News*, September 17, 1987.

30. Gurley Library scrapbook.

31. Huntsville Library Board archives.

32. *The Huntsville Times*, November 17-19, 1988.

33. Ibid., November 25, 1987.

34. Ibid., March 20, 1988.

35. Unidentified footnote to protect the blockhead's identity.

36. Huntsville Library Board archives.

37. David Lilly, interview, March 9, 2004.

38. Huntsville Library Board archives.

Chapter 11 – Fort Book

1. *The Huntsville Times*, June 19, 1984.

2. Ibid., September 23, 1984.

3. Ibid., September 23, 1984.

4. Ibid., May 7, 1985.

5. Ibid., October 9, 1985.

6. Ibid., September 1, 1985.

7. Ibid., February 19, 1986.

8. Ibid., March 30, 1986.

9. A Tradition of Leadership, undated pamphlet, circa 1985.

10. *The Huntsville Times*, May 23, 1986.

11. Ibid., August 10, 1986.

12. Ibid., December 7, 1986.

13. Huntsville Library Board archives.

14. *The Huntsville Times*, March 27, 1987.

15. Ibid., April 26, 1987.
16. Ibid., September 4, 1987.
17. Ibid., November 11, 1987.

Chapter 12 – Library Activists in New Hope
All information taken from the minutes of the meeting of the New Hope Friends of the Library, unless otherwise noted.
1. Maples, Mayme Claire, telephone interview, August 17, 2004.
2. Markham, Susan, interview, August 24, 2004.
3. New Hope Library archives.
4. Ibid.
5. Ibid.
6. Ibid.
7. Ibid.
8. Ibid.
9. Ibid.
10. New Hope Library Volunteer Handbook, undated.
11. New Hope Library archives.

Chapter 13 – Outreach and More Outreach
The Library Board minutes are identified by the date and a hyphen, for example, "August 4, 1936 – " when the date is at the beginning of a sentence or paragraph.
1. *Huntsville News*, January 29, 1990.
2. Huntsville Library Board Archives.
3. Ibid.
4. *The Huntsville Times*, April 1990.
5. Ibid., October 21, 1990.
6. Ibid., April 11, 1991.
7. *Cover to Cover*, Friends of the Library newsletter, July/August 1991.
8. *The Huntsville Times*, August 25, 1991.
9. *Huntsville News*, October 22, 1991.
10. *The Huntsville Times* and *Huntsville News*, August 30, 1991.
11. Huntsville Madison County Public Library Strategic Plan 2003 To 2008.
12. *Huntsville News*, September 1991.
13. *The Huntsville Times*, October 17, 1991.
14. Ibid., December 15, 1991.
15. Ibid., April 2, 1992.
16. *Huntsville News*, April 8, 1992.
17. Ibid., June 14, 1992.
18. Huntsville Library Heritage Room, undated.
19. *Huntsville News*, September 28, 1992.
20. *The Huntsville Times*, September 29, 1992.
21. Ibid., September 27, 1992.
22. *Huntsville News*, October 28, 1992.
23. Ibid., October 28, 1992.
24. Huntsville Library Board Archives.
25. *Huntsville News*, September 1992.
26. *The Huntsville Times*, October 29, 1992.
27. Ibid., April 12, 1993.

28. Huntsville Library Board Archives.

29. Ibid.

30. Ibid.

31. *The Huntsville Times,* August 1993.

32. Huntsville Library Board Archives.

33. *The Huntsville Times,* December 19, 1993.

34. Ibid., April 3, 1993.

35. Ibid., April 5, 1993.

36. *Huntsville News,* April 7, 1993.

37. *The Huntsville Times,* April 7, 1993.

38. Ibid., February 17, 1994.

39. Huntsville Library Board Archives.

40. *The Huntsville Times,* February 20, 1994.

41. Ibid., March 4, 1994.

42. Ibid., April 1994.

43. Ibid., May 29, 1994.

44. Ibid., June 12, 1994.

45. *Economist,* March 27, 2004.

46. *The Huntsville Times,* December 1999.

47. Ibid., November 22, 1994.

48. Huntsville Library Board Archives.

49. Ibid.

50. Ibid.

51. *The Huntsville Times,* March 20, 1995.

52. Ibid., March 20, 1995.

53. Huntsville Library Board Archives.

54. *The Huntsville Times,* December 8, 1995.

55. Ibid., July 14, 1997.

56. Ibid., October 7, 1997.

57. Welch, Joyce, interview, March 24, 2004.

58. *The Huntsville Times,* April 26, 1997.

59. Shepherd, Melissa, interview, November 17, 2004 & www.gatesfoundation.org.

60. *The Huntsville Times,* March 20, 1998.

61. Ibid., April 30, 1998.

62. Ibid., October 1, 1998.

63. Ibid., October 2, 1998.

64. Ibid., October 20, 1998.

65. Ibid., October 30, 1998.

66. Huntsville Library Board Archives.

67. Schremser, Donna, interview, January 26, 2004.

68. *The Huntsville Times,* December 31, 1998.

69. Huntsville Library Board Archives.

70. Ibid.

71. Ibid.

72. Ibid.

73. *Speakin' Out News*, October 13, 1999.

Chapter 14 – And the Beat Goes On
The Library Board minutes are identified by the date and a hyphen, for example, "August 4, 1936 – " when the date is at the beginning of a sentence or paragraph.

1. Thrasher, Lucy, and Thrower, Teresa, interviews, July 21, 2004.
2. Thrower, Teresa, interview, July 21, 2004.
3. Purinton, Judy, interview, May 27, 2004.
4. *The Huntsville Times,* December 27, 1988.
5. Huntsville Library Board, April 19, 2000.
6. Welch, Joyce, interview, March 24, 2004.
7. Ibid.
8. Huntsville Library Board Archives.
9. www.hpl.lib.al.us/locations/rrvan/.
10. Huntsville Library Board Archives.
11. www.al.org/PrinterTemplate.cfm?Section=lsta&Template=…
12. Huntsville-Madison County Public Library Strategic Plan 2003 To 2008.
13. Ibid.
14. *Cover to Cover*, March/April 2002.
15. Ibid.
16. Ibid., November/December 2002.
17. Ibid.
18. Huntsville Library Board Archives.
19. *The Huntsville Times,* March 31, 2004.
20. *Cover to Cover*, September 2003.
21. Fitzpatrick, Jack, Auburn University, e-mail, 8/13/2004.
22. *The Alabama Librarian.*
23. *The Huntsville Times,* March 31 & April 3, 2004.
24. Bradford, Sarah, interview, and McLemore, Kate, interview, October 27, 2004.
25. *The Huntsville Times,* May 30, 2004.
26. Huntsville Library brochure.
27. *Cover to Cover*, July-August 2004.
28. Ibid, September-October 2004.
29. Huntsville Library flyer, undated.
30. Dovers, Stormy, interview, October 22, 2004.
31. Corley, Anne, interview, November 5, 2004.
32. Huntsville Library invitation.
33. Huntsville Library flyer, undated.
34. *The Huntsville Times,* September 19, 2004.
35. Ibid., October 2, 2004.
36. Ibid., October 3, 2004.
37. Markham, Susan, phonecon, October 4, 2004.
38. Dilworth, Kathryn, interview, October 12, 2004.
39. Huntsville-Madison County Public Library Digital Collection Plan 2004-2009.
40. Huntsville Library Board, April 28, 2004.
41. Shepherd, Melissa, interview, November 17, 2004.
42. Lee, Helen, interview, October 22, 2004.

Bibliography

www.abebooks.com

Alabama Legislative Act, December 29, 1823.

Alabama Librarian, The.

Alabama Republican.

American Association of University Women. *A Half Century of AAUW in Alabama, 1927-1977.* Tuscaloosa, Alabama: Drake Printers, 1977.

American Library Association Yearbook, 1976.

Armour, Richard, *The Happy Bookers.* New York: McGraw Hill Book Company, 1986.

Asheim, Lester, *Persistent Issues in American Librarianship.* Chicago: The University of Chicago Press, 1960.

Augustine, Norman. *Augustine's Laws.* New York: American Institute of Aeronautics and Astronautics, Inc., 1982.

Baker, Sharon L. and Wallace, Karen L. *The Responsive Public Library.* Edgewood, Colorado: Libraries Unlimited, 2002.

Basbanes, Nicholas A., *A Gentle Madness.* New York: Henry Holt and Co. 1995.

Bellingrath, Al, interview, October 25, 2004.

Blackwell, Julie, interview, October 7, 2004.

Bobinski, George S. *Carnegie Libraries.* Chicago: American Library Association, 1969.

Bradford, Sarah, interview, October 27, 2004.

Chapman, Elizabeth Humes, *Changing Huntsville, 1890-1899,* Huntsville, Alabama: privately published, 1972.

Conaway, James, *America's Library.* New Haven, Connecticut: Yale University Press, 2000.

Constitution Village Script, May 2004.

Cook, Mrs. Robert, correspondence, December 1, 2004.

Corley, Anne, interview, November 5, 2004.

www.coursesa.matrix.msu.edu.

Cover to Cover, July/August 2004.

Dilworth, Kathryn, interview, October 12, 2004.

Dovers, Stormy, interview, October 22, 2004.

Economist, March 27, 2004.

Elizabeth Carpenter Public Library Volunteer Handbook.

Ennis, Philip H., *Seven Questions about the Profession of Librarianship.* Chicago: The University of Chicago Press, 1961.

Fisk, Mrs. Burke S., President, Huntsville Historical Society, typed vertical file in Heritage Room, November 4, 1968.

Fitzpatrick, Jack, e-mail, 8/13/2004.

Galvin, Hoyt R. *Planning a Public Library,* Chicago, American Library Association, 1955.

Garrett, Marie, interview, October 27, 2004.

www.gatesfoundation.org.

Gingerich, Owen, *The Book Nobody Read.* New York: Walker & Company, 2004.

Graham, Patterson Toby, *A Right To Read.* Tuscaloosa, Alabama: University of Alabama Press, 2002.

Grand Jury Report, Circuit Court, County of Madison, State of Alabama, January, 1978.

Grant, Nancy L., *TVA and Black Americans.* Philadelphia: Temple University Press, 1990.

Gurley Branch scrapbook, undated.

Hackworth, Nellie, interview, October 28, 2004.

Hamilton, John Maxwell, *Casanova Was a Book Lover.* Baton Rouge, Louisiana: Louisiana State University Press, 2000.

Heritage Room vertical files, undated paper.

Herrin, Mrs. Claude, *History of the Huntsville-Madison County Public Library, Huntsville Sesquicentennial-1955 Commemorative Album*. Nashville: Benson Printing, 1955.

www.hpl.lib.al.us/locations/rrvan/.

Proceedings of the City Council of the City of Huntsville, Alabama at its Regular Meeting held Thursday evening, February 8, 1940.

Hughes, Larrell, interview, July 15, 2004.

Huntsville Historical Review, The, Summer-Fall 1995, Volume 22, No.2.

Huntsville-Madison County Public Library Annual Report 1975-1976.

Huntsville-Madison County Public Library Digital Collection Plan 2004-2009.

Huntsville-Madison County Public Library Strategic Plan 2003 To 2008.

Huntsville-Madison County Public Library brochure.

Huntsville Mercury-Banner, April 15, 1915.

Huntsville News.

Huntsville Times, The.

Impact, Model Cities, Vol.2, No. 15, May 1971.

Johnson, Elmer D., *A History of Libraries in the Western World*. London: The Scarecrow Press, Inc., 1965.

Jolly, Geoffrey, interviews, July 15 & 29, 2004.

Karolides, Nicholas J., et al., *100 Banned Books*. New York: Checkmark Books, 1999.

Lee, Helen, Interview, October 22. 2004.

Liaw, Barbara, interview, July 21, 2004.

Library Board Minutes.

Library Notes, Friends of the Library.

Lilly, David, interview, March 9, 2004.

Maples, Mayme Claire, telephone interview, August 17, 2004.

Markham, Susan, interviews, August 24 & October 19, 2004; conversation, October 5, 2004.

Maulsby, Ann Geiger, The Dulcina DeBerry Library, *Huntsville Historical Review*, Volume 22, #2, July 1995.

McLemore, Kate, interview, October 27, 2004.

McMillan, Malcolm C., *The Land Called Alabama*. Austin, Texas: Steck-Vaughn Co., 1968.

Munford, W.A., *A History of the Library Association, 1877-1977* (British). London: The Library Association, 1976.

(www.newdeal.feri.org/eleanor/er4b.htm)

New Hope Friends of the Library, minutes and files, many dates.

Old Huntsville, #132, Huntsville, Alabama, February, 2004.

OPTIONS, Volume 1, Issue 4, October 1989, Huntsville Public Library.

Paine, Thomas, *The Rights of Man*. New York: Anchor Books, 1989.

Phillips, Ann Lee, interview, October 28, 2004.

Phillips, Gail, interview, March 16, 2004.

Piszkiewicz, Dennis. *Wernher von Braun*. Westport, Connecticut: Praeger, 1998.

www.etc.princeton.edu/CampusWWWCompanion/whig_cliosophic.

Proceedings of the City Council of the City of Huntsville, Alabama, February 8, 1940.

Proceedings of the First Meeting of the Alabama Library Association, November 21, 1904. Montgomery, Alabama: The Brown Printing Co., 1905.

Pruitt, Ranee, interview, October 13, 2004.

Purinton, Judy, interview, May 17, 2004.

Record, James, *A Dream Come True*, Huntsville, Alabama: John Hicklin Printing Company, 1970.

Redstone Rocket, June 25, 1969.

Roberts, Mrs. Roscoe (Jane), telephone conversation, March 20, 2004.

Royer, Sue, interview, November 17, 2004.

Russell, Mrs. C.H. *History of the Huntsville-Madison County Public Library, Huntsville Sesquicentennial-1955 Commemorative Album.* Nashville: Benson Printing, 1955.

Schremser, Donna, interview, January 26, 2005.

Scott, Priscilla, interview, June 1, 2004.

Sentinel, Scottsboro, Alabama.

www.server2.walkerweb.net/carlelliott/.

Shepherd, Melissa, interview, November 17, 2004.

Shera, Jesse H., *Foundations of the Public Library.* Chicago: University of Chicago Press, 1949.

Shirer, William L., *The Rise and Fall of the Third Reich.* Greenwich, Connecticut: Fawcett Publications, Inc, 1964.

Simpson, Fred B., *A Walk Through Downtown Huntsville, Then and Now.* Boaz, Alabama: Boaz Printing Company, 2002.

Sisk, Alice, interview, November 3, 2004.

Stieg, Margaret F., *Public Libraries in Nazi Germany.* Tuscaloosa, Alabama: The University of Alabama Press, 1992.

Snyder, Sarah, typed manuscript, D.O. Class of 1947, Heritage Room vertical files.

Speakin' Out News, October 13, 1999.

Thrasher, Lucy, interview, July 21, 2004.

Thrower, Teresa, interview, July 21, 2004.

Torrence, Missouri L., *Dulcina DeBerry: Door Opener,* Huntsville, Alabama: Golden Rule Printing, 1996.

Towery, Martin, interview, October 7, 2004.

www.ushistory.org.

Venture, Volume 1, Number 9, November 1970.

Welch, Joyce, interview, March 24, 2004.

Wiley, Peter Booth, *A Free Library in this City.* San Francisco: Weldon Owen, Inc, 1996.

Winger, Howard, *Seven Questions about the Profession of Librarianship.* Chicago: The University of Chicago Press, 1961.

INDEX

Cliosophic Society, 7
Clowers, Cecil, 103
Cockerham, John M., 181
Colson, Rob, 222, 231
Comprehensive Employment and Training Act (CETA), 140-1, 158
Conroy, Pat, 274
Conwell, Larry, 231
Cooke, Virginia, 133
Cooper, E. Cantey, 113-7, 167
Cooper, Regina, 175, 222, 241, 263
Courtenay, Carolyn, 267
Covey, Richard, 86-9, 102-4, 107-8, 113
Craig, Jerry, 173, 181, 187, 194-6, 208, 223, 243
Cramer, Robert E. Jr. (Bud), 159, 266
Crawford, Leon, 136-7, 156
Culp, Mr. Jesse,, 198
Davis, Mrs. Claude, 33, 38, 45, 50, 73, 89, 95
Davis, Claude, 92
Davis, Joe, 111, 169, 181
Davis, Kyle, 173
Davis, Nora, 13, 30-1
Darwin, Mrs. James L. (Mattie), 28, 31, 34, 36, 54, 57, 64-5, 70-1, 99, 105
Deal, Maurice, 137
Decatur Carnegie Library, 16, 31, 143
DeLaine, Kevin L., 247
Deschere, Allan, 92-3, 95
Dewey Decimal System, 10, 28, 76, 166-7, 203
Dewey, Melvil, 10, 49
Dickerson, George, 153, 156
Dilworth, Bernice, 199
Dilworth, Kathryn, 278
Dovers, Stormy, 273
Dulcina DeBerry Branch, 56, 77-8, 83, 91, 95, 104, 235
Duncan, Arlene, 198
Dyer, Faye, 223, 240
Dyer, Tom, 221, 241
Easley, Nevada, 134
Ehinger, John, 227
Eigenbrod, Marie, 246
Elbert H. Parsons, Sr. Law Library, 133, 145, 209, 214
Eleanor Murphy Branch, 145, 160, 176, 213, 217, 228, 248, 267
Elizabeth Carpenter Library, 199
Elliott, A.D., 92, 98
Elliott, Carl, A. Sr., 106, 161-2
Elsner, Silvia, 284
Erskin, Irmgarde, 198
Fearn, Thomas, 2-3, 5-6, 29
Ferranti, Mrs. A.L., 92, 107
Ferranti, Angelo, 92
Fish, Carl Russell, 8
First Alabama Bank, 185

Library Management Network, 165, 168
Library of Congress, 125, 236, 258
Library Services and Construction Act (LSCA), 99, 131, 133, 164, 216, 221
Library Services and Technology Act (LSTA), 247, 258
Lilley, David, 176, 229, 253, 284
Liddon, Gabrielle, 236
Linde, Walter, 153
Lockhart, Kenneth, 219
Loughead, Thomas, 115
Lowe, Mrs. Robert J. (Jane K.), 67, 108, 111, 117, 247
Lowell, James Russell, 179
Lowndes' Bequest, 35, 64, 70
Luttrell, Linda, 222
Lyon, Misty, 196
Mabry, Jane, 136
MacLeish, Archibald, 15
Madison Branch, 140, 147, 176, 224, 233-5, 237, 259, 271, 282-4
Madison, City of, 231, 233-4
Madison, James, 2, 258
Madison Mall Branch, 165, 175, 253
Madison County population, 5, 43, 61, 79, 97, 109, 233, 277
Madry, Carol, 181
Mailer, Norman, 113-4
Mann, Barbara, 197,
Mann, Carolyn, 196
Mann, Charlotte, 191-2
Mann, Horace, 8, 34
Maples, Mayme Claire, 186, 189, 191, 195, 196, 199
Maples, Tressy, 195
Markham, Susan, 167, 187-97, 199, 208, 212, 233, 237, 241, 247, 254
Maslow, Abraham, 255
Mastin, Elizabeth, 38
Matthews, Etta, 12
Mathews, Louise, 186-8, 207-8
Maxwell, Ida, 44, 71
McCanless, Christel, 124
McCrain, Beverly, 196
McCullough, David, 274
McDaris, Sarah, 110, 132, 163, 177
McGreuder, Loy, 191
McLain Eugene, 133
McLemore, Kate, 266
McMillian, Barbara, 196
McNaron, Abner, 153
McNaughton Books, 250
McQuiston, Rev., 89
Metrick, Diane, 251
Mickle, William, 92,
Milam, Carl H., 73
Miller, Emma, 241
Minor, Henry, 2-3, 5

Sirsi, 229, 259, 281

Slayden, Mrs. Howard A., 92

Smith, Barbara, 191

Smith, Betty, 172-3

Smith, Jeff D, 92

Smith, Jennie, 198

Smith, Jerry L., 244

Smith, Robert B., 118

Smith, Mrs. Wayne L. (Joyce), 103-4, 216, 235, 253

Snodgrass, Horace P., 60, 66

Snodgrass, Reverend, 91

Speake, Paul, 13

Spencer, Guy J. Jr., 181

Spencer, Loretta, 239-40, 247

Stevenson, Grace, 87

Stokes, Susan, 244

Stone, Anthony, 172-3

Stone, Mrs. Marty, 173

Stone, Roy, 81, 173

Strong, Dale, 267

Subregional Library for the Blind and Physically Handicapped, 103, 109, 216, 225, 235, 253-4, 264

Tappey, Reverend Francis, 23, 25

Tate, Judy, 125-6, 128

Taylor, John M., 2

Teledyne Brown, 183

Tennessee Valley Authority (TVA), 33, 36, 73

Terry, Mrs. E.T., 30, 47, 50, 100

Thrower, Teresa, 251-2

Ticklin, B.L. 117

Tillman Hill Branch, 147, 229, 237

Tomme, Virginia, 134, 152-6

Towery, Martin, 139, 160

Townsend, Carol, 247

Triana Branch, 157, 227, 237, 243

Tuchman, Barbara, i

Tucker, Lady Shivers, 257

Turner, Floyd, 251, 266

Turow, Scott, 273

TVA Regional Library Service, 36-40, 43, 50-2, 60, 68-9

Vann, Mae Rose, 190

Von Braun, Wernher, 96, 100, 116, 212, 214

Vought, Sabra, 48

Walker, John W., 84

Walker, Stephenie, 271, 282

Walker, Townsend, 220

Wall, Jimmy, 138, 175

Wallace, George, 133-4, 154

Wallace, Mary, 267, 276

Washington, George, 35, 165-6

Watkins, Miles S., 5

Watson, Elbert J., 108-11, 120, 122-5, 128-9, 133, 136-8, 153-6, 160